ROYAL

A Thousand Years of Jewish Life

in and around

the Royal County of Berkshire

Jonathan Romain

Grenfell Publishing
Maidenhead

First published 2013

Published by Grenfell Publishing, Maidenhead

www.maidenheadsynagogue.org.uk

Copyright © Jonathan Romain, 2013

The moral right of the author has been asserted

ISBN   978-0-9576986-0-4

Cover & design by Benedict Romain

All rights reserved. No part of this publication may be reproduced, stored in or introduced into a retrieval system, or transmitted, in any form or by any means (electronic, mechanical, photocopying, recording or otherwise), without the prior written permission of both the author and the above publisher of this book.

Printed and bound in Great Britain by
CPI Antony Rowe, Chippenham

Jonathan Romain

Born in 1954 in London, Jonathan Romain spent his early years in Ruislip, Middlesex. He studied for the rabbinate at Leo Baeck College, London and obtained his Ph. D from the University of Leicester in Anglo-Jewish history. He is minister of Maidenhead Synagogue in Berkshire. He writes periodically for The Times, Guardian and The Jewish Chronicle and is often heard on the BBC. He received the MBE in 2004 for his pioneering work nationally in helping mixed-faith couples. He is chaplain to the Jewish Police Association (Metropolitan Police), a board member both of the Council of Christians and Jews and of the Three Faiths Forum, chair of the Accord Coalition (which campaigns for inclusive education), and a Patron of Dignity in Dying.

Other publications by Jonathan Romain

Signs and Wonders (Beginners Hebrew) 1985

The Jews of England 1988

Faith and Practice (A Guide to Reform Judaism Today) 1991

Tradition and Change (A History of Reform Judaism), with Anne Kershen 1995

Till Faith Us Do Part (Couples who Fall in Love across the Religious Divide) 1996

Renewing the Vision (Rabbis Speak Out on Modern Jewish Issues) (ed.) 1996

Your God Shall be My God (Religious Conversion in Britain Today) 2000

Reform Judaism and Modernity (A Reader of Reform theology) 2004

God, Doubt and Dawkins (ed.) 2008

Really Useful Prayers (ed.) 2009

Great Reform Lives (ed.) 2010

A Passion for Judaism (ed.) 2011

For Timothy

… a royal Jew

CONTENTS

Introduction	p. 6
Notes on the Text	p. 9
List of Illustrations	p. 10
Maidenhead and its origins	p. 13

Part I - Beginnings

Chapter 1	1066: The First Jews	p. 16
Chapter 2	1656: Absence and Return	p. 56
Chapter 3	1838: The Railway and the River	p. 75
Chapter 4	1914: The Impact of the First World War	p. 91

Part II - The Second World War

Chapter 5	1939: The Evacuees	p. 110
Chapter 6	1939: The Refugees	p. 130
Chapter 7	1939: Jewish Life in Surrounding Areas	p. 152
Chapter 8	1940: The Birth of the Synagogue	p. 172

Part III - Communal Life

Chapter 9	1945: Becoming Reform and Acquiring a Home	p. 193
Chapter 10	1955: Life at Studlands	p. 211
Chapter 11	1960: Sinking and Swimming	p. 227
Chapter 12	1970: Preparing for the Future	p. 245
Chapter 13	1980: A Full-time Rabbi	p. 261
Chapter 14	1980s: A Decade of Transition	p. 287
Chapter 15	1990: Expansion and Development	p. 306
Chapter 16	2001: Grenfell Lodge	p. 328
Chapter 17	Trends and Changes	p. 347

Appendix 1	Communal Leadership	p. 363
Appendix 2	Association of Synagogues in Berkshire	p. 366
Appendix 3	*Bar/batmitzvah* Statistics	p. 367
Appendix 4	Map of the Synagogue Membership	p. 370
Appendix 5	Marriage Statistics	p. 371
Appendix 6	Funeral Statistics	p. 373
Appendix 7	Time-line since 1940	p. 375
Bibliography		p. 377
Index		p. 382

INTRODUCTION

The County of Berkshire has long been known as 'the Royal County'. Even before William I built Windsor Castle in 1070, the royal palace of Edward the Confessor had been situated in Old Windsor. The relationship between crown and county was maintained when William's castle was transformed from a defensive fort into a royal residence by the 12th century. This association was strengthened over the centuries as the place where various monarchs were born (Edward I), married (Henry I) or buried (Edward IV, Henry VIII, Charles I, and those from George IV onwards), as well as the long periods spent there by both Queen Anne and Queen Victoria. It was no surprise, therefore, that when the royal family felt that it was inappropriate to still bear the name 'Hanover' during the First World War, it chose 'Windsor' as its new surname, adopting it formally on 17th July 1917.

The royal connection also led to a series of salacious associations that cascade across the ages. Examples range from Nell Gwyn, mistress of Charles II, who occupied Burford House in Windsor, to Lillie Langtry, mistress of Edward VII, who resided at Bray Lodge. During the early 1900s, the town's reputation for dalliances away from spouses in London led to the reputed saying 'Are you married or do you live in Maidenhead?' The Profumo Affair at Cliveden in 1963 - a mixture of high class sex along with accusations of military secrets being revealed and national security being jeopardized - reinforced the area's reputation for scandal.

More positively, Berkshire boasts the agricultural pioneer, Jethro Tull, the first female MP, Lady Astor, the artist Stanley Spencer, playwright and composer, Ivor Novello. Oscar Wilde was here temporarily, although against his will, imprisoned in Reading gaol in 1895. Another visitor was Charles I who is thought to have said goodbye to his children in Maidenhead High Street before he was tried and executed in London. On the religious front, there was the Vicar of Bray - both the one who continuously changed his faith to keep his job, and the later one who mistook the king for a scrounger and refused to pay for his lunch when asked to help out. Brunel left his mark with his world famous bridge, which had the widest and flattest arches in the world, and which was immortalised by J.M.W. Turner's painting 'Rain, Steam and Speed'. Meanwhile the Thames continues to flow through the county. It has witnessed Viking warships, horse-drawn barges, steam-boats, punts and motor cruisers, but carries on regardless.

Amid this setting there are also Jews - extending from today to as far back as Norman times when they came over with William I. In some cases, only their name survives because of a fine that was recorded as being owed to a medieval monarch; in other instances their life story is well-known. Over the centuries, Jews have varied from individual traders to groups of war-time evacuees to the thriving community today. Amongst famous names who have been associated with the area are the Rothschilds, Benjamin Disraeli, and Rufus Isaacs, but as much part of the local story are Sarah of Windsor, Private Jack Stollerman, Ada Lewis, Sidney Rich, Jessica Blooman, Alec Belkin and Nicholas Winton, not to mention hundreds of others who made their mark in different ways.

The Synagogue in Maidenhead today is based in the centre of Berkshire but its membership extends throughout the Thames Valley, and also takes in parts of Buckinghamshire, Oxfordshire, Surrey and other adjoining counties. The initial chapters of this book therefore follow Jewish life in the same terrain, and any individual who has been located within those boundaries is recorded. The paucity of Jews in the area in those early centuries also makes a wide panorama sensible. However, from the 1850s onwards, when the railways meant that Maidenhead was more accessible and the local Jewish population grew, the attention of the book shifts more locally and narrows to the settled community that emerged.

There has not been a continuous narrative across the centuries, so each period is treated in a slightly different way to reflect its particular character. Thus in the medieval section, in which Jews were treated as group with specific laws governing their behaviour, the chapter traces the wider historical trends epitomised by the lives of individuals who were present locally. In this chapter, sub-headings are given for the different towns that are covered. After the readmission of the Jews in the seventeenth century, when Jews were generally treated in an individual capacity, the chapters deal predominantly with the personalities living in the area. Some of these chapters are given sub-headings to highlight major themes. Once Maidenhead Synagogue is officially established in 1940, the focus is more on communal life. However, records are often missing and it is only from 1980 that copies of the monthly newsletters and Council minutes are intact. Moreover, in the more recent period, the historical sources change from being entirely written records to include oral history, noted down either from private interviews or from a reunion of all former members in 1990 to celebrate the community's fiftieth anniversary. When describing the Synagogue's activities, a principle has been adopted that when a new venture is described – such as the *Kosher Shop* – the person who initiated it is mentioned but not necessarily those who took it over in subsequent years, otherwise the book would become an unending list of names, however worthy. An unfortunate gap in modern times is that even though an organised community existed from

1940, no institutional records from then are extant, and the first set of surviving Council minutes are not until 1955. It means that the main sources of written information about the community from 1940 to 1955 are external, such as notices in the *Jewish Chronicle* or remarks in the Reform movement's journal *Synagogue Review*.

I am grateful to the many members of Maidenhead, past and present, who gave interviews about their knowledge of the community. Thanks are due to Marc Saperstein for his help with sources. Equally to Jews College and its librarian, Mrs Erla Zimmels, as well as the staff at both Maidenhead Library and the Hartley Library, University of Southampton. I am grateful to those who helped with advice on specific parts of the book: Raymond Goldman, Anthony Grenville, Jo Hillaby, Bridget Hole, Griselda Hurley, Michael Jolles, Elias Kupfermann, Pam Manix, Robin Mundill, Luke Over, Edgar Samuel and Carolin Sommer. Also to Brian Humphreys for proof-reading.

This book covers almost a thousand years of Jewish history in Berkshire and the surrounds. It welds together disparate lives - medieval and modern, little known and famous, religious and secular - who shared a Jewish identity and who eventually formed a surprisingly vibrant Jewish community. This is their story and a record of a Jewish life that has not been told until now.

Jonathan Romain   September 2013

A montage of personalities associated with the area

NOTES ON THE TEXT

BOOK REFERENCES

Books are generally referred to by author and date of publication. Full details can be found in the Bibliography.

ABBREVIATIONS

The abbreviations below are used in the text or notes

AJR - Association of Jewish Refugees
ASGB – Association of Synagogues in Great Britain
BJRC – Berkshire Jewish Representative Council
CCJ - Council of Christians and Jews
JC - Jewish Chronicle
JJBS – Jewish Joint Burial Society
MA – Maidenhead Advertiser
MRJ – Movement for Reform Judaism
MSC - Maidenhead Synagogue Council
RSGB – Reform Synagogues of Great Britain
RSY – Reform Synagogue Youth
SR – Synagogue Review
UOHC – Union of Orthodox Hebrew Congregations
US – United Synagogue

LIST OF ILLUSTRATIONS

A montage of personalities associated with the area	p. 8
Maidenhead Bridge in 1810	p. 14
Mosse-Mokke, who lived in Norwich in 1233	p. 19
A chirograph of the sale of land to Jews in York in 1230	p. 22
A Jew weighing coins to guard against coin-clipping, 1233	p. 24
Memorial to Robert of Reading in the ruins of Osney Abbey	p. 30
The house in Lincoln where Belaset's daughter lived	p. 34
Isaac of Norwich, 1289	p. 38
A starr, Jewish legal document c. 1236	p. 41
A 1275 manuscript forbidding Jews to practice usury	p. 44
Woodcut illustrating a fox fable	p. 46
Letter granting safe conduct for Jews leaving England, 1290	p. 49
Aaron of Colchester wearing the Jew badge, 1277,	p. 51
A medal to commemorate the accession of Edward VI in 1547	p. 57
The Earl of Berkshire	p. 59
Francis Henry Goldsmid	p. 61
Goldsmid Road	p. 62
Reading Hebrew Congregation	p. 64
Gravestone of Sarah Hawkins	p. 67
Nathaniel Rothschild's seal as Lord Lieutenant of Berkshire	p. 68
The memorial to Disraeli in Hughenden	p. 72
Sam Lewis	p. 77
The Ada Lewis fountain in Bridge Gardens	p. 78
Craufurd College	p. 80
David Woolf Marks	p. 83
Jews' Free School teachers boating through Maidenhead	p. 85
The statue of Rufus Isaacs in Eldon Square	p. 88
41 High Town Road	p. 94
Maidenhead Advertiser, 27th March 1918	p. 97
Mr & Mrs Levene's shop in Queen Street, Maidenhead	p. 103
Ronald Barnett	p. 105
Israel Madenberg, Maidenhead Home Guard	p. 112
Air crew about to board Q-for-Queenie at RAF Burn	p. 114
Evacuee children trying out their gas-masks	p. 116
Annie Saville, December 1939, aged 16	p. 118
Rowledge House plaque	p. 121
Refugee children at Woodcote, Ascot	p. 123
Kindertransport children at Liverpool Street station	p. 131
Nicholas Winton with one of the children he saved	p. 137
Statue of Nicholas Winton at Maidenhead Station	p. 138

Fritz Lustig during the war	p. 140
Gertrude and Eva Evans	p. 145
Ludwig Guttmann	p. 149
Jewish children at the Dovercourt summer holiday camp	p. 150
Meir Zvi & Chanoch Ehrentreu	p. 156
The Jewish Chronicle in High Wycombe during the war	p. 159
Jacob Ferber	p. 162
Ian Mikardo	p. 164
Julius and Paula Jakobovits	p. 167
Shardeloes House	p. 170
Yechiel Galas	p. 174
Drill Hall, Marlow Road	p. 177
The Ark built in memory of Jack Stollerman	p. 179
Monycrower Drive	p. 181
Simon Joseph as a grandfather	p. 183
Harry Madenberg letter from a German prisoner of war camp	p. 188
Young Zionists training at Hurst Grange, Twyford	p. 195
Carmel College, Wallingford	p. 197
A *Hanukah* Party in a member's home, 1951	p. 198
Studlands, 9 Boyn Hill Avenue	p. 202
Erwin Rosenblum	p. 205
Order of service for the consecration of Studlands	p. 206
The Synagogue Dinner and Dance 1958 – the Ladies	p. 215
The Synagogue Dinner and Dance 1958 – the Gentlemen	p. 216
Alec Belkin	p. 220
Order of Service for the presentation of the Schwab Hall	p. 223
The wedding of Monte Margo and Hilke Englander	p. 230
Alf Shear	p. 232
Induction Service of Henry Silverman	p. 233
Batmitzvah ceremony of Judith Bernie and Amelia Frank	p. 234
Children from the Religion School 1965	p. 237
Murray Bernie and Israel Madenberg 1966	p. 241
Hashomer, the Maidenhead Guardian	p. 247
Summer Fete in the Synagogue's garden, 1970	p. 250
Robert Frankl, Mayor of Slough 1973-74	p. 253
Jessica Blooman, with Princess Margaret	p. 255
Members gather by the Thames for *Tashlich*	p. 263
The Holocaust Candelabra lit at *Tishah B'Av*	p. 265
Momma's *Kosher* Kitchen	p. 269
The Synagogue First XI	p. 272
The Synagogue rowers	p. 274
Operation Goodwill at St Mark's Hospital	p. 278

Hanukah Hymnalia	p. 280
Christian, Jewish, Muslim and Sikh leaders at the Synagogue	p. 282
The Borovinsky family	p. 289
Yoram Margai	p. 291
Headlines from the Maidenhead Advertiser, 1984	p. 300
The doors to the Prayer Hall	p. 302
Cartoon for Hadashot	p. 303
Knocking on doors	p. 305
Princess Margaret at the Synagogue's Jubilee	p. 308
Religion School teachers graduate with their diplomas, 1990	p. 310
Religion School teachers gain their diplomas, 1998	p. 312
A plaque is unveiled on the wall of Kojetin's synagogue	p. 314
Fiddler on the Roof cast and production team	p. 320
Memorial service for the Halifax bomber crew	p. 323
Lord Janner unveiling the Dedication Service plaque	p. 329
Jon Berman at work in the Prayer Hall	p. 331
Her Majesty the Queen at Ravenswood	p. 335
Jonathan Romain celebrates 25 years at Maidenhead	p. 340
Members of the choir perform for the BBC	p. 342
The High Holy Day tapestry	p. 345
The Ganon class practise the Sabbath blessings	p. 349
The summer Ulpan recreates the Temple	p. 353
Members of the youth club	p. 356
The Wednesday Social Club hold a play-reading session	p. 360
The fountain at the entrance to the Synagogue	p. 362
The *bar/batmitzvah* class of 2000/2001	p. 369
The Jewish section at Braywick cemetery	p. 369
The ark and reading desk	p. 397

MAIDENHEAD AND ITS ORIGINS

It could be said that the Jews appeared in England before Maidenhead did. They came over with William I, yet the name Maidenhead does not appear in the Domesday Book he commissioned, for in 1086 it was referred to as Elentone, which then became Ellington, a term still used for part of the area to this day. Elentone was a settlement comprising 360 acres, largely used for arable farming, part of the fertile lands of East Berkshire that had previously been cultivated for the growth of wheat and cereals in Roman times to feed the army in Wales. Berkshire itself had come into existence sometime before 860, when it is first mentioned, and takes its name not from any main town, as many counties do, but from the word 'beorc' (birch), a reference to the extensive woods there (1). Officially, Elentone was a hamlet, as no church is mentioned, unlike those in nearby towns of Bray and Cookham, now both much smaller than Maidenhead but then considerably more important, with Cookham being one of the sites where the Witan met under Ethelred the Unready in 997. All three settlements were situated along the River Thames, which formed a natural border between the kingdom of Wessex to which they belonged and the neighbouring kingdom of Mercia. Other notable locations in the area - all much larger then than Elentone - were Taplow, the site of a major Saxon burial mound; the Dane stronghold of Reading; Wallingford, where William had crossed the Thames after defeating Harold at Hastings, going to Berkhamsted where he received the English surrender; Windsor, where he built a castle that is still inhabited to this day; and Dorchester-on-Thames where Saint Birinus first raised the flag for Christianity amongst the West Saxons four hundred years earlier.

As local historian Luke Over has noted: 'It was the act of bridging the river Thames which eventually dictated the site of the present town of Maidenhead. Before the bridge was built the small hamlet of South Ellington existed on the spot, being one mile south of the Domesday site of Elentone, or North Ellington as it was later known' (2). The timber bridge was first erected around 1250, was rebuilt several times since then and is now a solid stone construction only a few yards away from the original crossing. The bridge had two enormously significant consequences. First, it resulted in the construction of timber wharves, which in turn led to an increase in prosperity and population locally.

Second, it became the main route from London to the west of England, and hence an important stopping place. This in turn led to hostelries and inns being established to cater for horses and travellers. By 1296 the name South Ellington disappeared from usage and was replaced by variations on the name Maidenhead. Luke Over records thirty-three versions of it, the effect of which is to hopelessly confuse its exact derivation. One possibility is that the name stems from 'mai-dun' - 'a fortified hill' - referring to the ancient fort on high ground at nearby Taplow. However, the most plausible assumption is that it developed from Maidenhythe – with 'maiden' meaning 'new' and 'hythe' meaning 'wharf' - and hence referring to the 'new wharf' that now graced the Thames.

1. Valerie Scott and Eve McLaughlin *County Maps and Histories: Berkshire* p. ii
2. Luke Over, *The Story of Maidenhead*, p. 20. I am grateful to Over for the material used in this and the preceding paragraph.

Maidenhead Bridge in 1810

PART I

BEGINNINGS

Chapter 1

1066: The First Jews

The Jews of England

History can be as much about frustration as information. That certainly applies to the early records of the Jews of England. We do not know, and probably never shall, who was the first Jew ever to set foot on English soil. It is likely that individual Jews came to this country as far back as Roman times, whether willingly as traders, or by force as slaves. Some of them may have been here only temporarily, others spent a considerable period here. However, it is impossible to talk of a settled Jewish community until the late eleventh century. It was then that William of Normandy, who became William 1 of England in 1066, brought over Jews from his French territory to help colonise his new kingdom.

William encouraged Jewish migration here for two reasons. First, it was obviously useful having people here who were both French-speakers and loyal to him. On the continent, Jews tended to be an urban population, not tied to the land and farms, much more mobile than most sections of society, and so were much more amenable to travel. Second, many of them performed a very useful economic function as moneylenders. This was not a matter of natural aptitude but of biblical interpretation. The Bible permits money-lending in principle, but stipulates several times that 'you shall not lend upon interest to your brother' (Exodus 22. 24, Leviticus 25. 35, Deuteronomy 23. 20). This begs the question as to the definition of 'your brother'? It was understood by rabbinic law to mean a fellow Jew, and that, as an act of kindness to members of the same faith community, one should not charge them interest, although one could do so to outsiders. Canon Law, however, interpreted the expression 'your brother' to apply to anyone, and held the verses to be an outright ban on levying interest. This may have been admirable in principle, but did not work in practice as there was a constant demand for loans, small or large, and at all levels of the social hierarchy; yet few people were prepared to make loans without charging interest, both so as to make a profit and so as to compensate for defaulters. With Christians being forbidden to enter such arrangements, here was an important economic vacuum. At the same time, medieval Jews were barred from many other occupations: they could not farm, as they were not allowed to own land outside towns that was part of the feudal hierarchy (1), while many artisan jobs were closed to them as they could not join the guilds, which had a Christian character and where the admission ceremony involved swearing an oath in the name of Jesus Christ. The coincidence of these factors led many Jews to engage in money-lending. It was an occupation that brought them many problems in the long term, for everyone welcomes the moneylender when in need of a loan, but tends to resent him when repayment is due. Thus anti-Jewish feeling became an inevitable by-product of their economic role in society. There was also the risk of clients being unable to repay their debts, along with the hazard of the king rewarding his followers by pardoning them of Jewish debts. However, the role did benefit future historians: many records of the Jews' financial transactions survive thanks to the Crown's interest in knowing the fiscal state of his most taxable subjects, and they provide glimpses into the life of medieval Jewry that we might not otherwise possess. At the same time, though, there is the danger of letting evidence of fiscal dealings dominate our picture of their lives simply because they are primarily the ones we possess today. Money-lending was certainly a Jewish occupation, but not all Jews were money-lenders.

There is another caution that needs to be added for the purposes of this particular study. The individuals mentioned below are identified in the records by local place names – with toponyms such as Moses of Aylesbury or Jacob of Wycombe. However, this does not necessarily mean that they were born in that location or that they lived there permanently (although that could have been the case). Their locative surname proves merely that they were associated with that town at some point in their life - whether through birth, later residence or business links - and it remained with them thereafter, even if they had left the area. Moreover, in the case of some individuals, they had variant names. Thus Jacob son of Moses was known as Jacob of Oxford when doing business in London, and Jacob of London when doing business elsewhere. Thus toponymic surnames are not evidence of long-term residence, therefore, though they can indicate a connection between Jews and those areas and serve as important clues for historians several centuries later.

The first Jews in Norman England may have settled in the London area, either because it was one of their points of entry or because it was the seat of royal power. The latter was important as the Jews were outside of the traditional feudal system, which was based on land and allegiance to local overlords. Instead, their right of residence was dependent on the will of the Crown, with a two-way relationship: they being answerable directly to the king and the king being their legal protector. Indeed, when their legal status was formalised, they were described as 'chattels' of the king and physically belonging to him. One result was that he could tax them directly without permission of the barons or Parliament. This, along with his ability to also fine Jews at will, is another reason why detailed records of their affairs survive, with lists of the royal penalties imposed on them, justly or unjustly. The Crown's fiscal power over Jews meant that it was in the king's interest to ensure their safety, although for his benefit rather than theirs. Henry III was to spell out in graphic detail the total subservience of the Jews to the Crown in his Mandate to the Justices of 1253, which declared that 'no Jew remain in England unless he do the king's service, and that from the hour of birth every Jew, whether male or female, serve Us in some way'.

The Jews largely remained in London until 1135, at which point Provincial Jewry came into existence. It indicated that the Jews felt able to leave the protection of the capital, although security was still a consideration. Thus when Jews did begin to branch out to other areas of the country, it was usually to places which were royal strongholds, often with a castle and Royal Constable who was responsible for their safety. As a generalisation, Jews tended to settle in clusters, preferring to be in close proximity to their co-religionists. This was primarily for positive reasons, so as to be part of a communal structure, and with the religious facilities that only a sizable gathering could provide, such as a synagogue, *mikveh* (ritual bath-house used for women), and school of instruction for children. However, individual Jews could also be found scattered in areas slightly further afield, but still with access to the town's Jewish life and never severing that umbilical cord. Of course, there were also negative reasons for staying close, as Jews were a double minority - both foreigners and non-Christians; in a world in which prejudice and superstition were rife, they could be easy targets if local disturbances arose. This was not often the case during the first hundred years of their stay in the country, but in the second century, when religious hatred of Jews was deliberately fanned by Christian clergy, it led to increasingly hostile relations between Jews and their neighbours. Despite the attention given to the Jews by the Church, whether in vilifying them or trying to convert them, the size of the medieval Jewish contingent was always modest. At its height in 1200, it was estimated to be four to five thousand, comprising 0.25%

of the total population of England and 1.25% of the urban population (2).

Mosse-Mokke, who lived in Norwich in 1233. He has a spiked hat, one of the marks of identity prescribed for Jews by the 1215 Lateran Council.

Local Jews

Just as the Jews attached to Maidenhead Synagogue today live throughout Berkshire, Buckinghamshire and Oxfordshire (along with parts of adjacent counties), so too there were medieval Jews spread throughout the area. However, it is impossible to locate the very first Jew locally. It is tempting, but fallacious, to seize upon a reference in 1075 by the 17th century chronicler Anthony Wood (3):

> About this time I find the Jews settled and their number great in Oxford, as in several scripts [letters] it appears, particularly in that of Brumman Ie Riche, made to the said church of St. George at its first foundation, by which giving to the canons thereof land in Walton, in the north suburbs of

Oxford, warranteth it to them 'against Jews'.

This warrant was intended as a guarantee that the rights of the land would not be transferred to Jews, which could later lead to the Crown claiming the land, as the Jews themselves were regarded as the property of the Crown. However, the stipulation could simply be the inclusion of a standard legal clause that does not necessarily indicate Jews were actually living in the area at the time. There is also doubt as to whether such a warranty - common in the thirteenth century - was in existence at that early period and the document may have been misdated. Another fascinating but inconclusive detail is a reference in 1086 in the Domesday Book to (4):

> Alwi sheriff holds from the king two hides [approx. 60 acres] and a half at Blicestone [Oxfordshire]. This land Manasses [Manasseh] bought from him without licence of the king .
>
> .... The same bishop holds Staplebridge [Dorset]. Of the same land Manasses holds three virgates [approx. 30 acres], which William, the king's son, took from the church without the consent of the bishops and monks

Here we have two possible clues: first, a Hebrew name and, second, mention that the king had not granted permission - which was not usually necessary in a private land deal but was common when the transaction involved a Jew - both of which might infer that Manasses was Jewish. However, once again care is needed, for non-Jews also used Hebrew names, with several occurring in the Domesday Book without any obvious Jewish connection, and so this excerpt cannot be claimed as definite proof of Jewish residence in the area.

Oxford

The first incontrovertible mention of a local Jewry is not until 1141 and occurs upriver in Oxford - although the reference implies that a community was well established there by then and so was formed earlier. It cites a tax that Matilda - then in the midst of a civil war with Stephen - imposed upon the Jews of Oxford. When the city was recaptured by Stephen, he too demanded a levy from them, although three and a half times as much as that given to Matilda, as a punishment for helping her. As for individual Jews, someone who left his mark on the town, albeit for the worse, was the son of Moses of Wallingford, known as Deus-eum-crescat or Dieulecresse. Some time before 1190 he was in the town and started taunting pilgrims on the way to the shrine of St Frideswide in Oxford, where miracles of healing were believed to be performed. According to Roth's description of events based on a chronicler's contemporary account (5):

> He showed his opinions in the most contemptuous and sacrilegious manner. He would pretend to limp, and then to walk freely, or else clench his fingers as though with palsy and then open them again, and afterwards inform the bystanders that these miracles were quite as genuine as any wrought by the saint and that they might as well let him have their alms instead of presenting them in church. His father told him to stop his antics, but Dieulecresse flatly refused, saying that he for one was not afraid of the saint. As a result the two had a violent quarrel; and whatever the reason, that same night the young man committed suicide by hanging himself in the kitchen of the house. There was at this time no Jewish cemetery in Oxford; and when the body was taken to London for burial (the Christian faithful fancied that the dogs bayed after it more than was usual) the coffin fell ignominiously from the cart, and the neck that had uttered the blasphemies was broken. The saint's triumph could not have been greater or more public

Oxford was the most important town in the Thames valley area, and had the largest Jewish community, with around 150-200 Jews living there by the end of the twelfth century, approximately a twentieth of the total Jewish population of England. Their economic importance was evident from the fact that it was one of a limited number of towns that had an archa: a locked chest (plural: archae) in which official documents of loans transacted by Jews were kept (6). The system was introduced in 1194 in the Ordinances of the Jewry. It is a remarkable example of early bureaucracy and provided an efficient method of record-keeping vital to both the creditor and debtor, as well as the Crown, which took a keen interest in the finances of its 'chattels'. The archae of each town were supervised by a group of two reputable Jews, two reputable Christians and two clerks. Each document - often referred to as a chirograph - was drawn up in duplicate (after 1239 in triplicate), with the copy being placed in the archa, which had three locks. Oxford Jewry was also one of a handful of centres in which Jews had their own cemetery. Until 1177 Jews who died anywhere in the country were taken to London and buried in the cemetery in Cripplegate, as happened in the case of the notorious Dieulecresse. After that date Jews were permitted to establish local cemeteries, which the larger communities did, and land was bought by Oxford Jews for a cemetery of their own outside East Gate (7). There were no limits as to where Jews could reside, but most chose to congregate together, be it for social reasons, ease of shared facilities or security concerns. The Jewish quarter ran from Carfax down St. Aldate's, roughly to the South Gate, and east and west along the sides streets. As for a synagogue, any building could serve as a place of prayer, with Jews gathering together in a large room in someone's home or workplace for weekly or Sabbath services, and so no formal synagogue was necessary. Still, it was desirable, particularly where there was a large community, and around 1228 an Oxford Jew - Copin of Worcester - purchased a house off Fish Street in St Aldate's parish, which he then dedicated as a synagogue for his co- religionists (8).

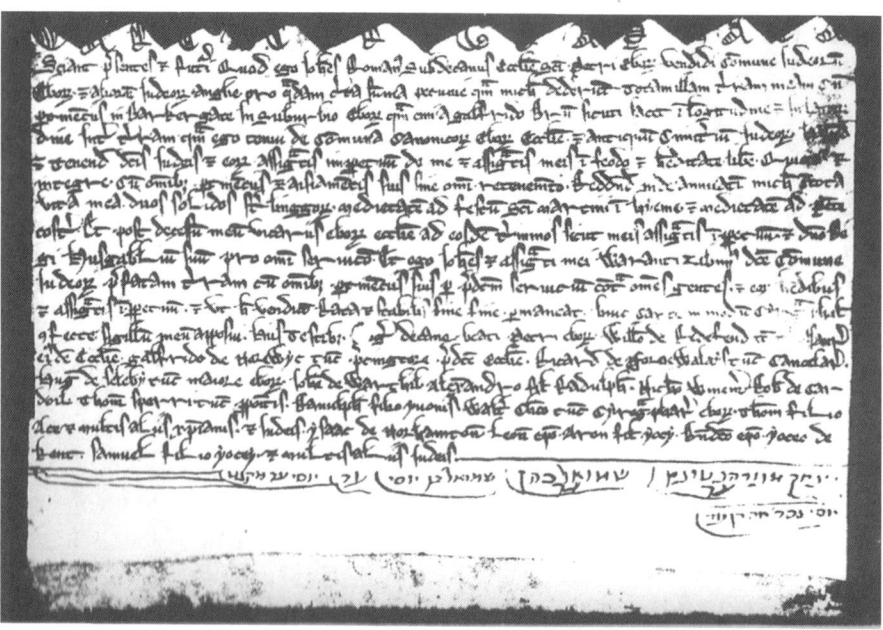

A chirograph relating to the sale of land to Jews in York in 1230

The Jewish community became caught up in another curious incident a few decades later. During a solemn procession on 17th May 1268 by the clergy through the Jewish quarter to St Frideswide, a Jew snatched the crucifix being held by the leader of the procession and broke it underfoot. Roth suggests that as no individual was apprehended, the incident is slightly suspicious, with perhaps a Jewish bystander falling accidentally against the bearer and tripping him up. Whatever the real cause, the entire community was held responsible and ordered to pay for a new portable crucifix, made of silver, as well as a permanent one of stone. There was some debate as to where it should be located: the initial idea was the spot where the incident took place; then it was suggested that it be erected opposite the synagogue, which would have been very provocative and the idea was vetoed by Henry III. Eventually, on 3rd February 1269, the crucifix was fixed in the grounds of Merton College, with an inscription bearing testimony to the event, although it is no longer standing today (9). Merton already had a loose Jewish connection, for in 1267, Walter de Merton, Henry's Chancellor and the founder of the College, had started it through purchasing some local houses from their Jewish owner, Jacob son of the famous Rabbi Moses of London (10). Detailed studies of the Jewish life in Oxford have already been published, and those interested in its story in general or the individuals within it are referred to them (11).

Windsor

If Oxford was the regional centre, there were many Jews living in other areas locally, either as satellites of the Oxford community, or families who moved out of London and gradually made their way along the Thames. The river had the same impact then as did the railways in later centuries, facilitating commerce and leading some traders to relocate their families in new areas. Starting down-river, Windsor was a natural point for Jews to settle, especially as it offered the protection of a royal castle. Among the individuals recorded was Hake of Windsor, on whose behalf the Exchequer of the Jews went to court in 1279 to claim 40 shillings owed him by William Chyvee. However, it was notable that the action was taken 'to the king's benefit' as that was where the money was going, with Hake, like so many Jews, merely being a conduit of income to the royal purse. (12). That same year we also hear of Lumbard of Windsor, along with his wife Sarah, albeit because he faced charges of coin-clipping. This involved filing bits of silver off coins in sufficient quantity to produce additional ones, thereby devaluing the currency. It was a crime that was common in the Middle Ages, and an accusation often levelled against Jews – fairly or unfairly - because their money-lending activities meant that they had more access to large quantities of coinage than most people. Lumbard did not face a trial as he died of natural causes before it could take place (13). However, before he died, he also suffered the additional woe of seeing his son Cresse being arrested on charge of theft and rape in Wilton, Wiltshire, where he was living. The records give graphic details of the alleged crime (14):

> Isabel of Rockeleye [or Lockerley] appeals [against] Cresse son of Lumbard, a Jew of Windsor, that whereas she was in peace of God and the king in Wilton on the Thursday after the feast of St Matthew the Apostle at the time of the curfew in the sixth year of the reign of the present king [1278] and was crossing East Street to the east of the bridge of Habbridge, Cresse had assaulted her and, as a felon, had robbed her of her surcoat of blue cloth with a fur of strandling worth fifteen shillings and another surcoat of squirrel fur worth six shillings; and subsequently the same Cresse, not content with this felony, dragged the same Isabel with all his force into his own house in which he lived in East Street and made her enter that house against her will and at once dragged her into a cellar on the north side of the house, knocked her down to the ground and choked her and had carnal intercourse with her.

A Jew weighing coins to guard against coin-clipping, 1233

Cresse denied both charges and elected to go before a jury. At the date set for the trial, he came to defend himself but Isabel failed to appear and the case was dismissed - although Cresse still had to pay the king half a mark to release the case. Jewish life in Windsor did not last much longer, for the rest of the community were expelled in an edict issued on 13th October 1283 (15):

> To Geoffrey de Picheford, constable of Windsor Castle. Order to be caused to be removed from that town certain Jews who have entered it and who inhabit it, without doing injury to their bodies or their goods, as, according to the custom of the king's Jewry, his Jews ought not to dwell in cities, boroughs or towns other than in those wherein there is a chest of the chirographers of the Jews and wherein they were wont from old time to dwell, and certain Jews have entered that town, wherein there is no chest of the chirographers and no Jew was wont to dwell of old time.

This expulsion edict takes it for granted that the Jews belong to the king - referring to them as 'his Jews' - while it also harks back to the Mandate to the Justices issued by Henry III in 1253 which had ordered that 'there be no synagogues of the Jews of England save in those places in which such synagogues were in the time of King John, the king's father.' It implies that Jews had not settled in large number in Windsor by the time of John (1199-1216), although it is hard to know whether the few families living there in 1253 had left and then returned later, or whether that edict had never been properly carried out and hence the 1283 expulsion. The edict may have been responsible for the fact that 'the son of Sarah of Windsor' was no longer in the town but living in Bedford when he was summoned to appear before the barons in 1287 to be informed of a tallage that was about to be exacted. Sarah was by then a widow, while her son's name is not given in the sources - perhaps Cresse, perhaps a brother of his (16).

There were also a number of Jews whose stay in Windsor was not for residential reasons but because they had fallen foul of the king's pleasure. Most prominent was Abraham son of Muriel, who lived in London, where he was an active financier and a member of one of the leading Anglo-Jewish families of the time. In October 1204, the Close Rolls record that (17):

> The King to Robert of Oldbrige. We order you to send to our Justices appointed in London for the custody of the Jews, Abraham fil. Muriel, whom you have in our prison in Windsor

The reason for his detention was that after the death of his father, Joseph son of Isaac, his mother married Isaac of Oxford in 1203. However, her new husband died that same year and both she and Abraham were accused of concealing his wealth, so as to avoid duties accruing to the Crown. They were fined the massive sum of 1,000 marks and given a strict deadline by when to pay it. Although they sold the property in England, and also travelling to Rouen to dispose of land there, they could not raise sufficient money to meet the penalty. Abraham was therefore imprisoned in Windsor before being summoned to face the justices of the Jews. Despite these tribulations and further fines, he was able later to restore his fortunes, to the extent that he ranked fifth highest in the 1239 London tallage list (18). It should be noted that it is unusual for a man to be called by the name of his mother rather than that of his father. In other instances this could be because the father is unknown, or of disreputable character, but in this case it is probably because his father died shortly after Abraham's birth.

The prison facilities at Windsor meant that over the years several other Jews living elsewhere in the country came to spend time in the castle. They included Hagin, son of the scholar Moses of London, who lived in Lincoln and who had been elected to the position of Arch-Presbyter, serving as adviser to the Crown on Jewish affairs in the realm. Hagin's long period of office from 1258 till 1280 was marked by traumas and controversies. This included having to flee the country after he concealed from the authorities the death of a child so as to save the family (his own relations) from having to pay inheritance tax. He was also accused of financial misdealings and in 1275 was imprisoned in the Tower of Windsor at the command of the king, where he died in 1280 of natural causes (19). A later inmate at the castle was Aaron Crespin of London. In 1275 he had been summoned before the courts in the capital on charges of trespass and fraud, but when he failed to appear it transpired that he was already imprisoned in Windsor owing to another accusation (20).

Runnymede

Not far away from Windsor is the spot at which King John signed Magna Carta in June 1215. The twenty-five barons who demanded the meeting were encamped at Staines, while the king and his retinue were staying at Windsor Castle. No Jews are associated with Runnymede itself, but it is notable that out of Magna Carta's sixty-two clauses, two relate to Jews and their money-lending activities (21):

10. If anyone who has borrowed from the Jews any amount, large or small, dies before the debt is repaid, it shall not carry interest as long as the heir is under age, of whomsoever he holds; and if that debt falls into our hands [if the Jewish creditor dies and the king takes over his bonds], we will take nothing except the principal sum specified in the bond.

11. And if a man dies owing a debt to the Jews, his wife may have her dower and pay nothing of that debt; and if he leaves children under age, their needs shall be met in a manner in keeping with the holding of the deceased, and the debt shall be paid out of the residue, saving the service due to the lords. Debts owing to other than Jews shall be dealt with likewise...

... Given under our hand in the meadow which is called Runnymede between Windsor and Staines on the fifteenth day of June in the seventeenth year of our reign.

The two clauses indicate that there was great concern over the effects that mounting interest might have on the under-age heirs and widow of debtors. The solution was a freeze on interest payments, while the debt was only to be paid once appropriate living expenses had been guaranteed. The insertion of the clauses also hint at the unpopularity with which Jewish moneylenders were regarded, even though it was the Christians who had entered into loans with them voluntarily.

Burnham

Continuing upstream, there are no references to any Jews in Maidenhead but there was a connection nearby concerning the Abbess of Burnham. In 1276 she was amongst several people summoned to court because she was the tenant of John de Boveney, who was in debt for 31s 1d to Bonevye, son of Jacob, and Elias of Bedford, and that amount was in turn owed to the king as part of their tallage. It is a good example of how the Crown gave considerable legal backing to Jewish claims against debtors, although largely in its own interest. It highlights the way in which the Crown used the Jews - via tallages which it could impose freely - to extract money that it could not have raised nearly so easily via taxes. Moreover, it is likely that, as in so many other cases, while the Crown was the main beneficiary, it was the Jews who - as the middlemen - were most resented (22).

Marlow

Further up the Thames, medieval Marlow can claim at least one Jew associated with it. Ursel (or Joshua) of Marlow is one of six Jews, along with six Christians, who formed a jury to hear a case in London in 1274 in which Isaac Le Eveske was beaten and wounded by Henry of Durham (23). Three years later Ursel requests a judicial investigation into some matter of his own, and is charged two shillings for it, although we do not know the nature of the problem (24).

Henley

Records for that same year indicate that another family had settled not too far away, in Henley, for Bonamy of Henley paid 40s for the privilege of erecting gates on his house (25). This passing reference to a domestic structural alteration is enormously significant. For a start, it must have been a fairly substantial property to be able to take gates, and indicates that he was a person of means. Whether this addition was for decorative reasons or defensive ones is open to conjecture, although given the hostile climate that existed in the last few decades of Jewish life in England, the latter explanation is the most likely. Moreover, this is clear evidence of a Jew actually residing along the Thames. Bonamy earned his surname not by doing occasional business in the area, but by actually dwelling there.

Caversham

Continuing along the Thames towards Reading, we hear of an un-named Jew in Caversham being fined £50 in 1275. This was a considerable sum for an individual to pay - although it could have related to the cost of a licence that was recorded as being granted to a Jew, permitting him to reside in the area - a requirement following the 1275 Statutum de Judeismo which restricted Jews to residing in towns that already had an archa (26). He may or may not have been Copyn fil. Bonavita who lived there at that time (27). It should be noted that a fine or imprisonment did not necessarily imply a legal misdemeanour on the part of the Jew concerned, as monarchs would often impose fines at will (and imprisonment to ensure rapid payment) for their own fund-raising purpose. An example is the donum levied in 1194 to pay for the release from captivity of Richard I during the Crusade.

Reading

Higher up the river, we hear of a Jew in Reading called Hakelot or Isaac. According to the deposition of Richard of Anesty in 1163: 'when I was in Reading, Hakelot the Jew, whom I found there, lent me thirty shillings at three pence a week for the pound, which I kept for five months and for which I paid usance of seven shillings and six pence' (28). The town nearly became interwoven with the land of Israel when Henry II was staying at the Benedictine Abbey there in 1185 and was visited by Heraclius, Patriarch of Jerusalem, and Roger, Master of the Knights Hospitallers of Jerusalem. They offered Henry, then considered one of the most powerful and effective rulers in Europe, the crown of the Christian kingdom of Jerusalem, which was facing grave danger from the Muslims. Despite an accompanying letter from the Pope urging him to accept, Henry declined the offer of an extra crown (29)

Still, Reading does have a special place in the history of medieval Anglo-Jewry, thanks to Robert of Reading (referred to in the sources as Robert de Reddingge). He was a Dominican friar, an order that had been increasingly active in the thirteenth century in whipping up popular fury against local Jews through preaching anti-Jewish sermons. They also went into synagogues and forced Jews to sit through sermons designed to convert them to 'the true faith'. It seems that Robert of Reading studied Jewish literature - in order to gain background material for his anti-Jewish activities - but began to become interested in the faith himself. The result was that instead of him leading the Jews to Christianity, he converted to Judaism in 1275. He adopted the Hebrew name of Haggai, and subsequently married a Jewish woman. The scandal of any Christian joining the unbelievers was bad enough, but the apostasy of one who came from the ranks of the clergy was even worse. The public disgrace brought upon the Church could only result in the severest possible punishment, but Robert/Haggai, along with his new wife, fled the country and disappeared from history (30).

His flight may have been hastened by memories of the fate of a deacon involved in a similar case, which took place in Oxford in 1222. He, too, adopted Judaism, and was brought to trial at Osney Abbey, just outside Oxford, with no less a figure than the Archbishop of Canterbury, Stephen Langton, presiding. The deacon was unrepentant. When presented with a crucifix, he declared, 'I renounce the new-fangled law and the comments of Jesus the false prophet', and apparently blasphemed the Virgin Mary. He was sentenced to death and burnt at the stake. A plaque in his memory was erected at the ruins of Osney Abbey in June 1931, although it names the deacon as Robert of Reading, probably because of a confusion with the latter's case owing to the similarities between them, despite occurring fifty years apart. Thus the plaque testifies to the martyrdom of 'Robert of Reading, otherwise Haggai of Oxford', who 'suffered for his faith on 17th April 1222' (31). It should be added that the religious traffic could be in both directions, and a few years after Robert of Reading we hear that Henry III was present to witness the baptism of Philip the Convert in 1234 near Reading (32)

Memorial to Robert of Reading in the ruins of Osney Abbey, Oxford

Wallingford

Moving up the Thames one comes to Wallingford. Its Jewish population had grown rapidly in the second half of the twelfth century. No community there is listed among the towns whose Jews were taxed in the 1159 Donum, but it is one of those in the 1194 Donum (the 'Northampton Tallage'), and had clearly sprung up in between those dates. Amongst the community at that time was Samuel of Wallingford (33), while another was Moses of Wallingford, a person whose integrity managed to bridge the growing Jewish-Christian divide, for the chronicler of Acta Sanctorum described him as 'a man less detestable than the rest of the Jews' (34). A later resident was Abraham of Berkhamsted, son of Manser. He had moved to Wallingford in 1242 after the Jews had been expelled from Berkhamsted that same year and was a moneylender of substance. He, too, was charged with coin-clipping, in 1251, but managed to resolve it by paying a fine. He had such a high number of financial transactions that an archa was established in Wallingford specifically to accomodate his business. In this, the lack of many other Jews in Wallingford presented a problem, for, as noted earlier, every archa needed two Jews to be amongst those supervising its procedures; the result was that they had to be brought from Oxford when the occasion required. Some of the loans Abraham contracted whilst there were still outstanding in 1267, for the chirographers at Wallingford were ordered that year to withdraw £40 'of the better and clearer' debts owing to him and to give them as part payment for his levy to the Queen, Eleanor of Provence (35). When Abraham died in 1272, Edward I was quick to order the chirographers to hand over charters of debts which had been due to him and over which the king now took ownership (36).

It should be noted that the authorisation for establishing the archa had come not from the king, as would normally have been the case for archae, but from Henry's brother, Richard of Cornwall, who owned both Berkhamsted and Wallingford. Indeed, for a period he had controlled Jews throughout the entire kingdom, for Henry had mortgaged the Jews of England to him for a year, both in 1255 and again in 1271 in return for loans (37). This was yet another example of how the Jews were seen and treated as the property of the Crown to be used, and disposed of, as any other holding. Henry had needed to raise extra revenues, and so had mortgaged his Jews. For his part, Richard envisaged that he would recoup his outlay through the fines and impositions he could levy from them. He had already benefitted substantially from Abraham in 1250 after the latter had been accused not only of maltreating an image of the Virgin but also of killing his wife Floria for her refusal to imitate him. It was claimed that Abraham had put the icon at the bottom of his privy, defecated on it and told his wife to do likewise, when she instead removed and cleaned it, he took her life (38). Richard gained his release from the charge on payment of a heavy fine. The inference is that he was innocent of such a crime, otherwise the case would not have been dropped, but he still had to pay for that privilege (39). Richard's dealings with Abraham extended to his son, Hagin, for in 1272 Hagin was involved in a dispute with another Jew, Jospin son of Solomon of Marlborough, over a deal with Richard, who is described by his subsequent title, King of the Romans, but who had by then passed away. The result was that Hagin, was taken from the hearing in Marlborough 'and thence carried by night to Wallingford castle, and there imprisoned for a year' (40).

A relatively minor incident, but significant for the individuals involved, was the case of a horse bridle lost in Wallingford in 1272. The details provide a fascinating glimpse into everyday barter in medieval England: Bonevie of Oxford (son of Vives) had hired a horse from Ralph Le Walle in order to journey to London. Bonevie accused Ralph of withholding a bowl of mazer-wood with a silver rim, but without a foot, valued at half a mark, which he had given Ralph as a pledge for the horse. According to Ralph, the mazer-wood bowl was indeed given as a pledge and the horse was hired for 16d. It was also agreed that if Bonevie exceeded the stipulated period of hire, then he would give Ralph 1d for every further day. Ralph claimed that Bonevie had kept the horse an extra twelve days, while he had used the horse on another occasion for ten days to go to Wallingford, where he lost the bridle, which was worth half a penny. Ralph also alleged that he had lent Bonevie's wife six pence, making a total of twenty-eight and a half pence extra being owed to him, and for this reason he was keeping the bowl. The incident is also a rare record of a Jew giving a non-Jew a pledge, whereas usually it was the reverse, while the non-Jew also lends money to the Jew. Bonevie hotly disputed the claim, and it was left to the Sheriff to try to sort out the conflicting evidence (41).

Another Jew associated with the town was Diei of Wallingford, whose life mirrored two of the dangers facing English Jews. In 1244 he has to pay 1 mark of gold as a pledge for his wife, Bona, who had been charged with coin-clipping, while his death in 1266 occurred because he was killed in disturbances involving the followers of Simon de Montfort. His wife, Bona, accused Hugh de

Kakesete and others of the crime, but it was never brought to court (42). An overseas visitor who became associated with the town was the scholar Josceus de Alemannia, also known as Rabbi Joseph ben Avraham of Germany and as Josce of Wallingford. In 1275 he had to travel to London to sit on a Commission of Inquiry (43). Apparently he dabbled in mysticism, for he and the famous Rabbi Elijah of London taught a student a magical formula to be recited over a particular plant in order to gain, either through a dream or by a flash of intuition, the answer to some specific enquiry (44). However, his supposed skills in this area did not protect him from brushes with the law - whether through his own malpractices or as a result of false accusation - for in 1278 he was accused of coin-clipping whilst still in Wallingford (45). It was a troublesome year for him, for he was also accused of trespass: of entering the house of Peter of Witton, in Wallingford, and carrying away goods to the value of ten pounds. The claim was subsequently proved to be false, for it emerged that, unbeknown to Peter, his wife had pawned to Josce some household items (46). No doubt the couple had a lively conversation after the case was dismissed.

Someone who found that the burden of being Jewish too much to bear was Agnes of Wallingford, who decided to renounce her faith and enter the Domus Conversorum (House of Converts) in 1280. This was a residential centre in Chancery Lane, London which had been established in 1232 by Henry III for the support of Jewish converts to Christianity. They lived there free of charge and with a daily allowance for their needs. Such support was necessary because the Crown had a legal claim on the property of any Jew who converted to Christianity - on the grounds that the possessions of a Jew were effectively the possessions of the Crown, and a Jew who became a Christian meant the Crown losing its assets unless they were surrendered upon conversion. Jews who changed faith thus not only relinquished any support they may have previously enjoyed from their family and the wider community, but also any property they owned. This was a major disincentive to any thoughts of baptism, quite apart from the social upheaval it would cause them, but the Crown was more interested in maintaining the fiscal value of Jews than the purity of their souls. However, in 1280, in order to encourage conversion, Edward waived for a seven year period his claim to the property of Jews who left their faith (47). It is not known what motivated Agnes - be it genuine religious conviction, exhaustion from all the financial penalties facing Jews, or fears for her personal safety - but whereas there had only been a small number of residents in previous decades, she was among nearly a hundred persons (48).

The house in Lincoln where Belaset's daughter lived

The pressure Jews felt at that time may be seen through another local Jewess, Belaset of Wallingford (also known as Bellasez), daughter of Solomon. She was a businesswoman and property-owner, yet also had a criminal record and had been condemned for felony five times (49). In 1278 she was one of two hundred and ninety-three Jews charged with coin-clipping, taken to the Tower of London found guilty and hanged in 1284. It may have been that she did engage in disreputable practices, but it has been suggested that the fact that the charges were simultaneously issued against so many Jews indicates they were trumped-up and motivated by the hostility of debtors and the greed of Edward I. As one of the king's chattels, Belaset's debts were automatically taken over by the Crown. These included bonds in Lincoln outstanding at the time of her death, and also a property she possessed there, one of the few medieval buildings still surviving today which was once owned by a Jew. Built in Norman times, around 1170, it is known as 'Jew's House' and attracted some attention in 1275 because of a young woman who lived there. She was Judith, daughter of Belaset (the daughter of Benedict of Lincoln, son of Moses of London, not the Belaset of Wallingford). In February of that year Judith was married next door in the building known as Jew's Court, which was thought to have served as the synagogue of Lincoln Jewry. Judith came from one of the most famous Anglo-Jewish families and her wedding brought guests from all over England to travel there. Belaset of Wallingford's house was valued in 1290 as 19s. 6d. - almost the highest figure in the list of properties formerly belonging to Jews (50).

Dorchester

Not far upstream, Jews could also be found in Dorchester, where a Jewish community sprang up in the mid thirteenth century. Individual Jews whose names survive are Solomon Episcopus, known formally as Solomon Episcopus de Dorcestria Iudeus, who is recorded as living there from 1241-1250. Although his surname might suggests some religious function, it had more of an economic significance, with a role akin to that of a royal bailiff, acting as an intermediary between the Crown and local Jewries (51). There was also Isaac of Dorchester in 1275, while Aaron of Dorchester is recorded there two years later (52). This was after the Statutum de Judeismo of 1275 whose provisions, as mentioned above, included restricting Jews to living in towns which had an archa, which Dorchester lacked. However, he was the beneficiary of special licences granted to individual Jews to dwell elsewhere. A few miles to the west, Abingdon had a small Jewish community, but none of the names of its members survive (53).

Wycombe

Away from the river Jews were scattered throughout the region. We know a number were present in Wycombe, for there was an edict expelling them from the town in 1235. We hear of one of them four years later, Isaac of Wycombe, for he had to pay a tax on a third of his property, although it is unclear whether this was in Wycombe or elsewhere (54). It does seem, though, that this expulsion was not wholly effective, or was later allowed to slip, for in the 1262 Oxford tallage are listed Moses of Wycombe and Ansell of Wycombe (55), while in 1286 we hear of Jacob de Wycumbe, who was accused of coinage violations, which is most likely to have been coin-clipping (56). Four years later, in June 1290, Jacob is found in Oxford where he was part of a jury of six Christians and six Jews empanelled to investigate an elaborate conspiracy to defraud the Abbey of Osney by Josce of Newbury (see below for details) (57). Leaving Wycombe and going further north, we hear of Moses of Aylesbury, who is listed as still being in arrears ten years after the amount he had been charged in the 1210 Bristol tallage (58). He would have needed to settle that debt fairly quickly, for the following year he faced more expenditure when he was one of those charged in the aid levied on Jews in 1221 towards the marriage of Henry III's sister Joan to Alexander II of Scotland (59). Josce of Aylesbury was another local resident who also found himself in difficulties, being accused of coin-clipping, for which he was indicted and bailed in 1247 (60).

Basingstoke

There were few Jews south of the area, but there is a passing reference to Ellis (Elias) of Fleet who had to pay 2 marks for the Easter tallage of 1254. (61). In the south-west was Lumbard (Longbeard), who paid four shillings and eight pence to gain a special permit to live in Basingstoke in 1273 (62). By this time, Jews were only able to live outside established communities if they purchased a royal licence to do so. Detailed records of his family tree survive: he was one of three sons from Licoricia of Winchester and her first husband, Abraham of Kent; his older brothers were Benedict (Baruch) and Cockerel (Isaac). After his father died, his mother married again, to David of Oxford, who was one of the wealthiest Jews of the town and whose business transactions covered several counties. However, the wedding nearly did not take place, owing to complications over David's divorce from his first wife, Muriel, possibly because she had not borne him any children. Muriel appealed to *a Beth Din* (rabbinic court) in France (English and French Jews had remained in close contact since Norman times, and the religious authorities there served both communities) to overturn the divorce on the grounds that it was against her will. The French Beth Din upheld her plea and an ad hoc English Beth Din ordered him to remarry Muriel, but David turned to the king, and no doubt made a gift at the same time. The result was that on 27th August 1242 Henry issued instructions to Moses of London, Aaron of Canterbury and Jacob of Oxford, the three members of the English Beth Din (63):

> We do hereby forbid you to hold henceforth any plea concerning David Jew of Oxford and Muriel who was wife of the same; nor under any circumstances are you to distrain him either to take or to keep that wife or any other. Know for a certainty that if you do otherwise, you will incur grave punishment therefore.

Lumbard's mother fulfilled her role to her new husband and bore him a son, Asher, in 1243 although David died the following year. So great was his estate that the massive death duty of five thousand marks was imposed, equivalent to £2,500,000 today (64). As a result, Licoricia was sent to the Tower of London as a way of preventing her fleeing abroad or defaulting. The majority of the sum was used for the king's construction of Westminster Abbey. David and Licoricia's house in Oxford was taken over by the Crown, with the rents arising being gifted to the Domus Conversorum in London. Licoricia moved to Winchester, where she was to meet a violent death in 1277 when she and her Christian maid were killed during a burglary. Lumbard himself had already moved to Basingstoke by then, while his son Solomon lived nearby in Odiham with his wife Joiette (daughter of Lumbard of Marlborough), having paid the king 28d. for the privilege of moving to an area in which Jews had not previously settled (65). Lumbard had not been alone in the town, for his brother – Jospin of Basingstoke – is recorded in 1272. They seemed to have had business links for Jospin, along with Lumbard and his other brother Isaac, were charged over a financial disagreement with Thomas de Chelwarton. On the day appointed for the hearing, none of them appeared in court, Jospin refusing to respond to the summons, Lumbard being out of the country and Isaac being sick in bed. By the time of the next hearing, Jospin and Lumbard were unavailable, both imprisoned in the Tower of London for non-payment of their tallages, while Isaac was still sick (66). No further details are know, save that Lumbard survived his period of incarceration and was still in England when the expulsion order was made in 1290 (67).

Isaac of Norwich, 1289 ('Hake' is a diminutive form of 'Isaac')

Newbury

There were also occasional Jews further west if we take a detour from the Thames, heading along the River Kennet, which intersects with it at Reading and leads to Newbury. When Bonefey or Bonevie left Bristol in 1231 to visit Newbury, he decided to remain there for a while, and gained permission to do so from Eleanor, Countess of Pembroke and sister to Henry III. He reappears in the records in 1241, accused of coin-clipping (68). He was also caught up in a violent incident that took place in the Warwick synagogue in 1245. It seems that Leo, son of Deuleben, along with his daughters

Anterra and Sigge, and his sister Muriel, all met Bessa, wife of Elias of Warwick at the door of the synagogue around midday on a Monday afternoon, whereupon (69):

> the said Leo kicked her with his foot so that she fell within the doorway in a fit as if dead, and the said Anterra, Sigge, and Muriel, and Henna, the wife of the said Leo, dragged the said Bessa out of the doorway by her hair and beat her and so ill-treated her that when she was brought home she miscarried of her infant, but the child was as yet too young for its sex to be distinguished...also that, when the said Bessa met the said Leo, Anterra, Sigge, Muriel, and Henna, she was wearing a buckle and rings of gold, but the number and quality of the rings are quite unknown; also that the said Bessa did not attack Anterra, daughter of Leo, nor beat or ill-treat her or gnaw her nose and ears; also that the said Bessa was carried home, and laid in her bed, and did not smear herself with the blood of animals, but, horrible to relate, was bathed in her own blood as she held her infant.

It is clear from this record that Leo was accused not only of assault, but also of theft, while his counter-claim was that Bessa had started the fracas by attacking his daughter and had then simulated injuries by covering herself with animal blood. In the event, Elias was fined for making a false charge of robbery, but Leo was found guilty of disorderly conduct and both he and his entire family were expelled from the town and banned from ever returning. Bonevie of Newbury was Leo's brother, and it is therefore to him that Leo turns when he has to provide someone willing to act as a pledge for Leo that no harm will come to Elias through Leo or from anyone acting on his behalf.

In the following decade a rare piece of information regarding personal possessions is revealed, for in 1253 the Sheriff of Hampshire, Henry de Farley, states that he has a valuable book belonging to Bonevie of Newbury - a Hebrew version of the Pentateuch - which he had given him as a pledge towards money owing to the king (70). After Bonevie died, his wife, Pucelle, carried on his business activities, although whether she was still living in Newbury or moved elsewhere is not clear. However, it seems that she died in suspicious circumstances, for in 1279 a warrant was issued for the arrest of John of Notley, then living in Winchester, to answer for her death (71). In 1272 the courts at Lincoln record a reference to Fluria of Newbury, widow of Bonevie of Newbury (which could be the same Bonevie just mentionned or a different person of the same name), and her decision not to prosecute a debt against the prior of Thurgarton (72). In the same year, Fluria appears before the Cambridge courts because she 'had lost the middle part of a chirograph for £20 under the names of Roger Russel and Abraham of Rye, which she had in her possession'. She is granted a writ for the chirograph in the chest and makes a payment for the privilege (73). There had been an expulsion of all Jews from the town in 1244, so either Fluria had returned there a few years later or the order had never been implemented fully. She was certainly not the only Jew living locally, for in 1275 we also hear of a Josce of Newbury (74). The following year, it is recorded in a then common but still rather delightful turn of phrase, that one of his clients, Alan de la Harloter, was now free from any outstanding debts 'from the Creation till the End of the World' (75). Josce was originally from Devizes and still had business interests there at the time of the expulsion, according to the bonds and money owing to him then: in the Oxford area, he was owed £23 11s 4d and 24 qtrs of corn amounting to £8, while in Wiltshire it was £22 6s 8d, along with 4 qtrs of corn worth £1 6s 8d (76). He may not have been able to collect those debts, for in October 1290, whilst other Jews were preparing to leave the country, he was on trial at the Tower of London, accused of forging three deeds of indebtedness to him for a total amount of £3,000 in the name of the Abbot and Convent of Reading and fabricating a copy of the Abbey seal on them. Owing to the indeterminate nature of the evidence, the jury was unable to reach a verdict and the matter dropped. It was this trial to which Josce of Wycombe had been summoned for jury service, as mentioned above (77).

<u>Hungerford</u>

Relatively nearby in Hungerford was Belia and her son-in-law Vivant. They were taken to court in 1244 by Hugh son of Hugh to contest a charge they made on him for 18 marks which he claimed he did not owe them (78). Meir of Hungerford can be dated there in 1253. By 1265 he is found in Oxford, where he had resettled with his wife Bassa (79). This was a typical feature of medieval Jews, who, unlike their Christian contemporaries, tended to be highly mobile. This was partly because they were not tied to land and could move their business easily to new areas, partly because they often had extended family living in other towns who could give them hospitality, and partly because local disturbances sometimes forced them to relocate. We know that Meir died sometime before 1273 thanks to a reference then to his death in a case over repayment of a loan taken out with Meir by Roger Gimel of Farindon, the ownership of which Meir had then sold to Gamaliel of Oxford (80). Apparently there was also someone Jewish residing on the outskirts of the town a few years later, for in 1287 the sheriff of Wiltshire was sent a writ to produce in court four Jews, one of whom was 'a Jew living at Caerleton outside Hungerford' (81). Another co-religionist a few miles to the north was Benedict of Lambourn, who we hear was owed four marks in 1278 by John de Rede of Upper Lambourn (82). Whether he had any Jewish company locally depends on whether he is the same as or different from the 'Jew of Lambourn' owed £2 13s 4d. in 1275 (83).

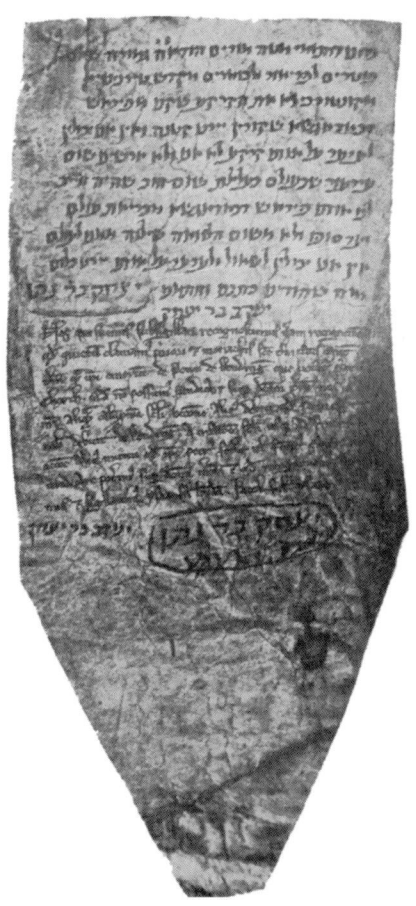

A starr, Jewish legal document c. 1236

Guildford

The vast majority of references so far to medieval Jews in the Thames Valley have been connected with financial transactions, as they are the main records to survive. As with the rest of Anglo-Jewry at that period, details of their social, cultural and intellectual life are far fewer, although attempts have been made to recreate a picture of their everyday life from the few hints that remain (84). Apart from documents, the only surviving physical item that may be connected with medieval Jewry in the region is the building discovered in 1996 beneath a property in Guildford High Street. It is speculated that it may have been the remains of a synagogue, or at least a private room belonging to a Jew's house. The structure is ten foot square and has a stone bench around the room. Possible clues as to its religious identity are the recess in the east wall, which may have housed an Ark, while scorch marks on the pilaster to one side of the recess may be from an Eternal Light (*ner tamid*). The building has been dated to c.1180 but its supposed Jewish connection is still not proven (85). There was certainly a Jewish community then, and it was also characteristic of Jewish homes to be built of stone rather than wood, which made them less vulnerable to attacks or fire should there be any local disturbances.

The names of some of the Guildford Jews later on are known thanks to their appearance in legal and fiscal records. One of the most famous residents was Isaac of Southwark, a Londoner who had extensive business interests throughout the southern England country, with dealings in Oxford, Cambridge, Surrey, Southampton and Devon. In 1274 he made a complaint to the Justices that the house in Guildford belonging to him and his wife Zipporah had been attacked, with the doors and windows broken, and his goods and chattels carried off. It is not clear from the records whether the family, including their daughter Slema, had been in residence at the time (86). When the incident came to court, the culprits were identified as Thomas, son of Martin, and William Haruwe, who broke in 'with force and arms', taking items to the value of 40s and causing damage worth one pound (87).

We also hear of other Jews who were subject to various fines in 1277: Abraham of Guildford (for trespass), Floria of Guildford (for a residency permit and erecting gates), and Josce of Guildford (for respite from prison). Josce's wife, Formosa, was also penalised. In her case, it was for missing an appearance in court after she had been summoned there, although the actual nature of the case against her is unrecorded (88). Josce (assuming he is the same person as Josceus of Guildford) appears to have then moved away and taken his family elsewhere, but it was not a wise decision, for he was killed by robbers near the town of Plumstead in 1281 (89). An inquiry as to his possessions at the time revealed that he owned no houses, lands or tenements but did have movable goods in the form of gold, silver, gages, jewels, bowls, brass vessels and cloths (90). However, even death was not the end of his woes, for his body was taken by cart for burial in London and as it passed through the highway of Southwark, it was overturned and trampled upon by a group of men, while those escorting the body were assaulted and beaten. The perpetrators were arrested but denied the offence, although one of them, Henry of Doneleghe, the bailiff of Southwark, did admit to stopping the cart and demanding two shillings as a toll, claiming this to be a long-standing custom. However, in an example of the courts upholding the rights of Jews to have freedom of travel along all public roads, it was ruled that (91):

> because he has no warrant from the king by which he may receive custom, since all Jews throughout the realm of England are quit by the king's charter of custom, the said Henry is committed to prison for the said offence until he has satisfied the king and the said Jews for it.

The final years: libels and fables

The flurry of court cases in that late period, both in Guildford and other towns, may have been connected with the Statutum de Judeismo (Statutes of Jewry) that was introduced in 1275 by Edward 1. It was an early experiment in social engineering that was very radical for its time. Edward was facing two problems: the vociferous opposition of the Church to usury, which was the mainstay of the Jewish community, and the deep unpopularity it brought upon them amongst the population at large. In addition, impoverished by formidable amounts of royal taxes and fines, the Jews were no longer of financial use to the Crown. He therefore ordered that they cease lending money on interest and instead turn to other trades, and become merchants, artisans and farmers. Various ordinances were made to accommodate this transition, such as Jews being allowed to hold land on ten year leases. However, a combination of other economic restrictions and the social antagonism between Jews and Christians meant that the experiment ended in failure. Jews were unable to make a success of their new businesses, with the result that some left England, and others secretly returned to usury. The increasingly difficult condition of English Jews may also have driven some to risk trying to make money by debasing existing coinage. This may then be reflected in the fact that in 1279 the sheriff of Berkshire, Alan son of Rowuld, was reimbursed for time and costs 'spent carrying various Jews arrested for clipping the king's money from Oxford to London' (92). In a similar note of recompense two years later, it is stated that as well as escorting Jewish prisoners to Newgate, he was also responsible for baptising some Jewish children (93).

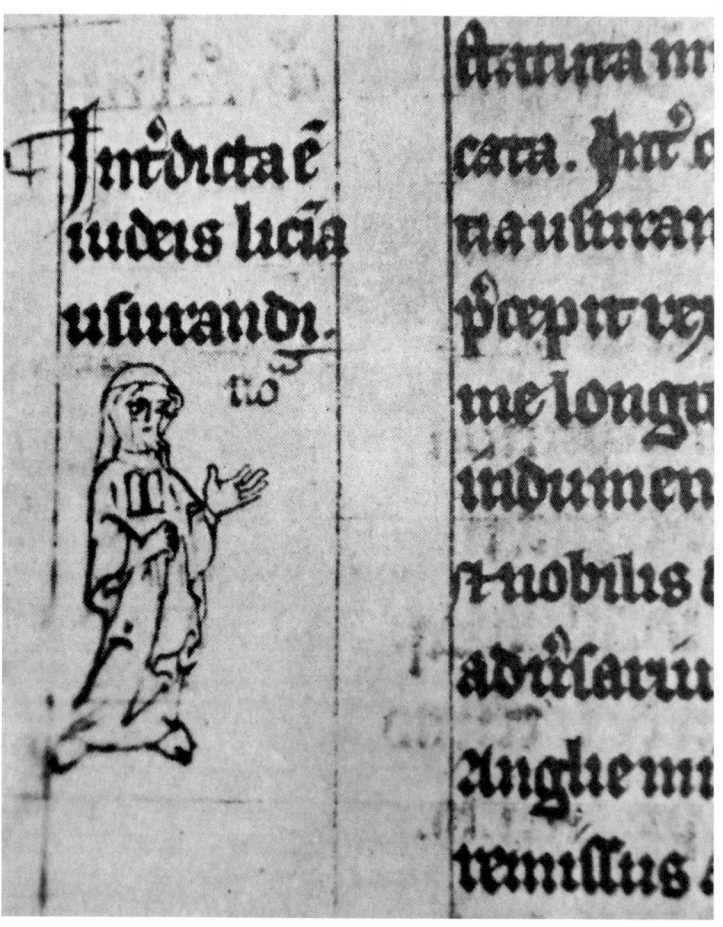

A 1275 manuscript forbidding Jews to practice usury, depicting in the margin a Jew wearing the Jew badge.

Of all the financial pitfalls and religious persecutions faced by Medieval Jews, perhaps the worst danger was the totally false accusation of Ritual Murder. It was claimed that, around Easter, Jews would crucify a Christian child in mocking imitation of the Crucifixion. There was no truth whatsoever in the libel, but the setting up of shrines with a reputation for procuring miraculous cures, persuaded credulous people, including King Henry III, that Jews were guilty of such atrocities. Every town felt it needed a martyr's shrine to cure the sick. From 1144 onwards, many English towns were the scene of Ritual Murder libels but there was no such occurrence in the Thames Valley. Still, from 1222, local Jews did share the indignity suffered by all English Jews of wearing the Jew badge, when the Council of Oxford introduced into England the provisions issued by the Fourth Lateran Council seven years earlier. The design of the badge varied across Europe, but in England it took the shape of the Two Tablets of Stone bearing the Ten Commandments, and had to be worn by all Jews over seven years old on their outer garment. Of course, the need for such a sign to designate a Jew implies that it was not always possible to discern whether a person was Jewish or not, and that they were not visibly different from their Christian neighbours (94).

On a more positive note, there is a suggestion of an important literary remnant from this time. As a generalisation, Medieval English Jewry was not renowned for its scholastic or literary ability. A few individual rabbis achieved recognition beyond these shores and had their opinions quoted in responsa abroad - such as Menachem of London (also known as Elias/Elijah Menachem) and Benjamin of Canterbury - but the great centres of rabbinic productivity were on the Continent and not to be found here (95). One of the few writers to achieve fame within the wider Jewish world was Berechiah ben Natroni Ha'Nakdan, the 12th century writer, grammarian and translator, sometimes described as 'the Jewish Aesop'. His works included Ethical Treatises, which summarised the views of Saadiah Gaon, as well as his translation of Adelard of Bath's scientific work *Questiones Naturales*. There has been much debate as to whether Berechiah can be identified as Benedictus Le Puncteur of Oxford (a nephew of Benjamin of Canterbury). Apart from having the same forenames and titles (Ha'Nakdan and Le Puncteur both mean 'the grammarian'), another possible hint as to this identification lies in Berechiah's preface to his most popular book, *Mishlei Shu'alim* (Fox Fables), where he refers to himself as 'a vagabond' in 'the island of the sea', a common description of English Jewry (96). Roth, for instance, places Berechiah as living in Northern France but asserts that he visited England and may have been recorded in the 1194 Northampton Donum (97). His correct identity is still under dispute, but in case he can be associated with England, it is appropriate to quote a short example of one of his 119 fables, written in Hebrew in rhymed prose, where, typically, he both tells his tale and comments upon it (98):

> A man taught the letters of the alphabet to a wolf. He said to him, 'Say *aleph*,' and the wolf answered, '*Aleph*'. The he said, 'Say *beth*,' and the wolf guarded the utterance of his lips and said *beth* and *gimel* after him. Said the man: 'Now listen to what I set before you, so that you may recognise the letters and put them together and so be able to pronounce what you will. When you combine the letters together, we shall be one people. Put *aleph* and *beth* together as I do.' The wolf responded 'Sheep! The parable is for one whose eye and heart are bent upon gain. His mouth will declare his wickedness and his lips will testify against him to reveal the frowardness of his heart .... He despises Jacob and chooses Esau.

Woodcut by Fritz Kredel illustrating the fox fable

As with the building in Guildford that may not have been a synagogue, the Fox Fables may not be from an English writer, and what could be two exciting structural and literary remnants of Medieval Anglo-Jewry may also prove fanciful myths.

What is much more certain is one of the very last references to local Jews: it concerned the sheriff of Berkshire, William de Greinvill, being ordered to bring Gilbert Wace to trial on 1st July 1290 over a hauberk (coat of mail) belonging to Roger de Clifford which Wace had taken from a Jew, Simon de la Haye. It is likely that Roger de Clifford had arranged a loan with Simon and given the hauberk as a pledge, and it had then been stolen from him by Wace (99). Simon was spending a considerable period in court at that time, for he was one of the jurors in the Abbey of Osney fraud case, mentioned above, that had been heard in Oxford the previous month. At the time of the expulsion a few months later, he is recorded as having bonds for 20 qtrs of corn worth £6 13s 4d (100). Of wider significance was the item which had allegedly been stolen from him, for a law enacted in 1181 had decreed that (101):

No Jew shall keep with him mail or hauberk, but let him sell or give them away, or in some other way remove them from him so that they may remain in the service of the king of England.

Having a hauberk as a temporary pledge may not have transgressed this law, but it reflected the fact that Jews, being outside the feudal hierarchy and chain of command, did not serve in the army. As a result they were not allowed to hold arms as this would effectively denude those who might be summoned to war and therefore also deprive the king of his full fighting strength. In some ways, bearing in mind the numerous wars through the early Middle Ages, this exemption was a great boon. However, it also meant that Jews had no arms with which to protect themselves during times of civil unrest and left them highly vulnerable when attacked by local mobs.

Expulsions – local and national

Throughout the thirteenth century Jews had suffered from a series of local expulsions in disparate parts of the country. In Berks and Bucks this included Wycombe (1235), Newbury (1244) and

Windsor (1283). However, in 1290 Edward I ordered the Jews to leave England entirely. It was the first time there had been a national expulsion of the Jews, either here or in any other country, although it was to be emulated in subsequent decades by France and later in Spain.

The official reason for the decision was that Jews had secretly engaged in usury despite the ban imposed in 1275. It was also alleged that Jews who had converted to Christianity had been persuaded to return to the Jewish faith by their co-religionists. Instances of both may well have happened, but they were not the decisive reasons. More important was the fact that - as a result of punishingly high royal taxation, ferociously hostile attacks by the church and a breakdown in relations with their non-Jewish neighbours - the Jews were now so impoverished and demoralised that they were of no use to the Crown. Their role over two centuries, in the trenchant description of Cecil Roth, as 'the royal milch-cow', had left them financially exhausted. The relationship between the king and his 'chattels' had always been based on their fiscal value. Moreover, expulsion would also bring Edward the political advantages of pleasing the Church, gaining popular acclaim and influencing Parliament to vote for extra taxes to bolster the royal revenues (102). The edict was issued on 18th July, which happened to coincide with the Hebrew date of 9th of Av, a fast day in the Jewish calendar, because on it occurred the destruction of the First and Second Temples (in 586 BCE and 70 CE) as well as other black events in Jewish history. Now one more disaster became associated with it. Nevertheless, it was an orderly expulsion, with Edward giving the Jews two and a half months in which to finalise their affairs. Moreover, they were allowed to take their cash and personal property with them. The actual edict has been lost, but the writ issued simultaneously to sheriffs remains (103):

> Whereas the king has prefixed to all Jews of his realm a certain time to pass out of the realm [the Feast of All Saints - 1st November], and he wills that they should not be treated by his ministers or others otherwise than has been customary, he orders the sheriff to cause proclamation to be made throughout his bailiwick prohibiting anyone from injuring or wronging the Jews within the said time. He is ordered to cause the Jews to have safe conduct at their cost when they, with their chattels, which the king has granted to them, direct their steps towards London in order to cross the sea, providing that before they leave, they restore the

pledges of Christians in their possession to those to whom they belong.

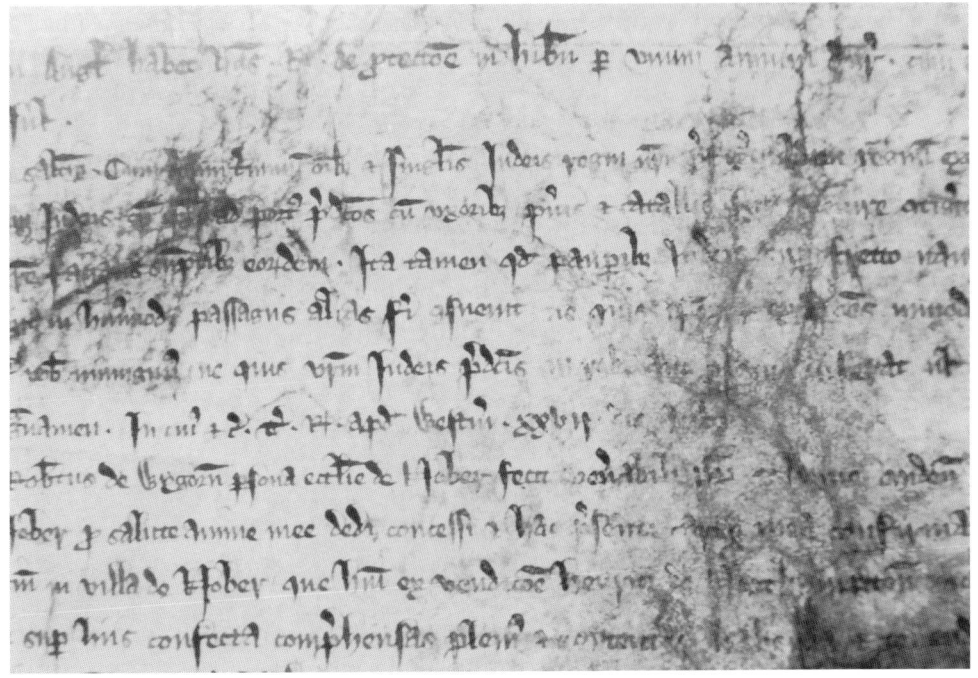

A fragment of letters granting safe conduct for Jews leaving England, July 1290

At face value, these terms were very generous. However, in reality, it was often hard for Jews to sell unwanted possessions for anything like the appropriate price, for purchasers knew that the departing Jews did not have time to hold out for higher offers. In addition, any bonds or real estate went directly to the Crown. More importantly, though, the Jews were guaranteed protection from harm, both in the intervening period and during their exodus from the country. According to instructions sent to the Wardens of the Cinque Ports (104):

> To each and every Jew of our kingdom we have fixed a definite time-limit for their departure from the kingdom. As we do not wish that they are harmed at all, whether in person or in possession during this period, we place these Jews in your care when they come to the above-mentioned

ports with their wives, children and belongings to cross the sea before the afore-mentioned limit. You should ensure that their passage is safe and speedy, and that their journey, for which they should pay the expense, is free from danger. In the same way, the poor amongst the Jews shall be treated sparingly when they come to cross the sea; and for others, according to their ability shall the charge be made, in a restrained fashion according to the type of passage they have. None of them shall be prevented from having passage by excessive or improper demands. We strongly lay upon you this grave responsibility, that no one shall be set upon the aforesaid Jews, whether against their person or their possessions in any way, and you shall not permit any injury, molestation, harm or impediment of any kind.

Not everyone heeded the king's command, and there was the notorious incident of Jews being left to drown on a sandbank in the Thames estuary and their goods stolen (105). However, most did depart safely, approximately 2,500 to 3,000 in number, a community that had already shrunk from its maximum size of 5,000 some fifty years earlier (106).

They settled largely in France, the community from which they had come two centuries earlier, and they disappeared from history as a recognisable group, assimilating into French Jewry and having to then endure further rounds of discrimination, persecution and expulsion. One of the last references to a local Jew is that of Meir of Oxford (also known as Myer of Cricklade, a small riverside town upstream from Oxford), who is recorded on a list of Jews living in Paris in 1296 as Mahy de Quiquelarde Lenglais (107). Jewish memories of the Thames meandering through Berks, Bucks and Oxon were not to be revived for several hundred years.

Apart from the possible, but by no means certain, discovery of the Guildford synagogue, no buildings or monuments remain to offer clues of the two hundred year residency of Jews in the area. Whereas London still has streets and sites named after them - such as Old Jewry and St Lawrence in Jewry - there are no equivalent memorials in Berks and Bucks, nor even in Oxford where the Jewish presence was greatest and they owned communal properties. The Oxford Jewish cemetery, which was adjacent to that of St John's Hospital, was taken over by it as an extension of its own land. The hospital later passed into the ownership of Magdalen College, which used the burial ground as a meadow and today it lies beneath the Rose

Garden, close to the Oxford Botanic Gardens. No tombstones remain, nor any records as to who rests there, although a memorial plaque has been placed on the site. The synagogue in Oxford - like all real estate owned by the departing Jews - fell to the king and he awarded it to William Burnell, the Provost of Wells, who donated it after his death to Balliol College. It was used as a tavern, known variously as Broadyates, the Pike Inn and the Dolphin (around 1520) before disappearing from history (108).

Aaron of Colchester 1277, labeled 'son of the devil' by a clerk who sketched in the records of a legal case involving him. He is wearing the Jew badge.

But for the fiscal records of Medieval Jewry that survive, their story might equally have been hidden from view. What is clear, though, is that while Medieval Anglo-Jewry may have congregated generally in towns and near royal strongholds, it also had a presence in more rural areas. Kings and bishops in urban centres may have been the clientele of the richer Jewish moneylenders, but most Jews operated on a smaller scale and their debtors included not only townsfolk but also villagers and peasant freeholders. Whilst the majority of Jewish moneylenders still resided in the larger towns and merely travelled to outlying areas for business, it is clear that others did settle further afield, including villages and towns along the Thames (109). Those Jews brave enough to venture into the more remote parts of the countryside between London and Oxford often found the Thames guiding their direction. Through the records of their financial dealings with non-Jews we gain an insight into the medieval 'river Jews' that might otherwise have sunk from view.

1. They could own houses in urban areas, whether for their own residence or to be rented out to others, although after 1271 this was limited to properties they lived in or rented only to Jews
2. Reva Berman Brown & Sean McCartney, 'David of Oxford and Licoricia of Winchester: glimpses into a Jewish family in thirteenth century England', in *Transactions* 39, 3
3. Anthony Wood i, p.129; quoted in Jacobs (1893) 4
4. Domesday 154, 160b; quoted in Jacobs (1893)
5. Blicestone is known today as Bletchingdon Roth (1951) 31; Richardson (1972) 127-132
6. At various times these included Bedford, Berkhamsted, Bristol, Cambridge, Canterbury, Colchester, Devizes, Exeter, Gloucester, Hereford, Huntingdon, Ipswich, Lincoln, London, Marlborough, Northampton, Norwich, Nottingham, Oxford, Stamford, Sudbury, Wallingford, Warwick, Wilton, Winchester, Worcester and York. Roth (1964) 91
7. Other cemeteries were established in Bristol, Cambridge, Canterbury, Northampton, Norwich and York
8. Roth (1951) 17
9. ibid. 151-154
10. Davis (1888) 369
11. These include Roth (1951), Cluse (2004) and several works since then by Pam Manix
12. Cohen (2005) 185, no. 960
13. Zefirah Entin Rokeah, 'Money and the hangman in late 13th century England', in *Transactions* XXXII, 201; Cohen (2005) 97, no. 115
14. Cohen (2005) 61 no. 372. A subsequent entry - 405A – describes how he 'with force feloniously opened the legs of the same Isabel with his left hand and by force oppressed her and made her bloody'.

15. Fodera p. 241; quoted in Ada Corcos, 'Extracts from the Close Rolls', in *Transactions* IV, 21 4
16. Rokeah (2000) 342
17. Close Rolls 13 October 1204; quoted in Jacobs (1893) 237
18. Joe Hillaby, 'The London Jewry: William 1 to John', in *Transactions* XXXIII, 34-36
19. Stokes (1913) 35; Roth (1964) 80
20. Rigg (1910) 229-230
21. Romain (1985) 47
22. Richardson (1972) 73, no. 236; Cohen (2005) 134
23. Rigg (1910) 129
24. Richardson (1972) 168, 192
25. ibid. 179
26. ibid. 120, no. 432; 131; Mundill (1988) 22
27. Roth (1951) 31
28. Palgrave, Commonwealth, ii, p. XXIV ff; quoted in Jacobs (1893) 41. With 20 shillings to the pound, and 12 pence to a shilling, the amount paid in interest was exactly right.
29. Phillips (1983) 27
30. Israel Abrahams, 'The Deacon and the Jewess: A Prefatory Notes' in *Transactions* VI, 259
31. F. W. Maitland, 'The Deacon and the Jewess', in *Transactions* VI, 260-276; see also Roth (1951) 19-21
32. Lauren Fogle, 'The Domus Conversorum' in *Transactions* 41, 6-7
33. Israel Abrahams, 'The Northampton Donum of 1194', in *Miscellanies* I, 64
34. Acta Sanctorum, lvi. 576 (19 Oct); quoted in Jacobs (1893) 68-70
35. Rigg (1905) 151
36. Rigg (1910) 188
37. Roth (1951) 32; Richardson (1972) 17
38. Mundill (1998) 51
39. Joe Hillaby, 'A magnate among the marchers: Hamo of Hereford', in *Transactions* XXXI, 34-35; Roth (1964) 56
40. Rigg (1905) 305
41. Rigg (1902) 63-4
42. Loewe (1932) II, 79; Rigg (1905) 73, 130
43. Roth (1951) 117, 134
44. Cecil Roth, 'Elijah of London', in *Transactions* XV, 53
45. Zefirah Entin Rokeah op. cit. 196; see Cohen (2005) 43 no. 272
46. Cohen (2005) 67 no. 406
47. Roth (1964) 79
48. Michael Adler, 'History of the Domus Conversorum', in

Transactions IV, 53
49. Lionel Abrahams, 'The Condition of the Jews of England in 1290', in *Transactions* IV, 64
50. Roth (1962) 52, 56, 304
51. Roth (1951) 6-7
52. Richardson (1972) 15, no. 45); Roth (1951) 31
53. Roth (1964) 277
54. Michael Adler, 'Jewish Tallies of the Thirteenth Century', in *Miscellanies* II, 18
55. Mundill (1998) 201-2
56. Zefirah Entin Rokeah op. cit. 195
57. Roth (1951) 164
58. Michael Adler, 'The Jews of Bristol in Pre-Expulsion Days', in *Transactions* XII, 144
59. Helena Chew, 'A Jewish Aid to Marry, A.D. 1221' in *Transactions*, XI, 101, 109
60. Zefirah Entin Rokeah op. cit. 196
61. Richardson (1972) 146
62. Rigg (1910) 104
63. Close Roll 1242 p. 464; see Roth (1951) 51-54 for a more detailed account the divorce proceedings.
64. A very helpful guide to rough comparative values is provided by Reva Berman Brown & Sean McCartney op. cit. 34, according to which the medieval sum of 1 mark - which was the same as 13s 4d (or 67p in modern usage) was equivalent to around £500 at the time of their research.
65. Rigg (1910) 163
66. Rigg (1905) 277, 294; (1910) 5, no. 14
67. For details of the rest of his family, see Brown & McCartney, ibid. pp. 1-34
68. Zefirah Entin Rokeah op. cit. 176
69. Rigg (1905) 103-4, 73
70. H. P. Stokes, 'Records of MSS and Documents Possessed by the Jews in England before the Expulsion', in *Transactions* VIII, 88
71. Cohen (2005) 185, no. 955
72. Richardson (1972) 9, no. 26
73. Rigg (1905) 311
74. Richardson (1972) 16, no. 55
75. Jenkinson (1929) 142
76. Lionel Abrahams op. cit. 101, 104
77. R. R. Mundill, 'The Jewish entries from the Patent Rolls 1272-1292', in *Transactions*, XXXII, 85; Roth (1951) 80

78. Rigg (1905) 81
79. Roth (1951) 31, 65
80. Rigg (1910) 115
81. Rokeah (2000) 343
82. Cohen (2005) 163, no. 877.
83. Robin R. Mundill, 'Lumbard and Son', in *Jewish Quarterly Review* LXXXII, 144 n. 24
84. Roth (1962) 26-45
85. Jewish Heritage Report, No. 1 (March 1997); further details on the excavation are available from Guildford Museum
86. H. P. Stokes op. cit. 90
87. Rigg (1910) 142
88. Richardson (1972) 151, 157, 158, 162, 164, 174, 180, 185, 188
89. Ada Corcos op. cit. 211
90. Brand (2005) 275, no. 1126
91. Brand (2005) 274 no. 1124
92. Rokeah (2000) 245
93. ibid. 258
94. Some Jews were able to purchase royal exemptions from wearing the Jew badge
95. For examples of the rulings of the two rabbis, see Jacobs (1893) 54, 288
96. Hadas (2001) 1
97. Roth (1951) 32 'It is impossible as yet to decide the argument fully one side or the other; the most that can be said is that there is considerable evidence in favour of the inherently improbable identification of Benedict Le Puinter in Oxford with Berachiah ben Natronai haNakdan, who was certainly in England about this time'.
98. Hadas (2001) 213
99. Rokeah (2000) 370
100. Lionel Abrahams op. cit. 101
101. Roger de Hovedene, Chronica, ii p. 261; quoted in Jacobs (1893) 75
102. For a full account, see Roth (1964) 68-90
103. Romain (1985) 58
104. ibid. 59
105. Roth (1964) 86
106. Causton (2007) 4
107. Robert Chazan 'Jewish Settlement in Northern France 1096 - 1306' in *Revue des Etudes Juives* (1968) 127, pp 41ff
108. Roth (1951) 100, 168
109. Mundill (1998) 11-12, 21-2

Chapter 2

1656: Absence and Return

In theory there were no Jews in England from the expulsion in 1290 until their readmission by Cromwell in 1656. In reality there were instances of individuals who made brief appearances. Some were officially invited here for specific purposes, such as the Italian Jewish doctors who were consulted about the health of Henry IV in 1410, or the rabbis whose opinions were sought as part of Henry VIII's attempt to find biblical justification to divorce Catharine of Aragon. Others came without official permission to be here, although it is only those whose Jewish identity was uncovered about whom we know. One such individual was found in 1450 living near Eton College, which had been established ten years earlier by Henry VI. Once discovered, the only way he could remain in the country was to be baptised. This occurred under the auspices of the king and he took the name Henry of Eton as a way of reflecting his loyalty to the monarch. He went to live in the Domus Conversorum in London, but left after three years, after which his whereabouts are unknown (1). A much longer resident was a Jew who converted and took the name Henry of Windsor, who stayed there from 1488 until his death in 1509. Although both parts of his name could have been adopted as a double compliment to the king, it is more likely that it meant that he had some connection to Windsor itself, for most others recorded in the list of inmates took names reflecting towns with which they had been associated or lived (2). The presence of both men in England before they had converted indicates that a certain number of Jews did enter the kingdom despite the ban. This trend increased as the woes affecting Spanish Jewry grew. After their expulsion from the Peninsular in 1492, whole groups of families sought refuge here, albeit posing as devout Catholics. In most cases, though, their stay was temporary and occurred in London.

Two practising Jews associated with the Thames Valley in the seventeenth century were attracted here because of academic opportunities at Oxford University. However, they could not remain for long as Jews. Jacob Wolfgang therefore converted in 1608 in order to become a permanent member of the University. Another scholar, Jacob Barnett, arrived in 1610 and toyed with the idea of conversion. However, when he failed to do so, he was forced to leave the country under the edict of expulsion (3). Another temporary Jewish resident in the town was known as Jacob - possibly Cirques Jobson - and was responsible for opening a coffee house there in 1650. It was the first such establishment in England, which he later transferred to Holborn, London, although it is not known how long he was able to stay in the country before having to either convert or depart (4).

Jews were banned from England from 1290 to 1656, but a medal to commemorate the accession of Edward VI in 1547 was inscribed in Greek and Hebrew

During this period, Maidenhead had acquired a fully independent existence as a town. Previously it had been under the jurisdiction of the Royal Manors of Cookham and Bray, with the former controlling matters concerning those north of the High Street and the latter overseeing those south of it. In 1582, however, Maidenhead was granted a charter by Elizabeth 1, designating it as a Corporation and henceforth responsible for its own internal affairs, including local statutes, court, market and a toll over the bridge (5). By then it was already a regular stopping point for the royal mail service from London that had been established three years earlier. Maidenhead was also sufficiently well-known to merit a line in Shakespeare's *The Merry Wives of Windsor* (published 1602), when Falstaff is warned 'there is a friend of mine comes to town, tells me, there is three cozen-germans that has cozened all the hosts of Reading, of Maidenhead, of Colebrook, of horses and money' (6).

The Civil War put Maidenhead at the centre of the conflict, midpoint between the Parliamentarians in London and the Royalist headquarters in Oxford, with constant troop movements in the area and two major battles at Newbury. The town was sympathetic to the Parliamentary cause and there was a large troop encampment on The Thicket. After the capture of Charles I, he was brought to Maidenhead to bid farewell to his children, which he reputedly did at the Greyhound Inn, now the site of the NatWest Bank. He was imprisoned in Windsor Castle where, after his trial and execution in London, he was brought back for burial. Cromwell's victory, like that of William 1, was to prove a decisive moment in Jewish history, for in 1656 he overturned Edward I's edict of expulsion and allowed Jews back into England after an official absence of almost 400 years. By that time, there was a small unofficial community living in the capital that was still claiming to be Catholic. They now openly professed their Jewish allegiance, rented a house for use as a synagogue and, later that year, purchased a cemetery. However, the death of Cromwell in 1658 and the return of the Stuarts two years later, meant that the position of the Jews, which had not been formally ratified and depended upon Cromwell's authority, was now in jeopardy.

It was at this critical moment that Berkshire first features in Jewish life after the readmission, in an incident that at the time seemed very dangerous but which turned out to be highly advantageous. In 1664 the Conventicle Act was passed, which banned services that were not conducted in accord with the liturgy of the Church of England. This had been intended as applying to Christian acts of worship, but the Earl of Berkshire tried to use it as an attempt to blackmail the Jewish community, suggesting that it applied to them too and effectively prevented them from holding their own services. He also informed them that in return for a payment, he would ensure that they were free from molestation and could carry on praying undisturbed. (It may be worth noting that his father, the Earl of Suffolk, had been responsible for expelling a group of Marranos caught living in England in 1609 when he was Lord Chamberlain). Instead of seeking the Earl's protection, the Jews immediately petitioned Charles II who assured them that they had no cause for fear, and on 22nd August the Privy Council declared that the Jews 'might promise themselves the effects of the same favour as formerly they have had, so long as they demean themselves peaceably and quietly, with due obedience to His Majesty's laws and without scandal to his government'. It was the first official confirmation of the legality of Jewish residence, and the Earl of Berkshire had unintentionally ensured that their stay here was henceforth legal and incontrovertible (7).

The Earl of Berkshire

The earliest reference to an individual Jews in Berkshire is not until the next century: Joseph Collins, a Jewish Freemason, who is recorded as belonging to the Mitre Lodge in Reading in 1725. Whether he actually lived in the town, or just joined the Lodge because of an acquaintance who was a member, is open to conjecture (8). More certain is the fact that Lyon Nathan had been living in Reading at some stage, as that appears in his records when he was naturalised in 1763, although by then he was overseas in Pennsylvania (9). Someone residing locally around that point was a Jewish jeweller in Twyford called Castelfranc, who was found in Twyford in 1764 (10). None of them stayed for long in the area, although the paucity of Jews did not mean there was no interest in them: in 1829 Henry Hart Milman, the vicar of St Mary's, Reading (later, Dean of St Paul's Cathedral) wrote his renowned 'History of the Jews'. It is quite possible that despite reflecting eloquently about Jews in the past, he never met a living one whilst writing the book. It was not until Isaac Goldman appears as a tailor in Reading in 1842, living at 42 Friar Street, that Jews started putting down roots locally, with their families staying there for several decades. Isaac Skitten also came to Reading at the time, and his grandson - born in Reading - was Rev. Dr Abraham Cohen, who was to become a leading scholar, whose works included a commentary for the *Soncino Chumash*, and who was the President of the Board of Deputies from 1949 to 1955 (11).

Given the rarity of Jews locally, it is somewhat surprising that when Jews were permitted to enter Parliament in 1858, one of the earliest Jews to take his seat in the House of Commons did so in Reading, when Francis Henry Goldsmid, took the seat as a Liberal MP in 1860 and became only the fourth Jew to sit in the House of Commons. The family already had a local connection as his father, Sir Isaac Lyon Goldsmid (the first Jew to receive an English hereditary title) had bought Whiteknights Park, Reading (12).

The grounds were held by the family until 1947 when they were purchased by the University of Reading. Born in London in 1808, Francis had initially trained for the Bar, becoming both the first Jewish barrister and Q.C. in England. Like his father, he had been deeply engaged in the struggle for Jewish emancipation, and contributed numerous pamphlets to the cause, including 'The Arguments advanced against the Enfranchisement of the Jews considered in a series of letters' (1831). Unlike some later Jewish MPs who preferred to hide their roots, he was not afraid to stand up for Jewish causes and one of his first acts in the House of Commons was to draw attention to the case of Edgar Mortara, a Jewish child abducted from his home in Bologna and baptised in Rome. Goldsmid was equally committed to reform in religious spheres too, and was one of the founders of the first Reform congregation in Britain, the West London Synagogue, which had begun in 1840. He worked tirelessly on its behalf and was widely regarded as a prime cause of its early success. He was active in wider communal life too, being a vice-president of the Anglo-Jewish Association which he had helped to establish in 1871. Perhaps because of his high Jewish profile there was a strong local antisemitic campaign against him during his first election contest, although it did not prevent him winning the seat. He remained MP for Reading for the next eighteen years, winning three further elections until his death in 1878.

Francis Henry Goldsmid

Goldsmid may have spent much time in his constituency, but his main residence was in London. A settled Jewish community in Reading did not start until 1886 when thirteen families joined together to form the Reading Hebrew Burial Society. It grew rapidly thereafter, with a place of worship established at 6 Anstey Road two years later that served a Jewish population of sixty to seventy adults (13). Further growth led to a splendid new synagogue being opened in October 1900 in Westfield Road (later renamed Goldsmid Road after a member of the Goldsmid family who had owned the plot of land and donated it to the community).

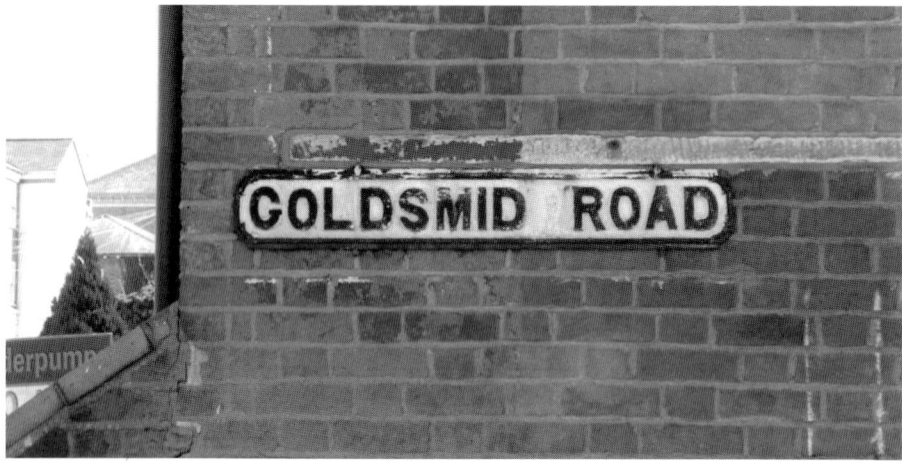

The inaugural service was attended by a host of London dignitaries, including the Chief Rabbi, Hermann Adler, the President of the Federation of Synagogues, Sir Samuel Montagu, and the President of the Anglo-Jewish Association, Claude Montefiore. The wide range of its communal activities - religious, educational and social - that extended far beyond provision of burial meant a new name was required and it became the Reading Hebrew Congregation.

The growth of the community owed much to an event far away and which was to be a key turning point in the history of British Jewry at large: the assassination of Czar Alexander II in 1881, which led to a wave of antisemitic pogroms orchestrated by the government and resulted in the mass emigration of Jews from Russia. Almost a million Jews went to the United States and around 100,000 arrived in Britain, with the vast majority settling in London and other major cities. Whilst their presence was eventually to prove highly beneficial, in the short-term it led to chronic overcrowding in unsanitary conditions, the growth of the notorious sweat-shops, and accusations that they were taking away jobs from local people. The established Jewish community had been in existence for almost two centuries by then and took pride in the way it had quietly integrated into British life and had become generally accepted. Nervous of the way in which the immigrants were bringing British Jewry under public scrutiny, the Jewish authorities were very keen to solve these social problems as quickly as possible. Alongside various attempts to assimilate the newcomers by founding institutions to anglicise them, another answer was to break up the urban concentration and encourage their dispersal around the country. It may well have been this factor that led so many of London's Jewish elite to be present at not only the launch of Reading's bid for a synagogue, but also the laying of its foundation stone a year later and then again at its inaugural service. Speaking at the second of those events, Sir Hermann Gollancz spelt out his motives (14):

> During the past twelve months, in the course of my enlisting the sympathy of the [wider Jewish] community on behalf of Reading, I have often been asked: Why do you take such special interest in this movement? And my answer has been: Because I believe that a great social problem is involved in the history of the Reading Jews. They hail for the most part from the congested districts in the East End of London, being sensible enough to understand that any movement tending to relieve such congested districts is a boon not only to the Jews themselves but also to the general population in whose midst they dwell.

In this respect, Reading was just one part of a general plan for the dispersal of East European immigrants out of London, with families being helped by Montagu's Jewish Dispersion Committee to go also to Leicester, Blackburn, Dover and Stroud (15). However, as Geoffrey Alderman has noted, Reading shone out: 'Efforts to persuade immigrants to leave or simply not settle in the capital were (inevitably) not a conspicuous success, the community established in Reading being the exception that proved the rule' (16). As well as a building, it had its own minister, Rev. Nathan Aarons (who also served as the local *shochet* - ritual slaughterer) and a religion school of over thirty children. The membership reflected the prevailing trades of the 'children of the ghetto': tailors and cigar manufacturers, along with shopkeepers, furriers and those involved with other aspects of the clothing industry. It was a solid beginning that was to stand the test of time, with the community still in existence today.

Reading Hebrew Congregation

A more temporary group who found their way into the Home Counties were some Russian Jews who came to Aylesbury in 1886. They were brought there by the Russo-Jewish Committee (headed, amongst other notables, by Sir Nathaniel - later Lord - Rothschild). As before, this was motivated by a desire both to help co-religionists and to lessen the embarrassment of the Jewish establishment. In this case, the object was to export the problem by training them as farmers on the Rothschild estates before sending them to the United States where the Committee had established agricultural settlements for refugees. Despite the short-lived existence of the venture, the Committee's report on the Aylesbury farm ended with high hopes (17):

> If the small settlements of Russian Jews which have been planted should hereafter develop into prosperous and thriving Colonies in the countries now in their infancy, then a lasting monument will have been erected, not only to the noble feelings of sympathy with a suffering race that were kindled in England in February 1882, but also to the vigour and endurance of the Jewish people, which enabled them to withstand all suffering and overcome every obstacle, to raise themselves from the

lowest depths of misery and destitution to positions of manly independence and peaceful livelihood.

Over in Oxford, Jews had been present after the Readmission for longer than those in Berkshire, with early residents including Manuel ben Hayyim Levy, who was born in Oxford in 1733 and was circumcised there by Isaac Carriao de Payba. Others began to settle there too, although they still belonged to synagogues in London and used their facilities both during their lifetime and upon death. Thus when Oxford resident Henry Isaacs died in 1812, he was taken to London for burial by the Great Synagogue, of which he was a member (18). By 1841 there were sufficient Jews in the town for an organised community to be formed, and premises for a synagogue were acquired in Paradise Square seven years later. Estimates based on the synagogue membership list, which generally recorded male members only, suggest that there were a maximum of 50 Jews living in Oxford then (19).

Other Jews were scattered in smaller towns in the area. Jacob Davis lived in Thame from 1806 to 1810. He had been born in Mulhausen, Germany and after he came to England he had married Anne Solomon in a London synagogue in 1805. After Thame, they moved to Cheltenham, where he set up as a pawnbroker, and later silversmith. One of their children was John Davis who became a successful manufacturer of miners' lamps, while another was Arthur Davis who was noted for his translation of the Jewish liturgy (20). Meanwhile in Wendover, Judah Samuel had established himself as a tanner sometime prior to 1778. He seems to have been very successful, for in the Parish Records of 1790 it states that 'Samuel the Jew owns six houses in Back Street'. No Jews are known of in Maidenhead at that time, but there were some in Windsor, for Myer Solomon, the *mohel* attached to the Western Synagogue in London records that he visited the town among the many places at which he performed circumcisions between 1782 and 1839 (21).

Further upriver, David Ximenes, a Jewish stockbroker from London and a member of the Bevis Marks Synagogue, bought Bear Place, Wargrave in 1784. The exotic associations of his name and faith in the eyes of the local population lead to much gossip, including the rumour that after buying the estate, the reason he then rebuilt the house on higher ground was because his hot Spanish blood was unable to stand the damp in low places (22). After his death two years later, the estate passed to his son Moses (1762-1837), also a stockbroker, who preferred to be known as Morris and who participated in social and cultural events locally. He raised a troop of territorials, known as the Wargrave Rangers whom he commanded in the Peninsular War and whom he housed in cottages on land adjacent to his property. He was an early example of those Jews who embraced wider society to such an extent that they abandoned Judaism altogether. He had long been a non-practising member of Bevis Marks Synagogue, but when he was asked to join the Mahammad, the synagogue council, this triggered his decision to resign and he converted to Christianity. However, his breach with the Jewish community was not rancorous, for he paid the traditional fine imposed by Bevis Marks for not taking up office and he informed the synagogue authorities that he would always be amenable to contributing to 'any of those charities that do so much honour to your heads and hearts, and in which no body of people are so particular as yourself'. His move into English society was furthered when he was appointed High Sheriff of Berkshire in 1805, knighted the following year and also became a magistrate (23).

Around the same time, we come across Jacob Levy (1774-1823), another Londoner who had moved to Berkshire, settling in Newbury. By contrast, he was from an Ashkenazi background, belonging to the Hambro Synagogue, and he maintained his Jewish connections throughout his life (24). Someone who may have lost contact with her Jewish family was Sarah Hawkins who died in September 1871 and lies buried in St Mary's Church, Winkfield near Ascot. She had lived nearby in Winkfield Street with her husband, Thomas, who is buried beside her. The fact that she was Jewish might be indicated by a large Star of David on her tombstone. If so, this may have been an early example of a mixed-faith relationship, with a Jewish girl falling in love with a non-Jewish man and marrying him. This possibility is reinforced by the fact that their grave is placed immediately by the church gate, which may be because she never converted to Christianity and so their grave (she died first) was placed on the furthest part of the cemetery.

Meanwhile the origins of a long family association with Slough began through Lawrence Lazarus. He was born in the East End of London and worked there in the cigar trade, later moving to Slough in 1865 to manage a pawn-broking shop. The family were to remain in the area, developing the business into a well-known furniture store - Isaacs - that continued up to 1987 under the guidance of several successive generations of the family.

Across the border in Buckinghamshire, the year 1833 was a notable date, marking the beginning of a long relationship between the county and the Rothschild family. It was then that the founder of the British branch of the Frankfurt family, Nathan Mayer Rothschild (1777-1836), rented Tring Park as a summer residence (25). It led to a major Rothschild presence locally through three of his children: his youngest son Mayer Amshel took up residence in Mentmore Village in 1842 and

Gravestone of Sarah Hawkins

then built Mentmore Towers; his second son Anthony bought the Aston Clinton estate in 1851; his eldest son Lionel purchased the Halton estate in 1853. The next generation, in the form of Lionel's children, continued the process: his oldest son Nathaniel Mayer acquired Tring Park and four thousand acres of land in 1872; his third son Leopold bought extensive lands at Ascott in 1873; his daughter Evelina married Ferdinand, from the Austrian branch of the family, who acquired land at Waddesdon in 1874 and built Waddesdon Manor, while his sister Alice established Eythrope nearby the following year. Their physical presence in the vale of

Aylesbury was extended even further by the Rothschild stag-hound hunts, which became a regular feature of the countryside from 1839 after kennels were established in Hastoe. No wonder that some locals dubbed the area 'Judea', while one squire (Duncombe of Great Brickhill) claimed that the hill on which his house was built was the only one in the neighbourhood that had not a Jewish owner (26).

Nathaniel Meyer Rothschild's seal as Lord Lieutenant of Berkshire, 1889

Land brought local responsibilities and political access. Mayer Amshel was appointed High Sheriff of Buckinghamshire in 1847, while Anthony and Ferdinand also occupied the position in 1861 and 1883 respectively. Nathaniel Meyer sat as MP for Aylesbury from 1865 until he was elevated to the peerage in 1886, becoming the first Lord Rothschild (of Tring Park). He was appointed Lord Lieutenant of Buckinghamshire in 1889. His brother-in-law Ferdinand took over the Parliamentary seat, serving till 1898. He was then succeeded by Nathaniel Meyer's son, Lionel Walter, who held it until 1910, whereupon it was taken up by his cousin Lionel Nathan until 1923. In effect, the Rothschilds represented Aylesbury in Parliament from 1865 to 1923, with four different members of the family holding the seat in succession, as well as taking a prominent role in local politics and honorary offices. It was a remarkable record over six decades.

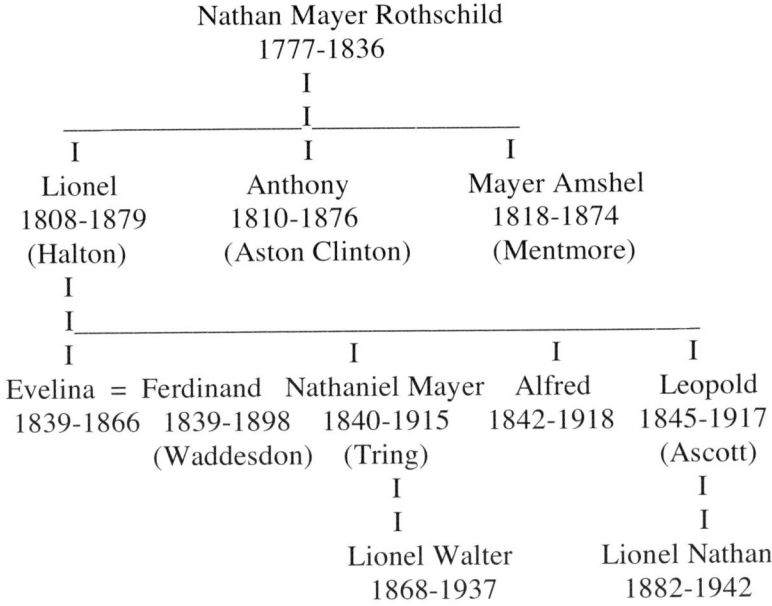

The social standing of the Rothschilds even led to a royal visit locally in 1890. In the words of *The Graphic* (27):

> On Wednesday last, her Majesty spent the afternoon with Baron Ferdinand de Rothschild, M.P., at his Buckinghamshire seat. 'Waddesdon Manor', the World says, 'is quite an Aladdin's palace. The site of the splendid house, which is crammed with pictures, old furniture, statutary, and priceless china, was simply a bare hill not many years ago; but now there are beautiful terraced gardens in what was formerly a mere waste, and a park has been formed by transplanting large trees from a distance. There is not a country residence in England which shows more forcibly how much can be done by the combination of unlimited expenditure and perfect taste.' Her Majesty reached Aylesbury from Windsor soon after one o'clock. The town was gaily decorated for the occasion with Venetian masts, flags,

banner and triumphal arches. Escorted by a detachment of Royal Bucks' Hussars, Her Majesty drove through Great Western Street to Market Square, where a loyal address was presented, and thence along the Bicester Road to Waddesdon. Her Majesty remained at Waddesdon, and inspected many of the priceless treasures.

The Rothschild estates also entered national history on 2nd November 1917 when the Foreign Secretary, Arthur Balfour, addressed a letter to Walter, the second Lord Rothschild, at Tring Park as the representative of British Jewry. The letter expressed the British government's favourable attitude to the establishment in Palestine of a national home for the Jewish people, and was a major boost in the campaign that led eventually to the creation of the State of Israel. It was received by Lord Rothschild in Tring. As Nahum Sokolow, one of the early Zionist leaders, wryly observed: the Declaration had been 'sent to the Lord and not to the Jewish people because they had no address, whereas the Lord had a very fine one' (28). For its part, Waddesdon was to be remembered for serving a very different function, as a hostel for evacuee Jewish children during the Second World War. The Rothschild estates were also occasionally used as discreet locations for diplomatic meetings when privacy was essential. Thus, during a period of rising Anglo-German tensions, Arthur Balfour met leading German figures at a conference held at Halton in February 1898, which by then had passed to Lionel's son, Alfred (29). Another common feature of the Rothschild residences was their reputation for exquisite hospitality. It was highlighted by the Liberal Prime Minister, Herbert Asquith, a frequent guest at Waddesdon, who recorded an example of the exchange between servants and guests (30):

'Which will you have, sir - tea, coffee or chocolate?'
'Tea.'
'What kind of tea, sir - China, India or Ceylon?'
'India.'
'What will you take with it, sir - cream, milk or lemon?'
'Milk.'
'What kind of milk, sir - Jersey, Guernsey or Alderney?'
I confess, added, Asquith, I should have been tempted to reply
'Sark'

A national figure of Jewish origins associated with South Bucks was Benjamin Disraeli. Born in London in 1804, he was baptised into the

Church of England at the age of 12 by his father, Isaac D'Israeli, not out of any sense of conviction but as a way of enabling his son's career to develop unhindered by barriers faced by Jews. In this respect, it was a very prescient move, leading to the highest elected office in the country. Benjamin's connection with the area started in 1829 when his father had first rented Bradenham House, near High Wycombe, as his country home. Benjamin often stayed there and went on hunts around the area. Moreover, his political career started locally, standing as an MP for High Wycombe on three successive occasions: in a by-election in 1832 and in the general elections the following year and in 1835, each time as a Radical. He was unsuccessful in all attempts, although he did achieve local office when he became a Buckinghamshire magistrate in 1836. He went on to enter Parliament as Tory MP for Maidstone twelve months later, which he held for ten years, after which he stood down so as to transfer back to Buckinghamshire when one of its sitting MPs died unexpectedly. He had always maintained his links with the area, and had become a Deputy Lieutenant in 1845. He was elected as one of its three County MPs in 1847. His father died the following year (and was buried in the parish church there) and Disraeli took the opportunity to buy the adjoining Hughenden estate (31). This had been a long-held ambition, partly so as to join the ranks of the landed gentry, and partly because of his love of the area. It was no surprise, therefore, that his local roots led him to take the title of Earl of Beaconsfield when he was offered a peerage after he retired as Prime Minister.

    Disraeli's residency at Hughenden led to many national personalities visiting him there, while it also brought Queen Victoria to the area when she had lunch with him in December 1878, only the second time that she had been the guest of one of her prime ministers. Royal approval did not stop his critics carping, with the historian Edward Freeman describing her as 'going ostentatiously to eat with Disraeli in his ghetto' (32). Lasting evidence of his attachment to the area lies in the fact that upon his death in April 1881, although eligible as a former Prime Minister to have a state funeral and burial in Westminster Abbey, he chose instead to be interred in a private ceremony besides his wife, Mary-Anne, who had been buried in the churchyard of St Michael and All Angels in Hughenden nine years earlier. Nevertheless, the funeral guest-list was an impressive one, including the Prince of Wales, other members of the Royal family, various ambassadors and leading political figures. Royal protocol meant that Queen Victoria did not attend the funeral of one of her subjects, but in a remarkable act of respect for her favourite prime minister, she made a pilgrimage there four days after his burial (33). Disraeli had remained a nominal Christian throughout his adult life, but he never shied away from his Jewish roots, and was accepted in Jewish society as a fellow Jew if not exactly a co-religionist. The attitude was epitomised by Louise de Rothschild's expression of 'a sort of pride in the thought that he belongs to us - that he is one of Israel's sons' (34).

The memorial to Disraeli in Hughenden

South Bucks was also home to Hermann Landau (1849-1921). Born in Poland, he had come to England in 1864. He started as a schoolmaster but later went into the Stock Exchange, and was involved with a number of Jewish and non-Jewish charitable endeavours, which included founding Jews' Temporary Shelter, a hostel for Jewish refugees. He received the OBE for his work on behalf of Belgian refugees during the First World War. He had a residence in London, but he also lived in Pipers Corner, Beaconsfield, where he was a familiar figure. A few miles away, Burnham became the country home of the London-based newspaper owner Edward Levy-Lawson when he purchased Hall Barn in 1881. His father had transformed the *Daily Telegraph* from its previously precarious existence into the best-selling newspaper of the day. Edward continued its success, and was raised to the peerage, taking the title Lord Burnham after his new home. Hall Barn became a centre of country pursuits, and the Prince of Wales (later Edward VII) stayed there every year from 1892 to 1910. Levy-Lawson took up local responsibilities, becoming High Sheriff of Buckinghamshire, as well as Justice of the Peace and then Deputy Lieutenant. He died in London in 1916 but was buried in Beaconsfield. Whilst he himself was Jewish, his wife Harriette Webster, was not Jewish. They married in church and he later converted to the Anglican faith. His son Harry Levy-Lawson succeeded him in the baronetcy, and was active in both political life and the Territorial Army. His chairmanship of the committee of teachers and local authorities led to the agreement over teachers' pay in 1920 known as 'the Burnham Scale'. Hall Barn remains within the family.

1. Michael Adler, 'History of the Domus Conversorum', in *Transactions* IV, 37
2. ibid. 39
3. Roth (1964) 147
4. Roth (1938) 223
5. The toll was maintained until 1903
6. Act IV Scene V
7. Cecil Roth, 'The Resettlement of the Jews in England', in Lipman (1961) 20
8. John M. Shaftesley, 'Jews in English Regular Freemasonary 1717-1860', in *Transactions* XXV, 196
9. W. S. Samuel, 'A List of Jewish Person Endenized and Naturalised 1609-1799', in *Transactions* XXII, 132
10. Roth (1950) 23
11. Krisman (2001) 4
12. Middleton (1975) 68-9
13. *Jewish Year Book* (1896) 86
14. Gollancz (1916) 139
15. Alderman (1987) 37
16. Alderman (1992) 166
17. Bentwich (1956) 3-4
18. Roth (1950) 89
19. V.D. Lipman, 'A Survey of Anglo-Jewry in 1851', in *Transactions* XVII, 182
20. Roth (1950) 19; correspondence with Dave Rimmer
21. Barnett (1961) 155

22. Malcolm Brown, 'Anglo-Jewish country houses from the Resettlement to 1800', in *Transactions* XXVIII, 31
23. Endelman (1990) 18; Gray & Griffith (1980) 195
24. Roth (1950) 19
25. Tring is in fact just on the Hertfordshire side of the border separating Herts and Bucks, but is considered by many locals to be in Bucks and was accepted as such by David Kessler in his study of the Rothschilds in Buckinghamshire (see below), as it is for the purposes of this study.
26. Kessler, 'The Rothschilds and Disraeli in Buckinghamshire', in *Transactions* XXIX p. 233; much of the material in this section is drawn from his article
27. *The Graphic*, 17 May 1890
28. Weizmann (1967) 78
29. Bermant (1971) 125
30. Asquith (1928) 187
31. The property is now owned by the National Trust, part of which is leased out and for many years was the home of Tilly Edelman, the wife of the Jewish MP Maurice Edelman. She was a member of Maidenhead Synagogue, and their daughter Sonia Greenwood still is.
32. Blake (1966) 607
33. Kessler op. cit. 244
34. Quoted in Endelman & Kushner (2002) 2

Chapter 3

1838: The Railway and the River

As for Maidenhead, for several centuries its population had not grown markedly and by 1801 only stood at 949 people. However, the introduction of long-distance coaches that operated by change of horses at major stops led to new trades springing up to meet their needs and increased the town's size. These included blacksmiths, saddlers, wheelwrights, vets and stable-keepers. A survey taken in 1834 found that over a period of two weeks 823 coaches passed through the town, involving the use of 3,000 horses (1). Shortly afterwards, Maidenhead experienced a major leap forward thanks to Great Western Railways, with the first train running to the town in 1838, providing a speedy and convenient way of transporting both goods and people. The journey from London was now about an hour, whereas previously it had taken much of the day by horse. It brought an end to the coaching trade, but led to Maidenhead becoming an attractive residence for those commuting to London, as well as a manageable destination for day-trippers.

The transformation of Maidenhead, from a small town out in the countryside to a bustling centre brought closer to the metropolis by the railways, began to attract the interest of Jews as much as it did that of others. From 1874 onwards there were regular advertisements in the *Jewish Chronicle* of properties for sale or to rent, while twenty years later it was considered worthwhile to advertise dance classes there (2). Moreover, fiction followed fact, as in the case of Julia Frankau's novel, *Dr Phillips: A Maida Vale Idyll* (written in 1887 under the pen-name of Frank Danby), which reflected, albeit in a highly critical way, the lifestyle of a particular group of affluent social-climbing West End Jews. Their visits locally are hinted at in an episode in which the evil Dr Phillips takes his non-Jewish friend, Mary Cameron, out on the river (3):

> He decided on staying at Skinner's, at Maidenhead. Now whenever the Israelites assemble in any force on the river, Maidenhead is the point of departure. At Oxford he might have been certain, or almost so, of escaping detection. At Maidenhead he would be running his neck right into the noose.

One of the first Jewish families known to have settled in Maidenhead was that of Alfred E. Davis, who was living in Farley Lodge, Ray Park with his wife Emma by the time of the 1891 Census.

They had a daughter in 1890, with two sons following in 1895 and 1896 (4). Jacob Prashner also came to Maidenhead, where he established a picture frame shop sometime before 1894, along with his wife Esther and four children. He had left London as he preferred to live outside a large city. The lack of local Jews led him to make contact with those in the Reading area, becoming one of the founder members of the synagogue there and its President in 1898. He also taught Hebrew at Reading University (5). The first recorded Jewish marriage to have taken place in Maidenhead occurred on 28th June 1892, albeit for a London couple. It was held at Holly Lodge, Ray Park, the residence of the bridegroom's sister, and was between Marie, the only child of Israel and Annie Cohen of Brixham, to Joseph, the second son of Israel Cohen of 56 Tavistock Square, London WC. Rabbi Dr Joseph Strauss, then minister of Bradford (Reform) Synagogue officiated, presumably because either the bride or groom's family had originally come from Bradford or had a personal connection with Strauss. Apparently 'It was a swell affair; the bridegroom, Mr Cohen, being the son of a wealthy importer of sponges' (6). Someone who died locally was Julian Arthur Lumley, who passed away in Bray in July 1894, although his business address was in London (7). Another Bray resident was Arthur Cohen, a tenant of Annie de Courcy, whose property in Fishery Road, Bray he was renting in 1896. The house fronted onto the river, and Cohen may have been there only for the summer season.

    This certainly applied to Sam and Ada Lewis, whose 'rags to riches' story epitomised the way in which some Jews climbed the social hierarchy with astonishing rapidity. He was reared in poverty in Birmingham and started up as a pedlar of cheap jewellery. He changed to being a moneylender and specialised in loans to the aristocracy, who often needed funds to keep up their large estates, finances, political ventures or to pay off gambling debts. He became highly successful, and very wealthy, moving in high society and owning fashionable homes in London and Hove. In 1895 he also acquired a property in Maidenhead, purchasing 'Woodside' from Lord and Lady Cowley for £11,000. It was a few hundred yards north of Boulters Lock, standing in two and a half acres and with a river frontage of more than 200 feet. The object was to have a local residence for June and July of each year, when the cream of British society occupied houses on the river, with royalty visiting too. The purchase was both to reflect his social status and to advance his business, entertaining clients and prospective clients. His acquisition of a yacht, the Isis Hathor, was also with both objects in mind. However, invitations were not just extended to the wealthy, but for good causes too, such as the occasion when fifty boys from the Old Castle Street Company of the

Jewish Lad's Brigade came to Woodside: 'After a short display of drill, dinner was served and cricket, rowing and swimming were indulged in, alternated by trips to Cookham by launch' (8).

Sam Lewis

Sam Lewis died in January 1901 but made his mark on the area for the next century. At the time of his death, he was described by the *Maidenhead Advertiser* as 'the greatest private moneylender in the world' and left £2.7 million (9). As he and Ada had no children, much of it was given to charity, either immediately or when Ada died, which occurred five years later. He especially favoured medical causes and housing for the poor. Among local beneficiaries were the Royal Berkshire Regiment, which was presented with three cottage homes, while £1,000 was left to establish a Working Boys' Club in Maidenhead. Maidenhead Cottage Hospital was gifted £10,000 for an entire new wing that was eventually opened in 1908 by Princess Christian, sister of King Edward VII, and was known as the 'Ada Lewis Wing'. The hospital was closed in 1977 and later demolished, but another gift, a drinking trough for horses, still remains, inscribed in memory of Ada. It was erected in 1908, with the unveiling performed by local MP, Ernest Gardner. Originally sited on the south west side of Maidenhead bridge, at the junction with Guards Club Road, it served the needs of horse-drawn taxis which used to go from the riverside to the town and back. It was moved across the road during the 1970s, to the north west side at the edge of Bridge Gardens, because it impeded the flow of traffic, and in 2010 was relocated to form the centrepiece of a new water feature in the middle of Bridge Gardens.

The Ada Lewis fountain, now in Bridge Gardens

In addition, £15,000 was left for 'charitable institutions in Maidenhead and Cookham' to be allocated by trustees of the will (10). Sam and Ada were members of the West London Synagogue and were both buried in its Hoop Lane cemetery. 'Woodside' still exists, although it is now divided into three large homes (11).

Despite the small number of Jews living locally, a Jewish boarding school opened in Maidenhead in September 1897, Craufurd College. The building itself had already served as a preparatory school, having been established some fifty years earlier by the educationalist and five times mayor of Maidenhead, J.D.M. Pearce. It occupied seven acres of land at the junction of Belmont Road and Gringer Hill. In its new incarnation it now catered for Jewish boys from eight to thirteen years old, run according to Orthodox principles. It was advertised as being eighty-three minutes from Paddington, with 'extensive premises' that included an 'ample playground, Cricket-field, Tennis and Fives Court, and a Swimming Bath', as well as a gym and chemistry laboratory (12). Its Principal was James Polack, previously headmaster of West Hampstead School, London for the past five years, and the brother of Joseph Polack, master of the Jewish House at Clifton College in Bristol. James Polack arrived with a considerable reputation as an educationalist, with the opening of the new school being attended by the leading metropolitan Jewish minister, Rev. A. A. Green. In keeping with the moderate Orthodoxy of the time, the school was keen to establish relations with the wider community. The local MP, Sir John Blundell Maple was invited to the inaugural ceremony, although he was unable to attend. The *Maidenhead Advertiser* was present and recorded that (13):

> Mr Polack is naturally supported by the people of his own faith; but we understand that with the exception of the purely dogmatic religious teaching, the school curriculum will be in all respects similar to that of an ordinary preparatory school where boys are intended for the Public Schools of the country. Thus there will be not the smallest objection to boys of all denominations joining in the ordinary school work and school games.

When the 1901 census took place, thirty-six boarders were recorded as being present, although by then the age-range had extended to being from eight to seventeen years. The great majority came from London, but included boys from Liverpool and Birmingham, as well as a handful from New Zealand, Australia and South Africa. The school roll had gone down to twenty-two on the 1911 census day. The school remained under the headship of James Polack until 1926, with his sons Ronald and Desmond both being born in Maidenhead and brought up at the school. It is noticeable, though, that key aspects of the family's Jewish life still centered on London. Thus James' father, Rev. Lazarus Polack, the former minister of Chatham Synagogue, died at Craufurd College in November 1900 but was buried in Willesden Jewish cemetery. When James became engaged to Miss Florrie Chapman the following year, they were married at St Petersburgh Place Synagogue, Bayswater (14).

The school received a boost in 1908 when the lease of Great Ealing School, West London, expired. Its headmaster was Rev. John Chapman, James' father-in-law, and the school's pupils were transferred to Craufurd. Among the latter's teachers was Herbert Loewe, a distinguished scholar who went on to become Reader in Rabbinics at Cambridge University. The school's Jewish pupils came not only from the London area but much further afield, including many from abroad. Amongst those whose subsequent details are known was Marcus Segal, whose family lived in London, and who later went on to University College School, Hampstead. He joined the army shortly after the First World War broke out, rising to the rank of Second Lieutenant in the King's Liverpool Regiment. He was killed by a shell in June 1917 (15). When the school closed, the premises were bought by Middlesex County Council and used as a mental hospital, later being taken over by Maidenhead College after the Second World War, and eventually demolished in 1949 to make way for housing.

Craufurd College

The arrival of the railway lines transformed Maidenhead and turned it into a desirable residence for those who wished to work in London but live elsewhere. It resulted in a dramatic expansion in the number of houses being built. By 1851 the population had tripled from the beginning of the century to 3,603, and by 1901 it was 12,980. The enlarged population led to the need for more shops, schools, churches, fuelling the growth of the town (16). The river area, once the scene of trade, had now became a magnet for those at leisure, whether in boats or walking along the promenade. Easy access meant it became a fashionable attraction for Londoners, be it for a weekend stay or even a day-trip, especially high society, including members of the royal family, with the highlight of the year being a parade of boats by Boulters Lock on Ascot Sunday in June. In 1909, for instance, over 5,000 people travelled from Paddington to Maidenhead by train for Ascot Sunday. Edward VII himself dined regularly at Skindles Hotel when spending weekends at stately homes such as Taplow Court with the Grenfells or at Cliveden with the Astors.

A notable overseas visitor was Theodor Herzl, who came to England in the summer of 1888 whilst he was working as a journalist for the *Neue Freie Presse*. He was on an assignment to write travel sketches, which eventually appeared in 1901. He described Boulter's Lock as 'a wonderful opportunity to see a procession of the most famous London stars in a mêlée of swells and sweets, in other words of dandies and their sweethearts.' He also spent time in Cookham and took a liking to one of its characters.

> The landlord at the Bel and Dragon is a good old man, in his late seventies, who carries his age well and with a good sense of humour. If he likes the look of a patron, Mr Worboys will sit down at his table for a chat, produce long lost liqueurs from a hidden stash, offer a little glass and tell tales of old. Only forty years ago he was still living in London, and by the sounds of it he was a bit of a ladies' man. He was a friend of the theatre, and he talks about Jenny Lind as if it were only yesterday that he heard her sweet voice for the last time. He preferred her over Grisi or Alboni. It is a bit like finding faded fripperies in some old junk room. And Mr Worboys laughs joyfully at these old memories, because he is still alive. There is only one thing that he really does not like, to the point where he becomes almost rude. You must not say 'Good-bye'. 'Good morning' or 'Good evening', yes, but never good-bye. It seems to make him feel the cold, like the Hare of Ueberlingen who did not want to die. So it is 'Good morning, Mr Worboys!' That's what he likes, and he shakes hands with every parting guest. His young eyes shine happily out of his smooth red face crowned by a white beard. One cannot think of a better illustration for the legendary good old days. Anyway, you can only learn about life from the elderly because only they know what it is.

A rare example of a rabbi who settled in Maidenhead, albeit in late age, was David Woolf Marks. Born in London in 1911, he had become an Orthodox minister, but became increasingly dissatisfied with some of the beliefs and practices he was obliged to uphold, such as the sanctity of the extra days that had been added by rabbinic tradition onto the original length of the biblical festivals. When the West London Synagogue was formed as an independent congregation that espoused modernist views, he applied to become its first minister. He held that position from 1840 till 1893, during which time he helped establish Reform Judaism as a permanent feature within British Jewry and developed much of its early approach and liturgy. In 1902 he was taken ill and spent some time recuperating at Thames Villa, River Road, Taplow near to where lived his daughter Frances Marks. In early 1908 he moved permanently from London to stay with her at Belmont House in Belmont Road, Maidenhead (17). His death occurred there on 3rd May the following year, and, from the account of his daughter, can be considered the perfect death after a long and eventful life (18):

> He was not ill at all on Sunday - on the contrary, that day he was bright, cheerful and full of animated conversation. He ate and drank well, had his favourite work of Dickens [David Copperfield] read aloud to him from 3pm to 7.30 pm, and had been up some two or three hours, walking from his bedroom to his library and back to his bed, with all his usual power. It was his custom always, after saying his evening prayer, to review his day, and on Sunday night, just before I left him to his nurse, he put his hands together and said: 'I thank thee, Lord, for a happy and perfect day, free from pain or care.' On leaving him I asked: 'How are you tonight, beloved?' and he answered: 'Quite comfortable, my child - good night and God bless you.' He slept from 9 to 12 pm, awoke then and took some brandy, slept again till 2 am, when he had some hot Benger's food, complained that he had a little flatulence after taking it, but laid himself down to sleep, and five minutes later, with a sweet smile on his face, which looked absolutely childlike - it was so peaceful - his great soul had passed away. I only venture to write you this that those who loved him so well may know that in very truth 'his end was peace'.

His body was taken to London and he was buried next to his wife in the Balls Pond Road Cemetery (19).

David Woolf Marks

Another person who retired to the area was the colourful Henry Louis Wallerstein. He was born in Frankfurt in 1849, as Heinrich Ludwig Wallerstein, and came to London as a young man, where he changed his name and worked as a journalist for *The Times*. Amongst other tasks, he covered the Berlin Congress as their foreign correspondent, before setting up a financial paper in the City called *The Daily Bourse*. He was often in conflict with leading Jewish figures, such as the Rothschilds whom he attacked for 'selling out' the Jews by arranging loans for Russia at a time when they were oppressing the Jewish population there. He also spent nine months hard labour in Pentonville prison on charges that he claimed were falsely concocted by his enemies after a libel action. After living in Essex and Kent, he and his non-Jewish wife moved to Bray in the early 1900s, where they lived in a house called 'The Cabin'. He became a familiar local figure, always going around with a rose in a glass buttonhole full of water. He remained there until his death in 1933 and was buried at the Jewish cemetery in East Ham (20).

Elizabeth Myers had also arrived locally in 1900. Her mother, Sara Myers, had shocked her family in Stoke-on-Trent by having a child out of wedlock, and had come down to Henley with her young daughter. Elizabeth grew up in the area, although she later returned to the family home in Stoke where she married out of the faith (21). Intermarriage, albeit higher up the social scale, led to another local residency. In 1881 Ellen Odette, eldest daughter of Henry Bischoffsheim, a London banker, married Ulick O'Connor, the fourth Earl of Desart, whose seat was in Kilkenny. After his death in 1898 she came to live in her English country home in Ascot, and became very involved in social and charitable work in the London Jewish community. She stayed in Ascot until 1912, returning to Ireland and later became one of the first female Senators in the Irish Free State. When it was suggested in the *Jewish Guardian* that she had deserted the faith, she wrote to the editor denying the 'unwarrantable assumption' and declaring that 'I am, as I have been all my life, a staunch and practising Jewess, far too proud of my faith and race not to feel extremely indignant at the slur you have tried to cast upon me' (22). It is not known for sure, but highly likely, given their name and occupation, that the Levi brothers were Jewish; they lived in Mount House (also known as Mount Farm House) in Spring Lane, Cookham Dean around 1910 and who were diamond merchants (23).

The families of those mentioned so far have long ceased to have any contact with the area, but this is not the case with Louis Oppenheimer who bought Waltham Place in 1912 and whose relatives still occupy it. He was in the diamond business and was the brother of Ernest Oppenheimer, the chairman of the De Beers diamond company in South Africa. His wife Charlotte was a keen gardener who added greatly to the estate's lavish grounds, and the sweatpea 'Carlota' is named after her. In the late 1920s, another brother, Gustav who also worked for De Beers, moved to Maidenhead with his wife Cecily and family. After living in White Waltham, they bought Raymead, near Boulters Lock. During the Second World War, the Oppenheimers moved out of Waltham Place and it became a De Beers diamond sorting office after its London premises had been bombed. After the war, their son Raymond moved back to the house, where he lived until his death in 1984. The property was then taken over by his nephew Nicky Oppenheimer (of Jewish origin but no longer Jewish) and his wife Orcillia, who have remained there since then (24).

If local Jewish residents were sparse, Jewish visitors were more common, and in the summer months there was often a boatful. This included teachers from the Jews' Free School in the East End of London who enjoyed an annual Westminster to Maidenhead boat trip during the early 1900s.

Teachers from the Jews' Free School boating through Maidenhead in 1911

Not long afterwards, in 1907, Sir Robert Waley Cohen, then one of the four Managing Directors of Shell and a future President of the United Synagogue, purchased a houseboat, the 'Natica', moored at Wargrave, which he used at weekends. In a description that captures the atmosphere of river life, his biographer wrote (25):

> The boat was well equipped and contained half a dozen cabins, as well as a saloon and kitchen. On the large, flat roof many a fine summer evening was spent with music. Two gangways led to the shore where Bob had purchased, with the 'Natica', a pleasant garden and tennis court. For the week of the Regatta, each year until the First World War and for a year or two after it, the 'Natica' was towed to Henley, where Bob and Alice gave large parties for sometimes more than forty people. Lizzie came from London to cook in the tiny kitchen of the houseboat, and Bob showed his skill at carving chickens as fast as she could roast them. When the Cambridge quartet played after dinner to the company, river craft would assemble silently from up and

down stream to listen. As the music stopped, applause came gently from the dusk.

There were numerous other affluent Jews from London who had additional residences locally, such as Samuel Heilbut (b. 1848), director of the Marine Insurance Company. As well as his Grosvenor Square home, he owned Holyport Lodge, which he and his wife used regularly. He was a keen gardener and in 1905 was awarded a Silver Medal at the Royal Horticultural Society's Temple Flower Show for his collection of fruit trees in pots, including nectarines, strawberries, grapes, prunes, cherries, and melon. He is still remembered amongst locals as the person who built the Real Tennis court in Holyport, which is in use to this day. He died in April 1914, and amongst the many charitable bequests in his will was £15,000 to the Guildhall School of Music in London, £5,000 to the Board of Guardians for the Relief of the Jewish Poor, £1,000 each to the London Hospital, St Mary's Hospital and Great Ormond Street Hospital, and £500 each to the United Synagogue and the synagogue in Brighton (26).

In similar vein was Abraham Hoffnung of both London and Rawdon Hall, Holyport. Born in 1833 in Poland, he was brought to England as an infant and spent his early years in Newcastle, where his father served as the local minister. As a young adult, he moved to Montreal where he established a successful business and later returned to England, settling in Liverpool in 1866 and later moving to London with his Manchester-born wife Esther. He represented Liverpool at the Board of Deputies and was on the Executive of the Anglo-Jewish Association. He was involved in two diplomatic incidents that provoked controversy. As a result of business dealings in Hawaii, he was appointed by the King of Hawaii as Charges d'Affaires at the Court of St James in 1877. This presented a difficulty as Hoffnung was British subject, and technically ineligible for the post. An exception was made and he became one of the first Jews to be part of the Corps Diplomatique to the British Empire.

That same year, he received an honour from the King of Portugal and was appointed a Chevalier of the Order of Christ of Portugal. However, when he attended the synagogue in Lisbon on the following Sabbath and was called to the Reading of the Law, two worshippers walked out in protest at his acceptance of a decoration so identified with the Church. The matter was referred to the Chief Rabbi in London, who ruled that it was permissible for a Jew to hold the award as it no longer bore any distinctive religious significance. In Holyport, however, he was associated more with local matters, being a regular benefactor of various charities and vice-president of Holyport Horticultural Society. The

Hoffnungs were also known in the area for their 'proverbial hospitality' (27). This was no doubt helped by the seven individuals at Rawdon Hall whose occupation was listed as 'servant' in the 1911 Census. Hoffnung died in Holyport on 5th April 1912, aged 79, and was cremated in Golders Green under the auspices of the West London Synagogue. At the time of his death he was also Chairman of the Anglo-Australian Exploration Company and three mining enterprises there (28).

Amongst other London Jews associated with Maidenhead in the early 1900s were Samuel de Lissa and Mr & Mrs Meyer Spielman, while K.S. Birnstingl and Alfred & Edith Picciotto lived there permanently (29). The Picciottos were listed as still there in the 1911 Census, residing at 64 Bridge Road, with his occupation being a 'financial agent'. Another example of intermarriage was that of a Jewish girl, Caroline Wolff, daughter of Alexander Wolff who had been Professor of Music at Oxford University in 1830. She married a Mr Rumball, and in the 1901 census they were recorded as living in Princess Street, Maidenhead, along with their three children.

Alongside the various individuals who visited, retired to, or had second homes in the area during this time there was one name of particular renown, Rufus Isaacs. He was born in London in 1860, went to sea as a ship's boy aged 16 and grew up to become one of the highest peers in the realm. Having studied law and built a successful career as a barrister, he entered Parliament as MP for Reading in a by-election there in 1904, representing the Liberals. When standing again two years later during the General Election, he was heckled by someone shouting 'Down with the Jews', but it was a lone voice and Isaacs was returned with an increased majority (30). He rose rapidly up the political ladder, becoming Solicitor General, Attorney General and then, in 1913, Lord Chief Justice, a position he maintained for the next eight years. His new office meant entering the House of Lords, and he took the title Lord Reading of Erleigh, resigning from his parliamentary seat. During his years as an MP he had resided at Fox Hill in Whiteknights Park and he kept the house until 1918 (31).

Isaacs went on to serve as Ambassador to the United States before being appointed Viceroy of India 1921-1926. In each of these positions, he was the first Jew to hold such an office. On his return to England he became Marquess of Reading, the highest honour ever held by a Jew. Moreover, before him, only two men who started life as commoners had reached the highest or second highest ranks of the peerage: John Churchill, first Duke of Marlborough, and Arthur Wellesley, first Duke of Wellington. A twelve feet tall statue of him was made by the Yorkshire sculptor, Charles Sargeant Jagger, and originally stood in New Delhi.

The statue of Rufus Isaacs in Eldon Square

After India gained independence in 1947, it (and that of other British figures) was no longer wanted for public display and eventually brought back to England. The statue now stands in the King George V Memorial Garden in Eldon Square, Reading where it was unveiled in July 1971, while Rufus Isaacs Road is nearby in Caversham.

Isaac's choice of title brought great pride not only to the town but to the Jewish population there, although some of the latter were upset at his lack of religiosity. He was a member of the West London Synagogue, but raised no objection, for instance, when his son Gerald Rufus Isaacs (1889-1960) married both in church and on a Saturday, while he himself saw no problem in chairing a meeting of the Fuel Conference on *Yom Kippur*, arguably the most sacred day in the Jewish calendar (32). On the other hand, once retired, he showed considerable interest in Jewish affairs and Zionist projects. In 1926 he became chairman of the Palestine Electric Corporation and six years later he made a tour of Palestine. But whilst encouraging such endeavours, he did not feel committed to Zionism. As he explained shortly after the Balfour Declaration was issued in 1917 - promising the British government's support for a Jewish homeland - which he had favoured: 'I have no great personal sympathy with Zionism. Why should I have? Here I am, Lord Chief Justice, Peer, and I started from nothing. I owe it all to England. I am English. How can I help it if I do not feel strongly about a national home for the Jews?' (33). On his death in 1935, Gerald became the second Lord Reading. Both he and his wife Eva were very involved in Jewish affairs, nationally and internationally, such as the Council for German Jewry and various Zionist causes, although having little active connection with Reading itself. During the Second World War, he was put in command of the Pioneer Corps, which was formed from Austrian and German Jews who had fled Nazi Germany but were classified as 'enemy aliens' upon the outbreak of war. After reconsidering their status, the British Government allowed them to join the non-combatant Auxiliary Military Pioneer Corps, the only unit open to them at the time. On his death in 1960, his son Michael Rufus Isaacs became 3rd Marquess of Reading, with his son Simon Rufus Isaacs becoming the 4th Marquess of Reading in 1980.

1. Over (1984) 38
2. JC (8 May 1974) 80; (14 September 1894) 2
3. Danby (1887) 94
4. JC (20 June 1890)1; (26 April 1895) 1; (15 May 1896) 1
5. JC (21 December 1894) 20; (17 June 1898) 27
6. Stroud (1974) 52; JC (1 July 1892) 1
7. JC (20 July 1894) 4
8. JC (19 September 1902) 20
9. MA (16 January 1901) 6

10. MA (23 January 1901) 6; (17 October 1906) 7; JC (18 January 1901) 11; (18 December 1908) 37
11. For further details about Sam and Ada Lewis, see Black (1992), from where much of this material is derived.
12. JC (4 June 1897) 1
13. MA (22 September 1897) 6
14. JC (2 November 1900) 12; (11 April 1902) 32
15. JC (18 October 1996) 26
16. Over (1984) 43
17. According to the 1911 Census, she was a servant in the household, with her occupation listed as 'farmer'.
18. Cassell 130; JC (14 May 1909)
19. JC (17 May 1909) 21
20. I am grateful to Claire Wallerstein, his great granddaughter, for providing this information
21. Interview with Elizabeth's daughter, Mrs Tyler
22. *Jewish Guardian,* 12 September 1930
23. Knibbs (1989) 164
24. Over & Oppenheimer (2001) 34-40; *Encyclopaedia Judaica* 12, 1425
25. Henriques (1966) 143
26. JC (2 June 1905) 20; MA (27 May 1914) 8
27. JC (6 March 1908) 16
28. MA (10 April 1912) 3; obit in JC (12 April 1912) 10
29. JC (27 October 1905) 11; (18 August 1905) 14; (29 March 1912) 35; (4 March 1910) 1
30. Jackson (1936) 109
31. Fox Hill is now a hall of residence belonging to the University of Reading
32. Jackson (1936) 286
33. Hyde (1967) 284

the Advertiser. On behalf of the Jewish community, he thanked the town for its hospitality and went on to attest to the common bond they shared (9):

> We are loyal subjects of King George; we are proud of our position as citizens of the British Empire, and to know that our children and brothers are fighting side by side with our Gentile brethren to bring this great conflict to a successful finish. We are glad to live in peace and concord with those who are of a different race and faith to ourselves. We only ask for the same tolerance to our faith and practice which we are ever ready to extend to those who conscientiously differ from us.....It is possible for Jew and Gentile to engage in manufacture, commerce and industry side by side, while each in matters of faith walks in the ways of his forefathers.

The letter also mentioned the gift of ten guineas from the 'Maidenhead Hebrew Congregation', organised by Mr H. Furman, as a 'thank-offering' which was being donated to the Red Cross Service locally.

This apparently amicable relationship received a brutal challenge only three weeks later when 'Our Looker-On' delivered a sharp complaint on the impact of Jewish community (10):

> When we Gentiles go shopping it is with extreme difficulty that a sufficiency of provisions can be obtained because of the 'raids' on shops and stores by Jews, whom we are sheltering from London air-raid dangers. Obviously these visitors 'do themselves well', and no wonder, for they are out and about early, and where it is a case of 'first-come-first-served' they invariably best the natives. It would appear with them that indoor duties, where performed at all, are set about after the larder has been well-replenished, and when later in the day some other folk go shopping, bacon is off, butter is unobtainable, tea-chests are empty, and other provisions are scarce. 'Shop early and often' is apparently the Jews' motto.

The lack of bacon implies either that the Jewish evacuees were extremely irreligious, or that the columnist was unfairly blaming the Jews for the faults of others. In fact 'A Jewish Resident' wrote a reply, not only protesting against the un-Christian spirit of the article, but pointing out how the citizens of Maidenhead were benefiting from the number of rooms, houses and hotels that were fully occupied. The correspondent also alluded to the peaceful presence of the newcomers: 'Has any case of drunkenness or disorder on the part of the Jews been reported?' (11).

'Our Looker-On' showed no sign of being chastened, but immediately replied in print with a protest of complete innocence, but which merely reiterated the hostile tone taken previously (12):

> I set naught down in malice. I have nothing to retract... there are Jews and Jews, orthodox and unorthodox, desirables and undesirables. You belong to the former and consequently would not presume upon our hospitality. But there are others, and these are a source of trouble to us. Happily they seem on the move, and we would fain speed the parting guests.

The lack of any correspondence in favour of the columnist might suggest that his feelings were not widely shared. Nevertheless, the attacks continued. Over the next two weeks the column complained of Jews taking over rented accommodation at inflated prices that allowed them to gain preference over others. Moreover, it was intimated that this was at the expense of existing tenants who were asked to move out for 'a consideration'. It should be noted, though, that a few weeks later the column quoted approvingly the donation of fifteen guineas by members of the Hebrew Congregation. It was organised by a Mr S. Lewis as part of a national collection on the Day of Intercession proclaimed by the King for the relief of sick and wounded soldiers. The columnist added (13):

> I gladly record these facts. They are a pleasing indication of that unity which a common danger has established among those who differ in race and religion and in peace times occasionally come into conflict. Today there is a united determination to win the war and united efforts to succour those who have suffered in the conflict.

It is not clear whether such words were a way of making amends for his previously derogatory comments, or simply in keeping with the professed distinction between 'desirables and undesirables'.

After a short interval, the Jewish issue returned to the pages of the *Maidenhead Advertiser*. It was highlighted by an anonymous correspondent who complained of both the anxiety and over-crowding caused by the 'constant and increasing influx of a certain class of visitors to this town' from the East End of London. He also helpfully informed readers that that area was currently suffering an outbreak of smallpox (14). Whilst Jews were not specified as being responsible for either problem, they were singled out the following week when a news item was headlined 'Russian Jews' Invasion of Maidenhead' (15):

Russian Jews' Invasion of Maidenhead.

WHAT THE LONDON PRESS SAYS.

We have frequently drawn attention to the hardships and inconvenience experienced locally by the invasion of Maidenhead by Russian Jews and have very strongly protested against house-owners selling houses to those undesirable visitors over the heads of respectable tenants who have occupied them for more or less lengthy periods. Now that well-to-do persons from London and elsewhere who have been accustomed to take houses for the summer season in Maidenhead and neighbourhood find themselves crowded out by Russian Jews, and excluded from the best part of the river Thames, there is a great outcry through the London press, as if the invasion was recent, whereas it has been going on since last June and in the meantime Maidenhead has been suffering in comparative silence, without any assistance from the London press or the people who summer or week-end here. Maidenhead is in the unenviable position now of having to tolerate the presence of some 3,000 aliens and refuse accommodation and hospitality to those who have hitherto seasoned here and been a real gain to the town. We give below some extracts from daily papers of last week:—

From Thursday's "Daily Mail."

At intervals last evening crowds of excited foreigners, women and men, flung themselves at trains on No. 2 and No. 3 platforms at Paddington Station, surging in knots round the compartments and addressing hysterical questions to seemingly comprehending compatriots within.

"That's funny," said an onlooker. "Party of aliens going home, I suppose. But why this way?"

"Yes, they're going home all right," remarked a careworn looking man who might have been a bank manager or a chief clerk. "Home to Maidenhead, and if you had to travel with them every

offer as much as £5 a week for a room in the poorer districts."

In one street an alien bought two small houses. He and his friends live in one, while the other is let at £1 a week. The normal rent was 6s. 6d.

Before he let the house a ticket in the window read :—" To Let. No English need apply."

The refugees are crowding out the regular business men travelling to and from London. The trains in the morning and evening are so packed that inspection of tickets on the train is no longer possible, with the result that the first-class compartments are frequently crowded out by third-class passengers. The aliens predominate among these blikers. Efforts are being made by local residential to persuade the railway company to restrict the issue of new season tickets to those who are prepared to take them for a year.

From the "Daily Telegraph."

Nothing has been decided so far as to the issue of permits for travel. There are two aspects of this travel. One is presented by the rush of aliens from London due to air-raid "nerves." We, in the metropolis, have no reason to desire their presence, which only makes for panic on raid nights. But they crowd trains to the prejudice of the regular traveller, and the areas they have swamped (save for a few "profiteers") cherish for them no hospitable feelings. They would gladly see the back of the last of these "raiders." But, instead, the tribe increases. The "Guard's" van queue grows longer daily.

How is the growing nuisance to be remedied? One suggestion is that if the highly "safety-first" flights are to be allowed to go on there should be "rationed areas." Registration provides the Government with the means of saying where all aliens are now. But there is no reason why they should continue to descend in platoons upon one or two places. They might be directed under a permit system to one or other of a number of specified points in accordance with the railway facilities available to these points and the quiet house supply. The wishes of the locality also could be taken into account. This, on the face of it, would ease the situation for everybody who need be considered.

The wider problem is that of permits for the public. Rolling stock available for passenger trains is steadily dwindling, owing to other demands on the companies, and anything like a holiday rush will probably produce a hopeless congestion. The experience of the coming Easter will doubtless afford some guidance as to the

Maidenhead Advertiser, 27th March 1918

We have frequently drawn attention to the hardships and inconvenience experienced locally by the invasion of Maidenhead by Russian Jews and have very strongly protested against house-holders selling houses to these undesirable visitors over the heads of respectable tenants who have occupied them for more or less lengthy periods. Now that well-to-do person from London and elsewhere who have been accustomed to take summer houses for the season in Maidenhead find themselves crowded out by Russian Jews, there is a great outcry through the London press as if the invasion was recent,

> whereas it has been going on since last June.... Maidenhead is in the unenviable position of having to tolerate the presence of some 3,000 aliens and refuse accommodation and hospitality to those who have hitherto seasoned here and been a real gain to the town.

There followed lengthy extracts from the *Daily Mail* and *Daily Telegraph* which spoke of Russian Jews having 'captured' Maidenhead and of them monopolising the crowded evening trains from London to the town. Maidonians were quoted in the London papers as saying that 'Their habits are not ours' and 'Their money never seems to run short'. There was also a letter in that same edition of the *Maidenhead Advertiser* from a local resident, W. Eglington, referring to:

> the indignities to which our townspeople are being subjected by the horde of human vultures that has swooped down from the East End, bringing with it all the unsavoury associations of the real Jew - the Russian Jew, perhaps the most vulgar, unscrupulous and grasping of a race known throughout the civilised world for its selfishness, greed an dishonesty....Maidenhead is being preyed upon by a mob of cowardly aliens, including men who are shirking their responsibilities to whatever country gave them birth. It is all very bilious and nauseating to Maidenhead, this ill-smelling, churlish, gesticulating rabble that struts along its streets and behaves with all the effrontery of its race!

What was much more significant than the vitriol of this particular individual was that the letter was followed by an 'Editors' Note' which not only endorsed its stance but castigated the author for not taking action sooner:

> We fear that if Mr Eglinton takes in the *Advertiser*, he does not read it, or he would have perused in the [previous] issues, some 'Looker-On' notes of protest against the invasion of Maidenhead by Jews...Had Mr Eglinton and others bestirred themselves earlier and not waited until within a few days of the river-season, they might have assisted us in checking the inrush of these undesirable aliens. They must not blame the *Advertiser*, but in some measure attribute the present state of affairs to their own supineness.

The *Jewish Chronicle* reported the accusations, although acidly dismissed them as the result of a well-known condition: 'It would seem that for some people the sight of a Jew has an intoxicating effect, so that they see him double, treble, quadruple or even a hundred-fold' (16). The spotlight cast on Maidenhead's 'alien invasion' by the London papers also prompted the Town Council to issue a statement, reassuring local people that there was no threat to public health and that if any diseases were detected, measures were in place to deal with them. The chairman of the Health Committee, Councillor Lever, also denied there was any danger from over-crowding or that conditions were becoming insanitary. Another member, Councillor Upson, dismissed the reports as 'sillier than the silly-season stuff. The aliens were orderly people and had brought no disease. They rather deserved sympathy in running away from dangers which the Maidenhead people had not been called upon to face' (17). Another councillor voiced suspicions that the objections came more from outsiders than full residents of the town: 'No one worried about this "invasion" till society people and others who have been in the habit of spending summer months in Maidenhead discovered that there were no houses for them to rent' (18).

The issue of Maidenhead's 'alien invasion' gained sufficient national attention to be mentioned in the House of Commons a number of times in April 1918. During one exchange, the Under-Secretary at the Home Office, William Brace, pointed out that 'the majority the migrants were neither aliens nor naturalised persons' (19). It also prompted Sir Samuel Stuart, President of the Board of Deputies, which represented the interests of British Jews in general, to meet with the Mayor of Maidenhead, Charles Cox. The result was a joint statement in which the Mayor stated that 'The number of alien Jews resident in the town, which has been stated as from 2,000 to 3,000 is grossly exaggerated'. He also 'deprecated the hostility which had been caused by the Press attacks, and expressed himself in entire sympathy with the views put forward by the [Jewish] deputation' (20). In a subsequent report, the Mayor estimated that the number of Jewish aliens in the town was nearer 300 than 3000 (21). The *Jewish Chronicle* placed responsibility for the scaremongering firmly on a hostile press (22):

> It is very difficult to preserve patience with the monstrous agitation which the Northcliffe and Hulton press have raised over the 'alleged' aliens influx into Maidenhead and other towns. We say 'alleged' because many of the people referred to are English-born Jews, who like so many aliens have sons or brothers or husbands fighting valiantly in the British army

today....this cruel and virulent Press persecution, the only redeeming feature in this wickedness being the ignorance on which it is based... any readers of their columns would suppose that the places to which they refer are swarming with myriads of aliens. Yet the number of aliens registered shows that they form a small proportion of those who, like them, desire to place their wives, their children and themselves outside the area likely to be bombed.

Examples of Jews connected with the area who lost their lives for their country include Major Ernest A. Myer (b. 1874) of the Sixth City of London Rifles who was killed in action in 1915 (23). He was a solicitor in London and a member of Bayswater Synagogue. He was very involved in social work, having helped establish the Brady Street Jewish Club in the East End of London, while he had also founded the Maidenhead Working Boys Club and managed it up until the outbreak of the war. Two years later, Second Lieutenant Simon Vanderlinde died of his wounds aged thirty in France, whose parents lived at Glen Cairn, Ray Park Avenue, Maidenhead (24).

A letter in the *Maidenhead Advertiser* after the House of Commons debate revealed that some anti-Jewish graffiti had been scribbled in chalk on the fence and pavement outside the temporary synagogue at 41 High Town Road. It also pointed out that 'people who start out to attack the Russian alien usually end up by dealing out condemnation to Jews of all classes' (25). Apart from these comments on the general issue of Jewish migration to the area, there were also a series of minor news items that were both critical and favourable: about a Jewish individual who wasted a loaf of bread by letting it go stale in a drawer; about another who illegally lent his train season ticket to a friend; a donation of twenty-five guineas by the Jewish community to the Red Cross Hospital; and Jews being granted extra meat rations in lieu of not eating bacon (26).

After a two-month lull, antisemitic remarks resurfaced in August 1918 over new regulations for obtaining train season tickets. 'Looker-On' had welcomed the development as a way of 'weeding out the "undesirables" who had invaded Maidenhead last summer' (27). In response, 'A Britisher' wrote to narrate how he had taken an early morning train to London and (28):

found things even worse than I expected. There were Jews galore, young and old, mostly the former, and I had great difficulty in getting beside someone who spoke English as well as myself... and to look at such crowds of young fellows without the thought that our fine boys, and now their very fathers, have to go and fight for these aliens, it makes one's blood boil. When the war is over.. the alien Jew will be the first to shake the German by the hand and buy from him, because he is so cheap.

The letter highlighted a feeling that had not been expressed before, but was certainly evident elsewhere in the country: the resentment that Russian Jews were not subject to conscription because they were foreign-born. Many were appalled at the sight of able-bodied young Jews engaged in commerce or at leisure when most English people's sons were away fighting and dying at the front. Support came two weeks later from 'Fair Play', who castigated the government for letting Britain become 'the dustbin for foreigners of every kind' and urged that a new policy be introduced, whereby there be 'English trains for Englishmen'. He also warned that Jews had started up a blouse factory in Maidenhead and that the 'sweated labour of Aldgate' was now being introduced locally (29). A rebuttal appeared from 'A Fair Play Britisher' decrying the revival of 'Jew Baiting', which led to two further exchanges between them, after which the correspondence petered out, no doubt aided by the Armistice being declared the following month and London becoming safe to live in again (30).

    It is clear that during the last two years of the war, the sudden influx of Jews to the area in large numbers had prompted unease or hostility in some quarters. Most notable were the unsavoury comments by both 'Looker-On' and the Editor of the *Maidenhead Advertiser* (who were, in fact, the same person, Mr Bannard). It was equally evident, though, that only a few correspondents entered the fray and that most felt obliged to do so anonymously. More importantly, apart from one instance of grafitti, there were no reports of antisemitic incidents in the town, so even if some Maidonians were upset by the newcomers, anti-Jewish feeling did not translate into anti-Jewish behaviour. Given the toxic mix of xenophobia, antisemitism, fears about food shortages and resentment over exemptions from war service, this was by no means assured. The peaceful atmosphere in Maidenhead outside the world of newsprint contrasts with other parts of the country, such as Leeds, where there was a street battle between Jewish and non-Jewish youths which led to a large mob of a thousand people attacking Jewish shops and smashing windows. Tensions were also reported in Manchester and Glasgow, particularly towards 'the Russian Jew who won't fight, but does eat' (31). In contrast, Maidenhead remained a place of calm and hospitality.

As for the internal life of the ad hoc Jewish community, the expectation of a quick return to London meant that little energy was put into developing local Jewish life other than services. An advert in the *Jewish Chronicle* in September 1917 invited those living in Maidenhead to attend a *minyan* being organised for the High Holy Days, with Mr Koppelman of Bridge Road being the person to contact (32). *Barmitzvah* celebrations also occurred locally, such as that of Meyer Simmonds, second son of Mr & Mrs S. Simmonds of Finsbury Park. The announcement not only declared that he 'will read a portion of the Law at the Maidenhead Synagogue', but also had the telling war-time addition of 'No festivities' that was a fairly common features of other such announcements (33). *Kosher* meat was available, for the temporary community enjoyed the professional services of a *shochet*, Abraham Shinerock, who was there during that period (34).

A rare cultural event was when the well-known Zionist speaker, Dr Jacob Samuel Fox, came from Liverpool to address an open meeting of the 'Maidenhead Jewish Congregation' on 26th May 1918. His topic was 'The Work of the Zionist Commission now in Palestine' and it was held at the Bear Hotel in the High Street. It came in the wake of the Balfour Declaration, issued the previous November, promising the British government's support for 'a national home for the Jewish people' in Palestine. The event was probably more testimony to the tireless efforts of the Zionist movement to garner support in all parts of the country than to the importance of the town's Jewish population. However, it does indicate that it was sufficient to justify the visit of such a prestigious figure. The message was clearly well received, for when details were given of those who had been honoured in synagogues at *Simchat Torah* later that year, they not only included mention of D. Mirner and M. Muer at Maidenhead, but also the information that £300 had been collected there for the Jewish National Fund (35). Amongst other Jews known to be in Maidenhead during the War were Henrietta Chumaceiro, the Gunzberg family, Jack Harris (of East London), Mr & Mrs H. Kaufman, Belle Morris, Max & Fanny Mushlin (of West Kilburn), Mr & Mrs Tobias (of East London), Mr & Mrs George Westrich (36) as well as Solomon & Eva Cohen with their children Sidney and Millie. There is also record of a Jewish wedding in the town towards the very end of the war, which was solemnized between Barnett Levine and Polly Brown on 6th October 1918 by Rev. Mendel Brown. Unfortunately, by the time the couple came to celebrate their silver wedding anniversary, the world was in conflict again and the announcement in 1943 concluded with the once more familiar refrain: 'No festivities are being held, because of war conditions' (37).

Between the Wars

With the war over and most Jewish evacuees returning to London, there was no active Jewish life in Maidenhead. As a result, no one who valued being part of an active Jewish community or wanted formal Jewish education for their children considered moving to the town. To the west, the Reading Hebrew Congregation, which had long pre-dated the war, continued. One of the few families that trickled into East Berkshire was that of Millie Levene, which arrived in 1919 from London to open up a tailor's shop when she was two years old. She recalled that the Reading minister, Rev. S. Fogelnest, visited their house occasionally to provide Hebrew lessons after his arrival in the area in 1923. The family left for Ilford in 1934 because her parents were concerned about her social life as there were 'too few Jews in the area' (38). Some years earlier, romance had led to another arrival. When Rosie Fenton from Sheffield fell in love with Max King, her parents refused to allow them to marry as he was much older than her. The couple eloped to the United States, where they married, eventually returning to England and living in Bray at Pomona Fruit Farm (now a caravan park) from 1930 to 1945, after which they settled in London.

Mr & Mrs Levene outside their shop at 77 Queen Street, Maidenhead in the 1920s

Other Jews living in the town were Mr & Mrs Sam Saleshaln and Isaac & Betty Freeman - both of whom had daughters born there in 1920 and 1923 respectively - along with Mrs Hyam Scott (39). The death of a number of Jewish residents are recorded between 1923 and 1937: Sydney & Alice Bennet, Bertram Fenn, Samuel & Rita Greenwood, Albert Jaffe, Hyman & Annie Lewis (40). Some held properties in both Maidenhead and London, including Mr & Mrs Littaur and Michael & Pauline Zeffert (41). A temporary resident was Walter de Frece, a music hall entrepreneur and theatre owner who was knighted in 1919 for services providing entertainment for the troops during the First World War. In 1922 he was appointed Deputy-Lieutenant of the County of Berkshire (42). He left the area the following year when he became MP for Blackpool for the Conservative Party. Some had reached the town via a circuitous route: Max Bilsky (born Poland) had met his wife Jane (born Russia) in Argentina. When they came to England in 1920, they settled in Maidenhead for a while before moving to North London. A more established family was that of the Dunkels. When Mina Dunkel died in Bray Lodge in 1939, it was noted that she was the mother of Ernest Dunkel - who lived at Woodhurst, Ray Mead Road and was 'a generous benefactor of the town' – while her son Walter lived in Windsor Forest (43). A non-resident who made his presence felt locally during the early 1930s was Leon Gaston Cohen, a Londoner who owned the then very fashionable Hungaria River Club, which was situated by Maidenhead Bridge opposite Skindles. As well as Jews who came to Maidenhead, there were also Maidonians who came to Judaism, such as Hazel Everett Jones, who was born in Maidenhead in 1927, eventually moved to London, converted to Judaism and several years later married Sir Sigmund Sternberg.

Most of the local Jews led lives that did not attract public attention. In contrast was Ronald Barnett, although details of his activities were revealed only long after his retirement. He came from a 'normal, reasonably Orthodox, middle-class family in Maidenhead' where he was born in 1922. His parents were from Poland and Lithuania. His father was a businessman, who died when Ronald was three. During the war he served as an RAF pilot and afterwards worked in London as a reporter for the *Daily Express*. In 1947 he began to work as an undercover Israeli agent. His first mission was in the South of France, working with Jewish refugees in camps in Marseilles, one of which was also a military training camp, preparing for the fighting that was to occur in Israel's War of Independence. Barnett was involved principally in taking immigrants from France to Israel by sea. He then performed a similar function for Romanian Jews.

HOME NEWS

The spy who came out of obscurity

By DAVID WINNER

To Arab rulers, Ronald Barnett was the perfect, dapper Englishman. They knew him as a former RAF pilot who ran an American, Mormon-owned airline.

He was on good terms with the Prime Minister of Iraq, Mr Tawfik as-Suwaidi, and senior officials in Egypt and Lebanon. He was a close friend of the Shah of Iran.

He was also one of Israel's greatest spies.

Between the end of the Second World War and 1952, Mr Barnett was personally responsible for the journey by air of between 350,000 and 400,000 Jews to Israel — from Iraq, Iran, Yemen and other Arab countries. "Including those who came by sea, the total wasn't far short of half a million," he says.

For 18 months, he masterminded the airlift of 120,000 Iraqi Jews. Mr Shlomo Hillel, now Speaker of the Knesset and the author of a recent book on that mission ("Operation Babylon"), was one of his junior assistants, working under the cover name, Richard Armstrong.

Mr Barnett, now 66, was formally and publicly recognised by the state when he was awarded a medal at a ceremony in Jerusalem a few weeks ago.

Few men have had a more profound effect on the shape of modern Israeli society than Mr Barnett, now long since retired and living in London.

Like most spies, he kept his silence for many years. But now, after nearly 40 years, he feels it is important that the contribution to the creation of the State of Israel of British Jews is recognised.

"We hear about the wonderful contributions to Israel made by the Wolfsons and the Sieffs and we hear how much American Jews did. But there were quite a few British Jews whose work and bravery have never really been recognised," he says.

Mr Barnett never learned a word of Hebrew. He was told not to bother in case it could be used against him to blow his cover.

He came from a "normal, reasonably Orthodox, middle-class family in Maidenhead." His parents were from Poland and Lithuania. His father was a businessman, who died when Ronald was three.

He was first approached to work as an Israeli agent after he had tricked his way into Brixton prison to interview the British traitor, William Joyce (Lord Haw Haw). He was working as a reporter for the "Daily Express" at the time.

His seven years of undercover work as a Mossad agent, which ended in 1954, started soon afterwards. His first mission was to the South of France working with Jewish refugees in camps

im Marseilles, one of which was also a military training camp.

He was involved principally in running immigrants from France to Palestine. On one occasion, his ship was intercepted by British warships. Mr Barnett flung his British passport overboard and was taken to a detention camp in Cyprus, from which he soon escaped. His captors never had an inkling that he was British.

Soon afterwards he helped to take Jews from Romania by negotiating a safe passage for their ships with Anna Pauker, the Romanian Foreign Minister, whose father, a rabbi, and uncle were on board.

After the creation of the State of Israel in 1948, Mr Barnett was asked to help with the aliya of Jews from Middle Eastern countries. His cover was his job as vice-president of the US-flagged Trans Airlines, and of Near East Air Transport.

He had a meeting with President Truman, who later began to exert pressure on Iraq to allow the Jews to leave. Many had already escaped to Iran.

"We had to get them out fast, because we were afraid that the Iraqis would change their minds and shut the door," explained Mr Barnett, whose codename was Boaz.

The codenames for the undercover agents were Operation Ali Baba and Operation Ezra and Nehemiah.

The Jews had to renounce their Iraqi nationality and although the Iraqi Government did not ask where they were going, their destination was known.

In fact, the Iraqis believed that by allowing so many refugees into Israel, they would be jeopardising its economy. When Mr Barnett reported that to the Israeli Premier, Mr David Ben-Gurion, he told him that quite the opposite was true.

His chief negotiations were with the Egyptian-born Iraqi Minister for Civil Aviation, Mr Ahmed Shafik, who was the Shah's brother-in-law. "He was a really nice guy — he was of inestimable

Ronald Barnett

After the creation of the State of Israel in 1948, Barnett was asked to help with the emigration of Jews from Middle Eastern countries. His cover was as vice-president of the US-flagged Trans Airlines, while his codename was Boaz. He had a meeting with President Truman, who later began exerting pressure on Iraq to let its Jews leave. Barnett also became a friend of the Shah of Iran and was instrumental in organising the airlift of Iranian Jews in 1950. Under his supervision, some 350,000-400,000 Jews went to Israel from Iraq, Iran, Yemen and other Arab nations in Operation Ali Baba and Operation Ezra and Nehemiah. His work as a Mossad agent ceased in 1954, whereupon he returned to London, only revealing his story in 1988 (44).

Maidenhead did briefly see the appearance of a rabbi when, on 9th May 1934, Rabbi Maurice Perlzweig preached at the West Street Congregational Church. At the time, he was one of the ministers at the

Liberal Jewish Synagogue, and had come to Maidenhead to participate at an inter-faith service to pray for oppressed Jews in Europe. The invitation had arisen because both he and the church's minister, Rev. Vanner Moore were members of the London-based Society for Jews and Christians, which had been formed in 1927. According to the *Jewish Chronicle*, such a joint service was unique and had led Rev. Moore to declare at the beginning of it that 'it implied no surrender on either side of distinctive religious beliefs'. The paper welcomed the gesture of sympathy for persecuted Jews, although it also wondered 'whether these days of religious slackness and drift are exactly the time at which Jews and Christians should fraternise in a Church and seem to lower the barriers of that separate their respective creeds' (45). In his sermon, Perlzweig referred not only to the problems in Germany but also to the antisemitism prevalent worldwide, as far afield as Eastern Europe, Brazil and Japan, In addition, he drew attention to the dire poverty of the Jews in Russia. His main message, though, was to assert that the situation should not be just a Jewish issue but a common concern, declaring that (46):

> When a Jew or the Jewish people is singled out for attack, it is something bigger than Jews being attacked...the common heritage of Jew and Christian, the foundation of faith....I conceive of the world in which we live today as being a great spiritual battle-ground. There is a titanic struggle going on - a struggle for the soul of mankind - and you have to choose on which side you will stand.

His words were to prove prophetic and five years later that titanic struggle came to a climax. In the meantime another minister, Sir Philip Magnus of the West London Synagogue, spoke to the Maidenhead Rotary Club at the beginning of 1937 on 'The International Situation'. Perlzweig addressed the same group later that year on 'Great Britain, Palestine and the Jews'. The two visits were organised by the Central Jewish Lecture Committee and were indicative both of the troubled times affecting the world and of the way in which Jews were a central feature (47).

    A meeting at the Baptist Church in Marlow Road two years later was also concerned with the oppression of German Jewry, but from a very different angle. It was addressed by a German Jew who had become a Christian and now worked in Berlin as a missionary. He told the audience both of his work in trying convert Jews, and of the persecution they were experiencing from the Nazis, including Kristallnacht. Responding to his remarks, the minister, Rev. Arthur Martin, said that 'Nothing had more profoundly shocked the feelings of all Christian people than the way in which the Jewish people were being called upon to suffer in this so-called enlightened age, than what had taken place in Germany during the past few months' (48).

The antisemitism abroad was not matched in Maidenhead. While Oswald Mosley's British Union of Fascists were active in London, there was little evidence of it locally. The only hint of antagonism was a correspondence in the *Maidenhead Advertiser* that was started in December 1938 when an open letter was addressed to the local MP – A. A. Somerville – accusing him and other politicians of showing preference to Jews over the British people. It was repeated twice in the following months by supporters of the fascist leader, Arnold Leese, asking why MPs were 'in the hands of Jews'. A subsequent letter appeared from a member of Mosley's party, claiming that 'a race that comprises about .06 of the population will not be allowed to dominate the country as they do today, or injure our relations with foreign powers in pursuit of a political vendetta'. This reflected the Fascist claim that the looming conflict with Germany was being engineered by Jews for their own purposes and was against the British national interest. It was perhaps a more accurate reflection of general feeling that the Editor added a note at the end of the letter stating that 'This correspondence must now cease' (49).

1. Woolf (1988) 41
2. MA (25 November 1914) 7
3. MA (9 December 1914) 7
4. Middleton (1975) 59
5. JC (25 September 1931) 1
6. MA (18 July 1917) 8
7. MA (19 & 26 September 1917) 8
8. MA (3 October 1917) 8
9. MA (31 October 1917) 8
11. MA (7 November 1917) 8
12. MA (14 November 1917) 8
13. MA (23 January 1918) 8
14. MA (20 March 1918) 8
15. MA (27 March 1918) 6
16. JC (8 April 1918) 7
17. MA (27 March 1918) 6
18. JC (5 April 1918) 6
19. JC (19 April 1918) 17
20. idem.

21. JC (26 April 1918) 6
22. JC (29 March 1918) 3
23. JC (16 April 1915) 21
24. JC (26 October 1917) 2
25. MA (10 April 1918) 2
26. MA (3 April 1918) 7, (10 April) 8; (24 April) 8; (12 June) 7
27. MA (14 August 1918) 8
28. MA (28 August 1918) 6
29. MA (11 September 1918) 8
30. MA (18 September 1918) 8; (2 October) 8; (9 October) 6
31. JC (8 June 1917) 14
32. JC (7 September 1917) 19
33. JC (12 October 1917) 1
34. JC (3 July 1931) 8
35. JC (27 September 1918) 12
36. JC (10 May 1918) 2; (6 September 1918) X; (9 November 1917) 1; (6 September 1918) IV; (18 October 1918) 13; (26 October 1919) 21; (6 September 1918) 16 & X
37. JC (8 October 1943) 11
38. Private correspondence, Millie Levene
39. JC (27 August 1920) 1; (1 June 1923) 28; (13 December 1918) 28
40. JC (22 July 1932) 2; (5 November 1937) 1; (23 December 1927) 2; (27 July 1923) 2; (6 January 1933) 2; (14 August 1936) 2
41. JC (18 September 1925) 1; (30 January 1931) 12; (26 August 1932) 10
42. JC (18 August 1922) 12
43. MA (2 August 1939) 6
44. JC (27 May 1988) 8
45. JC (11 May 1934) 8
46. MA (9 May 1934) 10
47. JC (29 January 1937) 41; (1 October 1937) 35
48. MA (25 January 1939) 5
49. MA (7 December 1938); (25 January 1939) 6; (15 February) 2; (22 February) 8

PART II

THE SECOND WORLD WAR

Chapter 5

1939: The Evacuees

The approach of war

The rise to power of Hitler in Germany in 1933 led to mounting tensions in Europe, which were exacerbated as his expansionist intentions became clear. Not all felt war was inevitable and Taplow became associated with the term 'the Cliveden Set', which was coined in 1937 to refer to the group of wealthy and influential individuals who would meet at the home of Lord and Lady Astor to promote a policy of appeasement of Germany rather than confrontation. However, the increasingly aggressive policies of Hitler, combined with Britain's foreign treaty obligations, meant that Britain found itself with few options. As the possibility of conflict loomed, the government designated Berkshire as a safe haven for evacuees. However, it still faced the threat of enemy bombs because of its proximity to London, while there was also the danger of German planes dropping any unspent cargo over the area on their route home.

There were also a number of important sites that might lead to Berkshire being specifically targeted. These included the Air Transport Auxiliary base in White Waltham and a major railway junction at Reading, while the Slough industrial estate was vital to the war effort, with its 700 acres of space being turned over to war production in 1939 and becoming one of the biggest armaments production centres in the country. In addition, Windsor Castle was not only the war-time home of the royal family but also of the Crown Jewels and other national treasures that were transferred to its dungeons. Destroying the castle would have presented a major propaganda coup for the enemy. Local preparations for war quietly took place well in advance. Eton had practised blackouts since May. In Reading, the Council prepared and published its Air Raid Precautions Scheme in 1937, while Windsor had taken action two years earlier. It was work well done and its extensive air raid defences proved to be a strong deterrent, bringing down at least three planes that ventured near the castle. Meanwhile there were severe police restrictions as to the movements of the civilian population in Crowthorne and Sandhurst, which became a military area, with huge ammunition dumps camouflaged in the surrounding pine forests.

War was declared by England on Germany on 3rd September 1939, but the mass evacuation of schoolchildren, mothers with young children and others had already been planned nationally by the government for 1st September 1939. There were also families who moved to areas such as Maidenhead of their own accord in anticipation of attacks on London. Over the next three days, an estimated total of 3,191,500 people were evacuated from major cities in England, the total population then being thirty-eight million. This included 1.5 million schoolchildren and toddlers and it formed the greatest population migration of its kind in British history (1). It was based on the widely held belief that the war would open with an immediate enemy air onslaught on civilian society so as to undermine the nation's will to fight. It was expected that London, the nerve-centre of the country and the largest concentration of people, would suffer first. (2). This view had been given credence by government's own warnings of such raids, with gas masks being issued to everyone over five years old, strict black-out procedures being announced and estimates suggesting that there would be 600,000 deaths in the first two months of bombardment. The result was that a total of 7,000 evacuees came to Maidenhead from London in September 1939, with 5,500 being children arriving en masse from their schools, largely from the East End and its high Jewish population. They increased the population of Maidenhead by 25%. Other areas were affected similarly and in total Berkshire took 46,722 evacuees, almost double the numbers expected. This included 25,000 evacuees who went to Reading in the first week of September 1939 and 5,000 evacuees who arrived in Windsor (3).

Among the famous evacuees to come locally was Queen Wilhelmina of the Netherlands, who lived in Stubbings House for the duration of the war, with her contingent of Dutch guards occupying part of Maidenhead Thicket where Nissen huts had been especially erected for them. Other royal visitors were Princesses Elizabeth and Margaret, who stayed at Windsor Castle for the duration of the war. King Haakon of Norway evacuated to Foliejohn Park in nearby Fifield, while Ascot became the war-time home of King Peter of Yugoslavia, the Grand Duchess of Luxembourg and King Zog of Albania. Amongst the Jewish 'celebrities' to come locally was the comedian Bud Flanagan who settled in Wargrave. At the same time, General Charles de Gaulle made Oakley Court the headquarters of the Free French movement. Maidenhead was further swelled by troops moved locally, including the 9th Devon and Royal Sussex who were billeted at Pinkneys Green brick kilns (4). At one stage there were 4,000 troops in Maidenhead, including a sizable contingent of the Fourth Royal Berkshire Regiment (5). There was a further influx from 1942 when American soldiers first arrived, while more of them came in ever increasing numbers in the build-up to D-Day. They were stationed throughout Berkshire, with many in Maidenhead itself.

With the influx of civilian evacuees and military personnel, the departure of many local men off to war, and women having to take over the jobs they left behind, Maidenhead was transformed.

Israel Madenberg (back row, sixth from the right), part of the Civil Defence Platoon of Maidenhead Home Guard

Maidenhead at war

The lack of any enemy attacks in the opening weeks of the war - the period of the 'phoney war' - led to many returning to London, only to re-evacuate once raids began in the summer of 1940. London underwent intense bombing from July to October 1940 - the 'Battle of Britain' - with raids continuing until early 1941. Maidenhead itself experienced an early raid in July 1940 (as will be seen below) and then a series of bombings during October 1940. Many explosives fell harmlessly into fields, while those over the town did damage to property, but there were only a handful of injuries and not a single fatality. Ruth Goldstone (nee Ellis) remembered that her brother was climbing a tree at the time of one of the bombs and fell out with shock. In 1941 the Luftwaffe was starting to run short of aircraft and also turning its attention to the Russian front, so there was a lull in activity over Britain in general. There were two sorties that affected Maidenhead in January, then one in December, and nothing at all in 1942 and 1943. Other towns nearby were not so fortunate, with a raid by a lone bomber on 10th February 1943 killing 15 people in Newbury and 41 in Reading.

The overall decline in air raids prompted many families to return to the capital, or mothers to bring back to London children who had been evacuated by themselves. Two more attacks occurred locally at the beginning of 1944, after which air raids ceased. However, they were to be replaced by what many considered a much worse threat, because of their lack of sufficient warning, the V1 flying-bomb (the 'Doodle-bugs'). An 80 day offensive began in June 1944, with the bombs being launched from northern France targetted on London and putting a stop to the homeward return of evacuees. Maidenhead was on the direct flight path of these missiles, and attracted the name 'Doodle-bug Alley'. However, only one V1 'flying-bomb' landed in Maidenhead, in Cookham Road in July 1944. Despite 64 casualties, largely from flying glass, there were no fatalities. When London suffered from the even more devastating V2s in early 1945, Maidenhead was spared its effects, with the only one arriving locally landing harmlessly in a field in Pinkneys Green in March.

Maidenhead did experience the death of six RAF personnel, including two Jewish airmen, when their plane crashed in Carpenters Wood, near Pinkneys Green. The Halifax - known as Q-for-Queenie - had left RAF Burn in Yorkshire on 18th July 1944 as part of twenty-one bombers from 578 Squadron heading south to strike at targets close to Caen in Normandy in support of troops engaged in the D-Day landings. It was about to fly over Reading when fire broke out in a starboard inner engine. Rather than bale out and leave the plane and its explosive cargo to crash into the densely populated housing below, the pilot – thiry-three year old Jewish Australian, Victor Starkoff DFC - diverted away from the town and into the countryside. He circled over Pinkneys Green looking for open land in which to bring the plane down, but in the process lost vital minutes and just as he gave the order to bale out, it exploded in mid-air, and only one person succeeded in parachuting to safety before the plane crashed into woodlands. The rest were killed, including the navigator, twenty-six year old Jan Fink from Finchley. No bodies were ever recovered. At the time, other members of 578 Squadron mistakenly reported that the Halifax had crashed in Buckinghamshire, so no memorial at the site was ever erected to the crew, although they were mentioned at Air Forces Memorial at Runnymede where they are listed as having no known grave. This was rectified five decades later after local historian Leslie Ritson-Smith pieced together the true story of the mens' heroic sacrifice.

Throughout the war, a key activity locally was the Air Transport Auxiliary. The ATA was a civilian organisation which ferried aircraft from the factories to their operational squadrons, and also returned planes requiring repairs to the maintenance units and back. It was not only

Air crew about to board Q-for-Queenie at RAF Burn

essential war-work but released RAF pilots from this job. There were fourteen 'ferry pools' scattered around the country, of which White Waltham Airfield (which opened in 1935) was Number One, the first site selected and the national headquarters. Set up in September 1939 it was a hive of activity until November 1945. The importance of the ATA in general, and White Waltham in particular, attracted enemy attention and was the scene of one of the first air attacks in England. A German bombing raid took place in July 1940 destroying seven Tiger Moths but causing no fatalities. Among the ATA pilots who may have been Jewish were Isy Rabinowitz, Frank Rosenberg, Harry Wolff and Paul Zimmerman (6).

Amongst the staff working on the ground at White Waltham was Peter Leapman who left his London home in order joined the ATA in 1943 aged seventeen. He was responsible for installing radios, the first FM radios to be used in Britain, which had arrived from the United States. During his time at the aerodrome he lived in digs in Maidenhead, but met no other Jews locally, even though there were a considerable number in the town. Speaking of that time, he said, 'I thought I was the only Jewish person there.' In 1944 he left to serve in the army (7). Others at White Waltham included Laurie Misener, working as equipment and uniforms officer, and who was to be chairman of Maidenhead Synagogue in the 1960s. In addition to its national role, the White Waltham ATA had considerable significance locally, both for those working there and the rest of the town: 'The ATA was quite an important bit of Maidenhead in the war. It was our bit of the frontline if you like, flying the aeroplanes from the factories to the squadrons' (8). Memory of the ATA lives on in the names of famous war-time planes that were given to streets in a housing area built after the war: 'Blenheim Road', 'Halifax Road', Lancaster Road', 'Lincoln Road', 'Stirling Grove' and 'Wellington Close'. It became known locally as 'Bomber Estate', although the passage of time means that many are no longer aware of the activities it commemorates.

Evacuees

The years 1939-1940 were a remarkable period in the Jewish life of Maidenhead and its surrounds. The area, previously populated by only a handful of Jewish individuals and devoid of any Jewish communal activity, suddenly became the receptacle of a massive Jewish inflow. This then resulted in the birth of an organised community, but first the story of those newcomers must be told.

For those who were evacuees, the initial days and weeks were a time of utter dislocation, suddenly cut off from their homes, family, friends and familiar surroundings. It was even more difficult for children: apart from the trauma of being separated from their parents and being billeted in the homes of strangers, many were experiencing the countryside for the first time and encountering strange beasts such as cows. It also presented a religious challenge - with Catholic children being put up in Protestant homes, Jewish ones ending up with Christian families - and the shock was for all the parties concerned. On arrival in Maidenhead, the children received a health check and, if necessary, a delousing, at the Wilderness Clinic in Cookham Road. They were then marched around Maidenhead where a billeting officer allocated up to three children per household. One of the first consequences was the overcrowding in schools, with many having to operate via two sittings, with local children attending in the morning and evacuees in the afternoon or vice-versa.

The stories of the individual evacuees are highly particular and often very disconnected to that of others, but added together they present a picture that reflects the massive disruption to so many ordinary lives. They also highlight a changed lifestyle that was to lead some of them losing all contact with Jewish life, but others re-establishing Jewish life in new areas and formats. The evacuees can be divided into two main groups: those who were British-born, predominantly Londoners and refugees from abroad who had already fled Nazism on the Continent. Each group can be sub-divided again into three futher categories: children who came alone, adults who arrived by themselves and those who journeyed together as families

Child evacuees

For many British-born children, the war was a time of enormous upheaval, not only departing from their homes but also being separated from their families. Many of them were evacuated with their schools on 1st September 1939. Among those that came to Berkshire was Stepney Jewish School with some 350 pupils, who were relocated to Windsor, while their own building was used an an emergency feeding centre. St Paul's School was evacuated to Crowthorne, with approximately 70 Jewish pupils amongst its 450 boys. They were billeted either in private homes in the village or some large hostels which the school had been able to rent. Lessons were partly conducted at nearby Wellington College - using their science laboratories and playing fields in particular - with the rest of the teaching done in a large country house set in Easthampstead Park, belonging to the Marquess of Downshire. Limited space sometimes meant that two classes had to be taught at the same time in one of its enormous rooms.

Evacuee children from London relocated to Windsor trying out their gas-masks

Amongst the Jewish pupils was Ralph Blumenau, who had come to England from Cologne with his family in 1937. As St Paul's in London was a day-school, it was a considerable transition for it to not only relocate but also turn into a boarding school. He recalled that there were no facilities for *kosher* food, but as most of the Jews were non-observant, this was not a problem. Jewish boys usually went into a separate room during Christian prayer assembly, although no alternative service was organised for them and they just sat around and chatted. Nor was there contact with any of the synagogues in the area. Proximity to a large army camp meant that the boys were caught up in occasional air raids, in one of which the headmaster of Wellington College was killed, although he was the only casualty the school suffered. Being a military area, special restrictions applied to those boys classified as 'enemy aliens', such as Blumenau. They were not allowed to move out of a tightly defined area, and if they wanted to go to the cinema in nearby Wokingham or Camberley, they had to receive prior police permission. Use of bicycles was even more prescribed, and they were only allowed to use them on the roads between Crowthorne and the school (9). Meanwhile the girls division of St Paul's went to High Wycombe, where it shared the site of Wycombe Abbey School and arrangements were made to hire a teacher to provide the religious education of the Jewish girls there (10).

Another day public school to evacuate en masse was Latymer Upper (Boys) in Hammersmith, which came to Iver Heath in August 1939. It was an example of the meticulous planning that had been underway in the months leading up to the war, with 500 boys being moved from London and settled with their billeting families in the space of three hours (11). Amongst the pupils was Michael Burnside, then living in Chiswick with his parents, who suddenly found himself billeted with a non-Jewish family. However, his stay in the area was short, because his family wanted him home for the High Holy Days. They themselves had moved to Eastcote, Middlesex by then, and once he was back with them he never left again (12). Regents Park School moved en bloc too. It was a boarding school that occupied a large house in Maresfield Gardens, Hampstead and was run by Alma Schindler. It moved to Haddenham, Bucks in late May 1940 (13). Amongst the many Jewish pupils was Charles Hoffner, who stayed there until 1943, after which he went to university (14).

Godolphin and Latymer Girls School also moved out of London and went to Newbury, where it shared premises with Newbury County School. The local children had lessons in the morning, with games and 'prep' in the afternoon, while the newcomers did the reverse. Someone who was part of the latter group was Annie Saville (nee Baskier), who had come to England via the Kindertransport. She had originally been settled in Brighton, but because of the public fears of German spies in 1940 had been sent inland and was residing at a Quaker hostel in Speen, near Newbury. She recalled being subject to no less than three curfews: the school insisted that she had to be indoors before dark, the hostel demanded that she be in by 8.00 pm, and the government ordered a 10.30 pm limit. She was joined at Godolphin by another German Jewish refugee, Amy Wieser (15). The sense of dislocation of the newcomers was evident even to local children: 'you would always know if children were evacuees, you could just tell. We didn't mix with them, they were at school in the afternoon and we were in the morning. I can't remember any unpleasantness or bullying, but they didn't want to mix with us either' (16).

Annie Saville, December 1939, aged 16

Not all children came with their schools. Sid Eckman was thirteeen when war broke out and he was sent away by his parents from his home in the East End of London to Clewer Hill Farm, near Windsor.

He had a happy experience there, going to school locally and helping out on the farm at weekends. When his parents moved to High Wycombe two years later, he joined them there, and the family returned to London after the war, albeit to a new home in Ealing. Years later, he became one of the leading organisers of the Zemel Choir. (17) Rosita Rosenberg (nee Gould) had been living with her family in Putney, South London. On the outbreak of war, she and her older sister, Isobel, were sent to Reading (18):

> [We] were billeted on a couple in Tilehurst who had never seen a Jew before in their lives, let alone two small girls with strange food requests. Staunch Catholics, they greeted us Sunday morning with a puzzled, 'I don't know why you won't come to church with us - after all, Jesus was a Jew!' Even the consumption of vast quantities of fried fish, regularly sent to us, failed to inculcate in them any understanding of Judaism.

When her parents decided to leave London to re-unite the family, they settld in Windsor and the two girls joined them there.

Some individuals experienced evacuation twice. Beryl Waldorf (nee Bloch) was evacuated with her parents in 1942 after their house in Hounslow was hit by an incendiary bomb. They relocated to Wargrave, while she went to a boarding school in Henley. She recalled that the other schoolchildren did not know at first that she was Jewish and when they asked her why she did not go to church, she told them that it was because she did not have enough coupons to buy a hat. When she eventually acquired a hat, she had to admit that the reason was because she was Jewish, although nothing untoward resulted from it. They all returned to Heston, London in 1944, but then returned to Wargrave shortly afterwards when the bombing raids resumed, this time with the 'doodlebugs' (19).

The move of so many Jewish children out of London was not welcomed in all quarters of the Jewish community and did attract some criticism. One of the *dayanim* (judges) of the London Beth Din exhorted Jews in the East End to stay where they were with their children (20):

> He argued that to send them away to the country would certainly destroy their Jewish identity, while to stay in London would create a doubt only about their physical security. In a conflict between a certainty and a doubt, we should opt for the doubt and keep the children in London. In any case, everything is in God's hands, he argued, so there is no sure way to escape one's destiny. Most parents were not impressed with the dayan's *halakhic* [legal] or theological observations and

continued to send their children away with the evacuated school groups. Thus, whilst Jewish education in Anglo-Jewry was never very good, during the war years it became a disaster.

It is certainly true that many children were billeted with non-Jewish families - some for the duration of the whole war - and saw no home Jewish life during their formative years. Celia Goodman typified the problems of maintaining a Jewish lifestyle. She had come to London from Vienna in February 1939 with her parents and attended a school in Bow, East London. When the entire school was evacuated to Wantage, she went to stay with a non-Jewish family nearby in Ardington. Acquiring *kosher* meat was impossible, so she became a vegetarian, but as this presented difficulties, she ended up eating non-*kosher* meat but avoiding specifically forbidden foods such as pork. However, she regularly ate rabbit, not realising that it was another of the forbidden foods (21). As British Jews tended to live in urban areas, it was inevitable that children evacuated to the countryside found themselves in places where there was no communal Jewish life or provision for any religious education. An attempt to answer these needs was made by the Zionist youth movements, which established hostels for evacuated Jewish children, which was co-ordinated by the Hostels Committtee for Evacuated Jewish Children under the Board of Deputies. They included Rowledge House, in Farnham, Surrey, which was run by Shalom and Edie Marcovitch through Bachad (an abrreviation of *Brit Chalutzim Datiim* – Association of Religious Pioneers), and catered for 32 children from 1942-1945. As one of them was later to record: 'My twin brother [Jochi] and I arrived there at the beginning of 1944, when we were eight years old, and stayed until the end of the war. It was an extraordinarily rich experience for a rag-tag bunch of children. I am certain that every one of us were coloured for the rest of our lives by the goodness, good will and nurture we received there' (22).

Amongst several others run by Habonim was that in Cefn Coed, South Wales, whose children were later moved to bigger premises in Woodcote, Ascot, a large country house directly facing the racecourse. It also acted as a visiting centre for Jewish children who had been evacuated nearby with their schools, such as City of London and St Paul's, who attended Woodcote for the Sabbath and festivals. According to Chaim Pearl, who ran the hostel (23):

> The Jewish education was Hebrew language oriented, and many Hebrew words and phrases became the natural means of expression in daily life, in the kitchen, dining room, classrooms and dormitories. The day started with daily prayers and there

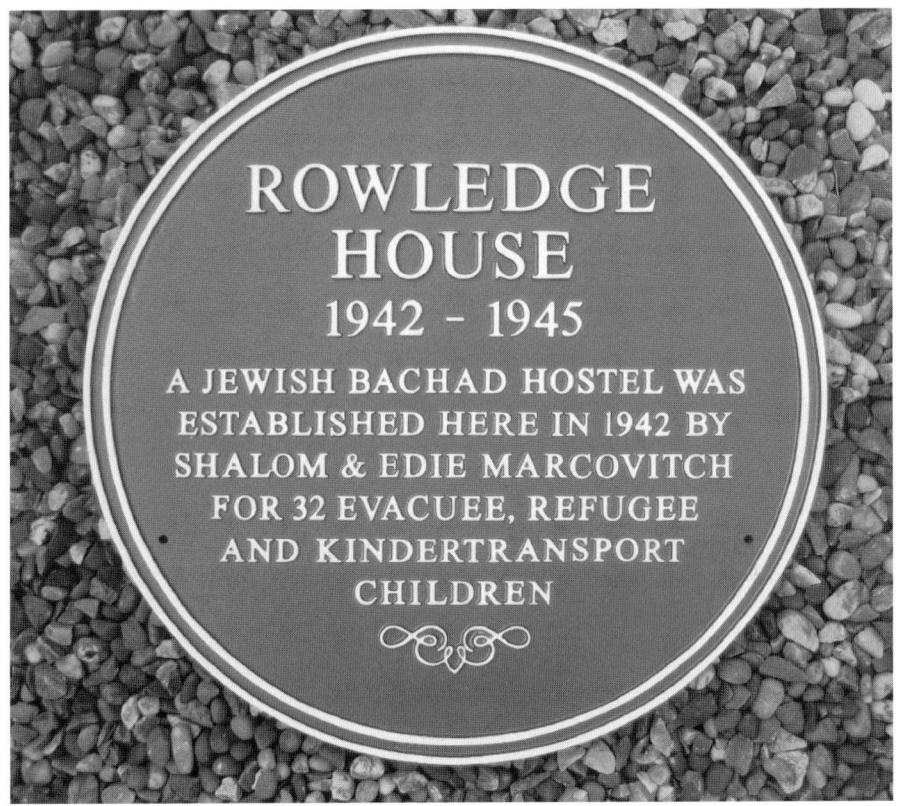

Plaque unveiled at Rowledge House in 2012

was always Grace before and after meals - during the week, the first paragraph only and on Sabbaths and festivals the long Grace enthusiastically sung by the entire gathering. Every Sabbath and festival was something special and we succeeded in combining traditional observance with a modern and dynamic approach. The children published their own house journal and were encouraged to participate in the daily discipline of the community through their own committees. This led to a natural acceptance of responsibility and personal involvement by each member of the hostel.....These little communities of evacuated Jewish children were islands in an otherwise hopeless area of Anglo-Jewish life.

After the war the evacuees who had resided at the hostels returned to their families, but their place was taken by 732 young concentration camp victims allowed into Britain for rehabilitation. Twenty-five teenagers from Buchenwald and Thereisenstadt came to Woodcote under the auspices of the Central British Fund for World Jewish Relief. One of the previous wardens, Manny Silver, stayed on to help the new arrivals (24):

> Shelter, food, clothing, security - all that they had tenaciously fought for was now theirs. But there were serious problems adjusting to a new way of life. In the camps, survival meant breaking the rules. 'Me first' was the only rule. But despite all this there were countless examples of altruism. Now, in Ascot, they were require to accept the control of staff who had to learn the hard way how to care for their wards.
>
> Boarding school discipline could not apply. After the Nazis, what punishment could there be for someone who stole food, refused to get up in the morning, did not come to class, disrupted others, or stayed out late at night? We devised a co-operative way of life, based on mutual respect and understanding of the different responsibilities of staff and youth and how best we could prepare them for the future.
>
> Although we were not qualified teachers, we taught them English, mathematics and geography in preparation for when they might be able to attend regular schools. Of course, we taught them Hebrew and Jewish studies, celebrating *Shabbat* and the festivals. All of them needed medical and dental help. Listed as orphans, they all cherished the hope that parents would be found alive. Gradually they accepted their new way of life and adjusted to the regimen. Eventually, some moved to Israel. Others were placed with Jewish families in towns.

Despite being havens of refuge for these children, Ascot had less pleasant associations for other Jews. In mid 1940 nearly 30,000 Germans and Austrian Jews living in Britain were interned owing to fears that they were fifth-columnists and a danger to British security. Many were taken to a temporary camp in Ascot before being transferred to the Isle of Man. Most were released within a few months once it was appreciated that the internees were the fiercest opponents of Nazism, but at the time it led to much anxiety for those whose lives had already been disrupted. Nearby, Sunningdale had been the temporary home of all refugee records kept by the Board of Deputies during the 'phoney war' period.

Refugee childen at Woodcote, Ascot

Not all evacuees remained in England. In June 1940, as Germany occupied France, a scheme was set up with the Commonwealth countries and America for Government-sponsored individuals to be evacuated abroad. Some 2,700 applicants left Britain, but the scheme was stopped after the 'City of Benares' was torpedoed and sunk in September of that year, with a loss of life that included 77 children. Daphne Woolf (aged thirteen) and her twin sisters, Ursula and Diana (aged six), were amongst those who went to the United States after they had been evacuated initially to Long Crendon, near Thame. Their father was in the army and their mother remained in West London. They were looked after by a Jewish family in Chicago, Al and Bea Neiman. Describing her experience long afterwards, Daphne expressed a scenario - and emotions - that were no doubt common to many others (25):

> I didn't want to go at all because I felt that I was nearly old enough to do something for the war effort, but they [my parents] wouldn't hear of me not going. I didn't believe we were going until we actually got on the way. Children were crying. We were miserable at leaving our parents. We didn't know what was going to happen.
>
> I helped sell war bonds and it was the thing to do to grow your own vegetables. I had a little vegetable garden; there was no

point in it because there was plenty of food, but I wanted to do anything that made me feel part of the war effort.

I'm sure that every child who was evacuated, even if it wasn't abroad, was changed. It was quite a thing to think that children could be lifted up and dumped somewhere else without any effect on their psyche. I blamed my mother when we were in America; I felt it was her fault, because of her nervousness, that we were away, but if I'd been in her place, I really don't know.

A recollection from Ursula highlighted another of the consequences of a six year evacuation: ' Our mother saved letters from us and they are sad to read. I finished mine, "love from Ursula Woolf", which isn't what a child would write to her mother unless she felt a stranger from her'.

Adult evacuees

Many of the adults who moved to Maidenhead saw it as a temporary stay to avoid the night-time bombs in London while they maintained their day jobs there. This applied to Helen Barnett (nee Levenson), who left London in 1940 aged 18 to stay at Whiteplace, a large mansion on the outskirts of Maidenhead in Taplow, where her uncles Barney and Bob Levenson were also renting rooms. She was working at the time for Palestine Potash Ltd (a Dead Sea company) and commuted into London by train every day. The move was a wise decision, as her Maida Vale home was later bombed and her father, who was still living there, was killed. She recalled that the owner of the house, Mr Stungo, had a step-son from his wife's first marriage, Gerald Joseph, who was a pilot with the RAF. When flying in the area, he had the habit of making a detour over the house and dropping his dirty washing from the plane. His low-flying escapades alarmed some locals, who called the police and the flights were stopped. Amongst other Jewish families also renting rooms in Whiteplace were Arthur Poliakov, a furrier; Len Suswin, a raincoat manufacturer, along with his wife Nini and daughter Muriel; Boyd and Helen Smith, who owned dress-shops in Chelsea; David and Freda Pell from Scotland; and a Russian pearl-merchant and his wife, Marcel and Beck. 'It was', Helen said, 'an extraordinary assortment of people'. She moved the following year to family in Storrington, Sussex, before returning to London and joining the WRENS (26).

Evacuees who came as a family

Sometimes extended families moved together, such as when Tom Cohen moved to Maidenhead from Stamford Hill in 1940. He not only brought his wife Esther and sons Harvey (six years old) and Paul (aged three), but also his two brothers and their offspring: Mick and Cissie Cohen (and daughters Barbara, Pamela and Marion) and Jack and Annie Cohen (and daughters Celia, Renee and Hazel), as well as his sister and her husband Ada and Rube Caplan (and their sons, Harold and Leon). Tom and Esther occupied a flat in Lassell Gardens and Harvey attended Maidenhead County Boys School. He recalled that his father, 'like most Jews', commuted to London every day, to his furniture factory in the East End, along with his two brothers and brother-in-law, playing bridge with friends on the train and using a briefcase on someone's knee as a table. In common with so many others, they not only returned to London at the end of the war, but, with their former home destroyed, settled in a new area, in their case going to Golders Green (27). As well as commuting to their businesses, the evacuees also returned to their metropolitan synagogues for special occasions. Aubrey Rose was living in Stamford Hill as a child and in September 1939 moved with his family to Melbourne Road, High Wycombe. This coincided with his school - Chiswick County School - moving there too and sharing the premises of the Royal Grammar School. London was still the main focus though: his mother worked in London and commuted back and forth every day, while Aubrey's *barmitzvah* took place as planned in North London (28)

An early evacuee who went elsewhere first before coming to Maidenhead was Rose Shackman who was living in West Hampstead with her husband Rube, a jeweller, when war broke out. She recalled getting up at 5.00 am to queue outside a local estate agent the next day, such was the enormous rush for property in the countryside. The business opened at 9.00 am and they took the first house available, down in Somerset. With Rube working in London midweek and seeing the family at weekends, it was decided to find somewhere nearer and they moved to Waltham St Lawrence. She was already familiar with the area, as she had been evacuated with her family to Henley when a child during the First World War. Rube was engaged in essential war-work, making ship's sextants, gun-sights for the army and technical cameras (one of which was used in the bombing of Hiroshima). His brother and Rose's four brothers all joined the army, two of whom were killed in action. When his factory was bombed in 1940, the government requisitioned new premises in Chesham to continue his work. After the war they remained in the area, and the factory switched to producing watches and bracelets. It later changed to industrial cameras and body scanners, and Rube was awarded the MBE for his enterprise. They eventually moved back to London in the 1960s (29). Another family that stayed in the area long after the war was that of Mrs G. Bidmead, who came to Maidenhead in 1940 with her parents and lived in Bray. Her father opened a shop in the High Street and the family remained in the area until 1957 (30).

In contrast, Yetta Michaels had no intention of leaving her home in the East End of London, but found she had no alternative when she and her husband were bombed out. They rented rooms in The Broadway, Maidenhead and commuted to London for work and shopping. They had no lack of friends, for they found many people in Maidenhead that they had known from the East End and it 'felt like one big happy family; life carried on'. One particular memory was that if someone had a *yartzeit* and wanted to say *kaddish*, they would wait at the station platform for one of the evening trains from London so as to gather together a quorum and go off for prayers. The family returned to the East End, where they had been allocated a new home, in 1942. They thought that the bombing had stopped but later found themselves under attack from the V1 and V2 rockets (31).

The family of Sidney and Lily Osborne were also bombed out of their home during the Blitz, which had been in Tredegar Square in the East End of London. They had to be dug out of the rubble covering the air raid shelter in which they had taken refuge. After being sent briefly to Taunton, they were relocated to Slough, where they remain to this day. Their bad luck seemed to accompany them to the area, when there was a confusion over their billeting address and they had to sleep overnight on the floor of the Slough Social Centre. However, it turned out to be a fortunate mistake, as they woke up the next morning to find that the place where they should have stayed the previous night had sustained a direct hit (32). Force majeure also brought Leonard Merran to the area. He left Clapton as child with his parents, two sisters and brother in 1940 when their house was bombed. They got off the train in Windsor and remained there ever after, with all the siblings marrying, having children and grandchildren in the area. He himself was a cabinet maker and worked on the 'stringers', the wooden wing parts of Hurricane planes at Langley during the war (33). Alfred and Leah Hammerson were also reluctant evacuees. They had been determined to stay in London and spent the Blitz there, but when they started a family, they felt it was time to leave, coming to Reading in 1943. At the end of the war, they returned to London (34).

One of the few to report difficult experiences with the local population, both adult and children, were Reuben and Mary Fogelman. When they sought to leave Hackney for a safer area, they automatically headed towards Maidenhead, as his parents had evacuated there during the First World War. However, when they rented rooms in Taplow in 1939, they received a request from some in the village to go elsewhere. They thought it best to comply and went to Courthouse Road, Maidenhead. Their daughter, Myrna, was teased by children at the primary school she attended, Alwyn Court, who chased her shouting 'she's got horns'. At the same time, she found very few Jewish friends as, according to her, 'most Jews kept their head down and only revealed their Jewish identity after the war' (35). Her father commuted to London where he ran a motor-tyre shop, and the family returned to North London in 1947.

For some, the route to Maidenhead was more circuitous. Edward Kessly's story of constant moves during the war was not untypical of some children, although at least he was with his family all the time, starting in Wales, going on to Manchester, then to London, before settling in Maidenhead in 1942. It meant that he was at nine different schools during the war years. His father commuted daily from Maidenhead to his ladies fashion business in Central London. Edward recalled attending Religion School, while services were held in a hall, led by Rabbi Munk, whom he described as 'an elderly German rabbi' who lived in the same road as the family, in Ray Park Avenue (36).

Maxwell Morrison represented a different pattern of arrival. He was born in 1936 and left Central London with his family on the outbreak of war to go to Ayr. They returned to their home in early 1944 when the danger of bombing raids seemed to be over, only to find themselves under attack from the 'doodlebugs'. As a result they were part of a much later and lesser wave of evacuees, settling in Fisheries Road, Bray. His father had been a regular synagogue-attender in London, but they had no contact with local Jewish life, although the family did employ locally-based Mr Joseph to come to the house to teach him Hebrew. His father commuted to London daily to run his fashion shop there, and at the end of the war they returned to London for good (37). There were also those who arrived locally by mistake. In 1939 Annie Skinner was intending to go to Chippenham in Wiltshire, but got off the train at Cippenham, near Slough when she misheard the station announcement. Her momentary mistake had long-term consequences, for she remained there until her death in 1996.

The biographical notes of Sophia Podguszer give an insight into some of the evacuees attitudes and experiences. In the spring of 1941, she moved from Stamford Hill, London to a house in Lent Rise, Burnham, which her daughter Anne had bought (38):

> where, apart from rationing and the war news, we were barely affected by the terrible daily air raids and bombing that took place in London and other industrial towns. Once every week I would travel by train to London and was horrified by the devastation that the Germans inflicted upon innocent people and property. Amongst countless women, I endeavoured to play my part in the war effort, by knitting gloves and scarves for the soldiers.

The reason for her weekly trips was that (39):

> In preparation for the Sabbath Friday evening meal, I would travel regularly by train each Thursday morning to Petticoat Lane. Arriving there with four or more stout empty shopping bags, I would make all the *kosher* food purchases for the following week. I enjoyed making the rounds of the innumerable small East End shops where surrendering money and ration coupons I could banter and talk in Yiddish, exchanging gossip with shopkeepers I'd known for so many years. I would then entrain that same afternoon from Paddington back to Taplow station and then walk more than a mile back home laden down with all those arm-wrenching shopping bags, full with every imaginable provision.

On one occasion, when another daughter, Betty, was travelling to Taplow by train, she happened to sit opposite a Jewish Canadian serviceman, Issie Glick, who was temporary patient at the Canadian Hospital there. He was invited back for a Friday night meal in Lent Rise, a relationship developed, they married and after the war they settled in Montreal. Sophia and Anne remained in Taplow until 1954, when the house was sold. Typical of so many other evacuees, Sophia did not return to her old area in North London, but instead went to St John's Wood.

1. Jackson (1960) 15
2. Titmuss (1950)
3. Hunter (1995) 136
4. Rosenthal & Danks (2004) 93
5. Over (1984) 53

6. Cheesman (1946) 239-245
7. Interview, Peter Leapman
8. Rosenthal & Danks (2004) 108
9. Private correspondence, Ralph Blumenau
10. JC (8 December 1939) 18
11. Details supplied by Latymer School
12. Interview, Michael Burnside
13. AJR Journal (June 2009) 5
14. Private correspondence, Charles Hoffner
15. Private correspondence, Annie Saville
16. Paddy Gibbons, quoted in Rosenthal & Danks (2004) 95
17. Interview, Sid Eckman
18. *ULPS News* (January 1992)
19. Interview, Beryl Waldorf
20. Chaim Pearl, 'Away and Home', in *Manna* (Summer 1991) 26
21. Interview, Celia Goodman
22. Private correspondence, Hanna Nyman (nee Isaacs)
23. Chaim Pearl op. cit. 27
24. Manny Silver, 'How CBF Changed My Life', in *Update*, (January 1995) 6
25. I am grateful to Anne Crabbe for this quote and that of Ursula below it, both of which were taken from her photographic exhibition 'With a label on my coat'
26. Interview, Helen Barnett
27. Interview, Harvey Cohen
28. Interview, Aubrey Rose
29. Interview, Rose Shackman
30. Interview, Mrs G. Bidmead
31. Interview, Yetta Michaels
32. *London Jewish News* (9 June 2000) 10
33. Interview, Stanley Merran
34. Stebbing (2003) 109
35. Interview, Myrna Julius
36. Interview, Edward Kessly
37. Interview, Maxwell Morrison
38. Powell (2010) 185
39. ibid. 190

Chapter 6

1939: The Refugees

Child refugees

The most well-known category of foreign Jewish children who arrived in the area were those who had come to England via the Kindertransport. This was the result of the British government being persuaded - following the widespread attacks on Jews and synagogues during 'Kristallnacht' - to provide refuge for ten thousand children. It started on 1st December 1938 when a train left Berlin carrying unaccompanied Jewish children between the age of three and seventeen to England. Subsequent trains left not only from Germany but also Austria, Czechoslovakia and Poland. Most went via Holland, crossed the sea to Harwich, and then continued by train to Liverpool Street, London. A smaller number sailed from Hamburg to Southampton, and then arrived in London at Waterloo Station. From there they were dispersed across Britain, some to family members, others to total strangers; some travelling alone, others with siblings; some speaking English, others having no command of their new language. The physical disruption to their lives was matched by the emotional dislocation they also suffered, cut off from their family, culture and even mother tongue, which many dared not speak as it was associated with the enemy. They were generally under the care of the Refugees Childrens' Movement who had taken responsibility for finding homes for them. Some came to the area directly, such as Victor Simons. He left Germany via the Kindertransport in April 1939 aged 14, although his parents were to join him in England later. He was placed with Ies and Dorothy van Zwanenberg, a non-observant Jewish couple who lived in The Arches, Willow Lane, Wargrave and undertook to support him. Victor was sent by them as a boarder to Shrewsbury School, which two of their own four sons were attending. He stayed at the school for the next four years, spending the holidays partly in Wargrave and partly with his parents. He left the area in 1943 to work as a farm-labourer and then as a coal-mining volunteer, one of the 'Bevin boys' (1).

For other children, the area was just one of many stops in a journey across the country. Kurt Beckhardt, for instance, landed in Southampton in June 1939 and then spent time at Barham Camp in Claydon, Ipswich. When the Battle of Britain began, he stayed in Wallingford at a Farm Training colony for a few weeks before moving on to Sheffield (2). This may have been the same 'agricultural training

Sculpture of Kindertransport children at Liverpool Street station

centre' that Claus Ascher (later Colin Anson) attended in Wallingford after he had come to England from Berlin with the Kinderstranport in February 1939, a few days before his seventeeth birthday (3). Another Kindertransport child, albeit who arrived in the area much later, reflected the story of those who not only changed countries and name but changed faith as well: Helga Richards (nee Nettel) came from Prague to England in

1939 via the Kindertransport aged twelve. As well as coming to a strange country alone, she also had to survive the trauma of her father being shot by the Nazis before she left. She was fostered in Northampton by a family from the Christadelphians, a non-conformist church who attached great emphasis on the importance of the Jewish people, and who, along with the Quakers, were in the forefront of offering hospitality to Jewish children. They did not actively proselytise, but it was inevitable that some children in their care would adopt their faith. This applied to Helga who became a member and remained a Christadelphian throughout her life and brought her children up in the church. After living in Scotland for a while, she and her husband moved to Berkshire (4).

There were also children who left the Continent via routes other than the Kindertransport. Kurt (later Robert) Klein was seventeen when he left Vienna for England in mid 1938. Thanks to the YMCA scheme, British Boys for British Farms, in 1940 he was sent to Rickett's Farm in Wheeler End, Bucks owned by the Hanson family. There he helped with the threshing and milking until he was interned on the Isle of Man as an 'enemy alien', after which he returned to the farm until emigrating to Africa in 1947 (5). Bob Kutner came as a young teenager from Kempnitz, Germany to England in 1939, travelling by himself via Italy, sponsored by Mr and Mrs Reigate, a London Jewish family. He was sent to work as a labourer on a chicken farm, White Hayes, near Streatley in West Berkshire, during which time he had no contact with any Jewish life. He recalled working hard and being fed well, with both he and the owners being tied to the farm every day of the week except Tuesday afternoon, when they went to the local Lyons Corner House for tea. (6). Where possible, siblings were kept together, and so Hans and Ernst Aris from Berlin – whose parents died in a concetration camp in 1942 - found themselves in Long Crendon, fostered by a local family (7).

Some children found foster homes in London but were then relocated to the Home Counties once war was declared. Beatrice Musgrave was sent to London from Germany with her sister in 1938. She then faced a further journey when her school was evacuated to Reading, experiencing both the best and worst of local families in the billeting lottery (8):

> This really was evacuation, totally different from the earlier experience of arriving in London from Germany and enjoying a quite glamorous time with our banking relatives, who'd already settled in England and treated us to teas in lovely hotels. My sister and I were billeted with three different families outside Reading, all of quite different backgrounds, two very hostile to

having young girls dumped on them. One, an old clergyman and his wife, more or less forbade us to be in the house during the day. Another, a vicious father with a terrified daughter, accused us of scribbling graffiti on his lavatory walls and got rid of us that way. The third family - a post office sorter with wife and son - were kind and cosy and provided our first experience of simple grass-roots English life.

A similar relocation happened with Hans-Wolfgang Danziger and his sister Marion (later Goldwater). They arrived in Liverpool Street Station in March 1939 via the Kindertransport aged five and eight respectively. They were one of the 'Sainsbury children', looked after in a home established by Alan, later Lord Sainsbury in Putney, South London for twenty-one refugee Jewish children. When war broke out most of the children were evacuated to Reading, although he and his sister were sent to the Sainsbury riding stables in Leighton Buzzard where the groom and his wife were put in charge of them. It was a mixed experience: 'Although I enjoyed riding the enormous hunters around the yard, Marion and I remember well the misery of trudging round the recreation ground in freezing weather to get fresh air. The smell of the iron swings is still with me and I avoided them when looking after my grandchildren' (9). Hans Rosenbaum (later John Rosen) and his brother Walter were amongst that same group of children, but they went to Reading where they were billeted in different private homes and remained there throughout the war. Even though Hans and Walter were then fortunate enough to be reunited with their parents who had also come to England - most of the other children had lost their parents in the Holocaust - Lord Sainsbury maintained contact with them, and sent them each birthday cards along with special gifts on their twenty-first birthday and wedding (10).

Alice Hubbers (nee Engel) had even more moves. She was born in Vienna and had come to England in December 1938 via the Kindertransport, leaving her parents behind. Her father had been interned in a concentration camp but was released in time to go with her mother to Shanghai before the war broke out. Alice initially stayed in the Dovercourt holiday camp near Harwich, which had been turned into a youth refugee centre, before spending two years in Scotland and then settling in North London. There she met Lee Davis, the daughter of Ben and Fay Davis who had evacuated to Maidenhead, and Alice decided to relocate there too in 1943. She rented a room in Alexandra Road with a non-Jewish family and worked locally as a bus conductress. She returned to London in 1945 (11).

There were also children who initially came to England with their parents but were then separated from them. Nine year old Henry Kuttner left Berlin with his family in February 1939, intending to go to Lima, Peru via Britain. However, the British authorities declared that their Peru visas were not valid and so they remained here. Having begun to learn Spanish in preparation for his supposed new home, his English vocabulary consisted of just four words. They lived in London, but when war broke out his parents wanted their two children to be out of the danger zone and they sent him to Crab Tree Farm, Eaton Hastings, near Faringdon, while his older sister, then thirteen, was evacuated to Wales. The city boy enjoyed learning to work in the fields and milk cows. He quickly picked up English through the local village school and his hosts, the Wilkins family. His religious education were weekly Bible lessons that were sent by Rabbis Harold Reinhart and Louis Cashdan of the West London Synagogue, using two volumes, appropriately called 'Out of the House of Bondage'. These were supervised by the local vicar, Rev. Girling, and were conducted on a one to one basis, as he was the only Jewish child in the area. Kuttner recalled that, 'At no time during my fourteen months there did I experience any antisemitism, so for a refugee from Nazi-infested Berlin, this was a breath of true British freedom, and I gulped at it'. His return to London was earlier than expected: 'I developed a nasty-looking and painful boil on the back of my neck. When I went home for the school holidays, my mother was so shocked to see me like this that she decided not to send me back to the Farm. So I had to endure much of the Blitz after all and later on the V1 and V2 Rockets' (12).

Another example was Nikki Van der Zyl, who was born in Berlin in 1935 and came to London with her parents in 1939. When they were placed in an adults-only aliens' camp two years later, she had to board at the Stoatley Rough school for refugees in Haslemere. She found it a difficult experience, being not only without family but also being unable to speak any English. The result was naughty behaviour that led to her being expelled, after which she boarded at a girls school in Farnham. 'But I was not any happier. I missed my parents and London. I used to go on long walks on my own'. She was reunited with them after the war and settled in North West London (13). For others the process of acculturation came quickly. Ruth Shire had left Bonn in 1937 as a sixteen year old and was transported to Great Milton in the Oxfordshire countryside, living with committed Christians, albeit both broad-minded and welcoming. When she left school she trained at Staines Hospital as a nurse and recalled a 'strange experience' when some friends had taken her to Virginia Water, near Ascot on one of her half-days in 1941 (14):

> Looking at this peaceful scene in the sunset, I suddenly felt I had reached a watershed, that I was stepping out of one part of my life and entering another. I felt I was no longer a refugee, a second-class citizen, but an ordinary young woman and that here I belonged

Some children arrived as a pre-formed group, such as the twenty-one children from the Flersheim-Sichel Stiftung, a boys' orphanage in Frankfurt, who came to England via the Hook of Holland and Harwich in March 1939. They were resettled at Cedars House in the grounds of Waddesdon Manor, near Aylesbury, the home of James de Rothschild. Nine other boys came over to join them in June. The orphanage was run by Hugo and Lilly Steinhardt, who came over with the children, along with their daughters, Lore and Helga. Following the violence of Kristallnacht, when hundreds of synagogues were burned and thousands of Jewish shops and synagogues attacked, the two girls had written to leading figures abroad to help bring the orphanage to safety. One letter had been addressed simply to 'Lord Rothschild, London'. He had passed it on to his cousin James, who had promised to help and who had acted as guarantor for the entire orphanage. He also provided furniture and basic necessities for Cedars House, which had originally been intended as a Maternity Home, but this had not materialised and the house lay empty. One of the boys, Hans Hellman (later Jack Helman) recalled that (15):

> The first day that we got to Cedars Lodge, the first thing we did was throw a soccer ball on the lawn and kick it around. The local boys came to see what was all of a sudden being brought into their village. They said, 'We'll see you tomorrow.' I was so excited. I was absolutely exuberant. I ran to my house mother and told her, 'Somebody who is not Jewish wants to see us tomorrow.'

Their refugee status did not stop some of them from having prejudices of their own. Another boy, Geoffrey Gert, remembered when a group of East European Jewish refugees were housed temporarily in Waddesdon recreation hall (16):

> The hall was packed full one day with a motley, unwashed crew. We were told that they too were refugees, but from the East, Ostjuden…The colourful D.P.s [Displaced Persons] were given to talking and gesticulating unintelligibly and to haggling

in the shops...I remember disowning them, saying: 'We (the German refugees) have nothing to do with them.'

The children went to local schools and Hugo Steinhardt took services at the hostel at weekends. He died in 1942, having been in poor health ever since his incarceration and severe beatings in Buchenwald concentration camp. After his death, Reform rabbis came to lead services, including Dr Georg Salzberger and Dr Hermann Schreiber, both refugees themselves. At High Holy Days, the children all attended a chapel in Aylesbury that was taken over by the Jewish community who had been evacuated there from London. When Hans (now in Israel as Hanan) Bodenheimer had his *barmitzvah* there in October 1940, James and Dorothy de Rothschilds attended. They often visited the hostel on other occasions so as to keep in touch with their proteges. Hans was tutored for his *barmitzvah* at the Cedars and recalled that 'We had several Hebrew classes, which considering that these were the war years, was quite an achievement. To me the Cedars group often seemed like a small island in a vast ocean. We were, of course, the only Jewish group in that area' (17). Another *barmitzvah* was in August 1943, that of Ulrich Stobieka (who later became Uri Sella after moving to Israel), none of whose family had survived. Once the boys were over eighteen, they were keen to go off to fight the Nazis. At first they had to join the non-combatant Pioneer Corps, but eventually they became part of the regular British armed forces. Those with German sounding names changed them in preparation for the invasion of Europe, so as to protect themselves if they were captured. Mrs Steinhardt carried on running Cedars by herself until 1950 when it closed. The 'children' dispersed, many of them going to the United States, Canada or Israel, often with their fare being paid by the Rothschilds, but she stayed in the area for the rest of her life (18). In 1983 a reunion of the 'children' took place at Waddesdon and ten years later a plaque was unveiled at the Cedars stating: 'This plaque is dedicated to the revered memory of Mr and Mrs de Rothschild by the Cedars Boys and Girls in gratitude for sanctuary at a time of conflict in 1939.' By then Waddesdon had been transferred to the National Trust and the Cedars had become a private house.

The plight of children endangered by the spread of Nazism was a particular concern of Nicholas Winton (b. 1909), then a Londoner but shortly afterwards to become a Maidonian and one of its most famous modern citizens. His parents were highly assimilated Jews and he received a nominally Christian upbringing at Stowe public school. In December 1938 he was working as a stock-broker at the London Exchange and was about to go on a skiing holiday, when he received an urgent call by a friend to come to Prague where the latter was visiting a refugee camp. Winton became alerted to the serious danger facing the Jews in Sudetenland, the Nazi-occupied part of Czechoslovakia and focused on the need to rescue the endangered children. He returned to England to persuade the Home Office to grant entry permits for refugee children who were not part of the Kindertransport arrangement and for whom he personally would find sponsors. He organised foster parents to provide homes for them, as well as the transport to bring the children to England. Each child had to have a £50 guarantor in advance, along with a family who would look after them until they were seventeen. This involved considerable amount of work, dealing with the Home Office, finding a large number of foster families and co-ordinating arrangements with the Czech authorities. The result was that in March 1939 a train left Prague carrying refugee children, journeyed through Germany and France, with the children then ferried across the channel and continuing by train to Liverpool Street station.

Nicholas Winton in Prague, January 1939, with one of the children he saved

Another five such trains were commissioned, bringing a total of 669 children to safety, most, but not all, of whom were Jewish. A further train was due to depart from Prague on 1st September, but was unable to leave because of the imminent outbreak of war. Only a few of the 250 children on that train are known to have survived. During the war Winton served first with the Red Cross and later in the RAF, and then moved to Maidenhead in 1948 for business reasons. His pre-war rescue work was largely unknown until 1988 when it was featured on Esther Rantzen's television programme 'That's Life'. It led to widespread praise for his efforts and a reunion of Winton's 'children', many of whom had become parents and grandparents by then. A number had become famous in their own right, such as Labour MP, Alfred (later Lord) Dubs and film director Karel Reisz, whose works included the *French Lieutenant's Woman*. The ring he received as a gift of thanks from his 'children' was inscribed with a line from the Talmud: 'Save one life, save the world'. Winton had received the MBE in 1983 for an entirely separate reason, his services to the local community, especially his work with MENCAP and Abbeyfield Homes. Winton House in Dedworth Road, Windsor is named after him in honour of his work to establish it. In recognition of his efforts on behalf of the children, he was knighted in 2002, while he was nominated by the Czech government for the Nobel Peace Prize. When he celebrated his 100th birthday in 2009 there was a re-creation of one of the train journeys he had organised from Prague to London, carrying his (by now much

Statue of Nicholas Winton at Maidenhead Station

older) 'children' who had gathered together from across the world in his honour. He was frequently referred to in the media as 'the British Schindler', a reference to Oskar Schindler, the German industrialist who used his factory in Poland to save hundreds of Jewish workers from the gas chambers. In 2010 a bronze statue of Winton was placed on one of the platforms at Maidenhead railway station (19).

Adult refugees

Whilst special arrangements were made to rescue children from Europe, there were also many adults who managed to seek safety in Britain and who came permanently or temporarily to the Home Counties. Some came alone, such as Marianne Grayeff (nee Zander), who was born in Berlin in 1910. She qualified as a teacher before coming to England in February 1939 by herself on a domestic permit and worked for a family in Beaconsfield. Unlike some of those who had a difficult relationship with their employees, she got on well with them. When war broke out and she was summoned to attend a tribunal to be interviewed as an 'enemy alien', her employer came with her to the tribunal, spoke on her behalf and ensured that she was classified as a 'friendly alien'. The following year she set sail for Australia, where she lived for many years before returning to England (20).

Another solo traveler was Fritz Lustig, who was born in Berlin and came to England in 1939. On the outbreak of war, he was interned on the Isle of Man. When he volunteered to work for the British forces, he became part of the Pioneer Corps in 1940 and was then transferred to the Intelligence Corps where he was sent to two Prisoner of War camps near to each other, Latimer House in Chesham and Wilton Park in Beaconsfield. There his role was to eavesdrop on high-ranking prisoners through electronic devices placed in their cells (21):

> A microphone was concealed in the light fitting, and we had to listen to their conversations in the hope that they would discuss something that might interest our side. There were always two prisoners to a cell, as far as possible from different services or units to encourage them to talk to each other about their experiences…..All prisoners were interrogated several times, always by officers not working in our monitoring section. We never dealt with any of them face-to-face. Their reaction to interrogation was often particularly fruitful. They would tell their cell-mate what they had been asked about and what they had managed to conceal from the interrogating officer

Fritz Lustig during the war

It was also there that he met another refugee working in the clerical department, Austrian-born Susan Cohn, who had arrived on a domestic permit the same year as he did, and who had joined the ATS (Auxiliary Territorial Service). They married, moved to London after the war, later settled in Middlesex, and then headed west to live in Reading in 1960 (22). Another person on active service in the area was Alice Anson, nee Gross, who had come from Vienna aged 14 in 1938, volunteered for the WAAF (Women's Auxiliary Air Force) in 1943 and then worked in photographic reconnaissance at RAF Bomber Command in High Wycombe. She was based in its underground photographic section and helped develop the first aerial photographs of top-security targets (23):

> We were responsible for processing 5 in wide film strips which came in from the bomber target cameras. Once developed and printed, the photographs were taken next door to the photographic interpreters. Sometimes they came back to us for enlargement depending on what the photographs had seen on

the image. On one particular occasion, a photograph was sent back to us and a section of it marked about the size of a postage stamp. We were asked to enlarge just that area. We had to photograph it using glass plates in those days and enlarge it to 20in x 16in. This was then sent back to the interpreters and that was how we found where the V1 flying bombs were launched in northern France.

For some refugees, the war changed not only their lifestyle but also their philosophy. When living in Vienna, Peter Arany had been a pacifist. After he fled Austria in August 1938, his initial stay in England was spent working on a farm in Hurley before being interned on the Isle of Man. He decided to jettison his pervious stance, joined the Pioneer Corps, volunteered for special duties and was one of eight commando units that landed at Normandy on D-Day. He later recorded his feelings as he crossed the English Channel (24):

I had the sudden realisation that this might be the last thing I would ever do. I tried to look back on my past life...I concluded that at twenty-two I had had a rich, full life and therefore could not complain if it were to end there and then. But before that I, who had been harassed by the Nazis, intimidated and targeted for extermination, would at long last have the opportunity to strike back.

Among the most common jobs for the refugees was as domestic servants, one of the few occupations for which a work permit was issued, owing to a shortage of British-born workers willing to fill the position. Hortense Gordon came to England from Breslau in 1939 aged nineteen, the daughter of an affluent doctor, gaining entry on a domestic permit. Her experience as cook-general in Farnham for two and half years came as a great shock, 'reminiscent of the servants' quarters in *Upstairs Downstairs* as she toiled from dawn to nearly midnight to supply a series of copious and frequent meals, and was treated strictly in accordance with her status in the kitchen' (25). Edith Argy, nee Tintner, who had come from Vienna in 1938 aged 19 found herself totally perplexed when initially working in London - 'I had never so much held a broom, and I was supposed to keep a fairly large house clean' - but found a more conducive job as secretary in an engineering firm in Maidenhead in Spring 1942. It was also where she watched her first ever game of cricket. Living in a boarding house, largely inhabited by non-Jews who had been evacuated with their firms, her experience was remarkably positive (26):

From their point of view, I was at best a Jewish refugee, at worst an enemy alien. Either way I was *foreign*, and they might have been forgiven if they had treated me, if not with hostility, at last with reserve. In fact, they did not just accept me but welcomed and even spolt me.

It was also common for spouses to work together as a team. This happened to W.W. Brown and his wife after they came to England from Vienna. The results were not untypical of others in that situation (27):

A well-meaning couple living on a large estate in Berkshire was rash enough to engage us. My wife had worked as a secretary in Vienna and knew little about cooking. I had spent my early life among books. Whatever I knew by then and was able to do did not include the duties of a butler.

My master told me to prepare his riding clothes for 8 am and an hour later his city outfit had to be laid out for him. Little did I know what English gentleman wore for riding or for the City, but when I got the wrong things out for him, he, fortunately, knew where to find what he really wanted. My wife, the cook had a kitchen maid under her; luckily that girl was a clever one and could teach my wife what she had to do. The arrangement did not last long though. After 3 or 4 weeks the Lady of the House told us that we were charming and pleasant people, but they needed experienced and efficient staff. The 'season' was beginning, guests were expected, so we would have to part company. However, they understood our position: they would advertise for us in the local papers to find us a job in a less grand household.

We started again, this time in Crowthorne in the service of a retired Indian Army Colonel and his wife. On the first morning the Colonel showed me his D.S.O. I had no idea what that was supposed to be but respectfully admired it. My early morning duties included cleaning the shoes, clearing ashes from the grate, laying the breakfast table etc...The 'Ohs' in various intonations and the 'It's not done' were early introductions into the English way of life. We laughed to ourselves when we first encountered them. Over the years we have learned to appreciate, respect and admire much of what seemed ridiculous at first.

Brown later joined the Pioneer Corps and then fought with the Royal Armoured Corps, being part of the advance into Germany after D-Day.

Leo and Sophie Ascher had a similar experience of a major cultural transition when they left their business life and soirees in Vienna in 1938 to become butler and cook in Gerrards Cross, a job for which they were both ill-prepared, albeit with occasionally comic results (28):

> Christmas Day was the big day in the house. An enormous turkey was prepared, mounted on a large serving plate, and wheeled into the dining room by the butler. The assembled guests eyed the bird hungrily. The cook was congratulated on presentation. The master of the house sharpened his carving knives ever so professionally and carved up the bird to great applause. He forced his fork into the wobbly carcass and began slicing but, to everybody's horror, the bird disintegrated. Tears rolled down the hostess's face. Silence prevailed during the entire meal. My aunt, unaware that she had spiked old tradition, cheerily informed everybody who cared to listen that in a civilised society people shouldn't be expected to chew meat from a bone in the company of others. Instead of bemoaning her ill-fortune, the lady of the house heartily agreed with my aunt that meat and poultry should always be carved in the kitchen and that the old tradition would be laid to rest. This incident became the talking point in the upper echelon of local society and crossed the Atlantic, there to be immortalized in the Hollywood production of *Mrs Miniver*.

After the war they bought a house in Reading, where they remained for the rest of their lives.

Another typical pattern was that experienced initially by Anna Lisa Kaufmann. Like many others, she was interned as an enemy alien when war broke out shortly after she had come to England from Germany. She was later released and trained as a nurse at Princess Christian Hospital in Windsor. She was then engaged as a nanny by William and Doris Cooper in Maidenhead in 1941. When their daughter Mary contracted a serious attack of smallpox, she nursed her back to health and managed to save her left arm, which had been particularly badly affected. Such is Mary's gratitude to her that, although not Jewish herself, Mary wore a Star of David around her neck ever after in her honour. She recalled that her mother occasionally received criticism from local people for employing a German nanny, but would robustly reply that she was a

Jewess and entirely different from the Germans whom the country was fighting. After two years, Anna Lisa went to work for a family in White Waltham before leaving the area. Meanwhile her father, previously a banker, was living in Reading, where he was employed as a bus conductor (29).

For some, war brought not only disruption but also romance. Cecilia (Celia) Ebner was nineteen years old when she left Berlin and reached England in the early hours of 1st September 1939, one of the last to arrive here before war was declared and immigration severely restricted. Initially she lived in London with family friends, Edward and Nita Miller, and when they evacuated to Maidenhead, she came with them. In December 1944 she attended a *Hanukah* party organised by the nascent Jewish community in the home of Israel Madenberg. Also present was Ellis Levenson from Glasgow, who had been serving in the British army overseas in the REME (Royal Electrical and Mechanical Engineering) and was then stationed in the town, holding the post of 1st Lieutenant in the Education Corps. They struck up a relationship and eventually married in 1948. As she did not want to move to Scotland, they remained in Maidenhead until moving to London in the 1960s (30). Another marriage arose when Ilse Illoway (nee Fuehrenberg) came to England in October 1937 from her home in Prague on a domestic permit and worked in North London. In 1940 she married Paul Illoway, a Jewish refugee from Vienna, after which they both came to Slough where his uncle had a mens' hosiery factory on the trading estate. Paul joined the army and after the war they remained in Slough permanently. They had numerous Jewish friends locally - all of them fellow refugees. As she put it, 'We were family for each other'. However, they had no contact with the synagogue in the town and did not provide their daughter with any home or Religion School education (31).

Gertrude Evans (nee Vanderwart) had the advantage of coming to England with her younger sister Eva. They were both born and brought up in Berlin, and crossed the channel in June 1939. Both were trained nurses and went to work at Borocourt Hospital in Peppard, Reading, which catered for adults with severe learning difficulties, in those days called 'mental deficiency'. She was officially classified as an 'enemy alien' but was not interned because she was needed at the hospital. She did, though, face restrictions as to her movements, not being allowed to travel further than five miles from Borocourt unless she had permission from the local police. She recalled several occasions when she was accused by locals of being a spy because she did not close her blackout curtains tight enough. Whilst there, she and Eva gained their RMPA (Royal Medical Psychological Association) diploma. She also met her future husband at the hospital, the son of a Christian minister who was a conscientious objector and was also working there. They married in 1944 and moved to London, while her sister left the following year and emigrated to America. The hospital itself was closed in the 1970s and converted into flats (32).

Gertrude and Eva Evans

Kurt Oppenheimer also had the company of family in his new country. He left his home in Mannheim, Germany and came to England by himself in 1937 when he was seventeen years old. He stayed with his uncle, who was already residing in England, until his mother managed to gain an entry visa, his father having died in Dachau where he had been taken following Kristallnacht. Kurt and his mother lived in Kingsbury for a while and came out to Maidenhead in 1941, living in Boyn Hill Avenue. He commuted to London for work, but was also responsible for fire-watching duties locally. It was during his time in Maidenhead that he changed his name to Keith Orpen. In 1945 they returned to London (33).

Refugees who came as a family

Some of the refugees were fortunate enough to leave together with their family. Thus Marion Koppel came from the Rhineland to England in 1939, aged fifteen with her parents. Her father had been sent to Dachau after Kristallnacht when thousands of Jewish males were imprisoned. On his release, they headed for Slough, where he had a business contact who owned a factory manufacturing margarine on the trading estate. They rented a house in Langley, which they eventually purchased in 1957, the same year that Marion left the area to live in London, and to which she later returned and in which she still lives (34). Another family evacuation was that of Kurt Ryz, who was born in Koenigsberg, East Prussia in 1938 and came to England with his family the following year, where they rented rooms for a short while in the East End of London. On the outbreak of war, they were evacuated, first to Egham and then to Reading, initially in Hosier Street and later to Waylen Street. As they had no home of their own elsewhere, they chose to remain in Reading after the war and his father opened a tailoring and menswear shop in Kings Road. They also became part of the synagogue and local Jewish life. Kurt recalled that although the immigrants were welcomed by the Jewish community, there was 'a slight divide' between us, with many of the German and Austrian Jews feeling closer to each other and mixing more amongst themselves rather than English-born Jews (35). Evidence, by inference, of a negative attitudes to refugees amongst some indigenous Jews can be seen in the wording of an advert placed by a Maidenhead family in the *Jewish Chronicle* in January 1942 under Situations Vacant: 'Pleasant person to run small house in safety area 30 miles from London; parents at business, two schoolgirls; comfortable home and good remuneration; refugee not objected to' (36).

One refugee family was in the unusual position of receiving royal help in their departure. The Duke of Windsor, the uncrowned Edward VIII, frequented the restaurant owned by Sophie Diener's father in Vienna, 'The Three Hussars'. The Duke had such regard for him that he offered to act as guarantor for the family in England after the Anschluss took place. Moreover, the Duchess brought jewellery belonging to Sophie's mother out of Austria and deposited it for her at Barclays Bank, Knightsbridge. It was much needed, as the family arrived in England with only seventeen shillings. They settled in London, but were bombed out and so moved to Wargrave, with her father opening another restaurant, The Green Monkey, in Earley, Reading. Both parents died in Wargrave, and Sophie later moved to Caversham, Reading, where she worked for the BBC Monitoring Centre for many years and remained in the area until her death (37). Some Jews found themselves on the wrong side of the law. Ellen Moses had arrived in England from Germany in 1936, since when she had been living in London. She came to Maidenhead in August 1939 but failed to register her nationality and other details despite several requests to do so. In December that year she he was brought before the local magistrates for breaching the Aliens Order and fined £5 (38).

Many of the above had left Europe in the months before war, but others had decided much earlier that it was time to depart. Stoke Poges, near Slough became the home of one of the leading opponents of fascism in pre-war Germany. J.P. Mayer was born in Frankenthal and later worked as a journalist for the newspapers sympathetic to the Social Democratic Party (SPD). When the Nazis came to power in January 1933, he went into resistance and helped plan an abortive SPD coup d'etat the following year that was called off because the Communists refused to join in it. During the 1936 Olympics, some of the anti-Jewish laws were relaxed by the Nazis and so Mayer, along with his wife Lola and one year old son Peter, travelled to England, ostensibly for a holiday but they did not return. In London, he continued his political journalism, as well as writing a book in 1939 on the French political thinker, Alexis de Tocqueville. This led to him being asked to edit the de Tocqueville family archives, work that engaged him for the next forty years. During the Blitz, the family rented rooms in Wexham Road, Stoke Poges. Peter recalled the bath being used to store coal, and also that when he attended the village school, the other children shouted 'Dirty German Jew' at him.

After the war, Peter's parents returned to London but then came back to Stoke Poges in 1949. They bought a plot of land in Plough Lane and built a house on it where they were to remain until their deaths. His father established a research centre at Reading University (where he became a Professor), while his mother became very involved in local affairs and served on the Parish Council for several years. Neither were practising Jews and they were both buried in St Giles' Churchyard - she died in 1979 and he passed away thirteen years later - although neither converted to Christianity. Peter never received any Jewish upbringing (39). The area also saw some German Jewish refugees gathering together as a group for retraining. This occurred at Tythrop House, Kingsey, near Thame, where young men and women spend several months training to work on a co-operative farm, with the eventual aim of going to Israel (40).

Many of the evacuees quietly came and went, but some left their mark on the area in various ways. Intalbury Avenue, Aylesbury was so named because it was built near a large smelting factory - International Alloys - established shortly before the Second World War by three German Jewish brothers, one of which was Dr Julius Jacobs, and another being David Jacobs. They reconditioned scrap aluminium, which was then transported elsewhere in usable form for the making of Spitfires. When the business came to an end, the site of the factory was redeveloped and now has a large Tesco store on it, but the road still remains. The brothers were also responsible for naming Devereux Place, which was in honour of a resident of the nearby village of Kimble, Mr Devereux, who had helped bring their family to England after the Nazis took power in Germany. He was a director of SMD, an engineering firm in Slough that has another Jewish connection in that, as will be seen in the next chapter, after the war it employed another Jewish refugee, Roman Halter, as a draughtsman and set him on his path as a renowned architect (41).

Not too far away, Dr. Ludwig Guttmann was creating his astonishing centre for the treatment of those with severe spinal injuries at the Stoke Mandeville Hospital. Born in 1899 in Upper Silesia, he had worked in the Jewish Hospital in Breslau until 1939 when he was invited to undertake research in Oxford. In 1944 he was asked by the British government to found the National Spinal Injuries Centre in anticipation of the heavy casualties expected during the D-Day landings. He remained there until 1966, by which time his pioneering methods had made it a centre of international renown. His mixture of physical and psychological techniques helped patients, who might otherwise have been considered beyond help and to have a short life expectancy, to lead long and fulfilling lives. He not only altered the public perception of paraplegics, but overcame the lack of self-belief that they themselves often felt too. As the Minister of Pensions, Sir Walter Womersley, famously said in 1945, 'Thank you, Hitler, for sending us men like these'. He and his family lived in High Wycombe in a house called *Menorah*. The success of his Stoke Mandeville Games for the disabled (which he had begun in 1948) persuaded the Olympic Games committee to hold the Paralympic Games immediately after the Olympics from 1960 onwards. He received a knighthood in 1966, amongst many other awards, and was a strong supporter of both Jewish causes and the State of Israel. He died in 1980, but his legacy has long survived him: 'Today, a simple, brilliant, humane idea that started on a Buckinghamshire lawn is the second largest sporting event in the world' (42).

Whilst much of the efforts on behalf of the evacuees had been undertaken by Jewish organisations and individuals, it is equally clear that many non-Jewish families had given them hospitality too, while some religious groups had taken especial interest, such as the Quakers and Christadelphians. There were also local non-Jewish groups established purely for the purpose of helping them. Even before the war, locals had shown themselves sympathetic to the plight of Jews. After the Archbishop

Ludwig Guttmann

of Canterbury, Cosmo Lang, had written a letter to *The Times* in November 1938 about the deplorable condition of Jews in Germany, Austria and Czechoslovakia, a committee had been formed in South Bucks to take action and it had established the Chesham, Amersham and District Refugee Fund. By February 1939, it has raised sufficient funds to rent a cottage in Ashley Green and bring over a family from Austria to live there, Mr and Mrs Neufield (43). The group also encouraged families to adopt or foster child refugees, householders to accept adult refugees as domestic servants, and employers to take men in the agricultural, cabinet-making and building trades. By June, another place of refuge was in operation, with three couples from Vienna (Roth, Schimunek and Gluecksmann) and the Kupfers from Munich being housed and supported at 4 Orchard Leigh Villas, Chesham. In similar spirit was the Gerrards Cross Child Refugee Aid Committee formed. It established a home for German Jewish refugee children at 769 London Road, Loudwater, suitable to house seventeen boys aged from nine to fourteen (44). One of the residents was Werner Conn, who was born in 1928 in Berlin, and who settled there are coming to England via the Kinderstranport in 1939. His parents and brother remained in Germany and died in the camps. He recalled 'a large house in spacious grounds' where the supervisors, Mr and Mrs Bolton, 'were strict but fair'. There was no contact with Jewish life in the area, although there was also no attempt at conversion (45).

Jewish children at the 1938-9 Dovercourt summer holiday camp

1. Private correspondence, Victor Simons
2. *Kindertransport* (September 2009) 8
3. Helen Fry (2007) 69
4. Rachel Pearson, 'Larkin was right' in *Second Generation Voices* (May 2008) 13
5. Private correspondence, Robert Klein
6. Interview, Bob Kutner
7. *AJR Journal* (July 2010) 6
8. Inglis (1989) 100
9. *Kindertransport* (May 2009) 3
10. *Kindertransport* (January 2009) 7
11. Interview, Alice Hubbers

12. Private correspondence, Henry Kuttner
13. Stebbing (2003) 307
14. Josephs (1988) 128
15. Godden
16. idem
17. Private correspondence, Hanan Bodenheimer
18. Interview, Helga Brown; private correspondence, Uri Sella
19. For further details, see Emanuel & Gissing (2002)
20. Stebbing (2003) 84
21. Fry (2007) 202
22. JC (7 September 2007) 35; *AJR Journal* (August 2009) 4
23. Fry (2007) 187
24. Masters (1997)
25. *AJR Journal* (December 2008) 1
26. Grenville (2010) 47, *AJR Journal* (June 2011) 3
27. *AJR Journal* (January 1988) 8
28. *AJR Journal* (June 1988) 5
29. Interview, Mary Cooper
30. Interview, Ellis Levenson
31. Interview, Ilse Illoway
32. Interview, Gertrude Evans
33. Interview, Keith Orpen
34. Interview, Marion Koppel
35. Interview, Kurt Ryz
36. JC (9 January 1942) 4
37. Interview, Sophie Diener
38. MA (20 December 1939) 6
39. Private correspondence, Peter Mayer
40. JC (1 September 1939) 20
41. Miss C.J. Humphries of 8 Intalbury Avenue, who used to work for the company's finance department.
42. Ben Macintyre in *The Times* (13 July 2012); see also Goodman (1986)
43. *Bucks Examiner* (10 February 1939)
44. JC (27 January 1939) 24
45. Interview, Werner Conn

Chapter 7

1939: Jewish Life in Surrounding Areas

Religious disruption

The disruption caused by the evacuation from London was felt by all those involved in the process, but particularly by the Jewish community, which was heavily based in the capital and probably suffered more upheaval than any other faith group. In Stepney, for instance, the Jewish population declined from around 60,000 in 1940 to not more than 30,000 in 1945 (1). The majority of them belonged to congregations affiliated to the United Synagogue, and as its historian Aubrey Newman put it (2):

> The needs for *kosher* food, for Jewish religious education, for any sort of Jewish observances, would have taxed any organisation, however efficient it may have been. But it had to be handled by an organisation [the United Synagogue] which itself had had to be evacuated, from the files and office routines of Woburn House [in Central London] to the outer fastnesses of the Edgware Synagogue Hall. Almost overnight London Jewish communities disappeared, secretaries were unable to keep track of their members, not knowing where their members had gone, and unable to organise any sort of services for them .... ministers [were] either being called on to act as chaplains to the forces or finding themselves obliged to meet new commitments in a wide variety of ways.

The result was that Jews who evacuated to areas without existing synagogues largely had to be responsible for organising services and childrens's religious education for themselves. Some families did so with gusto; others regarded their evacuation as so temporary that it did not merit putting effort into such activities, and they either commuted back to their London synagogues or put Jewish observances on hold until they returned to their homes. In some cases, those observances, once dropped, never returned. The exigencies of war-time life were highlighted from the very start, when the BBC broadcast a special announcement by the Chief Rabbi, Joseph Hertz, in which he gave permission to relax the dietary laws, declaring (3):

> The Chief Rabbi has been informed that some difficulties have arisen as a result of the strong desire of Jewish children brought up in religious homes to carry out their observances in regard to food in their new surroundings. He wishes to draw attention to all Jewish parents and children in reception areas to the fact that, in a national emergency such as the present, all this is required of them is to refrain from eating forbidden meats and shell-fish.

In evacuation areas where there was a large concentration of Jews who had belonged to the United Synagogue in London and who requested help, the United Synagogue felt obliged to act. This was both to help those concerned and to protect its membership, anxious that the dispersed Jews did not cut off ties with it and suspend their fees. As a result, it set up local 'Membership Groups' through which it channeled financial or ministerial help in return for the subscriptions that individuals continued to pay to their respective London congregations. Although the United Synagogue had always limited itself to London and the surrounds, its members were evacuated throughout the country, and so Membership Groups were set up as far as Torquay and Macclesfield. The following are brief resumes of the ad hoc communities that suddenly sprang up in the Home Counties, in towns which are now covered by membership of Maidenhead Synagogue.

Amersham

There were a few Jews already living in Amersham before the war, such as the Amar family, who had left London out of a desire to live in the country. In September 1939 they were joined by the evacuees, who started holding Sabbath services in their homes. They took place initially at that of Mr and Mrs M. Levy in Highfield Close. As the community grew, local halls were rented instead. When King George VI issued a call for a Day of National Prayer on Sunday 26th May 1940, the Jewish community held a service in Sycamore Hall, Woodside Road, part of Amersham Free Church. It was attended by over a hundred people (4). A similar Intercession Service was held on 13th November that year - coinciding with Armistice Sunday - at St Leonards Hall, Chesham Bois. The following year the community organised a *kosher* canteen for Passover, where eighty people attended a *seder* and fifty-two people were supplied with food throughout the festival (5). A Hebrew Education Board was established to co-ordinate the religious instruction of children in the area (6). By June the Religion School had forty children attending (7).

In June 1942 work started on erecting a pre-fabricated hut to be used as a permanent synagogue in Woodside Road by the corner of Sycamore Road. It was consecrated in August with Rabbi Harris Swift of the United Synagogue officiating. The ground was donated by the Hirschfeld family, the timber by Max Kirchner and Mr Kahan, while some of the furniture came from bombed out synagogues in London. Under the terms of the emergency building conditions by which it was permitted to erect the synagogue, it could not remain after the conclusion of the war and had to be at the disposal of the local Council until then should an emergency arise for its use. (8). Nevertheless, it was an historic moment, for it was the only example in the country at large in which land was acquired and a synagogue built during the war, and was a remarkable act of commitment by the local members. All other evacuee congregations were content to borrow rooms or hire halls and did not seek to make any lasting arrangements. As well as being for the conduct of services, the synagogue was also used to provide classes for the children and a venue for social functions. The community consisted of some 60 families and had an acting minister at the time, Rev. (later Rabbi) Isaac Rapaport. Speaking to the Bucks Examiner, he preferred to describe the new synagogue as a 'war nursery and army hut', perhaps wishing to downplay any hint of Jewish advantage at a time of national frugality and little building work. The community also benefited from Rev. Sonny Bloch as assistant minister, who helped with teaching classes and acted as a *mohel*. When the full extent of the horrors being perpetrated by the Nazis on continental Jewry began to come to light, the South Bucks Zionist Society held a public meeting at the synagogue in January 1943. Its purpose was both to protest at the atrocities and to urge the British government to save Jews by allowing those able to flee to safety to enter Palestine (9). Amongst other groups who used the synagogue for meetings was the Amersham Jewish Forces Club, which met regularly on Wednesday evenings. A change of religious leadership occurred in January 1944 when Rev. Rapaport left to become an army chaplain in HM Forces, while in August Rev. Bloch (two of whose brothers were on active service) was appointed as chaplain to the RAF in August 1944. Their responsibilities were taken over by Rev. Jonah Indech, who remained until the end of the war. There were regular services on Friday evenings and Saturday mornings, as well as for festivals.

The community was sufficiently stable for the United Synagogue to agree to the purchase of a minister's house in July 1944 (10). Several *barmitzvah* ceremonies were held during the war. Amongst the members were Maurice Edelman, who was to become MP for Coventry in 1945 and to remain in Parliament until his death thirty years later. He and his wife Tilly lived in Clifton Road, Chesham Bois throughout the war and stayed for several years afterwards before returning to London. They returned to the area in 1972, living in part of Hughenden Manor, Disraeli's country house. Many synagogue members served as Fire-Watching or Air Raid Precautions wardens, and played their part in the defence of the town. Despite being newcomers, several members made their mark locally, with Mrs Lissak being prominent in the Womens Voluntary Service, Kurt Nathan founding the local St John Ambulance Brigade (a room is named after him in their current bulding) and George Marks being a founder member and President of the Amersham Players.

One of the many benefits of VE Day for the Amersham Jewish community was that it coincided with the arrival home of the son of one of its members, John Jacobs who had spent five years in German prisoner of war camps. Once the war was over, most of the evacuees returned to London, although some did stay locally, such as Ivor Delman (originally Deitchman) who had arrived with his family in 1940 as a schoolboy and remained until 1954. He later moved to Reading, becoming bursar at Carmel College in Wallingford and, in the 1980s, honorary treasurer of Maidenhead Synagogue. Amersham's decline was delayed by those in the Chesham area who transferred to it when the community there disintegrated after the war. Nevertheless, it was significant that the minister's house was sold in 1946 (11). By 1950 it was known as the Amersham, Chesham and District Hebrew Congregation, and was affiliated to the United Synagogue. As time passed, the congregation shrank in size and was no longer active. However, under the Declaration of Trust established in 1952, the value of the land which the community owned could not be realised unless there were less than ten members of the congregation who were resident in Amersham and paying their subscription. When this situation was reached in 1966 it was decided to dispose of the land. It was sold in July 1968 for £9,750 and the proceeds distributed to the Jewish Blind Society, Jewish Orphanage, Jews College, the new synagogue in Oxford and the West London Youth Centre. The three scrolls that had been lent to the war-time community - one from Cricklewood Synagogue and two from the United Synagogue Head Office - were returned to them.

Chesham

Chesham attracted many evacuees, including Jews, who sought safety there or in surrounding villages. The Federation of Synagogues catered for the more observant amongst the Orthodox element of London Jewry. When war broke out, it kept its headquarters in the East End open, but transferred much of its administration to an emergency office in Chesham. This may have been one of the factors behind many ultra-Orthodox Jews evacuating there and establishing their own congregation. They were boosted by the arrival of Rabbi Yisroel Ehrentreu, who had come from Germany to England just before the war started with his wife and two sons, Meir Zvi and Chanoch. Their departure had been delayed as he had been incarcerated in Dachau concentration camp and it took the intervention of family members in London to get him released. Whilst in Chesham, his two sons went to nearby Amersham Grammar School. Another leading rabbi present was Eliyahu Dessler, renowned within the pietistic *musar* movement. By December 1939, the *Jewish Chronicle* was reporting the existence of a 'healthy congregation' in Chesham (12). Services were held at the Chesham Cricket Pavillion, while a youth club was formed for the evacuated children. By early 1941 there were around fifty children attending the Religion School, which was led by Rabbi Ehrentreu under the auspices of the Keren Hatorah and Beth Jacob committee (13). Close links were established with the nearby Amersham community, and in February they formed a joint Zionist Society, which organised speakers and film evenings.

Meir Zvi & Chanoch Ehrentreu

The Pavillion canteen was used for families who wished to eat meals during Passover under strictly *kosher* conditions. The question of *kosher* food for the rest of the year caused some controversy which exercised the Chesham Food Committee and spilled out into the local press. The Jewish community wished to use the canteen to provide *kosher* meals for its schoolchildren - estimated at seventy-five in total - and wanted the necessary permits to secure the food. The Food Committee faced difficulties not only in obtaining supplies but also in ensuring this would not result in Jews having double rations if families still retained their meat coupons. There was also the danger of the public wrongly perceiving that the Jewish community was enjoying privileges denied to others. The persistence of Julius Jung on behalf of the Jewish community, along with the goodwill of the Food Committee members, resulted in the canteen being permitted to open on a daily basis in September 1941 (14). Ironically, many of the Jewish children returned home in the next few months and within a year the canteen was being used almost exclusively by non-Jewish children. Another development was that in August of that year ORT - an organisation that encouraged vocational training for Jews - opened a centre locally to give free instruction to anyone who wanted to learn a trade (15). The wider community also benefited from the Rothschild family donating Shardeloes House in Chesham Bois to be used as a Maternity Hospital. It opened the day the war started and two thousand babies had been delivered there by the end of 1942.

One of the main organisers of the Jewish community was David Goldberg, who wrote to the local paper at the end of the war (16):

> As Chairman of the Hebrew congregation for more than four years, I feel that I cannot leave Chesham without expressing our appreciation and gratitude to the people here who have helped us find refuge in their midst. Your municipal officers; your food office staff who made great efforts in our food problems; your Cricket Club Committee (especially Mr Viner), who have done their utmost to help us. To the Headmasters and Mistresses and their staff, we owe a special words of thanks, for it is through their interest and efforts that our children have received the ideal education that will enable them to become true British citizens. I would also like to voice appreciation to your tradespeople. They have always been civil and helpful to us, although short handed and working under difficult conditions.

We came to Chesham at a time of great distress; but retain now only happy memories of these years between. So, 'Good-bye Chesham', and on behalf of us all, 'Thank you'.

Whilst many ex-Londoners moved back there, others went elsewhere. Thus the Ehrentreu family went to Manchester, where Meir Zvi eventually became head of its main *yeshivah* and Chanoch was made head of its Beth Din, and later of the London Beth Din (17). Those who did remain in the area were unable to maintain a viable Jewish life and joined the Amersham community.

High Wycombe

There were already enough Jews in High Wycombe by *Rosh Hashannah* of 1939 for a service to be held to mark the New Year. It took place at the home of Mr I. Daniel, with some forty people present, and was described afterwards as 'probably the first ever' Jewish service to be held in the town (18). One of the main organisers was F. M. Landau and the services were led by Rev. Dr Isaac Rapaport. Specific activities for children were organised by the Joint Emergency Committee for the Religious Education of Jewish Children, with Sabbath services for them (and adults if they were accompanied by parents) at the Friends Meeting House and Sunday morning classes (19). In addition, a group of members from the Golders Green Bet Hamedrash used the Tylers Green Hostel to provide extra Hebrew tuition for children relocated to the area (20). Amongst the Jewish evacuees was the weekly newspaper, the *Jewish Chronicle*, which described itself as 'the organ of Anglo-Jewry'. In September 1939 emergency printing and editorial offices were opened in High Wycombe (at 20 High Street), from where it was published thanks to the assistance of the principal local newspaper, the *Bucks Free Press*. It was a very inter-faith arrangement, as the *Jewish Chronicle* shared its new headquarters with the *Catholic Herald* and a Church of England journal, the *Guardian* (21). It proved to be a very wise move, as its main office in Moor Lane, London was destroyed by fire during a bombing raid in December 1940. Even the temporary offices to which the London management moved were in turn destroyed by enemy action in May 1941.

In April 1940 a United Synagogue Membership Group was established after a meeting of local Jews was addressed by Rev. Harris Swift, who also conducted occasional services over the next few months. thereafter regular services were held in members' homes, with the community's first *barmitzvah* - that of Stuart Lever - occurring in July (22). By November there were at least two hundred Jews present, with twenty-eight children in the Religion School and a Young Israel Society formed for those over seventeen years. In the same month, the community appointed Rev. Dr Rapaport as its minister (23). Jews continued to move into the area from London, so much so that a branch of the Walford Road Synagogue, Stoke Newington was formed (24). When a *Hanukah* party was held at the end of 1940, around two hundred children attended (*25*). Further growth meant that Rabbi Morris Swift was seconded to the community from his synagogue in Brixton and he was to remain a visiting minister until 1946. A Ladies Guild was formed, as was a Zionist Society, while childrens' classes were transferred to Tudor Hall in the High Street.

The Jewish Chronicle being printed at the offices of the Bucks Free Press in High Wycombe during the war

Such was the sense of local community that there was a strong move to establish an independent congregation - rather than be a United Synagogue Membership Group with members owing prime loyalty to their original London synagogues - although the move was narrowly defeated at a special meeting (26). During Passover 1941 the Mayor gave permission for the community to use the Oak Room in the Town Hall. Two communal *sedarim* were held, led by Rabbi Swift, while a total of two hundred and thirty people had meals there during the week (27). By

June numbers had swelled further and the *Shavuot* service attracted almost four hundred people, while a Habonim group was started for the youth. Of course, there were many members who were part of the community but not particularly observant, as was indicated by a sermon from Rabbi Swift the following week condemning Jewish women who went shopping on Saturdays (28). The number of Jews in the area was swelled further by Americans who were stationed at the United States Air Force base nearby at Daws Hill. As a result, the base offered its premises for the use of the entire local Jewish population, and services were held there.

After the war and the departures back to London, a sufficient number of Jews remained in the area for the community to continue. Its status changed into a more established congregation when it was admitted as an affiliate member of the United Synagogue in 1948. At the time it had fifty-seven male seat-holders - the method by which the United Synagogue measured membership - a much lower figure than that during the war. The community was served by a succession of ministers: J. Mayer (1947-9), H. Freed (1949-51), M. Miloslower (1951-54). Thereafter, services were led by lay members. It never had a purpose built synagogue, but continued at the Daws Hill base until the latter closed in 1969 and services were transferred to the homes of members By 1960 it had experienced a sharp decline to thirty male seat-holders and although the following decade saw a rise to forty-two, it decreased thereafter, partly because more Jews moved out of the area than into it, and partly because those with younger families usually joined Maidenhead which offered greater facilities through its religion school and youth club. By 2010 the community consisted of some twenty-five families, a loyal remnant who still managed to hold services fortnightly on Friday evenings and major festivals.

Marlow and surrounds

Despite being a small town, Marlow had a sizable influx of Jews during the war, attracted by its combination of being away from obvious bombing targets and having a railway connection to London where many evacuees still had their business. A number lived in Glade Road, where there were newly built houses available for rent. Amongst them was the family of Newman Morris, whose daughter, later Jennifer Sampson, said that an added reason for her family choosing that area was that it was not too far from Crowthorne, where her brother John had gone when St Paul's relocated there. Other Jewish families in that same road included Jack and Mabel Caine, the Vellermans, Mr and Mrs Barnett, the Creamers (whose daughter was born on V.E. Day and named Victoria), the Khans, Phil and Busie Green (whose daughter, Ruth Jewell, remained in the area and later became chairman of Marlow Council), Fay Schneider and her husband, and the Bogods. Jennifer recalled how, on one occasion, she (29):

> was woken up in the middle of the night by my grandmother (a frequent visitor) to move over in my bed for her to get in with me. The next morning I discovered that my father had met a Dutch family on Paddington Station. They had been bombed out of their home in Amsterdam and had somehow managed to get to Paddington. They had nothing but what they stood up in and had nowhere to go. My father brought them all home for the night.

Most of these families had children, who used to travel to High Wycombe once a month for religion classes with Rabbi Dr Arthur Katz who came from London to teach them. However, this arrangement did not last long and their Jewish education was extremely sporadic. There was, however, unexpected contact with a source of Zionism, for when Jennifer went to Maidenhead County School for Girls in Castle Hill, she found that the headmistress was Miss Monica Wingate, the sister of General Orde Wingate. She would tell the Jewish pupils about her brother and his Zionist sympathies. Bertha Ahrend (nee Goodman) reported the same experience from when she was at the school.

By January 1941 there were sufficient number of Jews in Marlow to start Saturday morning services at the home of Mr and Mrs J. Goldblum, who lived at 10 Claremont Road (30). By March these had grown to include a Saturday afternoon service as well as classes for boys over 10 years old (31). There were also social activities, such as a talk given by culinary expert, Florence Greenberg, on Jewish war-time cookery (32). Marlow also enjoyed the temporary services of Rabbi Jacob Ferber. He was born in Riga, Latvia in 1909, and had been brought to England three months later by his father, the famous Rabbi (Zvi) Hirsh Ferber. Living initially in Manchester, he moved to London with his parents, studying at the Etz Chaim *Yeshivah* and also becoming a qualified *mohel*. His first post as a minister was in Marlow in 1942, looking after the evacuee Jews there for a few months, before moving to Cheltenham and then becoming a chaplain to the RAF (33).

There were enough Jews elsewhere in the area for the United Synagogue to establish several smaller Membership Groups. The one in Beaconsfield began in April 1940 and was led by Joe Fraser, with services

Jacob Ferber

being held in the Girl Guides Hall in the Old Town (34). Rabbi H. L.Solomon helped found a community in Aylesbury in June 1940, with Mr D. Rose as Chairman. Rev. M. Davidson became its minister the following year, with Saturday morning services being held at the Friends Meeting House. There were also Religion Classes on Saturday afternoons, Sunday mornings and Tuesday evenings (35). In January 1941 regular Saturday morning services were held at the home of Mrs Weinman in Denham, while a Religion School was set up, using the premises of Denham School. The community celebrated its first *barmitzvah* that May (36). The following month services began in Thame at the home of Harry Marks. A religion school was also established (37). By July 1941 there was a separate group in Gerrards Cross, which linked up with Denham to establish a joint youth club (38). Its President was Mr H. Gavento and it had a lay minister in the form of Mr M. Richardson, who conducted services at the Congregational Church Hall in Packhorse Road. That summer a small group also started in Wokingham and planned to hold High Holy Day services (39). None of these groups survived the war, all collapsing when members returned to their London homes.

Reading

Reading was the only town in Berkshire to have a synagogue in existence before the war. Amongst the many evacuees it attracted were numerous Jewish individuals and families. Some became involved in synagogue life, whereas others saw their stay as too temporary to warrant any local involvement. For its part, the synagogue offered its communal facilities to the newcomers, with the Sir Hermann Gollancz Hall being used as a hostel for those whose homes in London had been bombed. In addition overflow services were organised for the High Holy Days in 1941 to cater for the extra worshippers, while local services for those living in Tilehurst were also arranged. The Tilehurst community continued as an adjunct to the main synagogue throughout the war and had its own warden, as well as its own minister, Rev. J. Wolf (40). Services also occurred in other part of Reading where evacuees were gathered, such as Caversham and Whitley. Later in the war, as Allied ground troops massed locally for the D-Day invasion of Europe, the synagogue organised a special *seder* [Passover meal] for the Jewish soldiers among them in April 1944. While the established Jewish community was committed to helping the newcomers, and did so in practice, there was also concern that its goodwill should not be taken advantage of without any form of reciprocation. Thus an entry in the Synagogue Council Minute Book for October 1940 records: 'The president stated that some means should be found to enable the congregation to benefit financially from all the Jewish people who had come into the town and were deriving the benefits of the congregation' (41).

One of those evacuees was David Lang, who was only five years old in 1939 when his family decided to leave London for Reading, where they remained for the duration of the war. He recalled the long walk from their home in Northcourt Avenue to the synagogue which he did with his father at High Holy Days. They would also bring back any Jewish servicemen, sometimes Americans, for lunch. He recalled that (42):

> A frequent and unforgettable sight, never to be seen again, was when the sky above Reading was filled with RAF Bomber Command Handley Page Halifax and Avro Lancaster four-engined bombers flown by brave aircrews fighting for our freedom by attacking enemy targets far from home. Even though some aircrew failed to return, we never had any doubt that the Allies would win the war.

He himself was to serve in the RAF during the 1950s.

The community took steps to acknowledge the contribution of those who were away on duty fighting for their country, determining that members of not less than six month's standing on joining the Forces would retain all benefits of membership, including rights under the burial scheme. The synagogue also had to take steps to look after its own safety with a rota being drawn up of members who would volunteer for fire-watching duties. One side-effect of the war was the leap in marriages experienced by the community. Whereas the synagogue marriage register recorded a hundred weddings in the period 1900-2000, which would suggest an average of one wedding a year, there were forty-two weddings between 1939 and 1945. The insecurity of the times meant that people sought ways of establishing a sense of normality and permanence, especially if one partner was a soldier about to go off on active service.

Ian Mikardo

Another sign of the times was the effect of food rationing and general frugality, which led to a resolution in the Council Minutes for October 1943: 'the honorary officers and minister….will withold their presence…from all festivities and functions (such as weddings and *barmitzvahs)* of an ostentatious or extravagant nature, or which are out of keeping with the present serious times'.

After the war, many evacuees returned to London, lowering the size of the Jewish community, although it was boosted by the return of servicemen who were de-mobbed and came back to their families. In 1947 they founded a Reading branch of AJEX (Association of Jewish Ex-Servicemen and Women) which not only ran its own events but took over many of the social activities of the community until it disbanded almost forty years later (43). The Jewish community boasted yet another local MP - following in the footsteps of Francis Goldsmid and Rufus Isaacs - in the form of London-born Ian Mikardo. He had come to live in the area during the war, where he worked in aircraft and armaments manufacturing at Woodley Aerodrome. In the general election of 1945, he won the Reading seat for the Labour party, overturning a large Conservative majority, holding it until 1959. He later returned to Parliament in 1964 to represent Poplar, London, remaining an MP until 1987.

Slough and Windsor

The Isaacs family were one of the mainstays of the small Jewish presence in Slough for nearly one and half centuries. As mentioned earlier, Lawrence Lazarus had been born in the East End of London, but had moved to Slough in 1865 to manage a pawn-broking business. After his death, it was taken over by his son-in-law, Nathaniel Isaacs. His son, Joseph, developed it into a furniture business, opening up premises in the High Street in 1904, and upon his retirement it was taken over by his son Lionel. A further two generations worked in the business before it closed in 1987, changing from a retail firm to a property investment company. There were only a handful of other Jews in Slough before the First World War, and whenever the Isaacs family attended services, they went to the Bayswater Synagogue in London. During the war, the local Jewish population was temporarily boosted by Jews who left London to escape the Zeppelin bombing raids. The added numbers allowed regular Sabbath services to be held for a period, but the newcomers returned to the capital once the danger was over. During the inter-war years, a handful of Jews came to nearby Windsor for commercial reasons, such as Bernard

Michaelson who brought his family there in 1937 when he found a job as a barber (44).

A second and larger influx to both towns occurred during the Second World War, this time made up of both Londoners and foreign refugees. Services in Windsor were held in a hall above the Baptist Church that was made available to the Jewish community, while in Slough they were in private houses. Sabbath services at each usually consisted of twenty to thirty men, along with women and children, with High Holy Days being much more crowded. Those attending services in Windsor had the problem of being in a venue that was dedicated to another faith, with the result that 'Early on Friday nights and Saturday mornings the warden of the synagogue would perambulate around the hall turning the pictures of Jesus to the wall. At the end of the service, Jesus was reinstated for the admiration of his Christian community' (45). The newcomers consisted mainly of shopkeepers and businessmen, most of whom commuted back to their workplaces in London on weekdays. There was also the staff and children of Stepney Jewish Girls School which had been evacuated locally under the guidance of its headmistress, Kate Rose. She led services for children on Saturday mornings, both those from the school and others living in the area. Religious education was also provided on a midweek evening at the home of Mr Isaacs, taught by Simon Joseph. In November 1940, Windsor witnessed what might well have been its first Jewish wedding, which was conducted by Rabbi Yechiel Galas (46). That same month saw the formation of the Slough Social Circle for single young Jews (47). By early 1941 the Religion School had forty children attending and moved to a local school in order to obtain larger premise (48).

Amongst those who had come from abroad was Rabbi Dr Julius Jakobovits, who had been head of the Rabbinical Court in Berlin (Av Beth Din). He came to England as a penniless refugee at the end of 1938, one of many Orthodox rabbis who were rescued with their families by Rabbi Dr Solomon Schonfeld. After working in London and then Bedford, he was appointed rabbi of the Windsor and Slough communities in 1942. His duties included officiating at each of the two communities on alternative Sabbaths, as well as overseeing Hebrew Classes in both towns. He lived in St Leonard's Road in Windsor, and so walked the two and a half miles through Eton to Slough every other week.

Among the English evacuees were Mr and Mrs Lewis Gould. On the outbreak of war, they had sent their daughters Rosita and Isobel to Reading for safety. After a few months, they decided to leave London as well and re-unite the family, and they all moved to Windsor, knowing that the Stepney Jewish Girls Schools had been evacuated there and so the area

Julius and Paula Jakobovits

had a large presence of Jewish children. Lewis Gould, became chairman of the Windsor community, even though he commuted to work in London not only midweek but also on Saturdays. Rosita attended Windsor County School for Girls, where she later became the head girl, the first Jewish one. Higher up the school at the time of her arrival was Shulamit Jakobovits, the daughter of Rabbi Julius Jakobovits. Reflecting on the compromises of that time, Rosita, who later became Director of the Union of Liberal and Progressive Synagogues, wrote (49):

> An Orthodox rabbi who sent his children to a non-Jewish State School! A chairman of an Orthodox synagogue who was not *shomer Shabbat* [Sabbath observant]! Services in English for children under Orthodox auspices. This was a tolerance born of war-time adversity. Through it, we retained our Jewish identities and proceeded to adult Jewish lives. Shall we see such tolerance again in 'normal' times? Unlikely! What is there in the Jewish psyche that makes us prepared to tolerate each other and respect each other's views only when we are living in exceptional times and under pressure? When not living in externally difficult times for Judaism, we seem to create the

adversity for ourselves internally. Is it some kind of chemical Jewish formula theoretically for survival, but, in fact, bringing us dangerously close to extinction?

During the war years, the Windsor community was visited by the then Chief Rabbi, Dr Israel Brodie, and Rosita was chosen to present a bouquet of flowers to his wife. Romance also blossomed during this period, for Isobel Gould met Michael Wagen, whose family had left Richmond for nearby Datchet. When the Gould family decided to leave Windsor in 1950 and return to South London - they would have left earlier but Rosita was in the midst of her Sixth Form studies - Isobel stayed behind to marry Michael; they lived in Slough for a while before moving to Bristol.

An English evacuee who made his mark on the wider life of the town was Barney Spivack. He was not only a senior manager at the Horlicks factory during the war, but was very active in organising lectures under the auspices of the Workers Education Association. They were held at a variety of venues, including Slough library. His sister had also moved to the area and ran a pharmacy in the Farnham Road. Barney himself lived in Losuce, Hill Farm Road, Taplow – a Grade II listed cottage, which he is credited for having given that name, which comes from an abbreviation of the line in Dante's *Inferno*, 'Loose all hope those who enter'. He remained in the area until his death in 1980.

Military uniforms were a common sight at services, either from soldiers stationed nearby or those on leave who were visiting their family. Jack Corman, who was living in Stamford Hill before the war, was warden of the Windsor community. Gaskell Jacobs, chairman of the Times Furnishing Company, who resided in a country mansion in Stoke Poges, was warden of the Slough community and overall president of both parts of the community. Each was designated as a United Synagogue Membership Group. There were good relations with the non-Jewish population, and Jakobovits invited local vicars to his home for a meal and theological discussion. All *kosher* meat was obtained from London. Sabbath strolls were often taken by him and his family along the Great Walk in Windsor Park. One of his sons, Dr Joseph Jacobs, recalled two occasions when they were 'gently hooted out of the way by a car with King George VI at the wheel, the Queen in the passenger seat and two girl princesses in the back seat. They were driving the three miles from Windsor Castle to The Royal Lodge. There may have been a war on, but a police escort was not thought necessary!' (50). Another of his sons was Immanuel (later Lord) Jakobovits, who was to become Chief Rabbi in 1967, but at that time was minister of Brondesbury Synagogue, London. In March 1941 the Windsor Borough Council gave the Jewish community exclusive use of a hall next to the Thames Hotel by the river, known as 'the communal', which was used for a wide range of social and cultural events, while it also provided *kosher* meals. It operated from 10 am to 8pm daily and was organised by the Board of Deputies and Chief Rabbi's Emergency Committee. It also provided activites for young children and teenagers, including a Scout troop, while over Passover two hundred people took meals there. It was formally opened by the Mayor of Windsor (51).

A few miles away a community had formed in Iver around the home of Harry Goodman in Old Slade Lane, where he had moved from Maidenhead. Services were held there, including the first known *barmitzvah* in the area in May 1941 (52). The sudden burst of extra activity in the vicinity prompted one irate neighbour to write a letter of complaint to the Chief Rabbi. As a result, services were moved to the Mission Hall in Iver. In 1944 Julius Jakobovits was appointed as a Dayan of the London Beth Din and returned to London, taking up similar responsibilities to those he had been used to in Germany. He was replaced by Rabbi Baum, who remained in Windsor for the next two years. The end of the war saw most Londoners return to the capital, although often to new areas as their original homes had been destroyed. Of the Jews remaining in the area after the war, a greater number resided in Slough, which became the focal point, with the few Windsor Jews left joining in the religious and social activities there.

By 1950 the community had consolidated into being the 'Slough, Windsor and District' community. It became an affiliate member of the United Synagogue and had fifty-eight male seat-holders. In 1955, the community purchased a house at 22 Grove Road, Slough, known as 'Lyndhurst', which was converted into a place of worship. It was consecrated in September of that year in a ceremony that also saw the official induction of Rev. B. Greenberg as the community's minister. The service was conducted by Rabbi Dr Louis Jacobs on behalf of Chief Rabbi Brodie who was unwell at the time. When Rev. Greenberg left after two years, he was not replaced. By 1960 membership had only increased to sixty, and thereafter it declined rapidly, with only thirty-five male seat-holders in 1970. The building was sold shortly afterwards and services were once again held in members' homes, though usually in Windsor where more of them now lived than in Slough. For large events, such as High Holy Days, the Quaker Meeting House in Ragstone Road was used. In the 1980s even this became impossible to maintain, and the dwindling community effectively closed by amalgamating with the Staines Synagogue and transferring all activities there.

Shardeloes House was used as a maternity hospital during World War II

1. Alderman (1987) 69
2. Aubrey Newman (1976) 148
3. JC (8 September 1939)
4. *Bucks Examiner* (31 May 1940). For this and subsequent information, I am indebted to Vivien Samson and her own local research. This resulted in a short history of the community, 'Landsleit of Amersham'.
5. JC (25 April 1941)
6. JC (8 November 1940)
7. JC (13 June 1941)
8. *Bucks Examiner* (12 June 1942)
9. *Bucks Examiner* (29 January 1943)
10. Minutes, United Synagogue Council (4 July 1944)
11. Minutes, United Synagogue Council (4 April 1946)
12. JC (15 December 1939) 21
13. JC (21 February 1941)
14. *Bucks Examiner* (28 March, 27 June, 12 September 1941)
15. JC (15 August 1941)
16. *Bucks Examiner* (10 July 1945)
17. JC (22 September 2000) 33
18. JC (22 September 1939) 15
19. JC (22 December 1939) 17; (5 January 1940)
20. JC (12 April 1940)
21. Roth (1949) 174
22. JC (19 April, 26 July 1940)

23. JC (8 & 15 November 1940)
24. JC (22 November 1940)
25. JC (3 January 1941)
26. JC (21 February 1941)
27. JC (7 March, 18 April 1941)
28. JC (13 & 20 June, 4 July 1941)
29. Private correspondence, Jennifer Sampson
30. JC (31 January 1941)
31. JC (21 March 1941)
32. JC (22 August 1941)
33. JC (22 May 1998) 23
34. JC (5 April; also 7th, 14th & 28th February 1941)
35. JC (28 June 1940; 22 August 1941)
36. JC (31 January, 19 May 1941)
37. JC (13 June 1941)
38. Minutes, United Synagogue Council (July 1941); JC (4 & 18 July; 22 August 1941)
39. JC (22 August 1941)
40. *Jewish Year Book* 1945/6
41. Krisman (2001) 26-8. I am grateful to Krisman for much of the material used in this section
42. Private correspondence, David Lang
43. Krisman (Krisman) 47-9
44. Newton (2001) 17
45. ibid. 21
46. JC (15 November 1940) 14
47. JC (29 November 1940)
48. JC (14 February 1941)
49. *ULPS News* (January 1992)
50. Private correspondence, Joseph Jacobs
51. JC (28 March, 25 April 1941). For a description of its activities, see Newton (2001) 54-59
52. JC (9 May 1941)

Chapter 8

1940: The Birth of the Synagogue

The first indication of an organised Jewish communal life in Maidenhead appeared in the *Jewish Chronicle* (JC) of 12th July 1940. It was written by Yechiel Galas and declared 'I should be glad to hear from any Jewish residents of Maidenhead where it is proposed shortly to form a Jewish congregation and Hebrew classes'. With the exception of the brief community of 1917, any mention of Jews in the local or Jewish press until this date had been associated with individuals; now the focus shifted to community. Two weeks later, the JC reported that: 'A Hebrew congregation has been formed and services are held regularly every Sabbath morning at 10 o'clock at 29 Laburnham Road. Hebrew classes are also being arranged by Rabbi J. Galas'.

The house in Laburnham Road was rented by H. A. (Harry) Goodman, senior vice-president of the Union of Orthodox Hebrew Congregations of Great Britain (UOHC). He had evacuated there from London at the beginning of July and had brought with him a Scroll of the Law, which he kept in the house. He commuted daily to his textile shop in Commercial Road in the East End of London. Amongst his many communal activities before the war, he had collected lists of Orthodox rabbis and their families trapped in Europe and given them to the Home Office, seeking permission for them to settle in England. In this work he was part of the Chief Rabbi's Religious Emergency Council and had attended a conference at St James Palace, London in February 1939 to facilitate its efforts. He also delivered annual broadcasts that were transmitted by the BBC European Service at the time of the Jewish New Year. These continued for some years, and as part of his broadcast in 1942 to Jews on the Continent, he declared (1):

> On this *Rosh Hashannah*, the whole House of Israel stands united before our Father in Heaven: we who live here in freedom, and you, all of you, in the ghettoes and in slavery. The destiny of mankind is being decided before our very eyes. Great Britain and her allies have been chosen by providence to save humanity, and to bring about a nobler, a better order. Eight million Jews in the free lands....send their fraternal greetings to those unhappy victims of the Nazi terror, to the millions now confronted with annihilation. As sure as the morn follows the night, victory will come. As sure as there is justice in heaven, there will be justice on earth.

Alongside these international concerns, his daughter Bertha Ahrend recalled a moment of local friction when, in preparation for the festival of *Sukkot*, he cut down a tree in the front garden of their house in Laburnham Road. It was the first time that the neighbours on either side had encountered the need to erect a tabernacle, and left them both puzzled at the cause and cross at the action.

Two of Goodman's sons saw active service during the war: Elie was an officer in the Intelligence Division of the RAF and stayed on after the war; Simon was in the army, was taken prisoner in Italy in 1943 and later released when the Allied forces invaded Germany. His youngest son, Jo(seph), attended Maidenhead County Boys School (now Desborough). Goodman had arranged with the headmaster that Jo would attend the Scripture lessons but not take part. This clearly displeased the RE teacher, Mr Barrington-Baker who, according to Jo, told the class, 'As the Jew boy is not taking part, he will sit at the back of the class'. Later in the lesson Jo was told, 'Stand up, Jew boy, and let the others look at you as an example of the Jews who betrayed Jesus to the Romans'. It was not only appallingly offensive and totally unprofessional, but highly insensitive given the sufferings of the Jews at that very time across the English Channel. The result was that Jo was ridiculed by his fellow pupils and beaten up afterwards. Apparently he took revenge some years later when he was twenty-two years old: he made a special journey to Maidenhead, looked up the teacher in the phone book, went to his house, hit him, and then caught the train back to London (2). In fairness to Maidenhead County Boys School, it should be noted that another evacuee, Maurice Rimel, later became Head Boy, probably the first Jewish one. He went on to qualify as a barrister and later emigrated to Israel, becoming a senior lawyer in the Israeli Attorney General's Office. The Goodman family kept a high degree of religious observance. One of the religious duties that Jo was given by his father was to go to Bray at the time of Passover to supervise the cows being milked. This was to check that the milk did not come into contact with any leavened produce, which would render it unsuitable for consumption during the festival.

Yechiel Galas had arrived with the Goodman family, with whom he lived; he was supported by them and in return provided religious education to their five children. He originated from Lithuania and had studied in the famous Slabodka *Yeshivah* there and gained rabbinic ordination. He had come to England in 1936 and taught at the Machzike Hadass synagogue in East London. Whilst in Maidenhead, he worked as Education Officer of Keren Hatorah, an educational arm of the UOHC. He also studied to become an opthalmic optician, taking his exams in Glasgow, with his expenses being paid by the clothing magnate Sir

Montague Burton, who originated from the same village as him near Kovno. In addition Galas gave Hebrew lessons to children in Maidenhead and in Slough, while he also helped supply families with *kosher* food, which Goodman bought in London and he distributed locally. Both he and the Goodmans moved to Iver Heath in May 1941 so as to have a larger house, whilst it also meant being nearer London. After the war Galas moved to North West London, where he set up an optician's practice, but also led classes in Jewish studies for adults at the Bridge Lane Bet Hamedrash, as well as becoming a regular contributor of articles on Jewish law for the *Jewish Review* (3). Another leading member of the strictly Orthodox group who had settled locally was Jacob Rosenheim, who had come to England from Frankfurt-am-Main in 1938 and who was Chairman of World Agudas Yisroel. He became the President of the nascent Maidenhead congregation until his departure in mid 1941.

Yechiel Galas

Whilst Goodman had held services in his own home for the initial influx of Jews to Maidenhead, the growing number of Jewish evacuees to the town meant that the house in Laburnham Road quickly became too small to hold services for everyone. From November 1940 they were transferred to a small hall in Brock Lane (now no longer existent), off the High Street, called Oddfellows, with Hebrew classes for children also taking place there (4). Many of the other evacuees were less observant than the Goodman circle, but they were still from Orthodox backgrounds and services were conducted in that manner. The hall was shared with a variety of other users during the rest of the week, including the local Christadelphians, and so everything had to be packed away after each service, including the Ark being turned around to face the wall.

The community became known as Maidenhead Hebrew Congregation, the standard nomenclature of Orthodox synagogues. Services were held both on Friday evenings and Saturday mornings. They were conducted by a variety of people, ranging from professional rabbis to competent lay members, depending who was in the area at the time. They included Rabbi Munk and Rev. Brazil, as well as Yechiel Galas and Lou Adelman. Others were Simon Joseph, Leslie Paisner, Alf Shear and David Silverman. The Council of the United Synagogue (US) took an interest in the situation in Maidenhead, as it had done in other towns where evacuated Jews had collected together. This was both for altruistic and selfish reasons, keen to help Jews dispersed into unfamiliar areas, but also anxious to ensure that they did not cut off ties with the US or suspend membership fees. It sent Rev. Isadore Swift to visit the community at the beginning of 1941, to investigate both the state of Jewish life there and the interests of the US itself. He reported that there was sufficient organisation happening through local efforts not to need the US to provide any facilities. He also addressed the other concern of the Council and reassured them that the US members temporarily located there would continue to pay their subscriptions to their London congregations (5). Maidenhead's self-reliance set the tone for the long-term character of the community throughout its subsequent transformations and changes of leadership. Whereas some other satellite communities were accustomed to expect help from a centralised source, Maidenhead was always very self-sufficient and did not look to others to assist it.

Another visitor from the Jewish hierarchy was Sidney Solomon, the Press Secretary of the Board of Deputies. He addressed a conference on 29th December 1940 at the Oddfellows Hall that had been called for Jewish groups in East Berkshire and Buckinghamshire. He spoke of the symbolic importance of the new community (6):

> Maidenhead was setting an example which it was ardently hoped would be followed throughout the country. Owing to the

Blitzkrieg there had a been a dispersal throughout England. This dispersal might remain after the war; indeed it might appear desirable that there might not continue the centralised conglomeration of pre-war times. The first step towards that objective was the establishment of new central congregations. Berkshire could find such a centre in Maidenhead, where there was happily already a throbbing Jewish life.

The conference had been convened by the 'Warden of Maidenhead', Harry Goodman who referred to the comparatively short space of time in which the community had grown 'from a scant *minyan* to a *kehillah* at which regular services were held and which on the High Festivals were attended by almost five hundred people'. He also announced that a youth club and ladies guild were being formed, while the Religion School had forty children registered, consisting of three separate classes. Galas was the headmaster and offered free transport to any evacuee children who were unable to pay the fare. Others present at the conference were representatives of Jewish groups in Windsor, Slough, Iver and Taplow.

In February 1941 a Jewish Social Club for young people was established, the first meeting taking place in the Oddfellows Hall, with Jewish members of the H.M. Forces being invited too. (7). Subsequent meetings - such as *a Purim* Dance were held at Prince Albert Hall, which offered larger facilities, and its growing popularity led to it soon having a regular Sunday evening booking at the British Legion Club. As a parallel activity, there were also periodic 'At Homes' held by members of the community that involved fund-raising for both Jewish and non-Jewish charities. The amounts raised were often impressive for relatively small gatherings: £60 for the Home for Aged Jews and £80 for the Maidenhead Prisoners-of-War. Larger sums were raised at dances held at the Riviera Hotel, such as that attended by the Mayor of Maidenhead in May 1943 which achieved £200 for an X-ray unit to be sent to Russia (8). In addition, a Zionist section was set up as part of the club. With Jews being persecuted throughout Europe, and often being refused entry by many countries, the issue of finding a safe haven in Palestine had become increasingly urgent and gave an added momentum to the cause of Zionism. Even those who had no wish whatsoever to go to the Land of Israel themselves, could see the value of a Jewish homeland where Jews in need were welcome and had full citizenship. The Jewish National Fund was amongst those who came to give a talk to the new group (9). With so many activities taking place, the community began looking for a venue where it could have sole usage. This was achieved at the end of 1942 when it moved to Woodcarvers Hall in Marlow Road, situated behind the

Drill Hall (which was knocked down in 1974 and replaced by the current headquarters of the Commonwealth War Graves Commission). Woodcarvers Hall had been found thanks to efforts of Alec Woolfe (brother of Frances Bernie) and a lease was taken out on it (10). As well as being used for services, it also housed social facilities with a table tennis table and half-sized billiards table.

Drill Hall, Marlow Road (with Maidenhead Technical - now Art - College to its left)

Most of the rituals objects necessary for synagogue usage were imported from London synagogues, such as scrolls and prayer books. However, the Ark, which contained the scrolls, was a new creation, made specifically for the community. Isaac Stollerman had evacuated from London to Maidenhead during the latter stages of the First World War. As he knew the area already, when the Second World War broke out, he brought his family back again in 1940, renting in Woodhurst Avenue, near Boulters Lock. He himself stayed in London, where he still worked, but visited at weekends. His son Sydney remembered the large garden belonging to the house that his father's brother, Bernard (also known as Philip) had in Maidenhead, which was turned over for growing vegetables and fruit as part of the 'digging for victory' campaign. Tragedy struck on 4th December 1940 when Philip's son Jack, who was the driver of a bren-gun carrier, was accidentally crushed by a tank during manoeuvres in Reading aged 22. Having fought with the British Expeditionary Force in France and escaped from Dunkirk, it seemed a cruelly unnecessary way to die after surviving so many other dangers. Both Isaac and Philip were cabinet makers, and they made an Ark from solid oak in his memory. In a remarkable twist of history, Sydney Stollerman, recalled what ensued when the family had a third encounter with Maidenhead (11):

> Another half-century passed before my family re-established contact with Maidenhead. By strange coincidence, my son Jonathan, having worked and lived in Hong Kong and Australia, returned to England, finally settled in Bourne End and joined my old community. My grandson William had his *barmitzvah* there in July 2000.
>
> Who knows what triggers long forgotten memories? Perhaps it was the warmth of the day, the heightened emotions of the occasion, the sight of my grandson reading from the scrolls? Perhaps it was some other force at work - who knows? It was only then that I suddenly remembered the 1940 Ark. After the service I asked the rabbi if he knew anything about it. After a moment's reflection, he led me to the top of the building and there, amazingly in the corner of a classroom, was the 'Lost Ark'. It was sixty years since I had last seen it and it was still in pristine condition.

An ad hoc group of lay leaders took responsibility for communal affairs. One of them was David Silverman, who had been living in Stoke Newington before the war and took his wife Hetty and children to live in Oxford in 1940. However, he found it too far to commute to his business in London and so moved to Maidenhead early the following year. By that time his oldest son had been called up to the army and was serving in the 17th/21st Lancers. Silverman had been secretary of an Orthodox synagogue in Vine Street, in the East End of London in the 1920s and took on the same position with the ad hoc community that he found already in existence. As a result, his son Maurice recalled that:

> After I had my *barmitzvah*, I became the unofficial collector of subscriptions. I cycled round Maidenhead each Sunday morning collecting - or in reality, attempting unsuccessfully to collect - the small weekly contributions from some members. In the main these were the members who rarely attended services. The experience was good for me; in my later life as a solicitor I was already well acquainted of the methods used by debtors as I tried to recover money due to my clients

The Ark built in memory of Jack Stollerman

Another lay leader was Leslie Paisner, who had come to Maidenhead with his family in 1940 and who commuted daily to his solicitor's office in London. He was Chairman of the Education Committee that was established in October 1940 and often gave sermons at the Saturday morning services. When he returned to London at the end of 1950 he was presented with an engraved cigarette box by the members in recognition of a decade's worth of work for the community.

For the High Holy Days, when there was a far larger attendance than weekly services, the community hired a large room on the first floor of the Town Hall (demolished in 1962, but which was then in the High Street at the junction with Queen Street). There was an attendance of around two hundred people at the first *Rosh Hashannah* service in 1940, which was led by Galas, while A. L. Klausner assisted him at the *Yom Kippur* service (12). For at least one of the annual attendees, it proved to be an exhilarating experience. Gerald Ansell (1922-1995) grew up in the East End of London. During the war his parents evacuated to Maidenhead, but he remained in London studying medicine. In September 1941 he went there to be with them for the High Holy Days in the Town Hall (13):

> The local press and wall posters announced the sale of tickets. My parents obtained some and we went to *shul* on *Rosh Hashannah*. I was used to praying in a large synagogue with cantors of the [famous] Kousevitsky family. People who know me realise the passion I have for outstanding cantorial artists. Entering the Maidenhead Town Hall, fully expecting wartime cantorial mediocrity, I was astounded at the most beautiful baritone renditions of our Holy Day prayers. Not only was the sound magnificent, but the fervour and passion of the man leading the prayers was overwhelmingly moving. To this day I have never seen or heard it repeated.

The cantor on that occasion was Abraham Reich. On another visit to Maidenhead a few months later, Ansell attended a Jewish social event held in a church hall and met a girl called Phyllis whom he dated. It turned out that she was Reich's daughter. They married and eventually emigrated to the United States.

The war impinged on religious activities in countless ways. The most obvious was the physical dispersal of previously well-established communities caused by the evacuation, while army-service resulted in a lack of teachers and ministers both for the existing ones and ad hoc ones. Black-out regulations meant that great care had to be taken over holding evening services, while access to *kosher* food was severely hampered. A relatively minor local concern, but indicative of the many adjustments that had to be made, was an intense discussion that occurred amongst synagogue-goers at the festival of *Sukkot*. The issue was whether it was safe or appropriate to carry *lulavim* from their homes to the services in Oddfellows Hall in the town centre, because there was a war-time restriction on carrying religious symbols in public. This ban had been formulated primarily to avoid Church processions becoming caught up in air raids, but no one schooled in rabbinic argument could fail to ask whether this also applied to palm, myrtle and willow branches (14).

The religious education of the Jewish children in the area owed much to Simon Joseph, a mathematics teacher (and, later, actor) whose previous posts included teaching at the Jews Free School in the East End of London. In September 1939 he had been sent to teach at a school in Ely, but in November he arranged to be transferred to Maidenhead, where his wife Beatrice and their children David and Miriam had been evacuated. He joined the staff of St Stephen's School, which had moved there from Paddington and was operating in a large house called Northfield. He realised that there were many Jewish evacuee children scattered in the area without their parents and that they were living with non-Jewish families, estimating there to be around eighty in total. Moreover, they seemed to be unknown to the Jewish community that was beginning to form. He obtained permission from the London County Council to visit local schools and make contact with the Jewish children. He then rented a hall in All Saints Avenue to hold services for them on Saturday mornings. This was done with the support of the Jewish Welfare Committee in London, who supplied a Scroll of the Law and prayer books. It also became apparent that some of the children were being taken by their billeting families to Church Religion School on a Sunday afternoon, so he also established Jewish classes at the same time so as to provide an alternative activity for them. They were held at the hall attached to Boyn Hill Church with the vicar's permission. They then moved to Monycrower, a large house at the top of Grenfell Road, since demolished and transformed into a drive with several small residences.

These initiatives resulted in conflict with the ad hoc Jewish community, which was organising classes in co-operation with Keren Hatorah, the educational arm of the UOHC. The latter felt that Joseph was acting unilaterally and undermining their own efforts at Jewish education. Among their teachers was Jacob Rosenheim's daughter, Adella, who taught the children at the Religion School and also organised *Hanukah* and *Purim* parties for them. The dispute reflected organisational tensions between the local community and the Jewish leadership in London, as well as religious rivalry between the UOHC and the United Synagogue. When the community's Religion Classes were inspected in August 1941 by the leading UOHC rabbi, Dr Solomon Schonfeld, one of the lay leaders, Leslie Paisner, criticized the fact that 'a London ecclesiastical body had authorized a local teacher to create classes competing with those of the Hebrew congregation'. He complained that this was divorcing children from communal life (15). The controversy eventually spilled over into the letters pages of the *Jewish Chronicle*, with Mr M. Sagan, Secretary of the Joint Emergency Committee, writing to complain that (16):

> An impression is being sedulously fostered by persons who ought to know better that the Joint Emergency Committee has interfered in an unwarrantable manner with the arrangements for the education of the Jewish children in Maidenhead. The facts are that the Joint Emergency Committee, before taking any steps whatsoever, took the trouble of consulting the local Community and arranged for certain activities to be conducted within the framework of the community. As a result of this effort, children are provided with services on the Sabbath in suitable premises and conducted in a manner which they can follow and understand. They also receive instruction from a competent teacher during the Scripture period in school hours.

The matter was resolved in the autumn of 1942 by appointing Joseph as Headmaster for the whole community, thus bringing the different initiatives together and catering for one hundred and fifty children in all. He also organised Childrens Services at Woodcarvers Hall during the High Holy Days. Amongst his pupils was Harvey Cohen, according to whom, Joseph was paid two shillings a morning and, without realising it, would mesmerise the children by playing with the money in his hand during the lesson. Others in his class at the time included Harold Caplan and Jerry Laurie (17). Joseph also gave private lessons and Maxwell Morrison recalled him coming to his parents house to teach him Hebrew.

Many of the boys had their *barmitzvah* tuition in Maidenhead but returned to their London synagogues for the actual ceremony. Harold Caplan, for instance, had his at the Shadwells Lane synagogue in Hackney, where his grandfather was the *shammas* (beadle). In contrast, Len Bernie was not only taught his portion by Simon Joseph locally but had his *barmitzvah* in Maidenhead. Others who had a war-time *barmitzvah* in Maidenhead itself included John Ellis, Michael Kremer, Jerry Laurie, Gerald Littlestone and Stanley Olman, as well as Joseph's son David, with the ceremonies before December 1942 taking place in Oddfellows Hall and those afterwards being held in Woodcarvers Hall.

Simon Joseph as a grandfather

Amongst those helping to teach the classes were evacuee ministers Rabbi Munk and Rev. Brazil. Another teacher was Lou Adelman, a dentist with a strong religious background, his father being Joshua Adelman, the *chazzan* of Philpot Street synagogue. During an era of rationing and blackouts, an annual *Hanukah* party was a regular highlight of the year as far as the children were concerned, and often attracted those who did not attend the regular classes. Joseph also held some classes for children in Marlow on Sunday morning and on a midweek evening for those in Slough, all taking place in private homes (18). A request was also received from the Czech Hostel in Bray, at which many Jews were in residence, for classes for the Jewish children there (19). The community had a youth club which largely met at Woodcarvers Hall but occasionally organised outings to visit the clubs attached to the communities in Reading and Windsor. Amongst the mainstays of the group were Harold Caplan, John Ellis, David Joseph, Stanley Olman and Maurice Silverman, with occasional attendance by girls such as Myrna Fogelman, Miriam Joseph, Suzanne Olman and Daisy Steiner. There was also a Habonim group that met on Wednesday evenings 6.30-8pm at Monycrower and arranged rambles on Sunday afternoons. Simon Joseph's contribution to the community came to an end in 1949 when his home in Stamford Hill, which had been taken over during the war by the local council, was restored to him, and he moved back there with his family.

Despite the attempts to establish a Jewish life locally, there was always a temporary feel to the community. Some *barmitzvahs* may have taken place in Maidenhead, but this did not apply to most other cycle of life ceremonies. There was no Jewish cemetery locally, so if any of the Jews in Maidenhead died, the funeral took place in London. London was also the venue for virtually all marriages, although one was conducted locally by Galas in December 1940 in a private home (20). An everyday concern was the provision of *kosher* meat, observance of which was still kept by many of the evacuees. Those who worked in London would often collect it themselves from butchers there, whilst it was also sent by train direct from Jewish butchers such as Blooms (in the East End) or Frohweins (in Finchley Road). Other options were *kosher* butchers in neighbouring towns, such as that in Reading or Philip Greenspan in High Wycombe.

Special efforts were made for Passover and in 1941 the congregation ran a *kosher* canteen for the duration of the festival. Given that many Jewish families were renting rooms or billeted in other people's homes with no control over the kitchen, this was a vital provision for those who were observant. The community also offered to provide *haggadot* and *matzah* free of charge to any refugee children in the area who could not come to Maidenhead (21). For those who were unable to look after themselves, a Jewish Convalescent Home was established in Cookham after the Association of Jewish Friendly Societies secured premises there in 1942, where it remained for the next eight years (22). There was also a private Jewish Convalescent Home, Restorea, owned by Mr & Mrs D. Fry near Courthouse Road, which transferred from London in 1943 and remained there until 1947. Their son had served in the RAF and had been shot down during a flying mission and his body was never recovered. Simon Joseph conducted a Passover Service there one year for the residents. During the war, the Jewish evacuees were scattered throughout Maidenhead and its surrounds, but in particular, many of them lived near the river and along the Cookham Road. This was partly because there were plenty of flats there and partly because of the proximity to the station, with many travelling daily to work in London. The vast majority rented accommodation, although some of the wealthier families purchased properties.

If the war brought London Jews to Maidenhead, it also brought American ones, for the USA troops who were staying in the area contained a number of Jewish soldiers, with many of the officers being billeted in houses near Boulters Lock. Among them was New Yorker Leo Leftkewich, one of several Jewish US army doctors stationed in Norfolk Road in the build up to D-Day. Many of them contacted the Jewish community and attended services or received hospitality from local families. As far as the latter were concerned, the American servicemen were fellow Jews, but there were occasional problems from the Americans' perspective (23):

> An American corporal arrived in *shul* one Saturday morning and was immediately 'kidnapped' and brought home for lunch after the service. It transpired that his name was Saul and that he was a medical orderly. At my parents' insistence he promised to look out for and tell other Jewish personnel that our house was always open to them as well as himself. He did exactly that; unfortunately, all the other Jewish personnel turned out to be medical doctors and thus commissioned officers. We never saw Saul again. As a corporal he was too embarrassed to be with, and to be seen to be with, captains, majors and a colonel, even though they were only doctors and totally uninterested in rank.

Such visitors did mean that the Jewish children were kept well supplied with chewing gum and Hershey chocolate bars. At the beginning of June the Americans suddenly all vanished without a word being said in advance - and shortly afterwards it became clear that this was the beginning of D-Day and the Allies' massive ground attack to liberate Europe. In some cases, though, the relationships continued after the war when the, by then, ex-servicemen wrote to their former Maidenhead hosts, and exchanged letters and even visits for several decades afterwards.

Some relationships were even more intimate, leading to marriage, such as that between Lt Edward Kellman of the US army to Sadie daughter of Mr. and Mrs. S. Markham, of Maidenhead. The ceremony took place in Maidenhead in August 1945 after he had returned from the war in Europe (24).

There were also Jewish servicemen amongst the British troops stationed locally, such as Londoner Harry Roos who belonged to the 1st Battalion Suffolk Regiment and found himself in Maidenhead for several months in 1943. He was given hospitality by Jewish families during his stay and received a butter dish inscribed 'from the Maidenhead Jewish Community' when he got married in April of that year, the ceremony taking place in the East End of London.

Some 60,000 Jewish men and women served in the British Armed Forces during the Second World War. 3,000 of them died fighting for their country. They served in the army, navy, air force and were also fire and police men, nurses, volunteers, miners, land girls and factory workers (25). Amongst members of the community who served in the forces was Harry Madenberg. He was captured early on in the war and was a prisoner until his release in May 1945. Some of his letters home during that time have survived and reflect both the frustrations of P.O.W. life and his dry sense of humour. As a sergeant, he was often in charge of the letters and parcels that arrived for all the inmates (26):

Dear Mum and Dad

Happy wedding anniversary. It should have been a pretty successful year for you without having to worry about me, for the first time in quite a while, not knowing my whereabouts when I do not come home at nights....

I received a consignment of boots for distribution last week. Somebody in the Ordinance Corps should have their bottoms kicked - the men are in great need of boots and I received a pair for nearly every man, but nearly half were size 6 and the rest nearly all sevens. That means that anyone taking 8, 9, 10 or 11 are unlucky and half the issue is completely wasted. I think it would be as well if you sent me a copy of your marriage certificate, because the comments of the dissatisfied men throw strong doubts on the existence of such a document.

Life goes on the same as ever. Nothing very much distinguishing one day from another. It is really difficult to fill a page nowadays, as the sole thing I can say is give my love to everyone.....Here is a little tale of P.O.W. life. One of us received a letter from his wife in which she said - 'I am sorry to say that I made a little mistake while you were away and have not yet decided what to call it. I am very sorry about this and if you will forgive me I shall get you anything you want'. He replied that he had always wanted a motor-bike, and if she would get him one, he would call it quits when he got back. All quite true, but the point of the story is - have you managed to find a bike for me yet?

Life here goes on as usual. I feel as though I were living a separate existence from you all. We seem to be detached from the rest of the world - a state of splendid isolation as it were.

Others serving in the forces who were members of the Maidenhead Jewish community, or offspring of members, included (with military details where known): Freddie Austin (Captain, RAMC), Gerald Baker (Major), Bernard Berman (RAF), Ronald Bernie (RAF), Morris Chodosh (Sgt, Burma), Alfred Davis (2nd Lieutenant), Alfred Gertler (REME), Charles Ludner (RAF), Arthur Mann, Edward Miller (Captain, Royal Artillery), Lesley Porter, Sydney Spiers, R.A.C. (Lieut., Italy and mentioned for gallantry in dispatches), Jerry and Toby Stanton, John Walters (RAF) along with members of the Bourne and Coville family. Among those who lost their lives were: Sergeant Cyril Berger of RAF (aged 20) who went missing, presumed killed during a mission in Atlantic in March 1943, while Boris Catsell died in Normandy in July 1944. There were no civilian deaths in Maidenhead, but relatives living elsewhere were killed, as in the case of Mr Lewis Trobe who lost his parents, sister and her two children during enemy bombing raid over Southend in September 1941 (27).

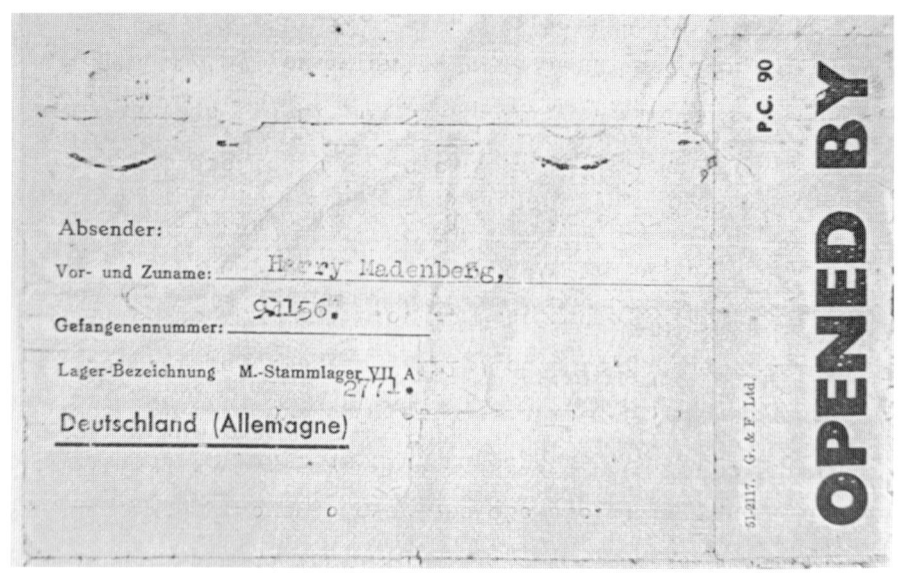

A letter from Harry Madenberg from a prisoner of war camp in Germany, 17th October 1942

There were also those serving in the forces who moved to the area at some point after the war and only then joined the synagogue. They included: Reg Ballantine (Burma and Malaya), Jessica Blooman (Captain, ATS), Tony Blumenthal (Major), Morris Brodie (RAF), Maurice Cooper, Jack Green (Royal Tank Corps), Ben Jewell (Royal Artillery, Lieutenant), Ruth Jewell (ATS, Captain), Dr Jack Lask (RMAC, Captain - Africa, Middle East and Europe), Alex Lawrence (RAF), Ann Leapman (WRNS), Denis Leapman (RAF - Italy and Burma), Ellis Levenson (REME), Alan Lyon (RAF Coastal Command), Edna Lyond (VAD - RN), Geoffrey Marks (RAF, Flight Lieut), Lewis Moss (Captain, Royal Artillery), Edward Peskin (Royal Navy), Daniel Romain (Merchant Navy), Vivian Sakal (Lieut. Commander), Ian Scott (Africa), Jack Sherman (Europe), George Supper (Radar Intelligence), Michael Wiseman (RAF - DFM), David Wolff (Royal Navy, Minesweeper Commander). Jewish residents in the town who were too old for the army were often involved in the local Home Guard, be it in Maidenhead, such as Victor Afia, or further afield, such as Albert Cowan in Henley. One member received a mention forty years later when Maidonian Enid Vickers reflected on her wartime experiences: 'I did stretcher training with Mr Olman; he was the only man short enough to manage the other end!' (28). There were also those who became involved in occupations they would never have imagined might apply to them when they were working in offices in London before the war. Thus Miss Wolff of Fifield, just outside Maidenhead, advertised herself in the Situations Wanted column: 'Jewish herdswoman (21 years) seeks responsible situation under bailiff or owner with pedigree dairy herd: five years experience.' (29).

Relations between the Jewish community and the wider population showed no sign of the public hostility with which Jewish evacuees in the First World War had been greeted. Perhaps they were judged as less uncouth than the 'Russian Jews', although some of them were the same families twenty years on. Perhaps townsfolk were aware of the sufferings of Jews in Nazi Germany, although German Jews were treated with suspicion as potential fifth columnists. The lack of religious tensions was all the more remarkable given that, from the point of view of ordinary Maidonians, the war was a time of great stress and disruption: many men were away on active service, women were taking over businesses and farmwork, rations were in place, German bombers went overhead coming and going from attacks on London, blackouts were imposed. To have one's town, and, in many cases, one's own home, filled with strangers was yet another unwelcome burden. The Maidenhead Debating Society considered the matter in early 1940, with a motion asking 'Is the Policy of Evacuation Desirable?'. It was carried by 15 votes in favour, 9 against and 24 abstentions, indicating that a large number of people were undecided (30). It was noticeable, though, that even those hosting evacuee children who complained about them in letters to the *Maidenhead Advertiser* - that they were behaving badly or causing too much stress - never made any reference to Jewish children specifically (31).

For its part, the Jewish community tried to identify with local activities. When £50 was raised during a charity collection, it was distributed between Jewish causes and the Maidenhead Spitfire Fund. A notable inter-communal event was a meeting at St Mary's Vicarage on 16th May 1941 to form a Friendship Committee of Christians and Jews in Maidenhead. It was initiated by its vicar, Rev. Raymond Lunt, who presided over the event along with Harry Goodman. Rev. W.W. Simpson, who was soon to become the first secretary of the Council of Christian and Jews, was another of the organisers. Other members of the committee were Rev. Eric Mees (Methodist Superintendent), Alderman Oldershaw JP, Mrs E. A. Vanner-More, Yechiel Galas and Leslie Paisner. It was decided to hold a public meeting at the Town Hall (32). This took place the following month with a large crowd in attendance. Councillor Oldershaw, a former mayor of Maidenhead, pointed out that 'The last occasion that I heard Jewish problems being discussed in this Town Hall was when a man who called himself Professor Joyce, and whom we now know as that arch-traitor "Haw-Haw" virulently attacked the Jews from this very platform.' Rev. W.W. Simpson declared that the Nazis were not just anti-Jewish but also anti-religion, and that the co-operation and friendship of Jews and Christians would bring about its utter defeat. On behalf of the Jewish community, Goodman noted that the Great Synagogue and Westminster Abbey were both bombed in London on the same night, a reminder that Jews and Christians should be 'each loyal to his own faith, yet each realising that the Fatherhood of God demanded the brotherhood of man' (33).

Other examples of interaction included a talk given to the Rotary Club by Marta Goldberg of Children and Youth Aliyah on its work, focusing particularly on its efforts to help Polish Jewish evacuees (34). When the rest of the town held special Intercession services in December 1942 - as did the country at large - the Jewish community held one too at Oddfellows Hall (35). There were also occasional joint efforts, such as the bazaar held between all the faith groups in the town in May 1944 in support of the Aid to China Fund (36). The potential for social disharmony was enormous, yet the relationships between townsfolk and newcomers were largely harmonious. Whether this was due to the British attitude of 'grin-and-bear-it' or to the camaraderie of the war effort, the result was that many Jewish children looked back on their evacuation here with warmth, while many adults chose to stay after the war had ended.

The Second World War was the key event in establishing a Jewish communal life in Maidenhead, just as the First World War had done so two decades earlier. The role of international conflict in twice bringing Jews to the town was epitomised by families such as the Stollermans and Fogelmans who had temporary stays here during both world wars. Even more important for the development of the community, though, were those like the Shackmans and Bernies who, having come and gone during the First World War, stayed on after the Second World War and turned an ad hoc synagogue into a permanent one. This time the Jewish community did not evaporate back to London but continued locally.

1. BBC, 11 September 1942
2. Interview, Joseph Goodman
3. These were later collected and published in a book, *Insights Into Halacha*, by the Mizrachi Federation in 1973.
4. JC (15 November 1940) 14

5. Minutes, United Synagogue Council (4 February 1941)
6. JC (10 January 1941) 13
7. JC (17 January, 7 February 1941) 14
8. JC (1 January 1943) 13; (7 May 1943) 11; (28 May 1943) 13
9. JC (14 March, 11 April, 20 June 1941) 13
10. The first event there was *Hanukah* Party that year took place on 6 December 1942 ; JC (4 December 1942) 9
11. Private letter, 15 November 2001
12. JC (11 October 1940) 17
13. Ansell (2000) 84
14. Unfortunately the person who supplied details of the discussion did not communicate the result.
15. JC (29 August 1941) 12
16. JC (16 January 1942) 19
17. Interview, Harvey Cohen
18. Joseph (1994) 51
19. JC (23 May 1941) 15
20. JC (6 December 1940) 13
21. JC (4 April 1941) 17
22. JC (2 January 1942) 21
23. Interview, Maurice Silverman
24. JC (10 August 1945) 11
25. For further details, see Kushner (1989) 65-77
26. They were sent on 2 February 1941, 29 September 1942 & 21 November 1943
27. JC (19 September 1941) 4
28. Testimony on display at 'Maidenhead at War' exhibition, Maidenhead Heritage Centre in May 1995. The reference is probably to Harry Olman who remained in the town for several decades and was a well-known shopkeeper.
29. JC (3 December 1948) 4
30. MA (3 January 1939) 7
31. MA (16 & 23 October, 6 & 20 November 1940)
32. JC (16 May 1941) 16
33. JC (4 July 1941) 16
34. JC (16 October 1942) 11
35. JC (11 December 1942) 5
36. JC (26 May 1944) 13

PART III

COMMUNAL LIFE

Chapter 9

1945: Becoming Reform and Acquiring a Home

Continuity and change

The arrival of peace could have spelt the end of Jewish life in Maidenhead, as it did for many war-time communities. In fact, many of the Maidenhead Jews had gone back to London long beforehand, from 1942 onwards, when the bombing seemed to be over, although they had failed to anticipate the V1 and V2 bombs. Most of the other evacuees returned to their homes at the cessation of hostilities. The number that had left by September 1946 was so high that it was no longer necessary to hold the High Holy Day services at the Town Hall and they were transferred to the smaller venue of Woodcarvers Hall. For the same reason, the Religion School, which had once boasted several classes, had declined to only one class by then. However, the number of those who elected to remain in the area was sufficient for Jewish life to continue. Some had established businesses locally, others still commuted to London but had grown used to the pleasures of living in the country. There were also parents with children who were settled at school or in the sixth form who decided to stay in the area so as not to disrupt their studies. This enabled the community's youth club to carry on for a while, and Jennifer Sampson recalled going to it by bus from Marlow on Sunday afternoons, while Rosita Rosenberg also visited it from Windsor. There were links with the youth clubs at neighbouring Orthodox congregations such as Reading, Staines and Ealing. At least one marriage resulted, that between Stanley Olman, who had come to Maidenhead with his parents during war, and Jean Kaufmann, from Reading Synagogue, whose family had also evacuated to the area. They were wed in 1959, albeit at a London synagogue. The Ladies Guild remained active. In August 1945, it helped collect thirty-two sacks of items for the Clothing Campaign for Liberated Jewry. The Guild held regular fund-raising activities in subsequent years, giving especial support to the Central British Fund and the Jewish Orphanage in Jerusalem (1)

Despite the general exodus, there were some Jews who moved into the area, usually those who were refugees from abroad. Some had come to England before the war and others afterwards, but in either case had no fixed homes to which to return once the war was over. One example was Gretel Jordan who left Germany for England as a child in 1939 via the Kindertransport. After living in Cambridge and qualifying as a nurse, she came to Taplow in 1945 where she worked in the Canadian Red Cross Hospital as ward sister on the gynaecological ward. She then moved to Stoke Mandeville Hospital as an administrative sister. She never had any contact with local Jewish life and kept her Jewish identity secret at both locations, although every year she asked for a day off that just so happened to coincide with *Yom Kippur*. After other posts elsewhere, she became matron of Bromley Hospital in South London (2).

Another local arrival was Roman Halter who was born in Poland in 1927. He survived not only the Lodz Ghetto, but also Auschwitz and then Allied bombing when working as slave-labour in Dresden. After the war he came to England, and then obtained work as an apprentice at an engineering firm, Structural Mechanical Development in Slough from 1947 to 1950. During that period he lived in digs in River Way, Windsor belonging to a Jewish landlady, Mrs Rachel Feldman. She had come to England from Poland as a child at the turn of the century and then spent her life in the East End of London until she moved to Windsor during the war. Her two sons had moved to Manchester and London respectively, while her married daughter had died of a broken heart after her husband, Bernard, was killed in action in Monte Cassino. She left a child, Clare Michaelson (later the author Clare Newton), whom Mrs Feldman brought up. By then most of the other Jewish evacuees had returned to London and Halter knew of only one other Jewish family in Windsor, that of Mr Markovitch, a presser who commuted to London every day. The Windsor synagogue had closed and there was little Jewish life in the town, although Mrs Feldman was able to buy *kosher* meat in Egham, where she went once a week. She remained in the area until her death. After Halter had gained his qualifications, he moved to London where he became a renowned architect (3).

In addition to individual Jews who arrived locally, there was also a stream of young men and women who came to stay for several months at Hurst Grange, a private house with a large garden in Twyford. It had been acquired by the Zionist youth movement, Habonim, as a training camp for those intending to emigrate to Israel. It existed from 1948 until it was closed down in 1955. It could accommodate up to twenty residents, who learnt agricultural and organisational skills that would equip them for life on kibbutz, as well as experience of communal living and how to speak Hebrew. Some of them worked on the farm itself, while others found jobs with local farmers. It was known as *Zichron Yeshayahu* – named after Yeshayahu (Isaiah) Morris, a former member of Habonim in England who had been killed whilst serving as an army doctor during Israel's War of Independence. It attracted leading Zionists who came to give talks to the trainees, such as David Patterson and Yigal Alon. They even received a visit in 1952 from Krishna Menon, the Indian Ambassador to Britain, who spoke on the Indian struggle for independence. The ethos of the Habonim was secular-Socialist-Zionist, and there was no contact with surrounding Jewish life. Most of the residents at Hurst Grange were British-born, but they included a few who, like Tom Behrman, had originated from the Continent and come to England before the War via the Kindertransport. Describing his time there, he wrote (4):

> There we were, a small group of city-bred youngsters of mixed sexes, living as a kibbutz in a dilapidated mansion in the middle of the English countryside. I doubt if any of us had ever really worked before in our lives. Now we were, transforming ourselves into farm labourers, doing the most menial jobs and at the same time trying to live an intense communal social and cultural life, preparing ourselves to become 'cultured peasantry'. Work was the dominant value. I suspect that for most, certainly for me, that task was initially more or less pure torture. In retrospect I suppose that learning to overcome, or at least endure, the physical hardship of farm work were a good education for all kinds of future situations.

Young Zionists training at Hurst Grange, Twyford

As for those Jews who had already been living in the area, a few of the war-time stalwarts still remained at the helm of the Maidenhead community for a while. In 1947, Leslie Paisner was President and David Silverman was Secretary, while Rev. Brazil was the part-time minister and ran the youth club. Services were still held at Woodcarvers Hall. One of the few details that survive from that period concerns an incident surrounding Christmas crackers. The *Hanukah* party held for the children in December 1947 was at a time when the austerity of the post-war years meant there was still rationing and a limited choice of goods. As a special treat Christmas crackers were placed on the table beside each child's plate, the first time they had been available for many years. The children were delighted, but their teacher, Simon Joseph, was horrified at the mix of Christian customs with Jewish celebrations. He declared publicly, 'I resign forthwith', and left the building. He was later mollified and withdrew his remark, but it left a lifelong impression on one of the young participants, Tony Miller, who recalled the incident fifty years later, including the confusion he felt at the time because 'we children did not know what "forthwith" meant' (5). Another member claimed that the incident was reported to the Beth Din, the Rabbinic Court. According to him, when the Orthodox judges were asked whether it was permissible to buy Christmas crackers, they asked 'What are crackers?'(6). It is not clear whether the Beth Din episode is a true story or one that grew over the years, but memory of the original incident has certainly survived a long time and indicates what a deep impression it made on youg minds at the time.

1948 was a milestone in Jewish history with the establishment of the State of Israel and the end of almost two thousand years of exile since the loss of independence in the year 70 at the hands of the Romans. Unfortunately no details are recorded as to whether there was a communal event or special service. However, a former member recalled that there was tremendous excitement when State was born, and that one member shocked everyone else by donating £100 (then a large sum) to the Jewish National Fund.

The year 1948 also had Jewish significance locally for an entirely different reason, for it was then that Carmel College was founded in Wallingford by Rabbi Kopul Rosen, who headed it until his death in 1962. It was a remarkable attempt to combine English public school values and education with Jewish life and learning. Most of the pupils were boarders, and the school boasted prowess both in sporting endeavours, such as rowing and cricket, as well as in Jewish studies and a beautifully designed synagogue. Many of its pupils came from London, and it also attracted those from abroad, but a few Maidenhead families sent their children there too. These included Elias and Mina Kupfermann, while some of those who had attended as boarders eventually moved to the area in adulthood, such as Michael Moher from Dublin and Morton Geppert from North West London. The school continued until 1997, when it closed due to falling rolls and financial difficulties.

Carmel College, Wallingford

By the end of 1950 all three of the post-war leaders - Paisner, Silverman and Brazil - had left the area and a new group emerged to head the community. They, too, had been evacuees but had not been in the forefront of their London congregations at the time, and so had not been amongst those who had automatically assumed leadership of the war-time community. Those who now came together to ensure that the post-war congregation survived included the following (with known occupations given in brackets): Victor and Rose Afia (who owned a carpet shop in London), Murray and Frances Bernie (he was a manager at the Rialto Cinema, Maidenhead, and also worked as a toastmaster), Rube and Ada Caplan (he worked as an accountant in London, while she had a women's clothes shop in the town), Regina Englander, Jack and Miriam Freedman (he owned a shoe shop in the High Street), Ellis and Celia Levenson (he ran a dress shop in Queen Street), Israel and Sarah Madenberg (he had a furrier shop in Windsor and she had a ladies outfit shop in Maidenhead), Arthur and Florrie Mann, Harry and Annie Olman (he was a corset manufacturer in London and she ran a corset shop in Maidenhead), Harry and Renee Otter (he was in the insurance business in London), Alf and Sam Shear (the former was a commercial traveller, the latter ran a local sweet shop, while their sister Miriam was married to Jack Freedman), Adolphe and Minnie Wiseman (he was a dress manufacturer in London).

Others who joined in communal affairs at the same time or shortly afterwards included Sam and Jean Cowan (he was a turf accountant, and also owned a garage in Henley), Ruth Doniger (a child psychiatrist based in Maidenhead but working throughout Berkshire, later to become the first single woman to be allowed to adopt a child), Arthur and Nita Duran, Will and Freda Goldstein (he worked in London in his father's firm - a public company - Ellis and Goldstein in London; they came to the area in 1946), Alec and Golda Hambury (he had a furniture factory in Shoreditch), Jack Krestin (a London solicitor), Edward and Nita Miller (he was stockbroker in London), Laurie and Iris Misener (he ran a men's outfitters in Maidenhead), Sidney and Jean Rich (he had a property and engineering business), Rube and Rose Shackman (he was a jeweller).

A brief glance of these initial members shows that there was a wide range of occupations, with a mixture of those working locally and in London, although largely the former. It is noticeable, though, that most worked for themselves in business or retail, whereas few were engaged in manual labour or were professionals. Nearly all had originated from London and come to the area because of the war. One of the exceptions was the Madenberg family who were living previously in Tunbridge Wells. They had opened a shop in Maidenhead in 1938 simply as a business opportunity and only moved there after the war broke out.

Hanukah Party in a member's home, 1951, (l to r) Robert Afia, Susan Cowan, Philip Afia, Barbara Rich, Margaret Rich, Gillian Otter, Charles Otter, Peter Afia, Patricia Wiseman, Sharon Krestin, Lewis Cowan

Changing to Reform

One immediate challenge facing the community was a place of meeting. The lease on Woodcarvers Hall had expired and so services transferred to the front living room of the home of Victor and Rose Afia at 17 Boyn Hill Avenue. They were held only on Friday nights, reflecting the fact that many members were shopkeepers and unable to attend Saturday morning. This also indicated that their level of religious observance was relatively lax, organising their Judaism around their work life rather than the other way round. By all accounts these services had a pleasant atmosphere, but it was clear that the community could not rely permanently on the hospitality of one particular family. Many other members did not have large enough premises to host services comfortably, while those that did often lived further afield in Marlow or Henley. A long-term solution was needed.

The community's search for a permanent home of its own was connected with another major issue it faced: what sort of synagogue should it be? It was not affiliated to any particular movement, but its services were conducted according to Orthodox rites. This had been dictated by the character of the original evacuees, most of whom had come from Orthodox backgrounds, including some who were highly observant. However, the community that remained was much less meticulous, almost by definition, for they were content to remain in an area which was non-Jewish and lacked proper facilities for *kosher* food and Jewish schooling. The membership was also less knowledgeable in terms of their Jewish education, and many of them found services entirely in Hebrew unsatisfying. This description applied to many other small provincial or suburban congregations, who simply carried on in the same Orthodox manner as before, if only out of habit rather than out of conviction. However, Maidenhead was to stand out for its willingness to challenge the religious status quo and change direction.

In this respect, Sidney Rich played a crucial role. He and his brother David had been living in London and had set up a factory in 1938 manufacturing electrical instruments, known as Taylor Electrical Instruments. The products had initially been for commercial use but once hostilities broke out, all such work was focused on the war effort, and the factory turned to producing 'degaussing' equipment that measured the magnetic attraction of the hull of a ship, so that it could be neutralised against German magnetic mines. Its importance for protecting ships was such that it was deemed safer if the factory was moved out of London and away from bombing raids, so it was transferred to the Slough Trading Estate in 1940, with Sidney Rich moving to Maidenhead at the same time.

He also developed a radio location system by which pilots could locate their exact position before the invention of radar. Amongst those who worked for him was a Jewish engineer, Wolfgang (later known as Simon) Newman, who had been born in Dresden. He came to England in 1939 and settled to Slough when the factory opened there.

In the summer of 1949, Rich had been in California where he was visiting family and also thinking of possible emigration to the United States. He attended a Reform synagogue there and was deeply impressed 'by the decorum, the absence of talking during services, the dignified way in which it was conducted, the use of English, the fact that men and women sat together, and the social gathering afterwards with coffee and cake provided'. On his return to Maidenhead, he related his experiences to others in the synagogue. It was an opportune moment, for many of them were thinking about the future of the community and wondering whether it could survive long-term in its current format. Moreover, many of them were personally sympathetic to the Reform approach of modernising the faith and felt it chimed better with their own attitude and lifestyle. Rich proposed that the community change to Reform and adopt the practices he had seen, insisting particularly that at least 50% of the service be in English, and that the Hebrew be read at the speed of comprehension and 'without any mumbling'. He set about trying to win over the membership (7).

Following a long period of discussion, a special meeting was held in mid-1952 for all members of the community - estimated at 30 families - at which the matter was discussed (8). Those in favour of becoming Reform argued for a service that they could understand; they included Victor Afia, Arthur Duran and Will Goldstein. Others supported the move be cause they felt that Reform was more 'respectable' than the Orthodox, by which was meant that it was perceived to be more in keeping with the integrated lifestyle in wider society that most members led (9). Another motive for change was that it was felt necessary to be part of a larger movement if the community was to have a future. As an independent Orthodox synagogue they received no external help, but as an affiliated member of the Reform movement they would be able to call on a variety of religious and educational resources. Those against the change wanted to carry on in the traditional manner and included Jack Freedman, Israel Madenberg and Adolphe Wiseman. No official record of the meeting survives, but the result was that a motion was passed to change to the Reform, although there is some dispute as to the size of the vote: '60-40' according to one source, but 'virtually unanimous' according to another (10). A few members were sufficiently unhappy with the decision that they held separate *Rosh Hashannah* service in the Orthodox manner that year, but by the time *Yom Kippur* came ten days later, they had decided to rejoin the rest of the community. If there had been another Orthodox synagogue in close proximity, some members may well have left Maidenhead and gone there instead, but as it was the only community in the town, they stayed together.

The significance of the transition from Orthodox to Reform went far beyond the effects on its own membership. It was also a 'first' in British Jewry. Other synagogues experienced break-away groups who left the congregation to go off and form a Reform community, but never before had an entire congregation changed its religious affiliation. It is notable that this has only happened twice since then, although in both cases they were struggling independent Orthodox communities that switched movements under the influence of nearby Reform synagogues that were already assisting them: Swindon in 1986 (which was being helped by Maidenhead Synagogue) and Darlington in 1989 (which became allied with Newcastle Reform Synagogue).

The main impact of the decision to switch affiliation was on the services, which now followed the Reform pattern of a mixture of Hebrew and English, along with men and women sitting together. It seems that old habits were not easy to change overnight, for according to Sidney Rich, at the very first service following the vote, he stopped the service after ten minutes because the reforms he had worked towards were not being implemented; apparently his intervention prompted more readings in English to be introduced.

Permanent premises

There were three far-reaching consequences of the change to Reform, for it began a process that led to Maidenhead acquiring a building, appointing a part-time minister and joining a national movement. The first was the impetus it gave the community to look for permanent premises, with a new sense of confidence and direction, backed by the financial commitment of Rich and others. At the very beginning of 1953, Victor Afia notified other members that 9 Boyn Hill Avenue - a large house on three floors in the same road in which they were already holding services - was on the market. The property, also known as Studlands, dated back to 1890, when it was originally owned by the local MP and public benefactor William Henry Grenfell, later Lord Desborough. It was currently in the possession of the brewery company Nicholson and Sons, whose directors were Thomas Stuchberry and Harold Jones. It was suddenly necessary for the ad hoc community to become a legal entity and it was formally founded as an unincorporated Society on 19th January 1953, at which time it was also resolved to purchase the freehold of Studlands. Sidney Rich approached the agents, Dudley Clifton and Son, but was told it had already been sold subject to contract. Rich felt that its size and location was exactly what was required and persisted with his attempt to win it. He discovered that the other party had offered £4,500 and so he immediately wrote to the owners, Nicholson Brewery, offering £4,600 for the freehold and enclosing a cheque of £460 as a deposit. Rich's bid was accepted.

Studlands, 9 Boyn Hill Avenue

Most of the balance outstanding was raised by donations from leading members of the time, although it was still necessary to borrow £1,000 from the Midland Bank to complete the purchase. The bank had agreed providing that ten people guaranteed £100 each 'jointly and severally'. Realising that this would mean that if nine guarantors failed to honour their pledge, the entire amount would fall on the tenth person, the then Honorary Treasurer, Ellis Levenson successfully persuaded the Bank to drop the condition that it be 'jointly'. The guarantors included Victor Afia, Alec Hambury, Sidney Rich and Adolphe Wiseman.

At the time of purchase, Studlands was occupied by one family, but on acquiring the property, internal work was done to make it more suitable for its new purpose. A description of Studlands shortly after it has been converted portrayed it as (11):

> a large mansion which possessed ample accommodation and a magnificent garden. The ground floor consists of the synagogue offices, spacious modern kitchen and cloakroom. Adjoining the synagogue is a conservatory, the roof of which is clustered with a flourishing vine. The first floor has children's classrooms, which are also used for receptions and other functions, and the minister's living quarters. On the second floor is a self-contained housekeeper's flat.

It was registered as a place of worship on 24th August 1953. The four trustees of the property were Victor Afia, Arthur Duran, Israel Madenberg and Sidney Rich. The name 'Studlands' had been given by the original owners who had been horse lovers, and initially proved to be a source of controversy, with some members regarding it as indecorous for a house of worship. This was to include the community's subsequent part-time minister, Erwin Rosenblum, but leading lay figures, such as Hambury and Otter, were also keen on horses and insisted on maintaining it. They won the battle, and although Rosenblum secretly took down the plaque bearing its name - for which he only admitted responsibility some forty years later - it was replaced and remained thereafter.

One immediate task was to give Studlands a Jewish character and to provide the usual furnishings expected of a synagogue. As the Stollerman Ark was no longer considered big enough, a new wooden Ark to house the scrolls was built into the wall. It cost £12. The red velvet mohair curtain which covered it was donated by Sam Cowan - valuable leftovers from material used to make the curtain for the Pathe cinema. Two scrolls were borrowed from Commercial Road *Talmud Torah* in the East End of London, for which a small donation was paid every year (12). Other items donated were chairs (by Harry Otter), the board displaying the Prayer for the Queen (by Alec Hambury) and bells for the scrolls (by Laurie Misener).

The purchase was a tremendous leap of faith. The community could have carried on using people's homes, or returned to renting part-time premises as before. It would have satisfied current needs but made little long-term progress. Acquiring a home of their home was a statement about a vision for the future and a determination to turn a community that had come into existence by accident due to external circumstances into a vibrant synagogue with a sense of its own purpose.

A part-time minister

Parallel with the acquisition of Studlands was the search for a part-time minister. An advertisement was placed in the *Jewish Chronicle* in June 1953 and it resulted in the appointment of Erwin Rosenblum shortly afterwards. He was born in Bratislava in Slovakia, but, luckily for him, had been in England in 1939 when war broke out, studying at the Manchester Talmudical College to train as an Orthodox rabbi. As a result he remained in this country and escaped the fate of his parents, two sisters and brother who were killed in Auschwitz. He went on to serve a Federation synagogue in London, the Maida Vale Beth Hamedrash in 1945, acting as both reader and headmaster. However, the effect of the Holocaust and his own questioning of religion led him towards Reform Judaism. After a period out of the ministry and in business in London, he decided to take up the offer to be Maidenhead's part-time minister (13). It was a mutually beneficial appointment, with the community responding to him warmly, while he found it restored his sense of vocation: 'Maidenhead was my way back to Judaism' (14). The synagogue was still using the Orthodox Singers prayer book, but he introduced the prayer book used by the West London Synagogue, which other Reform communities also used, and which was designed for a mix of readings in Hebrew and English. He was employed to take Friday evening services, with the only day-time ones being the High Holy Days, other festivals and Saturdays when there was a *barmitzvah*. Rosenblum's blend of traditional background, modern approach and tenor voice was ideal for the community. He also taught the Religion School on Sunday mornings. An issue that arose after his appointment was the question of whether the new minister was merely the person who conducted services or whether he had religious authority over the community. Clearly the latter was merited by someone of Rosenblum's learning, although until his arrival all such decisions had been made by the Council. The matter was discussed at the Council meeting of 1st May 1955 and it was agreed that 'The Minister be accepted as the Spiritual Leader of the Community and its adviser in religious matters'. Maidenhead was fortunate that its two major developments - a new identity and a new building - were accompanied by the acquisition also of a part-time minister. His presence gave both of them an added impetus and helped ensure that their benefits were realised.

Consecration of the new synagogue took place on 26th July 1953, with Rabbi Dr Harold Reinhart of West London Synagogue - one of the leading Reform rabbis at the time - coming down to lead the service in

Erwin Rosenblum

conjunction with Rev. Rosenblum and Alf Shear. Amongst the guests were various Honorary Officers from the Reform movement, the Association of Synagogues in Great Britain (ASGB), along with the Mayor and Mayoress of Maidenhead, Councillor and Mrs T. W. Stuchberry, and the minister of the nearby All Saints Church, Rev. Eric Perkins. Sidney Rich, President at the time, gave a vote to thanks to the ministers on behalf of the community. Other honorary officers were Ellis Levenson, the Honorary Secretary, and Adolphe Wiseman, the Honorary Treasurer. The only discordant note for some was the omission of a prayer for the State of Israel upon the insistence of Rabbi Reinhart, who had trenchant views that Judaism was purely a faith and not a race, and who opposed the influence of Zionism in Jewish life. (15) However, what could not be overshadowed was the significance of the day - heralding the transition of the community from a collection of Jews who had ended up in Maidenhead to a group for whom Maidenhead was their home of choice and who were committed to ensuring it had a Jewish future.

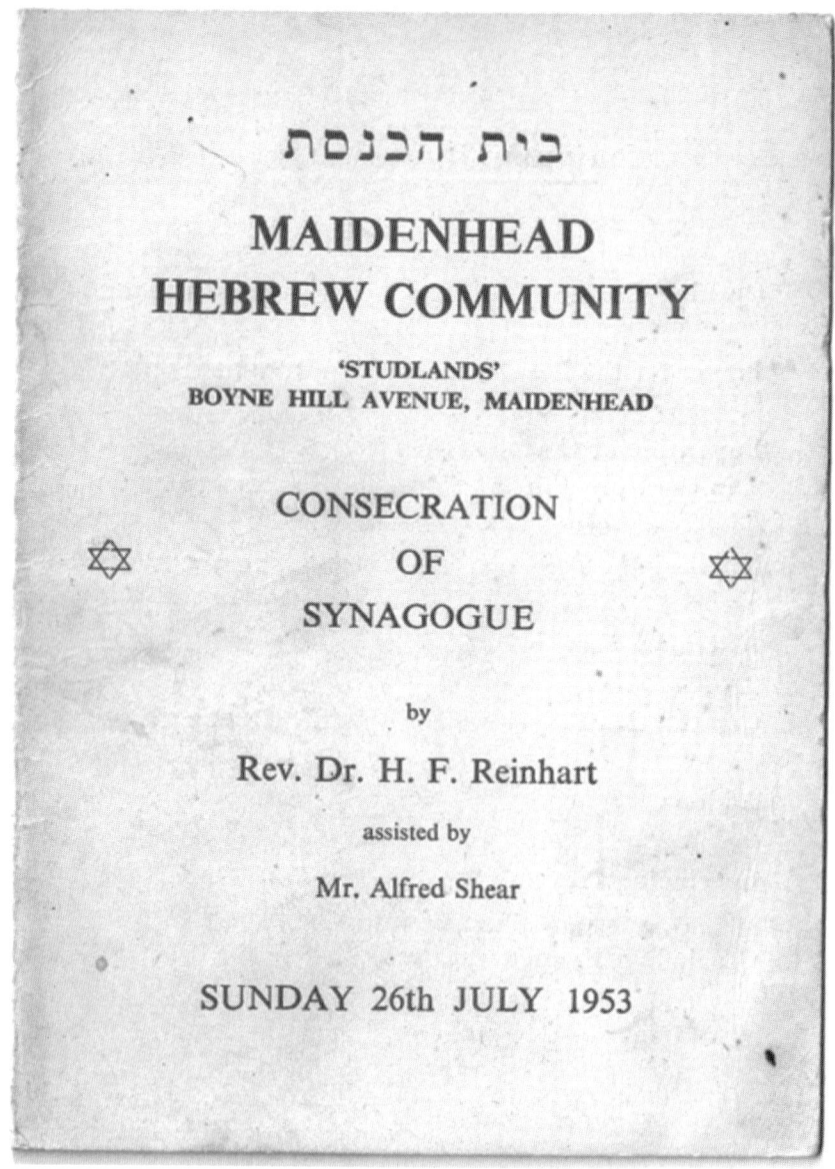

Order of service for the consecration of Studlands

Joining the Reform movement

The third major consequence of the change to Reform meant that the community was now no longer completely on its own, but part of the wider Reform movement. This not only gave the community access to support and expertise, but also suited its independent spirit: whereas constituents of the United Synagogue had their buildings owned by the US and their finances overseen by them, Reform synagogue were completely autonomous but voluntarily linked together. In 1953 in response to approaches by Maidenhead, Gus Radges of Alyth Synagogue and Chairman of the ASGB Expansion Committee visited Maidenhead to discuss its possible membership, along with two other members, Leo Bernard and Rabbi Harold Reinhart (both of West London Synagogue).

Radges reported to ASGB Executive meeting on 21st December 1953 that Maidenhead had fulfilled the condition for joining the Association of having regular services for the past twelve months. He said that the membership consisted of thirty families and his opinion was that 'there was not much likelihood of that number increasing to any extent.' Formal application to join the ASGB was duly received and was the subject of discussion at the 8th March 1954 meeting. Some members of the Executive felt that more information was needed about the congregation before it could be considered, while it was also reported that 'their opinion as to association with the United Synagogue or with the ASGB was divided.' It was agreed to put the matter on hold until greater investigation had been made, and a questionnaire was sent to the congregation. The matter was discussed again on 28th April. Julius Hart (of West London) felt that consideration should be deferred in view of the small size of the congregation, a view rebuffed by Radges who testified to the enthusiastic nature of the community. He also reassured the Executive by stating that he had told the Honorary Officers of Maidenhead that membership of the Association would not mean involving the ASGB in any financial commitments. At this point Rabbi Dr Van der Zyl - minister of North Western Reform Synagogue and a leading figure within the ASGB - declared that 'he could not understand why so many questions were being raised. The congregation had shown initiative. They had their own synagogue and minister and also children's classes, all without the help of the Association.' This comment reflected that fact that Maidenhead stood in contrast with other communities that the ASGB had actively helped nurture into existence, whereas Maidenhead was both fully formed and a self-supporting before seeking to join. Other members of the Executive agreed, with Sidney Kingsley taking the view that 'it was the association's duty to bring them in.' A motion by Radges to recommend to the movement's Conference that Maidenhead be accepted as a constituent member of the ASGB was carried by a large majority. An amendment by Hart that this be deferred until the Executive had had an opportunity to see the accounts of the community was lost.

It was decided to follow the procedure that had applied to other applicants, namely to invite Maidenhead to send two observers to Conference, who would state their case and answer any questions posed to them. They would then retire while Conference voted on their application, and, if accepted, would return as delegates. It was also agreed that, if accepted, Maidenhead should send an observer to all meetings of the Executive. The person would have no power to vote, but it would be a way of developing the community's ties with the Association and give it a better knowledge of the ASGB's work (16).

The Annual Conference of the ASGB was held over the weekend of 7th-9th May 1954 at West London Synagogue. Maidenhead's application was heard at the evening session on 8th May. The then President and Honorary Secretary, Victor Afia and Ronald Bernie, were present as observers. Bernie reported that the membership stood at thirty-four families and had eighteen children at the Religion Classes, while it already had its own premises and minister. In reply to a question from Hart, he said that the decision to apply for membership of the ASGB was 'a unanimous one.' This may not have been the case originally, but it had become so by that stage once those dissenting either had been won round or had come to accept the inevitable. The motion to accept Maidenhead was then put and passed, with Maidenhead becoming its fourteenth constituent congregation. In welcoming Maidenhead, the editor of the movement's journal *The Synagogue Review* hailed the moment as highly symbolic and stated that through it (17):

> we became aware of the new responsibilities and tasks within the Anglo-Jewish community. The great problem of our generation is the problem of the lonely Jew, who must, at all costs, be united with the rest of the community... [there is] an entirely new trend in the distribution of the population as a whole and the Jewish community in particular throughout the country. Given the blessing of lasting peace, the distribution of Anglo-Jewry throughout the land may well depict a different aspect due to the emergence of dormitory towns, development areas and the like. With the acceptance of Maidenhead within its fold, the ASGB has broken new ground in the right direction. If we are at all concerned with the survival of Judaism, no unit, however small, must escape our attention.

The ASGB provided support through a variety of important ways, such as the use of its prayer books and access to its Beth Din. It also tried to have a physical presence through occasional visits of key personnel. Thus Rabbi Dr Werner Van der Zyl came to lead a Sabbath morning service in November 1954. A Brains Trust consisting of leading lay and rabbinic members of the ASGB was held the following month. The panel featured Dr Ernst Cohn (lay leader from Alyth), Raymond Goldman (General Secretary), Rev. E. K. Sawady and Rev. E. Rosenblum; the question master was Ronald Bernie. Rabbi Reinhart returned in May 1955 to conduct a Friday evening service. For its part, Maidenhead sent delegates to the movement's Annual Conference. The two appointed to that in June 1955, the first one after gaining membership, were unable to attend (Laurie Misener and Rev. Rosenblum) but Victor Afia and Harry Madenberg went to the May 1956 Conference, with the latter elected onto the Executive as Maidenhead's permanent representative.

A new name

The new affiliation also led to a new name. Up till this point, the standard format of most Orthodox congregations had been used - Maidenhead Hebrew Congregation - but at the AGM of 19th January 1955, it was resolved that the name become 'The Maidenhead Synagogue'. The move was partly to mark a new chapter in its religious direction and partly to reflect the fact that it now possessed a building of its own. It was noticeable, however, that it did not become 'Maidenhead Reform Synagogue', the standard description of many others in the ASGB. This could have been in order not to antagonise those members who had not wished to change to the Reform and a way of keeping them part of the community. It might also have been a statement of inclusivity: that Jews of all backgrounds were welcome, with the synagogue being conscious that it was the only one in the area and therefore tried to be open to all Jews locally.

1. JC (24 August 1945) 13
2. Interview with Gretel Jordan via her carers
3. Stebbing (2003) 99; extra details from interview, Roman Halter
4. Tom Berman, 'Memoirs' unpublished mss.
5. Interview, Tony Miller 1st April 1997

6. Interview, Harold Caplan July 2009
7. Interview, Sidney Rich
8. Interview, Ellis Levenson
9. Interview, Harold Caplan July 2009
10. According to Harry Madenberg, it was 60-40 in favour of becoming Reform; according to Ellis Levenson it was 'virtually unanimous', with Ron Bernie agreeing with the latter version
11. SR (August 1954) 399
12. According to the Synagogue Council minutes of 1 March 1955, this was initially three guineas; in the 1970s it was five guineas
13. According to one source, contact with Rosenblum happened because Sidney Pettle of West London Synagogue recommended Rosenblum to Sidney Rich; according to another source, Rosenblum was working part-time for Victor Afia
14. Interview, Erwin Rosenblum November 1986
15. Interview, Ellis Levenson who had an argument with Reinhart over the omission
16. Minutes, ASGB Executive (7 May 1954)
17. SR (June 1954) 317

Chapter 10

1955: Life at Studlands

In terms of the religious life of the community, services continued to be held on Friday evenings, with Saturday morning ones occurring only when there was a *barmitzvah*. The starting time of the Friday evening service was at 8.30 pm throughout the year, rather than varying it depending on the season and at what time the Sabbath officially began. This was set as a matter of convenience for those whose work timetable meant that they could not attend any earlier, especially those commuting to and from London. An important aspect of those Sabbath eve services was that they were always followed by tea and socialising, which helped bind members together and also provided refreshments for those travelling from outlying areas. It was to prove a key part of the 'Maidenhead *minhag*' and one that survives to this day. During the 1956 ASGB Conference there was a discussion about encouraging new synagogues to hold not just Friday evening services but also Sabbath morning ones. The community's delegate, Harry Madenberg, pointed out that Saturday services would be impossible in Maidenhead's case as most of its members did not have a five-day week. Attracting attendance during the week when festivals occurred then was even more difficult and meant making compromises. Thus festival services were sometimes held instead at the nearest weekend so as to facilitate attendance, such as the *Shavuot* service in 1959 which was celebrated on the morning of Saturday 13th June whereas it actually fell on the Friday morning. It was more common, though, just for evening services to be held for midweek festivals, with midweek morning services taking place only at the High Holy Days.

The first *barmitzvah* at Studlands was that of Lewis Cowan on 3rd July 1954 followed by Robert Afia two years later. Both were sons of members who took a key role in communal affairs and it highlights one of the motives for their involvement: providing Jewish facilities for the next generation and ensuring that their children had a Jewish upbringing. It became traditional at such occasions for the *barmitzvah* boys to be given books of Jewish interest, although occasionally a *tallit* was presented instead. One notable *barmitzvah* was that of Paul Freedman, who had learning difficulties and later went to live in Ravenswood. His parents had assumed that he would not be capable of having a *barmitzvah*, but Rosenblum encouraged him to do so to the best of his abilities and it was a memorable occasion. An organ donated for the new synagogue was used at special events, although it seems to have fallen out of favour and it was disposed of by July 1959. Innovations and changes occurred on an ad hoc basis. At the August 1955 Council, for instance, it was proposed by Mr Levenson that there should be no allocation of seats for the High Holy Days and that the principle of 'first come, first served' should be observed. Mr Afia spoke very strongly against the motion stating that people liked to feel that seats were reserved for them. However, he proved to be in the minority and when the resolution was put to the vote it was carried by ten votes to one. A more minor development that could never have occurred in an Orthodox synagogue came when the Council agreed to modify for electricity the silver candlesticks donated by Mrs Hambury. This was so that the candles could appear lit at the beginning of Friday evening services without being physically lit - as the service often began after the Sabbath had started after which it is traditional not to kindle a light - and they were simply switched on beforehand.

The acquisition of the building not only enhanced the religious life of the congregation but acted as a major spur to social activities and permitted a range of events not previously possible. 1954 saw a Communal *Seder* at Studlands, a Garden Party there in July attended by one hundred and seventy people, a Ladies Committee film evening in November on the work of WIZO, and the annual *Hanukah* party for children in December. There was also a *Purim* tea dance at the Hotel de Paris, Bray (which was owned by members of the community, Mr and Mrs Westerman, and which was to be demolished and replaced by the Braybank flats in 1964). Studlands had brought a feeling of permanency and confidence to the previously ad hoc community.

Relations with the wider community began to develop. The Maidenhead Branch of the Church of England Men's Society attended Sabbath evening service in January 1955, along with their minister Rev. Perkins. Welcoming the guests, Rev. Rosenblum said that (1):

> We were apt to be distrustful of the unknown. The mistake in the past had been that instead of stressing the moral and ethical laws which unite us, too much emphasis was placed on theological differences. Although, because of these differences, it was neither possible nor desirable to merge one church with another, we could and should all work together for the good of mankind.

This was a very different atmosphere from the meeting of the same Church of England Men's Society in 1914 that had been so hostile to Jews. Another group visit was of twenty-five members of the Boyn Hill Christian Association, who attended a Friday evening service which was conducted by guest preacher Rabbi Curtis Cassell of West London Synagogue in May 1957. Occasional donations to local causes were made by the Council on behalf of the synagogue, such as to an appeal from the Mayor of Maidenhead towards special nursing staff to deal with multiple sclerosis, and then again for his Christmas Cheer Fund for Old People. Rev. Perkins, who was also minister of All Saints Church, which was in the same road as Studlands, was often invited to services and functions, while the Mayor came for a civic service. Their presence epitomized the good relations with the rest of the town.

The synagogue also began to look further afield and take a minor role in the affairs of British Jewry at large, partly by being represented on communal bodies, but also in hosting special activities for them. Thus it organised a River Trip for fifty-one members of the Jewish Blind Society in the summer of 1955 and again in 1958 (2). There was a proposal by the Council to link with Reading Synagogue to celebrate the Tercentary of Jews in England, which occurred in 1956, although there is no record of a response, nor of any joint event taking place (3). The community decided to inaugurate Zionist activities in late 1955, with a meeting to launch a JNF box campaign (4). It also organised a Brains Trust in conjunction with the Anglo-Jewish Association in November 1959. The panel featured Rev. A. Rose (Sutton Orthodox Synagogue), Rev. Michael Leigh (West London Synagogue), Daniel Schonfield (ex-President of the Bnai Brith First Lodge) and Mr H. D. Barnard (AJA); it was chaired by the AJA's Victor Lucas.

A landmark event for the community occurred on 19th June 1955 when the first wedding in the synagogue took place, that between Mr Frank Burns and Miss Rita Willis. To commemorate the occasion, the couple were presented with a pair of silver candlesticks by the Council. Ellis Levenson had been appointed as the synagogue's Marriage Secretary three months earlier, allowing such ceremonies to be civilly valid as well as religiously so (5).

One of the regular social events throughout the 1950s was an annual Dinner and Dance, intended partly as a social activity and partly as a fundraising exercise to cover the cost of the conversion of the flats and refurbishment of the synagogue. The first one was held at the East Arms Hotel, Hurley in February 1953. It was very successful both socially and financially. The only hiccup was a miscommunication over food: the catering manger had been told to avoid meat and serve only fish - and was therefore most surprised when synagogue members objected to the shrimps he put on their plates. Subsequent annual balls in 1955 and 1956 were held at the Hotel de Paris, Bray. They transferred to Skindle's Hotel the following two years and returned to the Hotel de Paris in 1959.

Throughout this period, the mainstays of the social committee included Rose Afia, Jean Cowan and Freda Goldstein. Other activities included a newsletter started by Yetta Bernie.

Maidenhead may have witnessed the blossoming of a Jewish community, but there was not sufficient customer demand for a *kosher* butcher to open locally. As in the war-years, *kosher* meat was obtained from London, either in person or sent by train. There was also a *kosher* butcher in Reading who sent meat by bus, which was picked up from Maidenhead bus stop. There had been a *kosher* butcher in High Wycombe during the war, but it had closed once the evacuees departed. The experience of Sylvia Newton indicates the difficulties faced by those seeking to keep *kosher*. She and her husband Edward had joined the community in 1958 when they came to Twyford from North London, attracted by cheap house prices there. She recalled (6):

> In the days before I could drive, I used to catch the train every Thursday from Twyford to Reading and then the trolley bus to Morry Goldstein's *Kosher* butcher shop, which was situated opposite Battle Hospital. After my second baby was born, it became impossible for me to manage the journey, so the meat was put on the train for collection at Twyford station. It often either 'missed the train' or was behind some huge freight, and I was invariably told to call back later.
>
> This was all very unsatisfactory and Morry suggested putting the meat on the bus. I had to find out where the collection point was, which he thought was the post office, but in fact was the pork butchers! Very much so as they used to keep live pigs in pens behind the shop! I was told to go to the cashier who gave me a most disagreeable glare and handed me a box covered in blood. I never went back.

Even those who bought their *kosher* food in London had occasional problems. According to Newton, Alf Shear used to bring meat from London: 'His sister told me that one day he arrived home in a terrible state. Apparently he put the meat on the parcel rack in the train and was horrified to see drops of blood dripping on the hat of a fellow passenger'.

Despite the departure of many children back to London, and also of adults who had acted as teachers during the war, the Religion School carried on. Members who had any Jewish knowledge were asked to teach, and parents who might otherwise not have done so sometimes had to step

The Synagogue Dinner and Dance 1958, standing (l to r) Jean Cowan, Nita Duran, Jean Rich, Diana Duran, Freda Goldstein
Sitting (l to r) Ada Caplan, Golda Hambury, Rose Afia, Minnie Wiseman

in themselves if no one else was available. When specialised tuition was necessary, such as for *barmitzvah* preparation, then someone from London or elsewhere within travelling distance would be hired to give private lessons. This happened, for instance, when Tony Miller was tutored in 1951 by Michael Wallach at the latter's home in Heston, Middlesex. The arrival of Rev. Rosenblum meant that a knowledgeable teacher was now readily available.

In 1955 the Council discussed whether children's lesson should be included in the membership fee or if parents should be asked to pay an additional amount for it. After much debate, it was decided to maintain free tuition, albeit with the proviso that parents of children attending should be approached for a donation (7). It was an issue that was to recur in Council over subsequent decades: did membership of the synagogue cover participation in all activities, or should those enjoying particular facilities pay extra for them On the one hand, the Religion School had high costs attached through teachers' salaries, books and classroom equipment. This meant that the membership fee of those members who

The Synagogue Dinner and Dance 1958, standing (l to r) Will Goldstein, Isidore Madenberg, Jeremy Gordon, Arthur Duran, Victor Afia, Harry Otter, Harry Olman, Harry Madenberg, Sam Cowan, Ellis Levenson Sitting (l to r) Sidney Rich, Jack Krestin, Alec Hambury, Adolphe Wiseman, unidentified

had no children, or children over religion school age, were subsiding those members who had young children. On the other hand, if payment was introduced for certain core activities, then it could be asked: what was the membership fee for? In addition, the principle of extra payment, once established could run amok; it might be argued, for instance, that only a minority of members attended regular services and so they were being subsidised by the once-a-yearers and should pay for the privilege. To date no extra charges have been added, but the debate still rumbles on.

The gap at the Religion School caused by Rosenblum's eventual departure was filled by Harry Melichan. He had already become the principal teacher in autumn 1955 when Rosenblum started teaching on Sunday mornings in London instead. He had arrived in the area shortly beforehand to lecture in Economics and English at the College for Further Education. He and his wife Sally lived at Studlands, renting the top floor flat. He occasionally assisted with other events, such as leading the

Communal *Seder* in 1957. On his appointment, an Education Committee formed, consisting of him, Ellis Levenson and Alf Shear to deal with all matters concerning the classes. His resignation as teacher four years later due to his return to London led to a report in Council on the state of the classes. The total number of pupils was between 12 and 14 children with average attendance being 8. It was stated that there were two standards, with only two children in the Senior Standard and the remainder being in the Junior Classes. This division related to Hebrew ability and meant that there was a large mix of age ranges in each group (8). Council expressed concern over the low numbers overall and that the synagogue was not offering proper facilities. It decided to advertise for a trained teacher and also to write to Rabbi Van der Zyl to see if he could recommend someone. He replied that there was a scarcity of teachers but he 'wondered if the teaching could be done on a weekday after school. Alternatively would we consider a lady teacher?' His reply implied there might be objections and suggests that Maidenhead had a reputation for not being fully attuned to Reform thinking. If so, it was wrong, for the Council did agree to a female taking classes, providing it was on a Sunday morning (9). The problem was eventually solved when Alec Belkin took on teaching duties.

Prior to Maidenhead joining the ASGB, funerals were still conducted in London, usually at Bushey Cemetery under the auspices of the United Synagogue, unless members belonged to the burial schemes of another organisation, such as the Federation of Synagogues. It indicates that many members of Maidenhead had retained membership of London synagogues, albeit often at a reduced 'country' rate, so as to secure their burial rights. This was either because they had already invested several years' worth of dues into those burial schemes and did not want to lose their benefits, or so as to be in the same cemetery as relatives who were already interred. Israel Madenberg, for instance, stayed a member of Great Portland Street Synagogue in Central London. This was clearly not a satisfactory position for a community that was seeking to establish itself in its own right, and so the Council sought ways of providing burial cover as one of the privileges of membership. This was achieved when the community became part of the ASGB, whereupon the West London Synagogue allowed Maidenhead to link into its burial scheme and have use of its cemetery in Hoop Lane, Golders Green. This was arranged on an individual basis for any Maidenhead member who did not have burial rights elsewhere, although it operated through the synagogue itself. Thus each individual paid their burial scheme dues to Maidenhead, who then passed them on to West London. It was also agreed with West London that if any family did not pay the costs incurred, Maidenhead would be responsible for them. However, this led to some consternation when West

London raised the cost of a plot from twenty-five guineas to fifty pounds in July 1955. This was felt to be too high and might endanger the synagogue's financial situation. The secretary was asked to find quotations from insurance companies as an alternative, but nothing resulted. At the January 1956 Council meeting the secretary stated that the Burial Fund was too great a liability to the synagogues finances, but several members disagreed, insisting that it was 'essential to the running of the synagogue' (10).

Much of the Council's time was devoted to supervising the state of the premises. The decline in Religion School numbers meant that the classes could be conducted on the ground floor only, allowing the first floor to be turned into a flat. At the same time, improvements were made to the top floor, providing it with its own bathroom and toilet. The Council was responsible for renting out or refurbishing the flats, chasing up unpaid rent, securing new tenants, and even ordering the removal of an old motorcar that had been left in the forecourt by a tenant. The tenants were usually not Jewish and acquired through the local newspaper or estate agents, although there were occasions when one of the flats was occupied by a member of the community if a vacancy coincided with them looking for accommodation. Whilst the flats brought an income to the synagogue, there was also the occasional disadvantage of sharing the building. Thus there was a complaint from one member during the High Holy Day services in 1959 over distraction caused by noise from the upstairs flat - after which, it was decided that some suitable underfelt would solve the problem (11).

There was also the upkeep and heating of the synagogue itself, while the long garden also demanded attention. Occasionally it suffered from periods of neglect that called for radical measures. Thus the July 1959 Council minutes record that 'On the matter of the rear section of the back garden, it was agreed that in view of the overgrowth it should be completely burnt down. At least it would keep the place tidy' (12). One particular episode has entered synagogue folklore. At an AGM in the 1950s it was noted that dry rot had been discovered, to which the then Treasurer, Adolphe Wiseman, commented 'We cannot afford dry rot!' - a remark that was remembered by several members over forty years later.

The success of Rosenblum at Maidenhead attracted the attention of others. In September 1955 he also became part-time minister at North Western Reform Synagogue, assisting Rabbi Van der Zyl there on Sabbath mornings, as well as being the Superintendent of the Religion School. However, he maintained his other duties at Maidenhead, with the congregation having 'first call' on his services for Friday evenings and festivals (13). Serving two communities simultaneously was not ideal and the opportunity to have a full-time post came when Leon Bressler, a member of the newly formed Brighton and Hove New Synagogue (Reform) who was a relative of the Madenbergs attended a Friday evening service at Maidenhead. He was so impressed by Rosenblum that he invited him to guest preach. This led to him being offered the position of their rabbi, which he accepted. However, the fact that Brighton had approached Rosenblum without notifying the Maidenhead Council caused considerable upset, especially as it was a fellow Reform synagogue that was perceived to have 'stolen' their minister.

The Council was informed in May 1956 that he had been appointed to a full-time post as minister of Brighton. The way in which the news was recorded hints that it was both against the congregation's wishes and also to its surprise: 'It was with great regret that the Congregation learned that the minister had decided to leave Maidenhead and seek fresh pastures' (14). This annoyance was voiced at the ASGB Annual Conference later that month by the community's delegate, Harry Madenberg, who complained about Brighton's behaviour. As a result of this intervention, it was agreed that a letter would be sent by the Chairman of the movement to all constituent synagogues that no minister should be approached direct by any other constituent, but instead they should either advertise the post generally or communicate with a particular synagogue's Council if interested in its minister (15). Despite the bad feeling at the manner of his departure, Rosenblum was given a warm farewell when he conducted his final service at Maidenhead in June 1956 (16):

> A large congregation assembled to wish him well. The President, Mr I. Madenberg, thanked him for the sterling work he had done since the inception of the synagogue and assured him that he took with him the thanks and best wishes of every member of the Congregation. Mr Rosenblum was presented with a set of books.

When news of Rosenblum's resignation first became known, Council immediately agreed that 'the future policy of the Maidenhead Synagogue is to call a resident minister, either full time or part time, as quickly as possible' (17). However, lack of suitable candidates combined with the problem of applicants being willing to travel to Maidenhead proved a problem. It meant that the most immediate task was finding someone to lead the New Year services. When Alec Belkin applied for the position of reader for the High Holy Days, he was interviewed by Alf Shear, who reported back to Council that he was 'ideal' (18). Belkin had originally started training for the ministry at the Etz Chayyim *Yeshivah*,

London, but the war had interrupted his studies. He got married during his military service and when hostilities ended he decided instead to go into commerce. However, his love of Judaism and *chazanut* (cantorial music) remained, and so he was delighted to pursue it via Maidenhead on a part-time basis, even though he was living far away in Stamford Hill. Belkin duly led the services, assisted by Alf Shear and Laurie Misener, and officiated also at *Sukkot*. Shear had undertaken all the preparatory organisation of the High Holy Days, while he also took over the regular Friday evening services. The praise given to him in the Maidenhead section of the *Synagogue Review* reflected both the appreciation of the community and the worries caused by the lack of religious leadership (19):

Alec Belkin

> The entire Congregation offers sincere thanks to its worthy Senior Warden, Mr Alfred Shear, for his sterling work in arranging the High Festival services. The enthusiasm and ability of Mr Shear has dispelled the doubts of those who feared that the Congregation could not carry on without the services of a resident Minister

However, the reliance on Shear led to great concern when he announced a year later that he might be leaving the area. He had regularly taken both Friday services and festival ones, and Council asked him 'to coach several members so that there should be a rota of members able to take the service if, and when, the time comes' (20). In the event, he remained in the area for several years further. Meanwhile, the search for a minister continued to be unsuccessful and so in June 1957 Rabbi Rosenblum, with permission of Brighton Synagogue, agreed to act as Honorary Spiritual Adviser to the congregation, dealing with any questions of religious procedure or status issues that arose. He also returned to conduct services whenever a *barmitzvah* occurred, doing so that year and twice more in each of the following two years.

Alec Belkin led the High Holy Day services again in 1957, assisted by Shear, Misener and Levenson. At the Council meeting afterwards it was noted that 'the services were discussed and whilst most comments were favourable there was some criticism of the Reader' (21). The nature of those objections was not revealed, but whatever the initial hiccups, it was an arrangement that not only became a fixture but was to have a remarkable longevity, with him travelling from North London and back for the next forty years. Moreover, his wife Peggy, who often accompanied him at services, became a much loved figure in the community. The family's involvement was completed in future years when his daughter Evelyn served as a Religion School teacher. The tradition of having a communal *seder* had been begun by Rosenblum in 1955 and after his departure was led by lay members - Melichan in 1957, Misener in 1958 - after which Alec Belkin took it over. For many years, Frances Bernie and Minnie Wiseman led a team of women in cooking, while Rose Afia and others saw to the tables and flowers. Not that everything proceeded smoothly all the time, for there were hints of occasional religious friction. According to the Council minutes of 23rd Sept 1959, the Honorary Secretary reported that the two Wardens were 'not in accord' with each other over their respective duties: 'Whilst Mr Shear said he was only too pleased for Mr Misener to assist in services, Mr Misener was of the opinion that this was not the case and that the Senior Warden was doing it all himself'. Council urged the two men 'to forget personalities and, in the cause of the synagogue, get together'. It was a sentiment that was no doubt repeated at some point in virtually every congregation in the land.

It was in the nature of the ASGB that communities which belonged to it ran their own affairs and were completely independent, but the ASGB still kept an eye on constituents that were facing difficulties. As early as September 1956, its Expansion Committee had expressed concern over Maidenhead's inability to find a minister after the departure of Rabbi Rosenblum. By 1959, when it seemed it was impossible to locate a successor, it agreed to arrange regular visits by other Reform ministers and Rabbi Charles Berg of Wimbledon Synagogue became the first to do so, taking a Friday evening service in September 1959.

The Schwab Hall

The absence of a minister may have affected the conduct of services but did not mean that the congregation remained static, and another significant advance was made to communal life through the building of the Schwab Hall. Hugo Schwab was born in Berlin in 1891 and came to England in 1938. His wife, however, was unable to leave and died in Bergen-Belsen concentration camp. He settled in South Wales, where he set up a factory making precision machine parts for the RAF. There he met and married Marjorie Hall, whose family owned a chemist shop in Maidenhead High Street. In 1950 they settled in Maidenhead, where he developed both an engineering and a building business. As well as supporting the synagogue, he was also a generous benefactor to various local causes. He built the extension to the King George VI Memorial Club in York Road for Elderly People, helped fund Castle Hill Youth Centre (now demolished), and bought Highview, a three-storey house in North Road to be used by the Maidenhead Society for Mental Health. The latter was opened by Lady Bowes-Lyon, a cousin of the Queen in April 1964. The plaque on the building revealed the particular motive behind his generosity: 'This building was endowed as a centre for the handicapped by Hugo Schwab and his wife, Marjorie, in gratitude for the kindness and friendship extended to him by the people of this country in time of trouble and persecution'.

Schwab was also a business partner of Sidney Rich and, according to the latter, benefited from half the profits of a venture that Rich had arranged but in which Schwab was not involved. As a way of recognising this, Schwab agreed to Rich's suggestion that he fund the building of a hall which would be an extension to the synagogue on the

> **"Honour thy Father and thy Mother"**
>
> THE SYNAGOGUE HALL
>
> *is presented by*
>
> HUGO SCHWAB, ESQ.
>
> in memory of his dear Parents

Extract from the Order of Service

ground floor. Its object was to provide extra room for the Religion School on Sunday mornings and better facilities for social events. Plans to build the extension were submitted to the Borough Council on 18th July 1957 and within a month permission had been granted. It was designed by the local architect, Ronald Beer, and it was presented in memory of Schwab's parents, Eugen and Bertha Schwab.

A special Service of Consecration took place on 13th July 1958 when the Schwab Hall was officially opened and dedicated in memory of his parents. The service was conducted by Rabbi Rosenblum, who returned yet again from Brighton. The many guests in attendance included Rabbi Dr Werner Van der Zyl and Leonard Mendel, chairman of the ASGB, while Schwab's sister flew over from America for the occasion. The hall was described as 'a further step forward in the progress of the synagogue', while Schwab said that 'he hoped the Jewish youth of Maidenhead would make good use of the new facilities' (22). Schwab's largesse to the community was to continue over several years, and he was also responsible, amongst other acts, for donating presents for the children at

Hanukah parties, installing the central heating system for the synagogue, and providing a hedge around the Jewish section of the cemetery.

In 1954 the membership was stated as being thirty families, consisting of eighty individual members and with the Religion School comprising around twenty children (23). This gradually increased to forty-seven families by 1959, no doubt attracted by the focal point of a building and the increasing number of religious and social facilities it offered. At the Kol Nidrei service that year, ninety-four people attended (24). A structural change in the community's leadership took place at the end of the decade. Initially the leader of the community was designated as the President, but from 1959 the President was a figurehead role and executive authority was invested in the Chairman. The prime motive was to find a way of acknowledging the great contribution of Israel Madenberg, who had been chairman for the past three years, but also of relieving him of the work involved. The position of Chairman was to be subject to annual election, but that of President was lifelong.

Virtually every Jewish family in Maidenhead had its distinctive story to tell, and one example of the many that could be told is that of Fritz and Toni Jacobs, who had a particularly unusual war. They were both German and both doctors, but she was Jewish and he Protestant. Before the outbreak of war, they made sure that their children were sent to safety in England, but he turned down a job offered to him in England, because it would be taking it away from a Jewish colleague desperate to escape, whereas he did not need such a lifeline. Other attempts to emigrate failed. The result was that they both stayed in Berlin throughout the war. His status acted as a protection for his wife, as Jews married to Aryans - *mischlings* - were not subject to the normal deportation process that befell their co-religionists. For six years they endured many difficulties and deprivations, but they survived. As they were living in East Berlin, they found themselves in the Russian sector after 1945 and were unable to leave for England until 1948. Meanwhile their daughters had attended boarding school in Scotland and then gone on to university, although one of them had been interned temporarily on the Isle of Man under suspicion of being a German spy. Fritz and Toni eventually came to Maidenhead in 1952, living in Wavell Road, while one of their daughters, Juliana Robertson moved down from Scotland with her family to be with them, living in Altwood Drive from 1962 to 1988. None of them, however, had any contact with the Jewish life locally (25).

There were also other Jews living locally who had little contact with communal life as they belonged to London synagogues. Their number included Miss Jeanette Halford OBE, who had been the Honorary Secretary for both the National Association for the Prevention of Infant

Mortality, and the Association of Maternity and Child Welfare for many years; Alexander M. Levy who left £800,000 in his will in 1956 to King Edward's Hospital Fund for London, as well as a sum to the Jewish Board of Guardians and the West London Synagogue, to which he had belonged; and Dr Herbert Levenstein, one of Britain's leading industrial chemists who had advised the government during the First World war on how to counter the German use of poison gas (26). There was also the Benedictus family in Cookham Dean, one of whom – the writer and theatre director David, who was brought up there – was later to be entrusted by the estate of A. A. Milne to write a *Winnie-the-Pooh* sequel novel, *Return to the Hundred Acre Wood*.

If the formation of a permanent Jewish community in 1940 counts as the most significant date in Maidenhead Synagogue's history, 1953 must rank as the second most important. It was then the community achieved the triple distinction of changing its affiliation from Orthodox to Reform, acquiring premises of its own, and gaining the services of a part-time minister. Moreover, this was in marked contrast with so many other wartime communities that had disappeared, or begun a period of inexorable decline, once peace arrived. Maidenhead did lose many members after 1945, but enough stayed on to keep the community a viable enterprise. In addition, there was no vacuum at the top, with new leaders stepping in to replace the previous ones. The Reform community of 1953 proudly based in Studlands may have been almost unrecognisable to the Orthodox one of 1940 renting Oddfellows Hall, but the two were strongly linked and there had been a remarkably smooth transition between them. They were each located in venues with names that were unusual for religious institutions, but they both fulfilled their mission admirably.

1. SR (March 1955) 224
2. JC (5 August 1955) 14; (12 September 1958) 22
3. Minutes, MSC (17 January 1955)
4. JC (25 November 1955) 21
5. However, the first wedding recorded in the synagogue's Register for Marriages is that of Maurice Dresner and Hazel Ord on 14 September 1955, suggesting that the Burns-Willis wedding was a religious ceremony only, with a civil ceremony having already taken place elsewhere
6. Private correspondence, Sylvia Newton
7. Minutes, MSC (1 February 1955)
8. Minutes, MSC (3 June 1959)

9. Minutes, MSC (26 August, 23 September 1959)
10. Minutes, MSC (27 November 1956)
11. Minutes, MSC (28 October 1959)
12. Minutes, MSC (15 July 1959)
13. SR (October & November 1955); Minutes, MSC (16 August 1955)
14. SR (August 1956) 399
15. Minutes, MSC (22 May 1956)
16. SR (August 1956) 399
17. Minutes, MSC (22 May 1956)
18. Minutes, MSC (6 June 1956)
19. SR (October 1956) 61
20. Minutes MSC (4 November 1957)
21. Minutes, MSC (12 November 1957)
22. SR (September 1958) 18
23. SR (August 1954) 399
24. Minutes, MSC (28 October 1959)
25. Interview, Andrew Robertson
26. JC (31 March 1950) p. 8; (27 January 1956) 11; (10 August 1956) 7

Chapter 11

1960: Sinking and Swimming

An article on Maidenhead by Laurie Misener appeared in *The Synagogue Review* of March 1961 that would have brought vivid images of the town to many readers:

> Nestling in the beautiful Thames Valley is the Riverside Town of Maidenhead. To those who remember it from pre-war days, the names conjures up a dormitory town of clubs, lazy summer afternoons punting through Boulter's Lock and evening dances at Skindles Hotel. Today, though the clubs are fewer, Maidenhead is a thriving residential town, but the scenery of the surrounding districts remain as lovely as ever - and it also boasts a synagogue.

The article went on to reveal that the membership was scattered throughout Berks and Bucks, with members living in Windsor, Slough, Reading, Marlow, Henley and High Wycombe.

Despite this rosy picture, the synagogue also faced serious challenges. They were epitomised by a significant departure at the very end of 1960, that of Ellis and Celia Levenson who left Maidenhead to move to Stanmore. It was not only a loss in terms of their high involvement in synagogue life, but it also highlighted a problem facing the community. They had met in Maidenhead during the war and had spent their married life there, but left when their children Sharon and David were eight and three years old respectively. The main reason for the move was the lack of Jewish education for their children. In fact Levenson had sometimes taught at the classes in the absence of any trained teacher; at the time, there was only one class consisting of seven or eight children. There was a real danger that Jewish families with young children would not wish to come to Maidenhead, while some already in the area would leave, and those who remained would not gain a sufficient Jewish identity. If the community was to prove viable in the long-term, this needed to be addressed. As it happened, Levenson's departure was balanced that same month by the arrival of Robert Goodman, who was to play a prominent role in leading the synagogue, but the question mark over the future remained

The 1960s showed that Misener's optimism and Levenson's pessimism were equally justified, with the community experiencing both successes and disappointments. Among the successes was an active social life, with a Dinner and Dance at famous venues such as Skindles in 1960 and the Guards Boat Club two years later. The Communal *Seder* continued as an annual event in the Schwab Hall, led by Alf Shear up to 1965 with around sixty people in attendance. The Ladies Guild, which had lapsed over the last two years, was re-formed in 1961 with Mrs S. Goodman (wife of Harry) as Chairman (1). It helped run the *Hanukah* party for children and put on its own events, such as a talk by a speaker from the Board of Guardians. The following year the Guild visited a local old age home and distributed seventy-five parcels for residents (2), while it also held a social event in aid of WIZO. Over next three years it helped cater the *seder* and arranged card evenings and dances. It disbanded at the end of 1964 through lack of support but was re-started by Mrs Berk in 1968 as a Luncheon Club. It helped with the highly successful garden party in September 1969, with proceeds being divided between the Leo Baeck College (£60) and the youth club (the purchase of a new record player). That year another new group started - the Young Marrieds - led by Jack and Judy Rosenbaum.

On the religious side Rabbi Rosenblum continued to return for special occasions: he led the second day *Rosh Hashannah* service in 1961 and conducted that for *Sukkot* the following year. The Reform movement - which by then had changed its name to the Reform Synagogues of Great Britain (RSGB) - also organised a succession of ministers to make occasional visits: Rev. Philip Cohen of North Western Reform Synagogue took a Friday evening service in June 1960, Rabbi Michael Leigh of West London Synagogue in June 1961, student minister Henry Goldstein in August 1963.

There was a rare mention of religious issues in the Council minutes when Israel Madenberg brought up the question of reciting *kaddish*: 'He felt that the majority of members objected to saying *kaddish* in unison with the reader and it was generally agreed that we should revert to the traditional way' (3). The discussion might also be seen as evidence that several members retained an attachment to more traditional practices and were not always comfortable with the Reform approach. Another example was holding a second day *Rosh Hashannah* service, which was not customary then among Reform synagogues but which had occurred during the war years when the community was under Orthodox auspices. It continued thereafter and had been recorded in the Council Minutes of August 1955 with what seemed like a semi-apologetic explanation of it being 'an extra service for those who wish'. There was no further discussion of it until the Council meeting of Sept 1968 when there was a debate as to whether to continue with the second day service. It was decided to count the numbers attending and make a decision afterwards. It emerged that there had been ninety-one people present on the first day, and twenty-five at the second day. There was clearly some support for it, albeit small, but it dwindled further and by 1971, the second day service was no longer continued.

Traditional leanings were also evident in a plea in the October 1966 Newsletter for members who were a Cohen or Levi to let the wardens know. This reflected the Orthodox practice of conducting the Reading of the Law by calling up first a Cohen, then a Levite, then an Israelite, a categorisation not maintained in most Reform circles. In fact, in a letter sent in February 1966 to Sigmund Schwab, chairman of the RSGB, Misener stated that 'quite a few of our members still retain their membership of the United, and it is these who form the nucleus of our Friday evening services'. Still, seeds of change were also apparent. The May 1965 Newsletter recorded that the synagogue Council 'would like to respectfully emphasise that all ladies are required to wear hats, or at least adequate head-covering, when attending services'. It indicates that some were choosing not to do so. In fact, this was the culmination of a long discussion within the congregation and which three years earlier had led the Council to write to the Assembly of Ministers, the professional association of Reform rabbis, asking whether women were expected to cover their heads during services. The minutes of the Assembly record that 'after discussion it was felt that it was usual for women to cover their heads, though there was no hard and fast rule, especially for young people' (4).

Whatever the religious inclination of members, the services themselves encountered various challenges. There was a plea for services to start promptly at 8.30 pm made at 11th Sept 1963 Council, but after discussion about the difficulties of those working in London being able to return in time to start punctually it was agreed that 'present arrangements regarding not-so-prompt starting would continue'. More significant, though, was the problem of numbers. At the Council meeting the previous month, Murray Bernie 'deplored that Friday night services were poorly attended'. The difficulty in attracting members to services are strongly implied in a letter by Laurie Misener published in *The Synagogue Review* of May 1964:

> The RSGB has been responsible for the realistic adaptation of some of our ancient Laws to conditions existing today…It would seem to me that consideration now be given to the Law that a mourner is not permitted to recite the *Kaddish* without the attendance of a *Minyan*. In a small synagogue where members

reside in outlying area, and in inclement weather, it is frustrating for one who has *Yahrzeit* to attend on a Friday evening and find to his consternation that there is no quorum.

Monte Margo and Hilke Englander leave Studlands after their wedding

Special occasions did attract extra numbers. This happened upon the death of Sir Winston Churchill in January 1965, when a memorial service was held at the following Friday evening service, with a photograph of him displayed on the reading desk and a Union Jack flying at half mast. Such was the general malaise, though, that the May 1965 Newsletter revealed that the traditional refreshments and chat after the service had ceased and called for it to be revived. Matters deteriorated to such an extent that the June/July 1966 Newsletter took pride that the synagogue was busy on Sunday mornings with children at the Religion School, but lamented the turn-out on Friday evenings with attendance having 'dwindled to less than half-a-dozen'.

There was a suggestion that if services were held on Saturday mornings it might prove more attractive. It was pointed out that this would have the added bonus of being at a time when children could attend, as at present they only came to festival services and were being instructed in Hebrew but with little opportunity to witness it being used. The editor also commented that the nature of the community had changed - no longer predominantly made up of shopkeepers who worked on Saturday mornings but now a more varied and larger membership, many of whom were free at that time. It was to be more than two decades, though, before such services became regular. It was also significant that, after two synagogue marriages in 1955, the next one to be registered was not until 1968 – that of Monte Margo and Hilke Englander - indicative of the fact that most couples opted for a London wedding, be it because of family logistics, larger premises or better facilities. One area in which Maidenhead could claim to be unusual compared to other synagogues was that it displayed both the British and Israeli flags in front of the reading desk, a visual assertion of dual loyalty that was common in the United States but rare in England.

In December 1964 Alf Shear retired and arranged to move to Hove, along with his brother Sam and sister Miriam. He had been the person most responsible for leading services and organising festivals in the absence of a minister for more than a decade, while he had regularly taught at the Religion School. His enormous contribution to communal life was recognized with the presentation of 'a radio and a length of suiting' in appreciation of his services just before his departure the following April (5).

The problem of filling the gap caused by his departure would have been extremely difficult had it not been for the almost simultaneous arrival in the area of Rabbi Henry Silverman, who had just retired after thirty years as the spiritual leader of the Jewish community of Jamaica. On his return to England, he purchased a home in Farnham Common and agreed to become the visiting minister of Maidenhead from June 1965. Rabbi Silverman was born in Bournemouth in 1894 and had served as Jewish Chaplain to the Forces in World War I, and later to the army of occupation in Germany. After his demobilisation he occupied pulpits at an Orthodox congregation in Manchester and then a Reform one in Elmira, New York State, before going to Jamaica in 1935 to become minister of the United Congregation of Israelites in Kingston. As well as working for the Jewish community there, he also participated in civic affairs, broadcast on the radio, helped with social service organisations and was a Justice of the Peace (6).

Alf Shear

Silverman was inducted on 20th June in a service led by Rabbi Van der Zyl, and in the presence of the Mayor and Mayoress of Maidenhead, Councillor and Mrs Maurice Hayes, along with Rev. Michael Ware, the vicar of All Saints Church. The chairman, Laurie Misener, presented the Mayor with a *Hanukiah*, and in return the Mayor presented the synagogue with an inscribed plaque of the Borough of Maidenhead arms, which was later affixed to the Reading Desk in the synagogue. The fact that the plaque included a depiction of a haloed Christian saint, who thereafter gazed out at members of the congregation at prayer, did not seem to bother anyone. It remained on the reading desk for the next thirty years, by which time the boroughs of Maidenhead and Windsor had been amalgamated and the plaque was eventually replaced with the new and saint-less emblem of the new Borough. In his induction address, the new minister said he would concentrate on 'instilling the fundamental principles of our faith' into the younger generation of the town (7).

l to r: Werner Van der Zyl, Laurence Misener, Henry Silverman and Israel Madenberg at the Induction Service

Silverman led the High Holy Day services in 1965 assisted by the now regular annual addition of Alec Belkin. The latter seems to have made more of an impression than the former, earning high praise in the Newsletter: 'This gentleman's beautiful voice seems to improve each year, and it was indeed a joy to listen to his rendering of the traditional tunes, some times breaking into operatic arias' (Newsletter December 1965). The Memorial Service was held in its usual spot in the afternoon, but it was indicated that it would changed in future to be during the morning of *Yom Kippur*. This change then became part of the Maidenhead tradition, with *Yizkor* being immediately after the morning service, rather than, as happens at most other synagogues, just before *Neilah* and the closing prayers.

Silverman's arrival led to various other innovations. For the first time there was a *sukkah* in the synagogue grounds that year, with Willy Frank donating the timber and Frank Burns building it. That, too, became an annual event. Another change was the invitation by Silverman in the Newsletter for parents wishing their children to have tuition for a *barmitzvah* or *batmitzvah* to speak to him. It was the first time the latter had been mentioned, although no one took it up until four years later when Judith Bernie and Amelia Frank took part in a *batmitzvah* ceremony in July 1969 with the former reading the blessings over the *Torah* and the latter reciting the Ten Commandments.

Judith Bernie and Amelia Frank at their batmitzvah ceremony

As well as conducting Friday evening services, Silverman led festive services, such as at *Purim* and the Communal *Seder*. However, his tenure was short-lived for he resigned in November 1966 after several disagreements with members of the Council, especially the chairman Laurie Misener, over his conduct of services. Unfortunately, an ugly situation developed as a result of this. It appears that Silverman - rightly or wrongly - became very resentful of the way he felt he had been treated. According to a solicitor's letter he publicly abused Misener on two occasions in Maidenhead High Street, shouting loudly 'You blackguard, you blackguard' and cursing him (8). He also verbally accosted Murray Bernie. Misener threatened to take legal action if this continued and asked the Assembly of Ministers to intervene. A meeting took place between one of the rabbis and Silverman, as a result of which the latter gave an 'assurance that he would keep away from Misener and would not speak to him or of him'. For his part, Misener was asked to 'ensure that nothing is said or done by himself or by his colleagues which could provoke Rabbi Silverman in any way' (9). The matter seemed to have simmered on for a while, for it was not until a meeting on 18th April 1969 that the synagogue Council was told that the libel action between Silverman and Misener had been settled, and that the costs paid by Rabbi Silverman had been donated by Misener to charity. Despite his resignation from the congregation, Silverman still gave occasional talks about Jewish life and values to local groups and churches. He later moved to Farnham Common to live with his son. He passed away in 1979, while his wife Carrie died in 1985.

With no minister and with Alf Shear now in Hove, Friday evening services were led by Murray Bernie, while special events such as the Communal *Seder* were taken by Belkin. The RSGB responded to pleas for help by sending Rabbi Lionel Blue to take a Friday evening service in May 1968 and then returning several times until illness forced him to stop the following February. His visits, though, did not solve the underlying problem. This became apparent when the Council were given statistics of the attendance at the last six Friday evening services in October and November 1968: four, four, two, eighteen, seven and four with the attendance of eighteen being when Blue had officiated (10). The figures were so dire that it was decided that Council meetings, which had previously been held midweek, should now take place on Friday evening at 7.00 pm, before the 8.30 pm evening service so as to boost attendance. The new measure started the following month and continued throughout 1969. It was also agreed to start monthly services on Sunday mornings as an experiment, led by Belkin. It was hoped this would enable children to participate and encourage parents to come to Friday evening services. An additional attempt to attract more participants was by inviting members of the community in advance to read the *Torah* portion of the week in English at the Friday evening service. However, this was often not taken up by those asked to do so (11).

Another area that experienced high and low points was the Religion School. The announcement in May 1960 that 'there is ample room for more pupils' was intended to sound encouraging but also had a rather desperate tone to it (12). Little immediate progress seems to have been made for by the end of the year there were still only eight children attending (13). However, three years later the number had grown to such an extent that the sole teacher could not manage and so the experiment was tried of having two separate classes, with one on Saturdays from 3.00 - 4.30 pm and one on Sundays from 11.00 am - 12.30 pm. The new arrangement did not continue for long and reverted to Sunday mornings (14). By December 1965, there were thirty children, with a class for the more advanced led by the recently arrived Rabbi Silverman, and one for the very young led jointly by Mrs Silverman and Mrs Marianne Philipps. By the following summer, numbers were thirty-four to forty children, covering an age span of four to thirteen years (15). An Education Committee was started under chairmanship of Robert Goodman to examine the problems of the Religion Classes caused by the fact that 'the number of children attending these is increasing rapidly with the influx of Jewish residents in the area covered by Maidenhead Synagogue' (16). It was a wonderful problem to have and included the need to find adequate teachers, but also to encourage parents to bring their children to services, as well as to ensure that their Jewish identity was maintained after *barmitzvah* age. A new headmaster was found in the form of one of the members, Max Holt, while other teachers were Willy Frank and Alec Belkin. By end of year they had expanded to five teachers and Hugo Schwab agreed to put in folding doors to partition the hall so as to create extra classes (17).

Unfortunately, matters began to deteriorate after a few months. Holt resigned a year later over criticism over the books in use and although Belkin took over as headmaster, there were complaints over poor levels of attendance (18). Council member Michael Wheeler wrote an open letter in the Newsletter expressing regret that only twenty children were attending regularly despite efforts at modernising teaching methods and increasing the number of staff. He appealed to parents to bring their children: 'I feel that our efforts are being wasted by the parents non-co-operation. Don't you think it is your duty as parents to get out of bed on a Sunday morning and bring your children to classes?' It was a plea that was not unique to Maidenhead and could be heard in many other synagogues. Matters did not improve, though, and the resignation of other staff meant that one teacher was catering for the 7-11 age group, despite wide range of abilities and interests within it. There were several reports of dissatisfaction with level of teaching throughout 1968 and 1969, and particularly over the poor standards of Hebrew. As well as the difficulty in obtaining teachers, there was also the fact that few of them had a Reform background and so they were unable to provide the children with a Progressive Jewish education, a problem raised at the RSGB Council meeting of 7th April 1968. More positively, a Youth Club for 14-18 year olds was formed in October 1968, led by the youngsters themselves, nine in total.

There was better news in the area of community communication. A magazine was started in February 1965, edited by Laurie Misener, called 'Maidenhead Synagogue Newsletter' and with the ambitious sub-title: 'The organ of Reform Jewry for Berks, Bucks and Oxon'. It ran very successfully for several editions, with up to twelve pages per issue full of news items, photographs and articles. When Misener had to give up editing it, it was impossible to maintain the high standard and it was replaced by a one-sided news-sheet put together by Robert Goodman. One notable item in the latter occurred in 1969 when an article appeared on the racial prejudice that affected attitudes to local immigrants from India and

Pakistan, and urging the synagogue's female members to assist with an Asian women's group that had been established, such as by giving car lifts, teaching English or helping with knitting. By way of response, the Council itself agreed to donate a sewing machine costing £7 (19).

Children from the Religion School in the sukkah, 1965

As in the previous decade, much of the Council's time was spent on maintaining Studlands. There were constant discussions over cleaning, maintenance of the garden, the best heating system, and supervision or replacement of tenants. A major addition to the garden occurred in November 1968 when Hugo Schwab volunteered to provide bannisters for the verandah so that nobody should fall down and hurt themselves (20).

Another ongoing discussion thoughout the 1960s concerned burial rights. This initially centred around negotiations with West London Synagogue over its burial scheme (21) and attempts to provide cover for all members, not just those who had personally opted into the West London scheme. It culminated in a proposal that would involve an annual charge of ten shillings per family for every family in the community, which should be borne by the synagogue funds and taken out of subscription income (22). This was eventually agreed by Council, but was still dependent on families opting into it (23). However, although this access to the Golders Greeen cemetery was welcomed by some, there were many members who wished to have burial facilities much nearer. This resulted in lengthy talks with local Borough Council about setting up a Jewish cemetery locally, which were led by Laurie Misener. When advice was sought from the RSGB about the attitude of Jewish law to a Jewish cemetery being a section within a municipal one, the Convener of the Reform Beth Din, Rabbi Michael Curtis replied that all that was essential was that 'the ground should be virgin, and that if possible a hedge be planted separating the Jewish sections from that of other denominations' (24).

At the January 1969 Council meeting, Misener reported that the congregation has been offered a plot of land within the Braywick Road municipal cemetery, sufficient to inter four hundred people. The Jewish section would be part of the overall cemetery but distinguished by a small hedge (this was duly planted and only removed in 2012 when space was needed for an extra row of graves). Schwab agreed to donate a stone tablet to mark the entrance. It meant that for the first time, burials in a local Jewish cemetery were now possible in addition to the London options through the different burial schemes to which individual members belonged. The Borough made it clear that the synagogue would not have exclusive rights, but that all Jewish people, whether or not members of the Congregation, could be buried there. The cost of burials would be borne by individual members, and it would be double for those living outside Maidenhead, which was a standard part of the Borough's charging structure. This was to prove a bone of contention in later years, as members of the synagogue who lived outside the area felt they were being discriminated against by the Borough. Many could not understand why membership of the local synagogue did not gain them access to the local cemetery at the local rate, whereas the Borough charged individuals according to their postal address. The absence of any local funeral directors who were able to perform the washing of bodies in the traditional way - *taharah* - was another unresolved issue, and so the community continued to rely on Jewish undertakers in London. The following month the synagogue was invited to join the Jewish Joint Burial Society, which offered a burial scheme of its own and had a cemetery in

Cheshunt but this was declined in favour of the new local arrangement (25).

The RSGB continued to take an interest in Maidenhead's affairs and be supportive. Thus there was a series of lectures on aspects of Judaism arranged by RSGB Congregational Development Committee. The lectures were delivered by rabbis from other congregations, including Henry Goldstein, Michael Goulston, Sonny Herman and Dow Marmur. Another visitor was Rabbi Curtis from the Reform Beth Din, who came to talk to the Council in September 1968 about the movement's policy on mixed-faith marriages. This was in response to a letter by the Honorary Secretary, Robert Goodman requesting information on the Reform stance on the grounds that 'we have a large number of mixed marriages in our congregation. The offspring may/often do wish to be *barmitzvah*/married according to Jewish rites' (26). Subsequent minutes do not mention what transpired, although the lack of a rabbi to arrange conversions for those who so wished meant that there was no local solution at that time. For its part, the synagogue usually sent delegates to RSGB Council meetings and its Annual Conference, with reports back to Council. However, as Misener pointed out in a letter to the movement, most ordinary congregants still did not relate to it: 'the majority of our members are quite unaware of the RSGB; their concern is that they belong to a Reform synagogue' (27). In effect they identified with Maidenhead, which happened to be Reform, rather than identifying with the Reform movement nationally. This was not unique to the congregation and was a common perception elsewhere, and the RSGB leadership often bemoaned the fact that it knew it had thousands of members but they often did not realise to what they belonged.

In terms of the wider affairs of British Jewry, Martin Savitt of the Board of Deputies came to the synagogue in June 1960 to give a talk on Jewish defense and on combatting antisemitism. This had been prompted by some problems in other parts of the country at the beginning of the year, but a Council meeting at the time had discussed the subject and concluded that there were no instances locally (28). Towards the end of the decade, the Council a received letter from the Board of Deputies warning all synagogues to safeguard their premises over the High Holy Days. Willy Frank had taken down the sign outside Studlands advertising the synagogue of his own accord, but other Council members were divided on whether or not this was desirable (29). On the cultural side, the AJA returned with a joint talk by Victor Lucas and Charles Spencer (30).

The impact of Israel was felt in the 1960s in a way that had never happened before. Like so many other congregations, especially Reform ones, Maidenhead had not particularly engaged in Zionist activities.

However, the threat to the existence of the nineteen year old state in June 1967 galvanised the vast majority of Jews and provoked an outpouring of money and practical offers of help. An emergency fund-raising campaign during the Six Day War led to £3,000 being raised from members of the community. This was followed by a film show by the Jewish Palestinian Appeal (JPA, later known the UJIA - United Jewish Israel Appeal) in September 1968.

The end of the decade saw two major changes in the leadership of the community. The June 1968 AGM was a watershed moment with Laurie Misener stepping down after a record eight years as chairman. The Annual Report by the Honorary Secretary paid tribute to his era: 'Until last year we had a heavy mortgage on the premises. Today, thanks to his generosity we have no mortgage and receive an income from two flats which, thanks largely to the generosity of Mr Schwab were converted to self contained units which are let.' In the following March, Israel Madenberg died after several years of poor health, aged 82. He had been a member of the community since its inception in 1940, a past chairman and then president since 1956. In paying tribute to him in the newsletter, Laurie Misener said he had been 'A father to the synagogue, an unofficial title that he alone had been qualified to hold - not because of his age, but for his knowledge of our faith, synagogue ritual and administration'. He had also been active in the Jewish Friendly Society movement, which provided a wide range of welfare and funeral benefits for its members, having joined the Order of Achei B'rith in 1920 and been 'an outstanding worker' ever since. Rabbi Rosenblum returned yet again to conduct the Memorial Service for him, which was held the following month. Misener himself was asked to fill the post of President in view of his many years of service. Sadly he resigned after two years following a series of disagreements, and although he remained in the area until his death, he joined a London synagogue.

Throughout much of the decade the finances of the community were strained, a fact that tended to be reflected in its payment of its dues to the RSGB. The April 1962 RSGB Executive meeting was told that Maidenhead had certain financial difficulties and had not submitted accounts for the previous two years. The assessment was paid in full by June, but questions over payment arose again in 1964. The following year, Misener wrote to the RSGB treasurer, Bernard Davis, saying that the synagogue found it difficult to pay its full assessment to the movement because of a combination of a modest subscription rate and bank loan repayment: 'It is only through the generosity of a few members who, from time to time, make donations that we are able to carry on ...assessments are a drain on our finances... [any increase would mean] that reluctantly we should be compelled to disassociate ourselves with the RSGB' (31). When Raymond Goldman, the General Secretary of the RSGB held a meeting with Misener in 1966 to discuss the issue, the latter reported that £2000 was still outstanding on the mortgage and was absorbing £200 in interest per annum. The accounts presented to the 1967 AGM reveal that income for the year was £2147, with the main sources being £1007 subscriptions, £114 donations and £553 rents. Expenditure had come to a total of £1791, the biggest items being repairs and maintenance, along with payments to teachers and cantor. The result was a surplus of £356 for the year. The accounts also show the start of a Building Replacement fund that year, which amounted to £426. The subscription that year was twelve guineas for a husband and wife, six guineas for a single person.

l to r Two Presidents: Murray Bernie (far left) and Israel Madenberg (foreground with scroll) at Simchat Torah 1966

The actual membership virtually doubled over the decade, going from forty-five households in 1960 (32) to eighty households in 1968, including seventy-nine children under twenty years. Amid the figures there was also a high degree of arrivals and departures, with a Council report in 1968 showing that some twenty families - a quarter of the community - had moved away in the last two years and a similar number had come to fill their places (33). Moreover, the membership covered a wide area, not only scattered throughout Maidenhead - Misener reported that only six lived in the immediate area of the synagogue - but from a wide radius outside the town, including Ascot, Henley and Frimley.

The growth of the community reflected the fact that by the end of 1960 Berkshire was the fastest growing county in England, with annual population increases, and prosperous businesses and industries. Unemployment was virtually unknown: in East Berkshire there were seven vacant jobs to every unemployed person. It had become one of the catchment areas for the flow of population from both Northern England and Greater London. Plans to connect both Windsor and Maidenhead with the M4 - each subsequently completed in 1972 - gave it important access routes. This, plus its proximity to Heathrow, meant it was a highly desirable area, and the result was a lengthening in the wait for housing and school places. Maidenhead in particular was fast expanding: whereas the town's population had been 26,790 in 1948, by 1965 it was 41,230.

One curiosity in this respect was a minute from 2nd November 1960 Council meeting at which 'Membership was fully discussed by the Meeting and it was agreed we would not approach famous people in the District'. There is no indication of what caused this decision, although it might possibly have related to an unsuccessful attempt made by the Council, largely made up of the same individuals, five years earlier to invite comedian and the local resident Bud Flanagan to join the synagogue (34). However, even if it was not interested in chasing celebrities, the Council was keen to attract ordinary members. To this effect an advertisement publicising the synagogue was taken out in the *Maidenhead Advertiser*, with the cost of it appearing fortnightly for a year paid by Schwab (35).

The move was a worthwhile one, as there were many other Jews in the area, some of whom may not have known of the community's existence. There were also those who did know, but chose to have no contact with Jewish life. There were yet others who retained a Jewish involvement but ignored the local community as they were members of London synagogues. A further group was made up of those who lived in London but also had weekend and holiday residencies in the Home Counties. By definition they were reasonably wealthy, and some were extremely so, such as business tycoons Jack Cotton, who lived at Thames Lawn, Marlow from 1945 till his death in 1964, or Charles Clore in his Berkshire estate, Stype Grange. There were also Jews who worked in the area and were well known to local people, but who lived elsewhere. Philip Engelberg, for instance, was born in Berlin in 1923, had come to England via the Kindertransport in March 1939. He later joined the British forces, ending up in the Eighth Army and serving in North Italy and Yugoslavia.

After the war, he lived in North London but he opened a clothing shop for women in Slough and another one in Maidenhead. They were both called Sylvan Fashions, and he commuted from London and back for ten years (36).

The synagogue ended the decade with no president and no rabbi, but with a new chairman for the first time, Bernard Feldstein. However, at a period when the Council should have been pulling together, the opposite seems to have occurred, with meetings being highly contentious. The minutes of the October 1969 Council meeting concluded with a remarkably candid entry under Any Other Business: 'As is sometimes customary, the meeting ended in some disarray with some items being left for a future date, and little positive policy decisions being taken.' That particular meeting had earlier heard threats of resignations over the question of using synagogue money to subsidise presents for the children at the *Hanukah* party, rather than take it from the parents social group. Similar threats –'resignations were offered freely' - were heard at the November Council, this time over the idea of paying for a coach to bring teenagers from London to the synagogue youth club. It was in reaction to such instances of disharmony that the Honorary Secretary, Robert Goodman, proposed a series of measures to reform the way Council operated. These included set duties for each Council member so that everyone had designated tasks allocated to them. He also urged that the Chairman should have the power to ask for the resignation of anyone who did not carry out their responsibilities or who 'consistently loses his temper at meetings'. Presumably there would have been no need to make such a proposal unless these occurrences were a regular feature of Council meetings.

An incident from the decade that is not of historical significance but remained in the memory of some for the next forty years was the behaviour of one member at *Yom Kippur* who normally took the festival very seriously. Because of a medical condition from which he suffered, he was obliged to eat food and told not to fast. However, rather than quietly leave the service and go outside the synagogue to have a sandwich away from the public gaze, he munched his lunch in the corridor in full view of others and loudly explained why he had to eat. From his point of view, it was a way of assuaging his guilt at breaking one of the strictest rules of the day, but for everyone else it was utterly infuriating. Such are the unintentional legacies which individuals contribute to synagogue legends.

1. SR (September 1961)
2. SR (October 1963)
3. Minutes, MSC (March 1960)
4. Minutes, Assembly of Ministers (31 October 1962)
5. SR (May 1965)
6. SR (May 1965)
7. JC (25 June 1965) 22
8. Letter 19 June 1967 from Cameron Kemm Nordon and Co, Solicitors to The Secretary, Ministers Assembly, RSGB
9. Letter 29 June 1967 from Martin Shaw Solicitors to Mr L. Misener
10. Minutes, MSC (November 1968)
11. Minutes, MSC (3 September 1968)
12. SR (May 1960)
13. SR (December 1960)
14. SR (September 1963)
15. Synagogue Newsletter (June/July 1966)
16. Newsletter 7
17. Minutes, MSC (November 1968)
18. Minutes, MSC (October 1969)
19. Minutes, MSC (April 1969)
20. Minutes, MSC (November 1968)
21. Minutes, MSC (February 1960)
22. Minutes, MSC (June 1960)
23. Minutes, MSC (14 August 1963)
24. Letter, 20 September 1968
25. Minutes, MSC (7 February 1969)
26. Minutes, MSC (June 1968)
27. Letter, 7 October 1965
28. Minutes, MSC (27 January 1960)
29. Minutes, MSC (September 1969)
30. SR (July 1960); JC (27 May 1960) 14/15
31. Letter, 7 October 1965
32. Minutes, MSC (February 1960)
33. Minutes, MSC (9 October 1968)
34. Minutes, MSC (5 July 1955)
35. Minutes, MSC (11 September 1963)
36. *Slough & Windsor Observer*, 'The Day We Went To War' (Supplement 1st September 1989) 7

Chapter 12

1970: Preparing for the Future

The beginning of the decade witnessed a series of highly significant developments that altered the character of the community and was to prepare the way for a subsequent leap forward. The 1970 AGM saw a major 'changing of the guard', with long-term stalwarts, such as Misener, Olman and Schwab no longer on Council and the leadership being transferred to a group of much newer and younger members who were to be at the helm of the synagogue for the next decade. Under the chairmanship of Ronald Bernie, they included Gerald Cohen, Jack Rosenbaum, Vivien Sakal, Bobby Salmon and Brian Shieldhouse. Significantly, many of them had children at the Religion School - unlike the 'old guard' - and therefore had a very immediate interest in its success. Unfortunately the 'takeover was to come at the cost of both Misener and Schwab resigning from the synagogue itself. The position of President was left vacant but was filled the following year with the appointment of Murray Bernie in recognition of his long service to the community.

1970 was also memorable as the year that saw the beginning of the student-rabbis. Following repeated requests for ministerial assistance that had failed to materialise in a sustained way, the RSGB began to use senior rabbinic students at the Leo Baeck college to help out for a year at a time, as it did for other congregations without a rabbi. The students would study midweek at the College, and then go to their designated community to lead services at weekends and teach at the Religion School. The first student-rabbi to be appointed to Maidenhead was David Lilienthal from September 1970, who was already familiar with the congregation from teaching at its Religion School. He was succeeded twelve months later by Robert Silverman who stayed for two years. He was followed in September 1973 by Ernst Stein, who also remained for two years, after which Michael Williams took over. Joost Cohen came in 1976, Chaim Wender the next year and then Jonathan Romain in 1978. Willy Wolff replaced him a year later, the last in a line of eight student rabbis before a full-time appointment was made (1). Service attendance improved, with fifteen to twenty people coming to Friday evening services and by the mid-70s Council meetings had returned to their midweek slot. The custom of women lighting the Sabbath candles at the beginning of the service – rather than doing so only at home – was introduced in 1974 and has remained ever since (2).

There were often attempts during this period to hold Sabbath morning services once a month, if not weekly, but they always failed to be maintained owing to poor attendance save on special occasions (3). Moreover, their character sometimes led to questions depending on who was leading it. Thus at one Council meeting: 'Some discussion took place regarding the length of services and certain resemblances to orthodox ones. The student minister agreed that at present it was not a reform service' (4). Other issues that arose were the mode of dress worn at services, with some members concerned at the informal attire that was developing, while others objected to those who smoked after services (5). When students were not present, services were led by members, while one notable occasion – for that period - was a *Shabbat* service taken entirely by women of the community, organised by Jessica Blooman in 1976 (and which she led again seven years later). The practice continued of holding festivals other than the High Holy Days at the nearest weekend, so as to facilitate attendance, rather than on their due date midweek.

A major change in the liturgy took place in 1977 when the RSGB brought out a new edition of the Daily and Sabbath Prayer Book. One of its many innovations was the use of modern English in the translation of the Hebrew prayers, instead of the by-then old fashioned language of the previous edition of 1931, including usage of 'thee' and 'thou' which had long ceased in everyday speech. The Prayer Book also took account of the major changes that had occurred within the Jewish world, including the impact of both the Holocaust and the birth of the State of Israel (6). The cost of switching to the new books was defrayed when one hundred and twenty copies were donated by Jenifer Goldstein in memory of her late husband Jack. Throughout this period, Alec Belkin, both taught at the Religion School and co-officiated at High Holy Day services, providing an invaluable degree of continuity despite the constant ministerial changes. It was also a testimony to his remarkable good-nature that he was able to work harmoniously with so many different (sometimes strong-minded and occasionally idiosyncratic) characters. He was a true 'servant of the community' and earned much respect and affection for it.

A new magazine started in the autumn of 1970, called *Hashomer: The Maidenhead Guardian*. It was the brainchild of Brian Shieldhouse. With glossy pages, a colour cover, professional lay-out and design, with each issue being twenty pages of Jewish articles, film reviews, comment on Israel, letters, photographs and adverts, it had a spectacular impact. It was even put on public sale. Sadly it lasted only two years and its remarkably high standard was not matched again till the next millennium. Its opening editorial displayed a vivacious optimism, claiming that by the twin events of engaging a student minister and producing a magazine

Maidenhead had thrust itself very firmly into the top half of the Reform League. It suggested that they would create an irreversible momentum and declared that (7):

> *Hashomer* has no hesitation in predicting that the next ten years will see a steady migration from North West London to rural areas, and that this will bring about a NEW DIASPORA, a new spirit, and the final abandonment of the theory that it is impossible to live as a Jew except under ghetto conditions.

Subsequent editions showed a healthy openness to controversy, allowing members to express their opinions and be lambasted or lauded by letters in reply. This certainly applied to the topic of Israel, and to what extent Jews should identify with the Jewish state, as well whether there was any need to be worried by antisemitism in Britain. Another fierce debate was over the nature of the Maidenhead community itself, with one correspondent asserting that it was very aloof and unfriendly, and others flatly contradicting him. The final edition had a stirring editorial entitled 'Divided We Stand', which strongly advocated serious consideration of merging with the High Wycombe community. The latter was affiliated to the United Synagogue but had a membership that could be described as 'Orthodox in allegiance but Reform in practice'. As it was a neighbouring congregation with a similar outlook, *Hashomer* asked whether it might be possible to link together, pointing out both the advantages and disadvantages of such a move (8):

> To remain apart is to preserve individuality - to cut down the opportunities of marrying; to call always on the faithful few to arrange the functions and attend to fund raising; to see the same faces. To combine wholly is an EEC dilemma in miniature - to lose individuality; to wrangle over rules and bosses acceptable to all and to water down two faiths and backgrounds to achieve one more variant.

It concluded that neither isolation nor combination were desirable and urged a middle path of great co-operation, such as regularly attending each other's services and working together on children's education. However, no practical steps were taken by either community and nothing resulted from this debate.

A new constitution - 'Laws of Maidenhead Synagogue' - was introduced and formally approved at the 1972 AGM. It defined the object of the synagogue as 'providing and maintaining a synagogue for the purpose of public worship and of advancing religious, educational and charitable activities' (Clause 2). Amongst the religious stipulations was that 'every service shall be formed partly in Hebrew and partly in English' (Clause 3). The definition of who was Jewish and therefore eligible for membership was 'as determined and accepted by the Laws of the RSGB' (Clause 5). This effectively meant anyone whose mother was Jewish or who had converted through a recognised Jewish authority. A crucial change to the management of the synagogue was in Clause 17 which stipulated that 'no Honorary officer shall serve for a consecutive period exceeding two years in the same office'. The clear intention was to prevent any individual dominating one particular position, as had happened previously, and to ensure that the Council was constantly invigorated by new people bringing energy and ideas with them. The AGM was fixed for June each year to prevent the fluctuations that had often occurred in the past.

The year 1970 also brought a double bonus for the Religion School, in that Leo Baeck College student David Lilienthal came on Sunday mornings to teach from the beginning of 1970, while he also helped to train two graduates of the Religion School, Judith Bernie and Amelia Frank, to be teachers themselves. During his six months at Maidenhead he also helped start a library and a parents-teachers group. At the time there were thirty-one children attending classes, which grew to slightly under fifty by 1975, consisting of five classes (9). Finding adequate space for classrooms was a constant problem. With the first and second floor rented out to tenants, the ground floor offered limited room and no way of preventing the noise from one class disturbing another class. A solution attempted in 1971 was to seek planning permission to erect classrooms in the back garden but this was turned down by the local authority (10). The problem was to remain throughout the decade, alongside the paucity of trained teachers, with parents often being brought in to teach even without any previous experience. It meant that there were years when the Council received complaints over 'the children were not learning, lack of discipline and boredom; it is difficult for teachers in making themselves hard above the noise, in handling unruly children and having different ages in one class' (11). It may not have been of any compensation, but similar problems were experienced in many other Religion Schools. The issue of space also affected the High Holy Day services when peak attendance made conditions very cramped. The Council investigated the possibility of holding the services at larger venues, such as Court Gardens in Marlow or Burnham Hall. However, eventually it was decided to solve the problem by holding a children's service at the synagogue prior to the main service. This would not only be more appropriate for the youngsters, but as many went home immediately afterwards with the mothers, that lessened the numbers for the rest of the day (12).

Another venture aimed at the youth was the start of a football club in 1971 for thirteen/fourteeen year olds under the guidance of Willy Frank, with matches against other synagogues or local school teams. He was manager, coach, organiser and occasionally referee if the usual officiant, Gerald Cohen, was not available. A typical team would have featured Ted Bechman, Philip Benjamin, Phil Bernie, Mitchell Coppel, David Frank, Laurence Morris, Chris and Simon Raine, Danny Reuben,

Mark Salmon, Henry Sherman, with Judith Bernie often a substitute and doing as well as any other member. One notable victory was beating North West Surrey 11-1 and matches continued for the next three years (13). There was an attempt to found a Brownie Pack from members of the community, open to girls from seven to eleven years, organised by Joan Sakal. However, there were not sufficient numbers to enable it to proceed.

Summer Fete in the Synagogue's garden, 1970

The year 1971 also witnessed the consecration ceremony of the new Jewish section at Braywick, which was led by David Lilienthal on 16th May. It was a highly significant moment, for in the past it was often the case that when a Jewish community formed, one of the first things it did was to establish a Jewish cemetery locally. This did not happen when the Maidenhead community was established in 1940 as the members saw themselves as Londoners temporarily living elsewhere, and they went back there for any funerals. This mentality remained for several years after the war amongst those who still resided locally. The consecration at Braywick indicated a change of attitude, in that members were here to stay and, quite literally, put down roots. The first funeral was that of Alec Hambury, one of those who had come to the area during the war, who died in February 1972.

When the charges for the cemetery imposed by Maidenhead Borough began to rise considerably, it was decided that the synagogue needed to be part of a burial scheme that gave cover to all members, and not just the few who were part of the West London and other schemes. This was achieved on 1st July 1977 by joining the Jewish Joint Burial Society (JJBS), which not only had a cemetery in Cheshunt, but also offered a burial scheme that, unlike all the others, was not tied to one particular cemetery. It gave members the opportunity either to be buried at Cheshunt, or to be interred elsewhere, such as Braywick, with the JJBS compensating for the equivalent costs. Full cover was offered to members under the age of fifty at the time of joining the scheme, while there was a sliding scale for those over fifty in which the benefits gradually decreased. In order for the synagogue to join the JJBS, the entire membership had to be included, for which an annual per capita charge was made. The result was that henceforth any member of the synagogue had a choice of two cemeteries and automatically received some degree of financial cover depending on their age. The benefits provided by the JJBS also extended to the costs of cremations, with facilities available throughout the area: Amersham, Bracknell, Slough and Reading. A Burial Fund was created by the Council so as to provide for extra expenses or the costs of members without means. This was later named the Israel Madenberg fund in honour of the latter's contribution to the life of the synagogue over many years.

On the social side, there was a new enthusiasm in the organisation of events. Some were 'up-market' Dinner and Dances, such as one held jointly with Middlesex New Synagogue at the Excelsior Hotel, London Airport in March 1972, which was a great success socially and financially with four hundred and thirty people attending, with another at the Esso Hotel, Maidenhead the following year. At the same time the Young Married Group proved very energetic, organising a range of activities, from barbecues to car rallies to discussion groups. It also had joint events with their Reading equivalent, going there for a supper dance and them coming to Maidenhead for a quiz evening. Meanwhile the Ladies Guild was reborn in 1973 and proved very active under leadership of Herta Orchudesh. The end of the decade saw the creation of a new social group called 'Beenagers' - open to anyone no longer a teenager and therefore, it was assumed, a 'has been'. It met in people's homes, rotating around different areas covered by the community.

The first one took place in November 1978 at the home of Andy Curshen in Bray. The initiative partly reflected the personalities in charge of social events and partly indicated a desire to holds events that were low-cost and accessible to all, alongside the more expensive dinners. Youth activities had began to blossom as well, with a Junior Youth Club (nine to thirteen years), Senior Youth Club (fourteen plus), while there was a residential weekend held at the synagogue for those over sixteen, held jointly with others from Bournemouth and North West Surrey Reform synagogues. The Communal *Seder* continued, although in a wide variety of locations, being held at Skindles in 1971 and 1972, before going for three successive years to Ken House Hotel in Amersham, owned by Vivian and Joan Sakal. It then transferred to Pinder Hall, Cookham. Communication of all these events was via *Hadashot*, which started off as a one-sided monthly newsheet and grew to eight pages by the end of the decade under the editorship of Veronica Lansman.

There was a still a Jewish presence in Maidenhead High Street with Warren Cahn having an art and boutique shop, Valerie Feldman a secretarial agency, Martin and Marion Kaye running Curtain Up, and Annie Olman selling ladies underwear. When she retired in 1985, she had been serving in her shop in Queen Street for 45 years continuously. Over in Windsor, Harry Madenberg maintained his fur shop opposite the castle while Susan Barclay ran an employment agency in Peascod Street. However, just as the Jewish community was undergoing a period of transition, so was the town itself - with half of Maidenhead High Street being paved over, a relief road round the centre, shops closing and being replaced by office blocks, along with a new town hall and library being built. For some, it meant that the once sleepy town had at last caught up with those around it and was just like any other bustling modern centre. For others, that was precisely the problem and they felt they no longer recognised their home town, as it had been stripped of its distinctive character. As the local historian, Tom Middleton lamented, 'So fast and complete were the changes that old Maidenhead was practically destroyed' (14). As well as this internal transformation, the town's identity was also affected by external factors. In 1974, the Local Government Act led to major boundaries changes, so that Berkshire gained Slough, Eton, Datchet and Wraysbury but lost Wallingford, Abingdon and Wantage. At the same time, the Borough of Maidenhead and the Royal Borough of New Windsor were joined together as a single entity, becoming the Royal Borough of Windsor and Maidenhead and a population of 133,000.

The synagogue itself was not greatly involved in local community affairs, but various individuals within it did play a role. Ruth Doniger was active in the Maidenhead Community Relations Council founded in 1970, working closely with Shreela Flather, who later became mayor of the town, while Sue Greenberg was secretary of the Wycombe and District Community Relations Council. A request from the Maidenhead CRC for the synagogue hall to be used to celebrate a Muslim festival was considered by the Council but turned down (15). The unease over incidents of antisemitism elsewhere in the country, though not locally, led to a discussion in Council as to whether to remove the 'Maidenhead Synagogue' sign on the wall, but it remained in place (16). Meanwhile Robert Frankl was Mayor of Slough in 1973 after many years as a local councillor. He had the distinction of being both the first Jewish mayor and the first foreign-born mayor of the town. Frankl's background epitomised the convoluted path to Maidenhead of many Jews.

Robert Frankl, Mayor of Slough 1973-74

He had been born in Bohemia in what was to become the western part of Czechoslovakia. He came to England in March 1939 to train in agriculture at the David Eder Farm in Kent, intending to go on to Palestine, but his plans were interrupted by the war. He worked in Oxford for a while as a milkman and then joined the British Army, serving in Italy as part of the 'Jewish Brigade' until 1945 and in India until he was demobbed in 1947. In 1948 he settled in Slough with his wife Charlotte, nee Kellerman, a refugee from Berlin, and worked as a draughtsman. He became a local councillor in 1961, standing for the Labour party. He demonstrated his political independence, though, when he backed the Conservative government's law requiring increases in council house rents in 1973 and was expelled from the Labour party as a result. Nevertheless, he became mayor later that year and was in office during the initial stage of the redevelopment of the town centre, opening major stores such as Tesco, C&A and the Holiday Inn (now the Heathrow/Windsor Marriott). He re-entered politics when the SDP (Social Democratic Party) was founded in 1981 and it then teamed up with the Liberals to form the Alliance. He stood for the Alliance in the local elections, but was not elected. There was the possibility of a Jewish MP for Windsor and Maidenhead - then a joint constituency - when George Kahan (not a local resident) stood as the Liberal candidate in the October 1974 election, but he did not succeed in what had long been a Conservative stronghold.

Another synagogue member who became a civic leader was Ruth Jewell, who had lived in Marlow since the war. She joined the urban council in 1957 and was chairman in both 1963 and 1969. During this period she campaigned vigorously for a swimming pool for the town. When the local Round Table organised a parade of decorated vehicles through Marlow in 1961, the theme of her float was 'We'll get that Pool, or my name's not "Jool"'. Eventually this was achieved and when it opened in 1974, she was the first person to swim a length. She also founded the Marlow Community Association, was active in the Marlow Players and the Town Womens Guild and was a J.P. for twenty-one years, receiving an MBE for her services to the community. Equally notable was Jessica Blooman, who became Chief Probation Officer for Berkshire, the first woman in the country to hold that post. She was also a leading organiser of the Girl Guides Movement. She was honoured in 1981 with an OBE for her work. Also in the public eye was Lewis Moss, who was chairman of Berkshire County Council from 1980-82, having served on it for the previous nine years. He was later made a CBE and was appointed High Sheriff of the Royal County in 1991. Bernard Falk, who resided in Maidenhead in the 1970s and 1980s, was well known as a journalist and television presenter, but he attracted a deluge of complaints in 1986 when he commented on the BBC that Henley Regatta could hardly be an exclusive event since they had admitted a 'little fat Yid'. What most listeners had not realised was that he was referring to himself (17).

Jessica Blooman, with Princess Margaret

A rare foray into international affairs occurred when an appeal was launched following the Pakistan Floods in early 1971, to which the Council send a modest donation. Although some members held that Pakistan's hostility against Israel meant it did not merit help, others felt that humanitarian considerations transcended all others. In most other cases, however, the synagogue took the attitude that it was not empowered to make donations to charitable causes with members' money and left it to individuals to respond privately (18). Thus during the Vietnamese 'Boat people' crisis in 1979, there was an appeal for members to donate funds that would be channelled through the synagogue. This applied equally to Jewish and Israeli charities, although the synagogue might promote them. During the *Yom Kippur* service of 1973, news filtered in that Israel had been attacked in what became the start of the *Yom Kippur* War. In the days following, the chairman, Gerry Cohen, organised an appeal and personally phoned many members, with the result that several thousands pounds were raised. The sombre mood of the community was reflected in a discussion as to whether or not to cancel celebrations at *Simchat Torah*, which followed shortly afterwards, but it was decided that they were sufficiently restrained to be able to go ahead (19).

In one of the few occasions when the synagogue expressed an opinion on national affairs, the chairman, Gerry Cohen, sent a telegram to the Maidenhead MP expressing regret at the government's decision to impose an arms embargo to the Middle East – a decision widely seen as affecting Israel more than the Arab nations. On the domestic front, a new development was that Herta Orchudesh became the first person to represent Maidenhead at the Board of Deputies in 1975. The possibility of having a representative had been discussed two years earlier but never carried out. The hesitation may have been because no one was willing to undertake regular travel to meetings in London, or because of the financial contribution that having a representative involved. The decision to now take such a step was indicative of Maidenhead's awareness of the role it was capable of playing beyond its local horizons. Meanwhile, Jews elsewhere were becoming acquainted with the waters of Maidenhead, thanks to the formation of Sephina, a Jewish Boat Club whose members – largely living in London and Middlesex – often sailed along the Thames, especially the Windsor and Maidenhead stretches (20).

The synagogue's financial situation had improved without the burden of mortgage repayments, while in 1970 the top floor flat was refurbished which brought in a higher income. This helped the synagogue to pay off previously unpaid RSGB assessments. Out of income of £2,204, majority was made up of subscriptions (£1,476 and rents £610). The expenditure amounted to £2,179, with the largest items being teachers pay, although Studlands itself was to cause periodic expenses, including major items such as subsidence at the front of the building, or with the wall at the back, which supported the building, beginning to bulge (21). A caretaker was used to keep the garden in order and the building clean. During most of the 1970s, the synagogue had an annual deficit of expenditure over income of four or five hundred pounds, but had a healthy General Fund that could accommodate such losses. Despite this, Maidenhead was fortunate compared to many other synagogues in having no overdraft and no mortgage. It was also able to rely heavily on the generosity of members for large capitals items. In 1975, for instance, Willy Frank donated the wood panelling that was to grace the synagogue hall for many years.

Amid the many successes in communal organisation, there were also occasional hiccups: a brief Council minute to the effect that *Yizkor* on *Yom Kippur* 'should not be said before the announced time' suggests that this did in fact happen and annoyed members who arrived at the due time to find that they had missed it (22). It seems there was dissatisfaction with the synagogue as a venue amongst some parents, as it was stipulated that 'all *barmitzvahs* should take place in the synagogue (and not private houses)' (23). Another Council minute indicates a co-ordination problem: 'It was suggested that someone should be aware of both religious and *barmitzvah* dates, as one *barmitzvah* was originally arranged for *Yom Kippur*!' (24). At one particular *barmitzvah*, there was a problem as to the standard of *kashrut* of the *kiddush*. The strong suspicion was not that the food was not labeled as *kosher*, but that it was of a type that could never be labelled as *kosher* (25). Meanwhile, a note from the Treasurer in late 1977, which seemed innocuous enough then, would have provoked raised eyebrows today: writing to a new member, he asked the person not only to send his subscription but also 'your full Christian name.'

An unexpected problem arose in August 1978 when the synagogue was asked by the Commercial Road *Talmud Torah*, situated in the East End of London, to return the two Scrolls of the Law that they had loaned Maidenhead more than twenty years earlier. It was amalgamating with another institution and now needed the scrolls for its own purposes, reqesting them to be returned after *Simchat Torah*. Writing to the RSGB for help, the chairman Robert Goodman, expressed his 'shock' at the news: 'The two scrolls have been in use by our congregation for more than twenty years. We fondly imagined that we would have their use until such times as we no longer required them' (26). An appeal was launched to purchase new scrolls, and eventually £3,000 was raised from the community. Jonathan Romain was the student rabbi at the time and helped obtain a scroll from the collection of Czech scrolls that were being cared for by Westminster Synagogue. The scrolls - 1,564 in all - had been taken by the Nazis as they rounded up the Czech Jews and sent them off to the concentration camps. The synagogues were destroyed or turned to other uses, the books burnt and the silver ornaments taken away.

Amid the tale of death and destruction, it is surprising that the scrolls themselves were meticulously collected and taken to Prague for storage. Each scroll was carefully numbered and its origin noted. It is not clear who organised the operation. It was originally assumed that it was the Nazis, who intended the scrolls to be a monument to a 'dead civilisation' after the war. However, it is now thought that it was a rescue mission conducted by Jewish curators keen to preserve the holy texts. Either way, they were kept in a disused synagogue in Prague and remained there undisturbed for almost twenty years. In 1964 they were brought to England and housed at Westminster Synagogue by the Czech Scrolls Memorial Trust. Those that were too damaged to be used were distributed to both Jewish and non-Jewish centres to be kept as a memorial to Czech Jewry. Those that were in fit condition, or could be repaired, were given on permanent loan to congregations who needed them, both in Britain and abroad. The scroll allocated to Maidenhead was from the town of Kojetin, situated in central Moravia, whose Jewish community dated back to at least 1562. Its synagogue had undergone renovations in order to cater for the expanding number of Jews living there, which grew to five hundred in the eighteenth century. The number declined thereafter as Jews moved to larger cities but was sufficient to still maintain a synagogue and communal life until the Second World War. This came to an abrupt end in 1942 when the entire community of fifty-eight individuals was deported to extermination camps and the synagogue was used as a stable. After the war it became a Hussite church. Four other scrolls from Kojetin were also redistributed and went to the United States: B'nai Jacob Congregation, Chicago, Illinois; Congregation Beth Am, Wheeling, Illinois; Temple Bat Yam, Fort Lauderdale, Florida; Temple Menorah-Knesset Chai, Philadelphia, Pennsylvania.

A second scroll was bought that was in a better physical condition but had a less dramatic history, having originated in Manchester some fifty years earlier. It was donated to the synagogue by Jenifer Goldstein in memory of her late husband Jack. In the interim period between returning the *Talmud Torah* scrolls and obtaining the new ones, a scroll was loaned to the community by Hendon Reform Synagogue. On 16th April 1979 there was a service of consecration for the new arrivals. 150 members attended and the guests included the Mayor of Maidenhead, Councillor Neville White. In his sermon, Jonathan Romain said that by giving a new lease of life to the scrolls, it would be 'both a memory and an affirmation, recalling past tragedies in Jewish history yet also being a resounding refutation to the forces that led to such events'. As it happened, a second Czech scroll was to find its way to Berkshire two years later, when it was donated to the Royal Library at Windsor Castle.

Following the AGM in December 1978 the new Council under the leadership of Robert Goodman set itself three ambitious objectives for the year ahead (27):

1. To increase the membership of the synagogue by 30% this year

2. To increase the number of synagogue activities undertaken, and the number of members participating and organising such activities

3. To hold monthly Sabbath morning services

If we succeed we shall be in a position to engage a full-time Minister to serve the Congregation in 1980

It had long been the aim of the synagogue leadership to have a full-time minister. They had been well served by those sent by the Leo Baeck College but the succession of different student rabbis meant that long-term planning was impossible. Some members were happy to maintain the status quo, but others felt that 'standing still' was not an option and the only way for the community to advance was by having a permanent rabbi. In fact, by 1976 Maidenhead was the only Reform synagogue apart from Harlow to be without one. A major stumbling block, though, was the lack of funds. Raising subscriptions a little would not produce sufficient income and raising them to a high level would involve loss of membership. It had been suggested in 1973 that the membership would need to rise to 130 families before employing a minister was a financially viable proposition. The community did experience occasional increases during the decade, but it never exceeded 100 households at any point.

The solution arrived thanks to the property market. The rear garden was some 250 feet in length and often so overgrown that much of it was unusable. The synagogue Council was therefore amenable to approaches made by local developer to sell part of it in 1973. However, the offer was withdrawn owing to the difficult economic situation at the time. At the beginning of 1979, another offer was made and part of the land at the furthest end of the garden was bought from the synagogue by developers for £24,000. They used this, along with the gardens of neighbouring houses to build a new road - Underhill Close - and several new houses. The synagogue now had the money to fund a rabbi. In June 1979 the chairman, Robert Goodman, wrote in *Hadashot* that 'A proposal has been made that the time has come for Maidenhead Synagogue to have a permanent minister. There are diverse opinions as to the benefit of this action, and as to whether we can truly afford it'. He invited comments from members, as well as offers to help fund such an appointment 'over three years'. He himself was a key advocate of such a move, but he also warned that subscriptions would need to be raised.

The matter was debated at the AGM that November. Concern was raised over the financial burden such an appointment would entail, although it was also argued that it would be an investment that would pay for itself because of the new members that would be attracted. It was agreed that the candidates be told that the state of synagogue funds as they currently stood meant that the post could not be guaranteed for more than three years and that it would not necessarily be renewed after that. The motion to seek a permanent rabbi was then put and carried almost unanimously, with only one objection.

1. Micha Konig had initially been appointed as the next student rabbi, but only took a few services before ill-health forced him to give up
2. Minutes, MSC (20 March 1974)
3. RSGB Conference report (1974 & 1975)
4. Minutes, MSC (18 October 1973)
5. Minutes, MSC (15 May 1974)
6. For an analysis of its many other features, see Kershen & Romain (1995) 227-232.
7. *Hashomer* (Winter 1970) 3
8. *Hashomer* (Autumn 1972) 3
9. RSGB Conference report 1975
10. Minutes, MSC (20 December 1971, 6 April 1972)
11. Minutes, MSC (15 May 1974)
12. Minutes, MSC (24 January, 11 May 1972)
13. Minutes, MSC (20 December 1972)
14. Middleton (1975) 128
15. Minutes, MSC (17 July 1974)
16. Minutes, MSC (16 June 1976)
17. JC (11 July 1986)
18. *Hashomer* 2
19. Minutes, MSC (18 October 1973)
20. JC (25 November 1977)
21. Minutes, MSC (20 March 1974, November 1978)
22. Minutes, MSC (21 May 1972)
23. Minutes, MSC (18 October 1973)
24. Minutes, MSC (19 July 1973)
25. Minutes, MSC (19 June 1974)
26. Letter to Raymond Goldman, 29 August 1978
27. *Hadashot* (February 1979)

Chapter 13

1980: A Full-time Rabbi

<u>Religious life</u>

The appointment of the synagogue's first full-time rabbi was to prove a turning point in its development. At that time, the membership stood at 80 households and used only the ground floor of Studlands. A decade later, the membership had quintupled, all three floors were in use and Studlands itself has been rebuilt to accommodate the multiple activities of the community.

The decision to employ a rabbi had been taken immediately after Jonathan Romain had completed his year with the community as its student rabbi. At that time he was in his final year at the Leo Baeck College, serving Barkingside Synagogue as its student rabbi and about to seek a permanent post. It was a happy coincidence, and led to Maidenhead offering him the position. He started on 1st September 1980 on the understanding that the synagogue only had sufficient funds for a three year appointment, although it turned out that he was still there three decades later. The formal induction service took place after a few weeks, with Rabbi Hugo Gryn, Senior Minister of the West London Synagogue, officiating. That autumn also marked another landmark occasion, the twenty-fifth anniversary of Alec Belkin's arrival. At the end of the *Yom Kippur* service, he was presented with a silver *etrog* holder as a token of the synagogue's appreciation for his long and affable association with the community, and which was to continue for many years further. The service itself had also epitomised the successful transition that was taking place, with the young Reform rabbi and older Orthodox-trained chazzan, both leading the prayers on the *bimah* together. It could have been a recipe for intense rivalry and ended in disaster, but proved to be the start of a harmonious partnership that both enjoyed and that satisfied the wide span of traditional and modernising elements within the congregation.

The most immediately obvious impact of having a full-time rabbi was the start of regular Sabbath morning services. Attendance in the first few months was sparse – varying from four to eleven people - but it was appreciated by those who came, while it was an important statement that Maidenhead was now able to offer full-time Judaism in a way that had not been possible before. As with the Friday evening services, there was always a *kiddush* afterwards, with the social element as important as the religious one. An innovation that helped increase attendance at services was sending out reminders of special dates in a person's life and inviting them to participate in the service that *Shabbat*. However, whereas many synagogues did this for *yartzeits,* Maidenhead did so also for birthdays and wedding anniversaries. It was the brainchild of Ian Scott, who established it in 1981 and wrote the letters for the next four years. It was then handed over to Sheila Veniar who, remarkably, has continued with it ever since then, despite the growth in the community meaning that the numbers of letters has increased correspondingly.

The letters proved a great success, bringing people to synagogue to read a prayer or perform a *mitzvah* when they might otherwise not have done so. Even those who do not take up the invitation to attend, still appreciate the fact that the synagogue remembers their birthday and, as one member put, 'doesn't just contact me only when they want a donation like my previous *shul* did'. A discernible trend in the practice of members themselves was that an increasing number opted to observe the *yartzeit* (remembrance) of relatives not, as was traditional, by the Hebrew date on which they had died, but the English date. This was because most of them had little knowledge of the Hebrew calendar, and so, for instance, losing someone on 9th Tammuz meant little to them, whereas the English equivalent of 25th June would always remain in their minds.

There was a pattern for the first Friday of each month to be a Family Service, held at an earlier time - 7.30pm rather than 8.30pm - and geared towards the younger age group. The third Friday of each month was designated an *oneg*, at which the rabbi led a discussion on a topical issue rather than give a formal sermon. It was billed as 'the congregation's chance to answer back'. The balance between prayers read in English and Hebrew on Friday evenings was roughly half each and with the service lasting 45 minutes. Saturday mornings service saw a similar ratio, while the service was longer – an hour and a quarter – although much shorter than those at most other Reform synagogues. This was due to a combination of factors: the rabbi tended to conduct it at a fast pace; there was only one call-up to the reading of the *Torah*; the lack of a choir except at a *bar/batmitzvah*. Within services, it became increasingly common for those having an *aliyah* to be called up by both their father's and mother's name, instead of just the former. Dress code gradually became more informal. With regard to ritual dress there were some women who chose to wear a *kippah* and *tallit*, but their numbers remained low, while it was noticeable that it was not the younger generation that were the more adventurous in this respect.

Another major change concerned the morning services for festivals, which had often not been held in the past if they fell midweek, but which now took place on the due date even if only a handful of people were present. In addition a variety of new activities connected with the festivals were introduced. The 1980 *Rosh Hashannah* witnessed the first communal *tashlich* - the ancient ceremony of symbolically throwing one's sins into free-flowing water. Elsewhere in the country it tended to be kept up only in very Orthodox circles, albeit as a family event rather than a communal one. However, with Maidenhead having the mighty Thames running through its midst, it was both an opportunity not to be missed and a sociable way of bringing members together. It took place at Abney Thatch, the home in Bourne End of Ian and Tanya Scott, whose garden backed onto the river. The well-attended afternoon consisted of three consecutive parts: throwing crumbs into the river to represent casting away the faults of the previous year; an informal study-cum-discussion group for adults whilst children played on the lawn; tea and cakes for all. It was a pattern that was to become an annual event at the Scotts for the next four years and then, after they moved house, at a variety of other homes of members who had river-fronting gardens, be it in Cookham, Bray or Maidenhead itself. Another High Holy Day innovation was having a communal breakfast at the end of *Yom Kippur*. It meant that members who lived far away did not have to elongate their fast, while it also offered an opportunity for everyone to socialise rather than rush off to their homes. It, too, has continued since then.

Members gather by the Thames for Tashlich

Another regular event that developed that year was the '*Sukkah* Crawl', whereby three members would each build a *sukkah* in their garden. Other members of the community would visit them in turn on the Sunday afternoon during *Sukkot*, with an educational activity and refreshments taking place at each one. That December, saw the start of yet another institution in the Maidenhead calendar, the Latke Party held at Rabbi Romain's house, when he would fry fresh latkes made from his own special recipe and up to a hundred people would attend. There was, however, always a 'price to pay' in the form of an educational quiz in the midst of the feasting. A similar mix of food and learning began the following May with the first Cheesecake Study Group after the *Erev Shavuot* service. Members were encouraged to bring a cheesecake, the festive fare, slices of which were exchanged with those of other people's cakes during the study group that took place after the service.

More controversial – although not in Maidenhead itself – was the decision not to have a separate commemoration for the victims of the Holocaust on *Yom HaShoah*, as most other Reform synagogues did, but to mark it alongside other tragedies in Jewish history at *Tishah B'Av*. This was partly to give a more contemporary relevance to the Fast of *Av*, as the destruction of the First and Second Temple two thousand years ago, or the massacres by Crusaders and Cossacks, had little meaning for most Berkshire Jews. It was also a matter of seeing the Holocaust, terrible as it was, as not unique but the latest in a long line of tragedies, each of which were devastating for those involved at the time. The *Tishah B'Av* service therefore began with the lighting of six candles in memory of the six million Jews who died in the Holocaust. A special candelabra was subsequently designed for this purpose by Harry Philipps, himself a refugee from Germany. The funding was taken from a bequest to the synagogue by Tom and Margit Sanders, who had also been refugees. From 2002, it became customary each year for a member of the synagogue who originated from Europe to speak of their experiences during the war years, with the first being Margaret Pordes.

As a generalisation for the 1970s and 80s, the further to the right a synagogue was on the religious spectrum, the more the gusto with which it celebrated *Purim* services, with ultra-Orthodox ones throwing off all inhibitions and Liberal ones barely bothering with it. Despite being a Reform congregation midway between these extremes, Maidenhead took the festival very seriously. This was particularly the case in the early 1980s when Laurie Tytel was teaching at the Religion School. Weeks of script-writing and practice went into producing *Purim* plays and such was the attendance that Bray Village Hall was hired for performances. Thereafter attention turned to the service itself and whereas for many years the tradition had been only for children to attend in fancy dress, adults were encouraged to do likewise. This became adopted so enthusiastically that by the 1990s it was the one or two individuals in ordinary clothes who stood out amongst the hundred or so more dressed more colourfully. Meanwhile, the Communal *Seder* continued to thrive at the Pinder Hall under Harry and Ruby Pitch, who organised it for twelve consecutive years, with some years being so oversubscribed that an overflow *seder* was held at the synagogue, with Rabbi Romain leading one and Alec Belkin the other. Other religious innovations were a Children's Service on the first Friday of every month, while a Junior Service for 5-8 year olds on the third Saturday of every month was introduced later on.

The Holocaust Candelabra lit at Tishah B'Av

The problem of accommodating the growing community was particularly evident at the High Holy Days. Within a year of the rabbi's appointment, the congregation was too large to be housed at Studlands and for the next three years services were held at the Riviera Hotel, Bridge Road, where the general manager, Ashley Corne was a member of the community and where the then ballroom accommodated the entire congregation. For many members, it had the added advantage of being alongside the river and offered a scenic view during services. The only disadvantage was that the ballroom backed onto the kitchen and led to some tempting smells wafting through during *Yom Kippur* when guests elsewhere in the hotel were being served. When in 1984 the Riviera underwent a major refurbishment that totally altered its shape, services were transferred to the Scout Hall situated in the grounds of Altwood School, where they remained for the next six years. A point of note there was that giant logs were stored in racks suspended under the roof and directly above the congregation, which appeared to some as if divine judgement was hovering over worshippers and lent an added urgency to the prayers.

The opposite problem applied to Seventh Day *Pesach* Services, in that attendance was very low, rarely more than a handful. This was partly because it had not been observed in previous decades and therefore lacked a tradition of attendance; it was also a problem inherent to the day itself in that many people reckoned that they had already 'done *Pesach*', while the fact that it ended the festival, rather than initiated it, meant that it was felt to lack importance. In an attempt to encourage numbers, in 1988 the *Erev* Seventh Day *Pesach* was relaunched as an 'Experimental Service': the service was held sitting in the round, with music and readings on the theme of Freedom. It proved successful and the pattern continued annually, with a different theme each year. Meanwhile, the desire for greater study of the weekly portion led to the birth of the '*Torah* Breakfast' in 1987, whereby a group of between five to twelve members would gather together at 9.15 am on the first Saturday of each month to study the relevant verses. A Sabbath morning crèche started a few months later, initiated by Cherrie Creager, for those who wanted to bring young children to the service but needed somewhere to deposit them when they became over-fidgety and disruptive.

That same year there were calls to improve the singing at Sabbath services and Jan Goodman established a choir which improved existing melodies and introduced new ones. Inevitably there were both positive and negative reactions. One member wrote to *Hadashot* to complain that (1):

> One used to be able to come to a service and know that, if nothing else, one would know the tunes, be able to join in and feel included; now it seems that we have expressions in sound unknown to all but the initiated; gone are the traditional tunes only to be replaced by those which make me feel like 'alien corn'.

The following month came a flurry of letters defending the changes and arguing for a variety of tunes to satisfy both the traditionalists and those preferring modernisation. Over the years, the same opposing arguments were to be aired regularly. The choir itself went through periods of dips and strength, depending on who was leading it. Initially it was present only on Friday evenings, with the Saturday morning attendees being more familiar with the service and able to produce a more melodious sound. Whenever there was a *bar/batmitzvah*, when there was often a large 'away crowd' who did not necessarily join in, Alec Belkin – who had usually tutored the child – was present and led the singing.

Female involvement in services was relatively modest, with many women happy to attend, but either feeling uncomfortable accepting any of the more important *mitzvot* (such as reading the blessings over the *Torah* and *Haftarah*) or reckoning that their Hebrew was too poor to do so. A Sabbath morning service was taken by a group of women in July 1983 in order to prove their ability to be equal in practice as well as in theory. Amongst the individual pioneers were Pearl Berman who was one of the first to wear a *tallit* (setting an example to younger women at a time when she was already a senior citizen) and Ruth Milton who regularly performed the act of raising the scroll (*hagbahah*), and showed others how easily it could be done. It was also extremely rare for a girl to have a *batmitzvah* and it took some time to persuade both them and their parents that it should be as natural for girls to read from the scrolls as it was for boys.

The first to do so was Ruth North in June 1982, and even though it became increasingly common, there were many girls who simply stopped Hebrew classes before they reached the age of thirteen and having a *batmitzvah* did not become automatic until the end of the decade. This reticence had nothing to do with ability and everything to do with assumptions. The new trend had the effect of galvanising a number of adult women, who had never had the chance of a *batmitzvah* because they had belonged to an Orthodox synagogue in their youth. They now took up the challenge. The first was Jan Goodman in July 1986 and she was followed by many others, including those who had converted to Judaism and so had not been part of a Jewish community when they were thirteen years old. There were also some men who decided to have a 'second *barmitzvah*' on a significant anniversary of their original one, the first of which was Harry Philipps who recited in November 1985 the portion he had had read fifty years earlier in Berlin.

Another consequence of the rabbinic appointment was the start of regular Adult Education classes. These took place on Monday evenings, with the first half devoted to languages and the second half to wider

Jewish themes. The former consisted of different levels of Hebrew reading, with classes for beginners (however old those beginners might be) and also for those who wanted to improve their fluency and comprehension. There were Ivrit classes for those who wished to speak colloquial Hebrew. For several years in the mid 1980s, classes in Yiddish were offered by Len Brown. In the second half, different themes were tackled each year, such as Jewish History, the 613 Commandments or Talmudic texts. These were led by the rabbi, although additional classes were provided in the late 1990s by Robert Goodman. The first decade attracted astonishingly high attendances, for instance forty-four people in 1985, perhaps due to the lack of such options beforehand, although in subsequent periods, numbers fell despite the overall membership increase.

Some of the classes were 'exported' locally, with Rabbi Romain teaching ones on Jewish festivals and the cycle of life at Bracknell College of Further Education from 1984-87. Although they were aimed at the wider community, they also attracted some Jews who were not members of the synagogue and who, through the courses, were brought into communal life. Another development in the field of education was the establishment of a Jewish Library. It had been much talked about as a desirability, but eventually came to fruition in autumn 1987 when David Cooper donated funds for shelving and the purchase of books. Harry Philipps became the first librarian and set up a catalogue system. Eighteen months later, a Children's Section was donated in memory of Michael Veniar.

One of the rabbi's aims was to make the synagogue as self-sufficient Jewishly as possible. A small Judaica Shop was established in December 1980 by Isabel Street. It sought to provide Jewish artefacts that were not available locally, selling articles such as New Year cards, *mezuzah* cases, *seder* plates and *Hannukkah* candelabras. Food was another issue. The absence of any shop selling *kosher* products had long been a cause for regret, but was simply a matter of market forces and the paucity of Jewish customers in the area. The growth of the synagogue spurred Ian Scott to approach local supermarkets to see if they would consider having a '*kosher* counter' at which such products could be available. When this met with no success, it was decided instead that the synagogue itself would set up a shop, albeit purely to serve its own members. In September 1982 'Momma's *Kosher* Kitchen' was established. It stocked a variety of frozen *kosher* items bought wholesale from London butchers and was run by Marie Sarner and Pat Elderton. The large freezer was initially situated in the kitchen until an expanding clientele meant that it required a room of its own and it was transferred upstairs. It quickly became a key part of synagogue life, not only supplying the needs of those who kept *kosher* but also catering for the larger number who did not do so, but who still liked *kosher* foods, such as beigels, latkes, viennas and schnitzel. It was also able to supply the special foods for Passover - from *matza* to cinnamon balls – that were in demand from members who did not use its services the rest of the year. It was open on Sunday mornings and attracted many who might not otherwise have come to Studlands so often. There were occasional attempts to arrange delivery of fresh *kosher* meat (2), but there was not sufficient demand for it to become a regular service.

Pat Elderton & Marie Sarner (right) serving customers including Leslie & Manon Bernstein, & Estelle Phillips at Momma's Kosher Kitchen

Social and cultural developments

On the social front, Beenagers – informal social evenings - continued to operate in people's houses, with venues deliberately chosen from different areas in which members lived so as to make them as accessible as possible. By 1987, though, the expansion of the community, coupled with the enormous dispersion of members across several counties, meant that there was a danger of people who did not attend events at the synagogue very often feeling 'cut off' and 'out of touch'. It became clear that a more institutionalised approach was needed, and so the concept of 'Networks' was born, spear-headed by Suri Poulos. Each of the major areas in which members were living had its own Network group set up, which arranged meetings in local homes on an occasional basis. The nature of their activities varied from area to area: some held purely social meetings, such as coffee evenings, whereas others organised debates or walks. A few also held quasi-religious events, be it a Friday evening supper or *Lag B'Omer* picnic. Initially each Network had both a Social Co-ordinator, who arranged the meetings, and a Welfare Co-ordinator, whose remit was to organise lifts for anyone needing transport or shopping for those unwell. However, the welfare side quickly evaporated and Networks developed purely as a social vehicle, providing a valuable local supplement to central activities. They served both as a way of linking up families who were living near to each other but might otherwise never have met, and as a means of involving members who found the distance from Maidenhead too far for regular attendance.

The first Network area was set up in Henley/Wargrave as a pilot project, and following its success, subsequent ones were: Bourne End/Cookham, High Wycombe, Marlow, Beaconsfield/Gerrards Cross, Slough/Farnham (initially known as The Beeches), Windsor/Ascot, Bracknell/Wokingham, and Camberley. There were so many households in Reading that the Network was divided into two areas – North-West and South-East – whilst Maidenhead, which had the largest numbers of members, was initially divided into three separate groups. Over the years, different Networks proved prospered and faltered, depending on who was leading them at the time or on the size and nature of the local catchment. There were also amalgamations of adjoining groups – such as Marlow and Bourne End. A specific post of Network Co-ordinator was created on the synagogue Council to monitor their overall progress and to assist the local co-ordinators.

Another important innovation that then became a familiar institution was the Welcome Mat – a midweek daytime club that was open to everyone, but primarily catered for those who were retired. It was launched in November 1981 by Marianne Philipps and was held fortnightly around mid-day on Wednesdays. It quickly became very popular, providing lunch, with some members then happy just to chat, others preferring games such as scrabble, and some setting up card tables. After organising it for six years, Marianne handed over guidance to Barbara Rosenberg in 1987. For some of those attending, it was their main social contact with other people and a vital lifeline to the outside world. Over time, not only have the numbers increased but so has the average age of participants, with several celebrating birthdays in their 80s and 90s at Welcome Mat. The team of helpers running it are also assisted by other members who provide lifts for those without transport. The range of daytime activities was supplemented in March 1988 by the Social and Cultural Society, aimed at 'the active retired', and which met on the first Thursday of every month to listen to a speaker followed by discussion and tea. The group was started by Vivienne Davis, along with Kenneth Doff, Maurice and Renee Cooper, Dennis and Anne Leapman. Talks during the first three months covered diverse subjects such as memories of Jewish life in the East End, a personal perspective of the police force and how to avoid the medical pitfalls of retirement. The group continued for twelve years, at which point falling attendances meant it was difficult guaranteeing a respectable audience for speakers.

A variety of other groups arose that were targeted at specific ages or interests: a Young Marrieds group was born in February 1983, although despite an initial meeting that was well-attended, it failed to last very long. Another attempt was made 1987 for newly weds, which met the same fate. One reason may have been that that once couples bonded with each other, they then made their own independent social arrangements and stopped attending the group events. As an organised activity, therefore, it failed, although it did lead to several friendships being formed. Another venture was M.R.S., which stood for Maidenhead Reform Synagogue (even though the word 'Reform' was not part of the synagogue's official title). It was chosen, though, as an appropriate title for a group aimed at women 'who wished to met together to talk about things other than the price of Persil...from "Why are women drinking more?" to TV programmes you love and hate' (3). It was the brainchild of Frances Lewis and led to a series of monthly meetings with discussions that ranged from private education to mixed-faith marriages. The group lasted a year, after which it found its initial momentum hard to sustain and gently faded away.

One of the problems that the group faced - along with many other women's organisations in society at large - was that a growing number of women were no longer 'housewives' with a certain amount of free time for social and welfare activities outside their domestic tasks. Instead, many were working part-time or full-time, some with child-care arrangements in place, and so the time available for voluntary activities was severely truncated. It was for this same reason that the Ladies Guild that had been so successful in previous decades collapsed in the 1980s. Herta Orchudesh tried to restart it in 1983 under the rebranded title of the Women's Guild, but found it impossible to do so. Perhaps it also reflected that fact that in previous times women did not play an active role in religious services, while the synagogue leadership was almost exclusively male, and so they had their outlet in the Ladies Guild. Now, however, women were as involved in all aspects of communal life as men, and no longer needed their own separate preserve. At the AGM that year, for instance, not only was a female elected as Vice-Chairman for the first time - Josette Clift - but Freda Lambourne became the Warden, responsible for the oversight of all religious activities.

The Synagogue's First XI
l to r: Jonathan Romain, Ron Newman, Julian Marks, Darrel Poulos, Braham Fredman, Adam Brookman, Daniel Brookman, Ivor Delman, Stephen Sommer, Michael James, Roger Rosenberg

The synagogue took the attitude that whatever Jews did, they should be able to do via the synagogue and therefore tried to offer wide range of social and cultural interests. It was also willing to back ideas proposed by members on the basis that if other members came along and supported it, then the event would succeed, but if no one was interested, then nothing was lost. Such projects included periodic successes such as the Bridge Club, which was launched in 1984 and then experienced a series of lapses and revivals in subsequent years, but is currently going strong. Similarly, a Music Group started, ran for a while, came to an end, and was then re-launched in a different format some years later. A horse-riding group was proposed but never succeeded, whereas a Cricket team did attract interest. It began under the captaincy of Braham Fredman in 1985 and continued for the next nine years, playing other synagogue teams. A report in *Hadashot* captured the enthusiasm it generated (4):

> After last year's humiliating defeat by Bushey Synagogue, the Maidenhead Synagogue Cricket Team set the tone in this year's

match taking a wicket with the very first ball of the game (ably bowled by Mike James). Although hampered by the absence of captain Braham Fredman, the team were in good form and Stephen Sommer took the helm. Wickets fell fast owing to excellent fielding, with good catches by Barry Walsh and Ivor Delman in particular and careful wicket-keeping by Stephen. Brian Pollock's bowling saw the fall of another three wickets and Julian Marks took two more. Bushey were all out for a mere 115. The Maidenhead batsmen struck out well, with Ivor and Stephen leading the scorers, and with good support from David Levene and Michael Warren. Their efforts, along with Adam Brookman, Jonathan Romain and Roger Rosenberg, took the toal to 87. The match was lost, but with honour, and next time…

Another sporting venture was rowing: when the Cookham Regatta was re-established in 1989, Rabbi Romain proposed that one of the races be 'the Clerics Challenge' – a contest between coxed four-man rowing boats from different religious groups, with each one led by their minister. The synagogue participated annually during the ten years in which the race was held and was rewarded with victory in 1994.

Another innovation was a series of social evenings targeted at particular nationalities. It started in 1987 with a gathering for South African families in the community at the home of Roger and Barbara Rosenberg, and was intermittently repeated, as were those held for Israeli families. A Thanksgiving Evening for American families began in 1994 at the home of Ian and Sandy Davis, complete with a *kosher* turkey. It has remained an annual event ever since. These were the three largest contingents of members born overseas, although the character of the area – with many computer and other 'high tec' firms located in it, as well as being near to Heathrow – attracted members from all parts of the globe. A get-together for students in the community at the rabbi's house started in 1985 during the winter vacation and became an annual event. There were also groups for 'young singles', as well as those unattached in their forties and fifties. Neither group proved long-lasting, although 'Fifth Friday' dinners did become more regular, which were held at the rabbi's house for those in their twenties and thirties every time there was fifth Friday in a month. Other social activities were geared to the community as a whole, ranging from riverboat trips to barn dances.

The Synagogue rowers power ahead
l to r: Jenny Gow, Mike Moher, David Lewis, Jon Berman, Jonathan Romain

There was never a regular Drama Group, but a one-off show took place that involved the talents of many members, including those who did not necessarily participate in other aspects of synagogue life. It took place in 1986 when the Town Hall was hired for a production of 'My Son the Rockstar' - subtitled 'A trivial pursuit through the music of the Fifties and Sixties' - featuring a variety of songs, sketches and magic. It was produced under the overall supervision of Mike James, with Ron Goldsmith being in charge of music. More dramatic for others were the difficult economic circumstances at the time. Towards the end of the decade, a 'Job Spot' column appeared in *Hadashot* both for those looking for work and for those seeking to fill vacancies. Over the years, a number of matches were made that proved mutually beneficial. Another one of the effects of the galvanised internal life of the community was a desire to have greater contact with Jewish life elsewhere. It started in 1981 with the rabbi hiring a mini-bus and driving a dozen members to Manchester for a guided history tour of the Jewish life there and also to see the art treasures from Prague Jewish Museum that were on temporary exhibition at the Whitworth Art Gallery.

The next generation

If the adult activities multiplied, so did those for children. A weekly Mothers and Toddlers group began in January 1981 led by Jannette Marlow. It has continued ever since, organised by succeeding generations of 'new mums', and has provided a place both to socialise and to discuss issues facing Jewish parents, from home ceremonies to school Carol Services. Initially meeting in people's houses, it then transferred to the synagogue, and depending on the number of births in any year varied greatly in attendance rate. It suffered from the wide dispersion of members, with some mothers unwilling to travel too far with a young child and preferring local non-Jewish groups; conversely, some of those in more distant areas religiously trekked to it and valued the chance to meet other Jewish mothers.

The Religion School also increased in size as the synagogue grew, with the 35 children on the roll in 1980 growing to 100 by 1984. It also grew in age range, expanding at both ends. Initially, the start age was six years old, but it was later changed to five, and then to four. This was in response to children starting school or pre-school classes at those ages, and with parents being concerned that their children hear not only about the Christian festivals but Jewish ones too. At the same time, children were encouraged to stay on after their *bar/batmitzvah*. At first, children left directly after their ceremony. This was then delayed until the end of the Religion School year - both so as to be supportive of those still studying and to continue their own Jewish education. A further extension was the formation of a Post-*bar/batmitzvah* Group. Over time, the novelty became the norm and the vast majority of pupils stayed on for it. The actual content of the Religion School was a mixture of Jewish history, religious life, Hebrew and ethical values. However, while Jewish knowledge was vital, the primary goal was to instil a positive sense of Jewish identity, without which that knowledge would be irrelevant. A third purpose was to provide contact with other Jewish children, as many of them were the only Jewish person in their class, and some were the only one in their entire school. Mixing with other Jews once a week on a Sunday morning was an important part of nurturing their Jewish awareness.

The youth group continued from previous years, but as well as regular club activities, the teenage section began to travel to places of Jewish interest. The first trip was to Amsterdam in 1983, as described enthusiastically by fourteen year olds, Beverley Brown and Steven Caplan:

We all gathered excitedly at the *shul*, There were twelve of us under the guidance of Laurie and Sheila Tytel and of course...Jonathan! The Diskins very kindly let us use their mini-bus in which Jonathan drove half of us to Sheerness, Isle of Sheppey. The rest of us went in the Tytel's car. After a night of barely an hour's sleep on the Olau Brittania, we arrived in Holland at 7.00 am. Holland was exactly how I had imagined it to be. We drove along spotless roads and took in the countryside dotted with poplars in perfect rows. Windmills galore! Our first stop was the Liberal synagogue on the outskirts of Amsterdam. We were shown round by an English speaking guide. It was a lovely large *shul*: it did, however, have two things in common with ours - membership numbers and a Czechoslovakian scroll. Another Jewish guide showed us Amsterdam with its many Jewish aspects. Typically, Laurie wore his white sun hat when it was pouring with rain. Having eaten in a *kosher J*ewish restaurant, we visited an old Jewish museum. On seeing Anne Frank's house, we were moved by walking through the 'annexe' where she lived those many years ago. The house was typical of Amsterdam, being narrow and cramped. The stairs were wearing thin but not the atmosphere. Next was an unexpected boat trip along the canal, which was relaxing. We walked back along the cobbled streets to the cars, via the 'Red Light' district; then dashed back to the port. After a filling meal on the boat we lived it up at the disco – and retired to bed. Most of us got three hours sleep – more than expected. Back on home ground Laurie and Jonathan managed to remember to drive on the right hand side of the roads. We all enjoyed ourselves and would like to thank everyone for making this trip possible.

A repeat trip was organised the following year for the next tranche of teenagers, while in 1986 the rabbi and Robin Lansman led one to Paris. Two years later, there was a trip to Lincoln to explore the remnants of its medieval Jewish life, this time led by the rabbi and Jenny Sakal.

An entirely new activity was the synagogue Girl Guide group, which was established in spring 1982 and became the first Jewish troop in Berkshire, known as 8th Maidenhead. It was founded and led by Jule North, a qualified leader who had recently moved to the area. It met every Wednesday at the synagogue, participated in activities with other Guide troops and held a summer camp. While many parents were interested in their daughters participating, their distance from Maidenhead meant that several joined local groups instead. Sadly, lack of numbers forced it to come to an honourable close after two years.

Relations with the wider community

Alongside the explosion of internal developments, the synagogue began to inter-act more with the wider community. The appointment of a full-time rabbi brought a flurry of requests for him to speak at a variety of local groups, from cubs to the Womens Institute to Rotary. There were also numerous invitations to talk to schools, both primary and secondary, both state schools and private ones. In some cases, he went to them, othertimes they came to the synagogue for a guided tour. This coincided with Berkshire County Council having recently adopted a multi-faith Religious Education syllabus and a widespread desire to cover the Jewish faith amongst others. Eventually the demands on the rabbi's time to speak to schools became so great that a team of members who could also do so was formed and is still kept very busy to this day. Relations between the synagogue and local churches also developed apace, with the rabbi establishing a rapport with individual clergy and often being invited to address church groups. On the welfare side, in 1984 Harry and Ruby Pitch initiated locally the Operation Goodwill project that had been developed nationally by AJEX (Association of Jewish Ex-Servicemen and Women). It involved members of the Jewish community taking over tasks such as washing dishes, cleaning floors and feeding patients at local hospitals or old age homes on Christmas Day. This was partly to relieve the workload of the reduced staff on duty, and partly to bring cheer to those who had no relatives to visit them. It was a way of helping out on a day that was unimportant to Jews but of great significance to others. It ran for the next ten years, while a Christmas lunch for senior citizens in Camberley was run for several years by members there. The synagogue itself became the home for two local voluntary groups looking for premises. It offered a central venue for a letter-writing circle attached to Amnesty International, sending messages of support to those imprisoned unjustly around the world. In 1987 it started hosting area meetings for mothers suffering from post-natal depression, while it also provided both some of those counselling them and some of those manning the crèche that looked after the children while their mothers were being seen. No charge was made to either group, and the 'PND' one still meets weekly.

The synagogue also become involved in some notable fund-raising activities for local causes. The first was in response to the

Maidenhead Advertiser's appeal to the town in 1984 to raise money towards a life-boat in conjunction with other provincial newspapers.

Operation Goodwill: Ruby Pitch and nurses at St Mark's Hospital

Rabbi Romain - who enjoyed rowing and whose father had served in the Navy during the Second World War – decided to support the cause by holding a 'Sponsored Non-Sermon' in the High Street. In a move publicised by the paper the week beforehand, he went into each shop and said that he was about to deliver a 30 minute sermon on the premises in aid of the lifeboat, but that if the shop-owner felt it might disturb his customers and wished to make a donation to the cause, he would desist from doing so. It raised £250 and was credited with helping enthuse the till-then flagging campaign, which eventually went on to reach its target of £1,000.

The following year, a local tragedy occurred when four teenage boys from Altwood School went on a school-trip to Lands End but were swept away in the sea and drowned. The parents launched a campaign to pay for a lifeboat in the area. In response, Rabbi Romain asked local people, including synagogue members, to sponsor religious jokes that would be told by him and six other ministers from local churches – who became known as 'the Sacred Seven' - at an 'Evening of Religious Humour' to be held at the United Reformed Church. The evening itself was a great success, attracting a packed audience and proved thoroughly entertaining, as well as an excellent example of inter-faith co-operation. It not only produced £2,000 but also attracted wide publicity nationally, dubbed by the press as 'Cleric Aid', while the group were asked to reprise some of their jokes on both radio and television. A lifeboat named 'The Four Boys' was eventually launched by the Duke of Kent, president of the Royal National Lifeboat Institution at Sennen Cove, close to Land's End.

Another unusual event took place in December 1987 when the rabbi organised a '*Hanukah* Hymnalia' by Maidenhead Station. He had noticed in previous years that there had been groups of carol-singers collecting money for charity and felt that the synagogue should do likewise with its own festive repertoire. This duly took place, with twelve members of the community singing 'Maoz Tzur' and other songs for an hour as evening commuters came home, with the donations going towards the Thames Valley Hospice that had recently been established in Windsor. Once again, it was a winning combination of fun and fund-raising, although it was quite possible that many of the commuters rushing by enjoyed the melodies but did not realise the words were being sung in Hebrew. A less public but equally novel charitable venture took place the following year in aid of the Royal Berkshire Hospital in Reading, which was celebrating its 150th anniversary and holding a major appeal to improve its cancer care facilities. As a way of contributing, the rabbi organised a sponsored non-stop reading of the 36 Books of the Hebrew Bible in English. The object was both to raise funds and to be educational, as not many people were familiar with books outside the Pentateuch. It also had a long-term benefit, as the readings were taped and then given to the Jewish Blind Society for those who might appreciate them. Thirty members participated, reading from 8.30 am to 11 pm, and a total of £1,532 was raised.

The more conventional way of raising money for charity - through an appeal at the High Holy Days - was followed, albeit through the newsletter and not done at the services themselves. This was on the grounds that financial appeals did not sit comfortably with the mood of prayer and reflection. A pattern developed of choosing three different charities each year: one connected with Israel, one concerning British Jewry and one serving the wider community locally. However, although the High Holy Day appeal raised a few hundred pounds, the annual response was fairly paltry compared to the much larger sums collected in other synagogues. Special collections were more successful and occurred whenever there was a need, such as in 1983 when £17,000 was raised in support of the Reform movement's campaign to purchase the Manor House in North London for its new headquarters. Two years later, £2,000 raised within a few weeks for 'Operation Moses', when thousands of Falashas were airlifted from Ethiopia and brought to Israel.

Hanukah Hymnalia - l to r:
Jonathan Romain, Stuart Pinkerton, David Banks, Barbara Rosenberg, Ruby Pitch, Sybil Romain, Barbara Shaffer, Naomi Hyamson, Harry Pitch

Inter-faith and inter-synagogue

The inter-faith relationships already mentioned continued on an ad hoc basis until the Berkshire branch of the Council of Christians and

Jews (CCJ) was formed in September 1986. Maidenhead Synagogue, Reading Hebrew Congregation and Thames Valley Progressive Jewish Community (a Liberal congregation) comprised the Jewish component, while all churches in the county were invited, under the chairmanship of Rev. Gerald Restall. The initiative had arisen from informal conversations when the Anne Frank Exhibition came to Reading some months earlier, which brought Jewish and Christian leaders together to support it. Both sides felt that it would be good to maintain the links that had been made and to set up an organisational structure to formalise them. Contact was made with CCJ's national body which was delighted to help set up a local branch in an area that had not previously had one. An average of four events were held each year from then on at different venues throughout Berkshire, with a mixture of talks, discussions, evenings of religious music and occasional visits to places of religious significance, such as Eton Chapel and Douai Abbey.

Amongst the memorable speakers who came to the events held at Maidenhead Synagogue were the Rt Rev. John Sentamu in 2004, then Bishop of Birmingham and shortly afterwards Archbishop of York, while Dr Anthony Seldon, Master of Wellington College came in 2010. The Berkshire CCJ has proved successful, both in terms of creating formal institutional links between Jews and Christians, and in providing a forum for individuals within each faith to meet who might not otherwise have done so. Moreover, the nature of its meetings changed over the years once a level of familiarity and trust had grown up between the regular participants. Thus the initial meetings concentrated on transmitting information (such as speakers on 'Introducing Christianity' and 'The Jewish Home'), whereas subsequent ones involved a sharing of personal perspectives (for instance, on religious artefacts or sacred music). An incidental result was a class on Hebrew at the synagogue specifically for local Christian clergy in 1993 that ran for two years, which both taught them linguistic skills and deepened relationships.

The inter-faith contact extended to other faiths too. The rabbi was at the opening of the Maidenhead Mosque in 1982. These and other ad hoc meetings were given much greater structure through the establishment of the Maidenhead Community Consultative Committee in October 1987, which brought together representatives of all faiths in the area – Bahai, Christians, Hindus, Jews, Muslim and Sikhs (with others joining later) – and organised regular social and cultural meetings. It proved a long-lasting development that significantly advanced inter-faith harmony locally, not just at leadership level but between members of the different communities. The synagogue took an active role both initially and throughout the next three decades.

Christian, Jewish, Muslim and Sikh leaders gather at the well-signed Synagogue

One of the arguments advanced by those opposed to religious dialogue is the danger that it might lead to conversionist activity. There were no attempts at this through any of the inter-faith bodies, although there were occasional efforts by individuals. Thus a Christadelphian who had attended services innocuously for three years was asked to leave after she began distributing conversionist tracts. The offer by local House Church group to make regular donations to the synagogue was gently declined lest it be part of a wider agenda. There was also an effort at Jewish missionary activity, when the ultra-Orthodox group Chabad sent two members to visit a member's home to persuade him to help establish a local group. It would have been very divisive in what was then still a small community, while it would also have excluded those deemed by Chabad to have status issues. The rabbi was asked to come round by the member's concerned wife while they were still there, and the plan came to nothing

The Berkshire CCJ had a significant, but unplanned side-effect: its purpose had been to bring Christians and Jews together, which it achieved, but it also brought together Jews from different denominations who rarely met in the then hostile climate between the different groupings within British Jewry at large. CCJ meetings saw members of the local Orthodox, Reform and Liberal synagogues find that they had even more in common with each other than with their Christian neighbours. Reform and Liberal leaders did meet from time to time – sharing a Progressive approach to Jewish life, while the rabbis came from the same rabbinic seminary, Leo Baeck College - but, they rarely saw their Orthodox counterparts. Now, all three of the Berkshire Jewish communities gathered together in the neutral territory offered by CCJ. Matters could have been left at that, with an occasional exchange of pleasantries, but it was felt that Jewish life could also benefit from intra-faith dialogue. A meeting took place in December 1986 between Rabbi Romain and Cyril Selinger, the chairman of Thames Valley Progressive Jewish Community - which did not have a rabbi – to start the process. The following month, Rabbi Romain wrote to Jack Album, President of Reading Hebrew Congregation (Reading) suggesting a closer relationship. It was written to him as it was felt that the lay leadership would be more sympathetic to such a proposal than the minister, Rev. Leo Sichel, although his approval would have to be gained at a later stage and was indeed granted (5):

> Would it not be possible – and very desirable – for the three Jewish communities in the Thames Valley region to get together for co-operation in certain areas. I realise that there are differences between us and that such links would have to be carefully thought out so as not to offend anyone. What motivates my suggestion is:
>
> a) Anglo-Jewry is a shrinking community – so we ought to pool resources
> b) It is also a divided community – and it would be wonderful if we could take a lead in promoting harmony
> c) Such co-operation would be mutually beneficial to all – and would be very helpful to each synagogue individually.

For the project to be even considered, let alone work in practice. it was important to choose areas of co-operation that would be free from religious controversy. Those suggested were Israel, Soviet Jewry and welfare.

Reading responded positively, leading to a meeting that same month of representatives of all three communities to discuss whether the project had any potential. It proved very amicable, following which the Reading Board of Management then authorised further talks to proceed. Other areas of co-operation agreed were Mothers and Toddlers,

Friendships Clubs, Women's groups and *kosher* food. The result was the formation of the Association of Synagogues in Berkshire in May 1987 and an announcement was put in the newsletters of all three communities. The Association's object was 'to provide a link between the synagogues in Berkshire so as to promote co-operation between them on matters of mutual interest, and to establish good relations between neighbouring Jewish communities of whatever religious affiliation. There is no intention to minimise religious differences, but rather to explore areas of common concern'. This object was to be achieved by a series of practical measures: the appointment of a liaison officer from each synagogue to be responsible for maintaining contact with the other two and relaying back to their respective Councils matters of common interest. The liaison officers would also receive the newsletters of the other synagogues so as to be fully informed about each other's activities. In addition, an information sheet was produced listing the names and phone numbers of those who organised events in the areas for which co-operation had been agreed. This was then distributed to all Council members and organisers so that they could liaise directly with others in their respective fields. It was a remarkable document, not only providing useful details, but encouraging tri-lateral links in many spheres without having to seek constant approval from each synagogue body (see Appendix 2).

These links were given further impetus in November when a meeting was held at Maidenhead Synagogue for all the activists and group leaders in each congregation, so as to facilitate face to face discussions. By this stage, other areas of mutual interest had been added such as AJEX, those unattached over 35, and security. Over sixty people were present, with everyone together for an initial plenum and then dividing into specific interests groups in which they shared both their successes and problems. There was a strong social element too, which was an important part of building up the trust and respect that were often lacking in inter-synagogual relations elsewhere and without which progress would be hard. The practical effects over the next few months varied depending on the different areas of interest: in some, it was a matter of sharing information, such as suppliers for *kosher* food deliveries; in others, it led to an occasional exchange of visits, such as the Reading Friendship Club coming to a meeting of Maidenhead's Welcome Mat and vice-versa; in yet other areas, it led to inviting members of all three communities to each other' events, such as the various activities for Israel Independence Day. There were also occasional events that were jointly organised, such as a cricket match between the communities. Such events, however, were strictly limited, both because of the need to avoid any of the 'difficult' areas that could be seen as religious co-operation, and so as to avoid stepping on the toes of existing activities by any one of the congregations.

The new Association attracted wide attention and was hailed at the first instance of a formal body between synagogue bodies of all three denominations in Britain. It made the front page of the *Jewish Chronicle*, with a lengthy report under the headline 'Link-up for unity' (6). The fact that story was not released until almost a year after the Association had been formed was no accident: it had been deliberately delayed lest the glare of publicity too early on cause any of the parties to withdraw their involvement, either because of their own nervousness or due to pressure by the movements to which they were affiliated. By waiting until the Association had taken root amongst the three congregations and gained popular acceptance, there was less chance of the publicity derailing the project. The fact that such a calculation had to be made indicated the adversarial nature of inter-denominational relations within British Jewry at the time; it also highlighted the pioneering significance of the Association, with the hope that publicity would encourage others to do likewise.

The co-operation continued throughout 1988 and included a visit of the Maidenhead Mothers and Toddlers group visiting the Reading Gan, as well as joint efforts in the Soviet Jewry campaign. The three communities also worked together when the Reading Council for Racial Equality appointed Lester Lewis as its Senior Community Relations Officer even though he was known to hold extremist views. However, the retirement of Rev. Sichel from Reading Hebrew Congregation in 1988 and his replacement by Rabbi Ian Goodhardt led to a change in the community's religious stance and to a discouragement of inter-denominational co-operation. Without Reading's involvement, it was impossible to continue. Personal contacts were maintained and Maidenhead still had good relations with the Liberals, but the Association of Synagogues in Berkshire effectively ceased to operate after that year. It seemed that the noble experiment had died after a short but meaningful life.

There were no other Reform synagogues nearby with whom to have a close relationship and, in terms of the Reform movement, Maidenhead was fairly isolated geographically. However, it was part of the Southern Region group, which arose in 1985 and linked non-London Reform synagogues in the South of England and organised an annual weekend away. A number of Maidenhead members attended, with Leila Blairman being a particular stalwart and Stephen Sommer organising several joint youth activities. Very few members were involved in other aspects of the Reform movement, apart from those representing

Maidenhead at its Council meetings. However, one notable contribution was Maidenhead's role in bringing a new community into the fold. Swindon was a small independent congregation that was organised under Orthodox auspices. It consisted of forty-two adult members, several being in mixed-faith marriages, and it lacked both a building and a rabbi, with members running the monthly Sabbath services and a visiting minister coming for the High Holy Days. In reality, most of its members were Reform in lifestyle and thinking. A number of them had approached Maidenhead to help with personal status issues and it became increasingly obvious that the community as a whole would be better served by changing to the Reform. Rabbi Romain visited the community several times to either lead services or to discuss the possibility of a transition. It was very much a parallel situation to Maidenhead's own decision to switch affiliation, with the majority of members ready for change but a number reluctant to relinquish the old ways. After much internal debate, a vote was taken in Spring 1986, at which point Swindon decided to become a Reform synagogue. It was only the second time that a community had moved as a whole from Orthodoxy to Reform, with the first being Maidenhead itself thirty years earlier.

1. *Hadashot* (March 1988) 4
2. *Hadashot* (May 1985) 3
3. *Hadashot* (June 1981)
4. *Hadashot* (July 1987) 4
5. Letter, 6 January 1987
6. JC (8 April 1988)

Chapter 14

1980s: A Decade of Transition

1987 saw the culmination of a great debate within all Reform synagogues in the country over whether to merge with the Liberals. Britain was the only country in the world with two Progressive movements and many felt that the historical circumstances that had led to their separate development were no longer applicable. Moreover, there was already much co-operation through joint institutions such as the Leo Baeck College. Merging the two bodies into one stronger larger Progressive movement had much to commend it. However, many on either side were concerned about their loss of identity, and there was also the feeling that some of the distinctive practices – especially the fact that Reform followed the matrilineal line, whereas Liberals accepted patrilineality – could not, or should not, be reconciled. Individual synagogues were asked to make their position known and Maidenhead voted in favour of the two organisations holding talks about joining together. For some, the fact that Rabbi Romain's wife was also a Liberal rabbi - then serving Ealing Liberal Synagogue, and known professionally as Sybil Sheridan - epitomised how much the two movements had in common and could live together in harmony. However, the joint working party established by both movements eventually decided to recommend that merger was not practicable given the divergent attitudes that existed between them. Instead, it urged closer co-operation in areas such as Education, Israel and Soviet Jewry. The failure to merge did not have a great effect on Maidenhead, although if it had gone ahead it might have led to closer relations with the Thames Valley Liberals or even a regional merger.

Soviet Jewry and Israel

The plight of Soviet Jewry has already been mentioned as an issue affecting synagogues of all denominations. Jewish life there had been suppressed for several decades under the Soviet policy of discouraging religious groups. However, the Six Day War and subsequent Israeli victory had stirred the latent identity of many Soviet Jews, who either sought to revive Judaism in Russia or applied to emigrate to Israel. This resulted in the state authorities actively persecuting Jews, both refusing to let them leave the USSR and denying them the ability to lead a Jewish life within it. With Soviet Jews unable to change the policies of a totalitarian regime, western Jews tried to alleviate their situation, both pressing for their rights and showing solidarity by travelling to visit them.

Like many other synagogues, Maidenhead organised a variety of events to highlight their cause. These included leaving an empty seat at the Communal *Seder*, as well as twinning those having their *bar/batmitzvah* with a 13 year old Russian Jew who was unable to have a similar ceremony of their own, symbolically calling them up by name and mentioning them in the sermon. Rabbi Romain had gone to the Soviet Union when a rabbinic student in 1978 and in 1979, and he did so again in 1980 shortly after joining the community, both visiting refuseniks and giving talks about Judaism to those who gathered in private houses for the clandestine sessions. On his return, he reported back on how those who wished to emigrate were punished by losing their jobs, having their telephones disconnected, finding that their children were denied university places and subject to police harassment. He explained in a sermon that their dependency on the Jews of the West was 'like someone stuck in a lift that is not working; they cannot do anything to help themselves. All they can do is hope that those outside will hear their cries for hep and respond'. When the Moscow Philarmonic Orchestra came to play at the Hexagon in Reading in both 1981 and 1982, members of Maidenhead staged a peaceful protest outside, along with those from other local synagogues, and handed out leaflets to those going inside, drawing attention to the human rights abuses in the USSR. The following year, the community participated in a nationally organised march in aid of Soviet Jewry starting from Hyde Park, with a coach taking twenty-eight members to it.

In 1984, the community adopted the Borovinsky family as honorary members: Semion and Natalia were both thirty-five, with two daughters, Zoya aged seven and Julia aged two. They lived in Leningrad in a flat of twelve feet by eighteen feet with no natural daylight, which had to suffice for all their activities, including eating and sleeping. They had a small kitchen, along with a bathroom, which was shared with eighteen others in adjoining flats. On applying to emigrate, Semion had been fired from his position as a computer programmer. However, they had been refused permission to leave on the grounds that Natalia's father had not formally given her permission to emigrate – which was technically necessary under Soviet law even though she was a fully independent adult. Her father had no objection to her going, but had not formally consented as he was a Professor of Marxism at the university, and was scared of losing his job should he do so. As a desperate solution, Semion and Natalia had got divorced, although they were still living together, in the hope that Semion could get emigration papers for himself and the children, and that she might be able to follow later.

The Borovinsky family

Julian Marks, Laurie Phillips and Rabbi Romain went to visit the family later that year, as well as seeing other refuseniks. Two years later, another visit was arranged and although the rabbi's visa was revoked by the Soviet authorities four days before the trip, Simon Jacobs and Barry Walsh did manage to travel there and see them. Other members of the synagogue wrote regular letters as a way of keeping up the family's morale, while their cause was publicised in local newspapers and in letters to MPs. In August 1987 the Borovinskys were allowed to depart and went to Israel to start a new life. The only sour note – apart from the fact that they had experienced unemployment, financial hardship and police surveillance for six years – was that when Semion's seventy-two year old father journeyed from Kiev to Leningrad airport to see them off, he was warned by the KGB that if he waved goodbye he would be committing a public nuisance and would receive fifteen days in prison. The family's struggle epitomised the traumas faced not only by Jews wishing to leave, but also by those staying within the USSR. Later that year, the community received a letter from Jerusalem from a re-named Shimon Borovinsky. His English writing may have been poor, but his sentiments shone through:

> We are now Israeli residents, but our way to freedom was neither short nor easy. During all that time of having been in refusal, we felt your support as brothers. Not all of your letters were answered – there were reasons: part of the letters never reached their destination; sometimes there was not a bit of strength to write; sometimes there was not enough time, but always they were desirable and looked for.
>
> I remember the time a year ago – the most hopeless time in my life – under the menace of trial, your letters were really like a breath of air as they made me sure I would not disappear from the earth without somebody's request and your living memory helped us break through the camp of socialism out.
>
> At present we are in Jerusalem attending Ulpan and trying to integrate with new life without losing our distinctive features. Our adjustment would be much harder if again there was not a friendship of those who knew us in our pre-life. Thank all of you – with deep respect to all members of Maidenhead Synagogue.

The synagogue's own links with Israel varied over the decades, depending much on whether particular individuals felt strongly enough to organise Israel-oriented activities. For many years, this role was held by Herta Orchudesh who arranged talks and film evenings, always accompanied by lashings of food. The meetings were invariably well-attended, although this was not so much due to the attractiveness of the events - which were usually of high quality - but to her tireless phone calls to members to drum up support. It was felt, though, that as well as holding educational evenings and doing general fund-raising for Israel, it would be good to engage more directly with Israeli life in some way. This was given personal shape in 1984 when it was decided to 'adopt' a twenty-four year old Israeli, Yoram Margai. He was paralysed from the neck downwards as a result of being wounded in the Lebanon war two years earlier, with only the use of his voice and brain. A campaign was launched to both establish a relationship with him and raise £2,000 for a special chair that would be built for him that could respond to voice instructions. This was achieved and, three years later, when Yoram was in a position to return to university and resume his studies, a further £500 was raised to purchase a tape-recorder that could be operated with a mouth-stick.

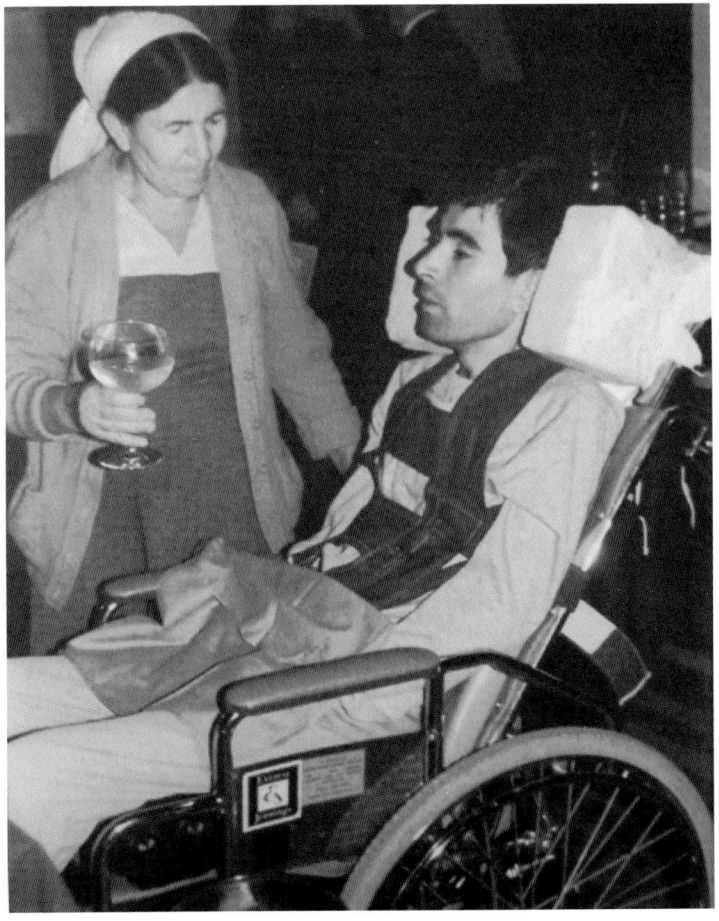

Yoram Margai

The community was very supportive of Israel – certainly of the state and the people, even if there was debate over particular policies of the government of the time. However, it was not actively Zionist in terms of encouraging members to make *aliyah* and emigrate there. For virtually all of the British-born members, their home was in this country. One of the few who did move to Israel was Alan North, who had had his *barmitzvah* at the synagogue but decided in 1986, when he was twenty, that his future lay in Israel. On arrival there, he changed his name to Ilan and eventually settled in Karne Shomrom. A more communal effort was the synagogue's first ever trip to Israel, which was led by the rabbi in March 1987, touring much of the country over two weeks. It proved a great success, but although there was talk of a further visit, the difficult security situation in subsequent years meant that attempts to attract a sufficient number of participants failed and the next trip was not until 2011.

The outreach campaign

One of the factors behind the success of the synagogue was the explosion in its growth rate, which both gave it the size to support such diverse activities and brought in those with the energy and expertise to organise them. Whereas in 1980 there were 80 households, within a year this had doubled, trebled by 1983 and quadrupled to 320 households by 1984. In 1986 it stood at 440 families and by 1989 it had grown to 500. This was not a spontaneous growth, driven by external economic factors such as the job market, house prices or transport links, but was the result of a carefully orchestrated membership campaign. It was predicated on the assumption that there were many Jews living in the area who had no contact with the synagogue. In some cases this was simply due to inertia; in other cases because of bad experiences with their previous synagogue before they moved to the area; yet others felt that they would not be welcomed because of their personal situation, be it single, divorced, in a mixed-faith relationship or same-sex ones. The motive for reaching out to them all was partly to gain members, but also because of the belief 'that they would actually be happier being part of the community and benefit from it' (1).

The campaign was spearheaded by the rabbi who collected names of Jewish individuals or families living in the area. This was done through asking members to relay the information to him, as well as through finding out if any Jews were present whenever he visited a school or hospital, or spoke to local groups such as the scouts or Rotary. Once identified, the person would then receive a copy of the newsletter, followed shortly afterwards by a phone call from the rabbi. Whilst many a phone ended with a definite 'no thanks, we're not interested', others resulted in the rabbi offering to visit when in their neighbourhood. The vast majority of people who received such visits said that it was the first time that they had had a rabbi in their house and enjoyed the opportunity to talk about their Jewish heritage or discuss a particular issue that had been bothering them. Although not all visits led to them joining, in many cases it was successful, with them either signing up there and then or doing so subsequently. It was not just a matter of 'the personal touch' that persuaded them, but also the inclusive approach behind it, which declared that there were many ways of being Jewish and that the synagogue could offer a home to all types of Jews. This was spelt out in one of the 'Ask the Rabbi' columns in *Hadashot* in response to someone wondering if they could belong even though they did not believe in God: 'being Jewish is not just a matter of faith, but of culture and identity too: one feels Jewish, eats Jewish, looks Jewish. The synagogue is not just a House of Prayer, but also a community centre, so that whatever kind of Jew you are, here you belong and here you will always find a welcome' (2).

During the rabbi's visits it quickly became evident that many people simply had not realised there was a synagogue locally. So another way of locating potential members was by having a high profile in the media so as to encourage them to make contact. This was initially done via the local papers and radio, with items of news interest regularly being placed in the *Maidenhead Advertiser*, *Reading Evening Post*, *Bracknell News* and others, or via interviews on BBC Berkshire. In time, this spread to the national media too, while great use was made of the *Jewish Chronicle*, on the assumption that someone reading it in North-West London might have a relative in Berks and Bucks and pass on details about the community. There was also the object of sending a message to those - particularly with young children - who were thinking of moving out of London and looking for property in an area which was not only in commuting distance but also had a vibrant Jewish community. Areas to the north of London, such as Radlett and Borehamwood, may have been the first choice for many such families, but it was important to put Maidenhead on the Jewish radar too. It was all part of the strategy to attract Jews who might otherwise not know of the synagogue's existence. Moreover, it helped create a feel-good factor amongst existing members who liked to see 'their place' being lauded. They became used to seeing the once virtually unknown synagogue being represented publicly, from the pages of *The Times* to Radio 4's *Woman's Hour* to BBC 1's *Ready, Steady, Cook*. A somewhat tongue-in-cheek letter to *Hadashot* showed how effective the wider media could be in making an impression on local lapsed Jews, in this case someone already a member (3):

> I write to you in despair. What can a member who pays their subscription regularly, do? You know you have earned the privilege of choosing not to come to *shul* very often. I know that Rabbi Romain ferreted me out in the first place to join, but I thought that now I was a member he would at least have the courtesy to leave me alone.

Suddenly, however, he invades my lounge on BBC television. So the following week I listen to Radio 4 instead: he is on again! In desperation, the third week I turn to ITV and, blow me, out he pops! 'He seeks me here, he seeks me there'. Okay, Jonathan, I give up. I am coming to *shul* next week.

The outreach campaign proved spectacularly successful and led to the synagogue first of all redeveloping on site, and later moving entirely, so as to accommodate the growth.

One of the consequences of the community not having had a permanent rabbi previously was that many status issues had gone unresolved. This included those who had divorced and obtained the civil certificate but not acquired a religious severance too, the *get*. It also applied to children who had non-Jewish mothers, but who had been brought up Jewish and considered themselves to be Jewish, but who lacked Jewish status. These issues were now addressed and several families sorted out such matters by going to the Reform Beth Din in London. A conversion class was also established for those who wished to become Jewish. It took place on a fortnightly basis before the Friday evening service, with the course lasting just over a year. In the vast majority of cases, it was taken up by those who had a Jewish partner. Whilst some synagogues, especially Orthodox ones, considered 'the marriage motive' to be a sign of insincerity and discouraged such applicants, the Reform took a much more welcoming attitude. However, even within the Reform movement, there were some synagogues who were reticent about conversion or who only ran courses if candidates came forward of their own accord. Maidenhead stood out in that the conversion course was seen as a normative part of synagogue life, not a concession granted to those who specially applied.

Maidenhead was also at the forefront of adopting a pro-active policy of offering conversion to non-Jews who had a Jewish partner. The rabbi was fully aware that not all of them were particularly religious, but was happy to accept them so long as they had an affinity with Jewish life in some other way, be it ethically or culturally. This was partly because they would have the benefit of Jewish support at home; partly because their conversion would help keep the Jewish partner Jewish; and partly because, if children were involved, it meant that Jewish life would be more likely to continue to the next generation if both parents were Jewish. The approach meant that there were many families who came to the community as mixed-faith ones but eventually became Jewish ones. It also meant that a high percentage of those converting did so after marriage, by which time the non-Jewish spouse had come to understand and appreciate Jewish life and wanted to become part of it themselves.

There were also instances of individuals who were themselves products of a mixed-faith marriage - especially those with a Jewish father and non-Jewish mother who lacked Jewish status but still had a sense of Jewish roots - who wanted to reclaim their Jewish heritage. They, too, were encouraged. Another category was individuals who had no Jewish family or partner who wished to join the faith. While some were accepted onto the course, many were not. This was because of the large number already converting in the former two categories, and a feeling that an influx also of those without any Jewish connection would put a strain on the identity of the community. Another, albeit much less common scenario, was when a husband and wife who were both new to Judaism but had separately developed an affinity with it, wished to convert, and there were three such instances during this decade.

The result of this pro-active policy was that, although Maidenhead was for many years among the smaller Reform congregations, it consistently featured in the top of the list for those sending most candidates to the Reform Beth Din. The overall effect was hugely beneficial in many different ways: it unified families religiously; it brought in new members; it gave a spiritual home to those who sought it; it educated the Jewish partners, who were obliged to attend the classes with their partner and who invariably gained a renewed sense of allegiance; it usually brought the active involvement of both partners in wider synagogue life, including serving on committees and taking up positions of leadership. During the 1990s, for instance, out of eight consecutive chairman of the synagogue, one was a convert and five were the partners of converts. Even more noticeable was the disproportionately high number of converts who went on to become Religion School teachers – at one point accounting for three out of nine members of staff – having a knowledge and enthusiasm to get up early on a Sunday morning while many born Jews preferred to stay in bed (4). A more detailed analysis of the conversion rate and trend is given in the final chapter.

The welcoming approach was extended just as much to mixed-faith couples where no conversion was anticipated. In 1986 an evening was held at Rabbi Romain's house for such couples at a time when they were generally rejected by the Jewish community at large. As an article in *Hadashot* explained, a new policy was needed (5):

> Whether one approves of inter-marriage or not, the fact is that a significant proportion of Anglo-Jewry - and of our community too - have married non-Jews. The attitude of previous decades

was to sit *shivah* for that person and shun them completely....but it has failed to stem inter-marriage and only succeeded in alienating the Jewish partner. Instead we should accept the reality of the situation, encourage the Jewish partner to maintain his/her links with Jewish life, welcome the non-Jewish spouse to family or communal events, and give the children the opportunity of learning about their Jewish heritage.

The object of the evening was for the couples to discuss some of the issues they faced, be it organising home life, dealing with in-laws or bringing up children. With hindsight, the event may appear perfectly reasonable, but for the 1980s it was revolutionary. It attracted a large crowd and not only proved helpful for those attending, but brought in non-members who had heard about it through members, including those living far away.

On a national level, it was clear that the evening for mixed-faith couples had answered a need that was not just in the Maidenhead area but applied throughout British Jewry. Intermarriage had always been present but had started growing rapidly in the 1930s as a result of increasing levels of integration and accelerated by the disruption to communal life caused by the Second World War. Whereas the synagogue marriage per thousand in the decade beginning 1931 was 8.4, for the decade beginning 1951 it had sunk to 4.6. Thus it had halved within two decades, even though the Jewish population had largely remained static (6). Whilst this was partly due to factors such as emigration of young British Jews to Israel, by far the greatest cause was Jews marrying non-Jews. The rate of outmarriage continued apace and by 1996, 44% of marriages that took place involving Jews were to non-Jews (7). Many communal leaders were worried about the implications for the size and sustainability of British Jewry and talked of 'dire consequences' and of 'the community haemorrhaging'. It was time for a more positive approach and the Maidenhead meeting was repeated at the Sternberg Centre, the Reform head-quarters in North London, advertised as *I'm Jewish, My Partner Isn't*. The title was carefully worded so as to be open to all those in a mixed-faith relationship, married or not. It also avoided terms that carried a value-judgement, such as 'married out', when very often the reverse applied and the non-Jewish partner felt that they had 'married in'. Nevertheless, it was the butt of considerable criticism by more conservative elements within the community, and much hostility was heaped on Rabbi Romain personally for 'encouraging' inter-marriage by accepting such couples. Almost two hundred people attended the seminar, and its obvious success led to it becoming an annual event at the

Sternberg Centre. It was also taken to provincial centres such as Bristol, Glasgow, Leeds and Manchester. Over the next twenty-five years, it attracted hundreds of mixed-faith couples and became a vehicle for many of them finding their way into the Jewish community. It also profoundly changed attitudes to mixed-faith couples and encouraged synagogues of all denominations to follow Maidenhead's lead in being more open to them.

On a local level, the evening epitomised the general attempt to make both the Jewish and non-Jewish partners feel at home in the synagogue. In some cases, the non-Jewish partners did not wish to participate, but were happy to know that they could do so if they wished; in other cases, they came along to social and cultural events and occasionally to services. In both cases, it meant that the Jewish partners felt able to join in Jewish life without worrying that either they or their partners would be turned away or subject to humiliating remarks, as happened in some other synagogues. Some non-Jewish partners wished to know more about Jewish life so as to better understand their Jewish partner and his/her family. The conversion course - which covered the basics of Judaism - was therefore opened up to them, so that they could gain the knowledge but without changing their identity. A few individuals in this situation felt sufficiently motivated to then apply to convert. However, this was not the object and in most cases they remained as they were, but emerged with a better Jewish understanding, as did the Jewish partners who attended with them.

Maidenhead also took advantage of a new policy that had been developed in 1983 by the Reform Beth Din which enabled the children of Jewish fathers and non-Jewish mothers to obtain Jewish status in their own right. In such cases, the mother did not wish to convert - either because they already had a faith of their own, or because they did not feel at all religious, or because it would cause problems with their own family - but were happy for their children to be Jewish. The procedure was for them to attend an Introduction to Judaism course (in Maidenhead, this doubled up with the conversion course), both so as to obtain Jewish background knowledge and to feel at home in what would be a predominantly Jewish household. They then brought the child to the Reform Beth Din who – after circumcision for boys and immersion in a *mikveh* for both sexes – was granted Jewish status. While this procedure was available to all Reform synagogues, Maidenhead adopted it more enthusiastically than most and many children who might otherwise have been lost to the community were brought up Jewish and the 'chain of tradition' was passed on to the next generation (8). From a membership point of view, the welcoming policy was highly successful, leading many families to not only join, but become actively involved in the life of the community.

A new building?

The rapid growth in the overall membership put pressures on the building. When a large hall in Rutland Road owned by the Parish Council became available in June 1981, an EGM was called and it authorised the Council to bid for it. The synagogue's offer of £30,000 was accepted, but a higher bid of £36,000 was made by the Sikh community, and the building became theirs. A variety of other sites were investigated, but none proved suitable. Not everyone was disappointed, as there was much affection for the existing building. This was given expression with a celebratory lunch marking its 30th anniversary, which included a speech by Sidney Rich who had been so involved in both the acquisition of Studlands in 1953 and in the community's change from Orthodoxy to Reform Judaism that same year. A commemorative brochure was published, containing reflections by a variety of members on three decades of Jewish life at Boyn Hill Avenue. It included an article by Alec Belkin which revealed his own religious transition, and which mirrored that of many others:

> Once upon a time, when I imagined that the wrath of God would descend upon me if I were to walk more than four cubits with my head uncovered, I never visualised in my wildest dreams that I would spend the next 25 years or so with a progressive community…In retrospect, how did I - a Talmudic student – cope with this new and almost revolutionary interpretation of our religion? The answer is that gradually I saw the other side of the coin and my understanding of the validity of Reform Judaism grew.

Another article highlighted the building's impact on so many individual lives:

> If you add up the thousands of people who have passed through that narrow and badly-lit hallway; the hundreds who have had baby blessings, *barmitzvahs* and weddings in front of that ark; the hours spent in prayer, voicing silently or aloud so many thoughts, fears and hopes; the long evenings devoted to committee meetings, discussing all aspects of the synagogue

from the existence of God to the purchase of toilet rolls; the ten of thousands of cups of tea, cakes and sandwiches that the ladies have produced for children's parties, communal *seders* and any other excuse for a nosh – add all these up and you will find yourself dealing with astronomical figures, and you would be overwhelmed by a crescendo of noise, greetings, emotional relatives, excited children, malicious asides, tearful *Yizkors*, ambitious plans, "good *Yomtov*'s", angry voices, *Purim* klappers, sizzling latkes, "*l'chaim*'s"…three whole decades worth of Jews.

Two weeks later, the AGM saw the election of a new Council, led by Ian Scott as chairman, who felt that with the community having expanded from 80 to almost 300 households and still growing fast, the time had come to seek more suitable premises as a top priority. A property at 101 Altwood Avenue, Garden Close, was viewed and at the same time, an offer was received for Studlands by Angie Best, former wife of the footballer, George Best, with the intention of turning it into a health studio. Both properties needed 'change of use' being granted. There were considerable objections by other residents of Altwood who protested against the disturbance that a public building would bring to a residential area in terms of noise and traffic congestion. The issue remained in the public gaze for several weeks through both the news and letters pages of the *Maidenhead Advertiser*. Approval was eventually given by the District Council on the casting vote of the chairman. However, the synagogue was then outbid by developers. The following May, when Franco's Cottage – a large house in Montrose Drive became available, an EGM was called to consider its purchase at around £210,000. Those in favour lauded its possibilities; those against were worried about the costs. After a three hours debate, two motions were voted upon. The first was 'That Maidenhead Synagogue as a Community is in favour of moving to a new building', which was passed by a very large majority. The second, in favour of buying Franco's Cottage, was passed by 48 votes to 13, with 3 abstentions.

David Brookman, as chair of the Building Committee, was responsible for much of the work in dealing with both the vendor and town planners. Matters moved fast and by August contracts had been exchanged on the property. As there had not been time for a fund-raising campaign, three members assisted the synagogue with a bridging loan. However, several residents of Montrose Drive objected to the idea of the synagogue moving to their small cul-de-sac, fearing the impact of the substantial number of cars that would be involved both mid-week and at weekends. Some members wondered if there was also an element of antisemitism, but this was never expressed, and the arrival of any public institution in a residential road would certainly have affected its character. As a result, in October 1984 the Borough's Planning Committee rejected the application for change of use by 13 votes to 4, even though it had been recommended by the Planning Officer. The grounds were that it 'would have a serious detrimental effect on the residential amenities of the locality by reason of disturbance'.

Headlines from the Maidenhead Advertiser, 1984

The negative publicity that arose in the *Maidenhead Advertiser* over both Altwood and Franco's Cottage worried many members, while others were appalled that the latter had been purchased without planning consent. Undaunted, the synagogue Council decided to appeal to the Secretary of State for the Environment. However, rather than deal with the matter in a short space of time and through written representations, the Secretary of State opted for a public enquiry. This now presented several difficulties: it would involve a new time-scale of several months before a decision would be reached; the short-term bridging loan that had been envisaged would become a long-term burden; the extra costs of hiring a barrister at the hearing would be incurred; and the whole issue would now become a major local controversy. All these factors, combined with the divise nature of the project within the membership itself, persuaded the synagogue Council to abandon the project and sell Franco's Cottage. The synagogue treasurer, David Cooper, was instrumental in overseeing the negotiations. The synagogue itself did not suffer financially, although many individuals had spent a great amount of time and some personal expense from the venture. Meanwhile, the offer for Studlands had failed to proceed - also being denied planning consent - and so, exhausted from the bruising experience, thoughts again turned to remaining there and renovating the premises.

The Building Committee - by now under the leadership of Howard Goodman and with the synagogue chaired by Peter Holt - developed plans for major internal alterations: on the ground floor, it would re-orientate the worship area and allow it to be expanded for when there were large attendances; on the upper floors it would convert the flats into classrooms; and a small office was created on the mezzanine floor. The proposals were put to the community at an EGM in May 1986 and overwhelmingly endorsed. Work started at the end of November, with Jex Construction of Henley being awarded the contract after it had gone to tender. The work was so extensive that it meant vacating the building entirely and establishing alternative venues for all activities over the next five months. Adult Education classes were held next door at Unity House; services were transferred to the hall of All Saints Church at the far end of Boyn Hill Avenue; the Religion School was held in All Saint Junior School in nearby Westborough Road; both Welcome Mat and Mothers & Toddlers was held at the rabbi's home; the *Kosher* Shop had to be closed until the synagogue re-opened. Careful planning meant that the disruption to communal life was minimised, while the willingness of the local church and school to share their premises was indicative of the good relations that had been established with the wider community. Apart from the oddity of having a Christmas tree present during the December services, the arrangements went remarkably smoothly.

The building work was finished a few hours before the first planned event in the new synagogue – the Annual General Meeting on 30th April 1987 – with a few cables and exposed wiring being proof of how tight the deadline came to being broken. The total cost was £140,000. A Service of Consecration took place the following month, with the packed congregation including those who had hosted the community whilst it was homeless, as well as local clergy, the Mayor and MP. The new facilities allowed the community to function much more effectively and were to extend its stay at Studlands for another thirteen years. One notable addition shortly afterwards was the donation of double doors to the prayer hall by Raphael Harris in honour of his wife and three daughters, with carvings depicting the four matriarchs. It was designed by another member, John Reynolds, and was rich in symbolism: in the background are two trees, signifying strength and endurance; each tree has six branches, making twelve in all, and representing the twelve tribes of Israel; Sarah is holding a rope, which was used to bind Isaac and which now symbolises the bond between Israel and God; Rebecca holds two flowers – her two sons – with the one only in bud being Esau while the other in flower and next to her heart is Jacob; Rachel and Leah are reaching out their hands to each other, being united in sisterly love and both married to Jacob. Equally memorable were the special fire escape chutes installed in 1988 for the classrooms on the first and second floors, with the Religion School children delighting in the annual practices which felt more like going down a fairground helter-skelter than doing a formal fire drill.

The doors to the Prayer Hall

Another consequence of the synagogue's growth was the increase in paperwork previously looked after by an Honorary Secretary in his or her spare time. It was decided to appoint an Administrator, with Shirley Brown taking up the post in February 1988. She was succeeded the following August by Barbara Rosenberg who remained in the position for the next ten years and proved vital to its smooth functioning. The nature of the Council itself changed. Instead of there being only four named positions – chairman, vice-chair, treasurer and secretary – with the remaining eight positions being undesignated – now everyone was elected to a specific post, such as social affairs or fund-raising, so that they each had a particular responsibility. A further development was the formation of a Security Team to oversee communal activities. It was started by Clive Creager, a dentist who was also part of the Territorial Army, although the initiative was more in response to attacks on synagogues abroad than any local threats. The team - initially men but later with female members - received both physical training and lectures about the nature of defence. It later became allied with the Community Security Trust. Members of the team were on duty primarily during Sabbath services and Religion School, as well as at High Holy Days. They never had any major incidents with which to contend, but they did act as a reassuring presence, particularly when events in the Middle East meant that tensions were raised around Jewish communities worldwide.

Throughout the period, *Hadashot* was the main means of communication with the membership, appearing regularly each month thanks to a succession of hard-working editors. Unlike other Council members, they had a highly visible monthly deadline that they had to meet and they always fulfilled it. Among the news items about the community and articles relating to wider issues, a distinctive feature were the cartoons that were supplied by Ian Scott, with the punch-lines changed by him to fit a Jewish context, as seen below.

"We're one short for a Minyan ....!!"

In January 1989, the rabbi took his first Sabbatical – a normal procedure for Reform rabbis after serving a community for six years or more. The object being both to 'recharge batteries', and also to undertake research and experience Jewish trends elsewhere that would not otherwise be possible. He spent part of the six months period in the United States and then went to Israel, during which time he completed his Ph. D, while he also wrote *Faith and Practice: A Guide to Reform Judaism Today*, which became the standard book on Reform Judaism in Britain for many years. Meanwhile, his usual responsibilities – from services to teaching to pastoral work - were delegated to members of the community, with Robert Goodman overseeing all arrangements. Alec Belkin was also on hand to provide his expertise and continuity, while a student rabbi from the Leo Baeck College – Miri James – helped with occasional services. It was a sign of the many individual talents within the community that, despite the massive expansion of activities over the decade, they did not need to hire another rabbi but could cover virtually all areas themselves. As the chairman, Stephen Sommer, wrote at the end of the Sabbatical: 'During the last six months we have found out a lot about ourselves and how, as a community, we have the ability to work together' (9).

The 1980s were clearly a time of enormous expansion for the synagogue, both in terms of membership and the range of activities on offer. However, there were also times of difficulty – as over Franco's Cottage – or ventures that succeeded for a while but were unable to be sustained, such as the Girl Guides. The wide dispersion of the synagogue's membership meant that events or projects that, in theory, should have been well supported, in reality could not always muster a good attendance. Amid the growth, there were also losses, with two deaths that held particular significance for the community at large. The synagogue's President, Murray Bernie, passed away in 1986. He had come to the area in 1940 and been a stalwart of both the services and communal organisation since then. Two years later the community lost one of its most ardent *machers*, Herta Orchudesh, whose passion for arranging events, especially connected with Israel or for children, and always accompanied by her strudel cakes, were unrivalled. Both of them – the Englishman who was evacuated to the area and the German refugee who found her way here – typified the twin strands of the early membership that had made the community's existence possible.

Knocking on doors; from the front cover of 'How To Grow'

1. Romain (1984)
2. *Hadashot* (August 1984) 1
3. *Hadashot* (August 1986) 1
4. For deeper examination of the effects of conversion, see Romain (2000)
5. *Hadashot* (March 1986) 2
6. Prais & Schmool (1967) 151-3
7. Miller, Schmool & Lerman (1996) 12
8. For details of status procedures, see Romain (1991)
9. *Hadashot* (July 1989) 1

Chapter 15

1990: Expansion and Development

The decade began with a very vibrant start, the ripple effect of which was to be felt for a long time afterwards. 1990 was the fiftieth anniversary since the community came into existence and a year's worth of diverse activities took place to celebrate it. As well as a Family Sports Day, Brain of Maidenhead supper quiz and a 1940s-style Tea Dance, it included a Re-Union for all former members in the previous five decades who had left the area and were invited back to renew acquaintances and exchange memories. The anniversary was shared with the wider community through a display of the Board of Deputies' 'Jewish Way of Life' exhibition that was held at Castle Hill Community Centre for two weeks and attracted many school visits. There was also a Choral Evening held at Eton College Hall with performances from the Zemel Choir, Maidenhead Choral Society and Desborough School Boys Choir. Two events that then became annual features were a Jewish Book Fair, bringing a range of books to the synagogue that were unavailable locally, and a Jubilee Lecture. The latter was given by writer and broadcaster Rabbi Lionel Blue and in subsequent years was delivered by prominent personalities within British Jewry such as Chaim Bermant, Judge Israel Finestein, Rabbi Louis Jacobs and Clive Lawton.

The Jubilee events all proved highly successful, although by far the most prestigious was the Thanksgiving Service on 11th May, thanks to the attendance of the Her Royal Highness, The Princess Margaret, Countess of Snowdon and sister of the Queen. On one level, her presence was not surprising, as the synagogue was the only one in the Royal Borough of Windsor and Maidenhead and so could be described as 'the Royal Synagogue'. However, royal visits locally are not automatic and so it was more a reflection of the reputation and impact of the synagogue. There was also a personal connection, in that the foundation of the community mirrored part of Princess Margaret's own life-story, as she too was evacuated from London to Berkshire in 1940, staying at Windsor Castle for much of the war. In his sermon, the rabbi summarised the origins and development of the community, but also suggested a motto for the future: 'Dare and dare again' – daring to uphold a message of faith in an age of skepticism, daring to assert that the best way to achieve individual satisfaction was through communal effort, and daring to believe in the future as much as previous generations did. The service concluded with Harry Pitch blowing the *shofar*, as was done at a Jubilee in biblical times according to Leviticus 25.10.

After the service, the chairman, Stephen Sommer, stressed both the sanctuary given by Britain to many continental Jewish refugees fleeing Nazi Europe and the contribution that they had made to the country in return. This was followed by tea and refreshments in a marquee in the garden. For her part, it was the first time that the Princess had attended a synagogue service. She was struck by the prayer for the Royal Family, saying that she had not realised that it was read out every Sabbath - 'they don't normally do that in church every week; I shall tell my sister'. During her walk-about, she spoke to members and recalled her own memories of the war years and the disruption it caused. The event was also attended by the Mayor, MP and local faith leaders. It was reported on local television news, while a brochure to accompany the occasion raised £7,000.

The energy and enthusiasm engendered by the Golden Jubilee was translated into a range of other activities in the years following: on the social side there was a 'riverboat shuffle', barn dance, skills auction, bicycle ride in Windsor Great Park and golf day (many of these being repeated subsequently). In addition, a series of new groups catering for specific interests began: Israeli folk dancing, a book club, music circle, young marrieds, as well as groups for the unattached in both the 20-35 and 35+ ranges. Most of the groups had a limited lifespan, running for two years but then petering out. Some were then relaunched at a later date, and proved more enduring second-time round, such as the Book Circle under the chairmanship of Bryan Robinson. On the pastoral side, a Befrienders Group was established for those who had suffered a bereavement, recently or at any point in the past, and wished to talk about it and how it had affected them.

A branch of the League of Jewish Women was established in 1991 by Ruth Bernstein, which both held monthly social meetings with guest speakers and performed a variety of practical tasks, visiting those in need, offering lifts and helping at local hospitals. It remained an important part of synagogue life - while its Summer Cream Tea was an annual highlight - until its demise several years later. Another initiative purely for women was the *Rosh Hodesh* Group. Based on the Jewish tradition that *Rosh Hodesh* – the first day of a new Hebrew month – was a woman's festival, it was a monthly get-together to discuss issues of interest to women, led by members themselves. It ran very successfully for two years, after which time it was felt to have served its purpose. A specific summer activity began in 1992 when the Mothers and Toddlers began holding weekly meetings in different parks in the area, open to older siblings too, a tradition that has remained ever since.

Princess Margaret being introduced to (l to r) Hanna Peyman, Stephen Sommer and Robert Goodman

A wider group was the Maidenhead JNF Committee, dedicated to support the work of the Jewish National Fund in particular and to raise awareness of Israel in general. It was spear-headed by Peter Holt and Hanna Peyman and held a variety of Israel evenings. This included organising a team of callers using an empty office with multiple phone lines to contact members to solicit donations for the JNF's Green Sunday Appeal. When the first Iraq War broke out in 1991 and Scud missile attacks were launched against Israel, it held an emergency phone-around and raised £24,000. The synagogue was also aware of the need to cater for members whose financial situation was far from happy. The Job Spot column in the *Hadashot* continued to offer extra options for employment, while in April 1992, a course was led by Suri Poulos for those who were out of work and wanted to discuss the issues arising. It covered not only advice on managing finances and preparing for job interviews, but also the effects on personal self-esteem and family life. It proved successful and became a regular self-help group that lasted several months until it dwindled as the economic situation improved. At the same time a 'Fighting Fund' had been established by Raymond Curtis and Ashley Brodin, which discreetly distributed help for families facing urgent needs and with nowhere else to turn.

Encouraged by the success of the Borovinsky family to emigrate to Israel, the Soviet Jewry Committee under the leadership of Debra Brunner adopted another family, Boris and Hannah Dubrov in Leningrad. When they too were allowed to leave, letters and support were directed to Mikhail and Elena Blank, from the same city. In the new era of *glasnost* (openness) the Soviet authorities were permissive about exit visas, but the flood of Jews arriving in Israel – up to 2,000 families a day - put a huge strain on the country's ability to absorb so many so quickly. In April 1990, the rabbi therefore launched an appeal to the community, asking members to join him in donating a week's income to help support the new immigrants. Not everyone was able to give such a specific amount and donated other sums, but £22,000 was raised within a few weeks.

The community itself continued to grow, increasing to 540 in the middle of the decade and adding another 130 by the end of it. The Religion School also expanded and led to the need for new teachers. Whereas previously they had come from members who either already had teaching experience or who made up with goodwill what they lacked in professional training, it was now felt important to ensure that all teachers had both Jewish knowledge and teaching techniques. In April 1990 a course lasting four terms was launched at the synagogue under the auspices of the Leo Baeck College that led to a diploma in Jewish education. It attracted both existing and prospective teachers, and resulted in the astonishingly high total of twelve successful graduates, most of whom were to be the backbone of the classes for the rest of the decade.

One development within the school was that it became customary for the *bar/batmitzvah pupils* to have a 'class graduation' at the end of the academic year by taking the *Erev Shabbat* service. This later changed to holding the evening in March and aso leading a *Shabbat* morning service in July. A discussion group was started for parents of children at the classes, known as ASK (Adults Seeking Knowledge). It was initially motivated by the fact that some parents had to travel so far to bring their children that it was not worth them going home, and hence the need for some productive activity whilst they waited. However, it proved a popular development and attracted those living nearby just as much. It was led by the parents themselves.

Religion School teachers graduate with their diplomas, 1990 (l to r) back: Jo Osborne, Doris Fisher, Sari Stacey, Jannette Marlow, Denise Williams, Sheila Veniar, Cheryl Weale, Rosalind Luper, Jill Wiltshire, Lesley Pinkerton; front: Diz Adelman, Michael Shire, Jonathan Romain, Clive Winston, Barbara Rosenberg

One issue that had been unresolved was that there was no provision for children too old for the Mothers & Toddlers but too young to join the Religion School. The result was that in 1992 there began a playgroup for two and a half to four year olds, known as Ganon, which met on Tuesday and Thursday mornings. The founding teachers were Hila Bram, Sybil Romain and Sheila Veniar and it has remained a part of synagogue life ever since, enjoyed by the children and appreciated by the parents. That same year saw another innovation that has also continued over the years: a summer camp, Ulpan, held in the synagogue during the summer holidays for children between three and thirteen. It was a mixture of fun and informal education, and proved an instant success, attracting 42 children. Subsequent years saw it expand to five days, while Super Ulpan was added, providing activities for older children, including outings and a sleepover. By 1995 the organisation of the Religion School had grown to such an extent that responsibilities for it were split, with the rabbi, previously the Head-teacher, becoming the Principal, responsible for overall direction and dealing with external matters (eg new children or parents), while Cheryl Weale became Religion School Co-ordinator and in charge of internal organisation. She was also instrumental in expanding activities through programmes for which she obtained funding from Jewish Continuity. These included away days, family learning and teachers' packs, as well as one-off events such as a Jewish Charities Fair.

Another development came in September 1996 when a GCSE Judaism group was launched under the tutelage of Sybil Romain. It not only ensured that the teenagers stayed connected with the synagogue for a further two years after the Post-*bar/batmitzvah* class, but they imbibed Jewish knowledge at an age when they had a much more sophisticated understanding. It proved a highly successful development, with students also being able to add another academic qualification to their CV, with the great majority obtaining a high grade. The first class consisted of Hannah Gold, Natasha Simon, Rhiannan Walton and Ruth Walton. The class has continued ever since, while many of the graduates then remained as part of the Religion School afterwards, acting as assistant teachers in the classes. Although they were paid for their efforts, it was less than what they could have earned from a weekend job and they stayed on primarily because of the social camaraderie. The result of the extra class was that children could receive a Jewish education from 4 to 16 years old, while if Mothers and Toddlers and Ganon are taken into account too, there was a seamless progression from birth. The expansion meant further teachers were needed and another teachers training course in Maidenhead resulted in a further eight emerging in 1998. The fact that one of them, Rebecca Fox, went on to become a form teacher was especially noteworthy, as she herself had grown up within the community from birth and had her *batmitzvah* in the synagogue. It was also a refection of the dramatic change in the community's membership that of both sets of the trainee groups, nineteen out of twenty had not been brought up in it.

At the same time, the youth club continued to provide social meetings for the younger membership, with both 9-12 and 13+ groups. A departure from the previous decade was that they became increasingly involved with the wider Reform youth movement, Reform Synagogue Youth (RSY). This involved having periodic joint meetings with other synagogue clubs, and the children attending RSY weekends or summer camps. As part of that process, the two groups took on parallel names to those of other synagogues, with younger club called *Garinim* and the older *Shtilim*. Both groups also benefited from RSY youth leaders making occasional visits to organise programmes or give some training. Over the decade the strength of the two groups varied depending on numbers and personalities, but both managed to survive the problem of Maidenhead being a widely dispersed community and children constantly being reliant on parental lifts.

More Religion School teachers gain their diplomas, 1998 (l to r): Elias Kupfermann, Hilary Harris, Varda Szablewski, Rebecca Fox, Jonathan Romain, Sue Altman, Sandra Moran, Alan Shorrick, Helen Gartner.

The growth of the community continued – by the end of 1997 it stood at 640 households. One of the consequences was a greater number of pastoral needs and it was felt that a formal structure was needed to help those experiencing difficulties of various kinds. A questionnaire had already been sent to all members to assess the most pressing needs and a Care Scheme launched in October 1993. The object was not to replicate what was done by Social Services or professional agencies, but to help with lifts, visits, shopping and gardening. These had been happening already through individual efforts or the League of Jewish Women, but needed overall direction. Denise Williams became the co-ordinator and set about collecting volunteers and matching them to requests for help as they arose. The scheme was an important initiative, but it was noticeable how few requests were made of it, and concerns that it might be overwhelmed proved unfounded. This was partly because many members had their own support groups already, be it family, friends or neighbours, whilst those who did not have them were often reluctant to ask for help out of pride or embarrassment.

An innovation in the religious activities was the start of monthly Saturday morning 'Senior Services' for children between 9-12 years to complement those already existing for younger children. There were also some venue changes: the Communal *Seder* transferred to Holyport Memorial Hall, while the High Holy Day services moved a few hundreds yards from the Scout Hall at Altwood School to its Sports Hall. In 1994 they changed to the Pearce Suite at the Magnet Leisure Centre, where they have since remained. Conversely, there was an occasion when the synagogue was taken over for a Christian ceremony, a memorial service for the leader of the missionary society next door, Unity House, which lacked sufficient space to accommodate the large number of attendees. The rabbi's second Sabbatical in 1995 hardly disturbed the flow of communal events, with a well-organised rota of members covering his various tasks and proving the community's ability to be self-sufficient. As previously, a Leo Baeck student – this time Maurice Michaels - took a monthly service. In subsequent Sabbaticals, the community had the benefit of other student rabbis: Laura Janner-Klausner in 2002, while both Lea Muehlstein and Andrea Zanardo came in 2009.

An addition to the religious life was the acquisition of a third scroll - acquired from Wolverhampton Synagogue for £850 in 1999 when it closed owing to falling numbers and sought to sell off its religious artefacts. It was the scroll from Kojetin, though, that began to become of increasing interest. Thanks to a series of articles in *Hadashot* by Len Brown on the history of the once thriving Jewish community there which was destroyed in 1942, it was decided to arrange a Maidenhead visit to Kojetin to mark its 50th anniversary. Len had already made a trip there himself and had discovered that the pastor of the church which used to be the synagogue, Dobromil Maly, was highly respectful of its Jewish origins and had, of his own accord, being holding an annual memorial service for the former Jews of Kojetin. In November 1992, twenty-three Maidenhead members went on a weekend trip to Prague to see the many Jewish places of interest there, visit the Theresienstadt concentration camp, and spend a day in Kojetin. The latter started with a civic reception by the town's mayor and other dignitaries.

When the group then went to the former synagogue for what they thought would be a small service led by Rabbi Romain, they found the building packed out with local townspeople, many of whom remembered the day when Jewish friends and neighbours had been deported and who wished to join in the tribute to them. The service included reading out the individual names of the fifty-eight Jews who had belonged to the synagogue and were murdered, most of them at Auschwitz or Treblinka, and saying *kaddish* for them. In his remarks, the rabbi pointed out that it was the first time that Hebrew had been uttered in the former synagogue for half a century. Afterwards a plaque commemorating the Jewish community was unveiled at the entrance of the church. The event was given extensive media coverage in both Czechoslovakia and Britain, including broadcasts on BBC Radio 4 and on Czech national television. As a way of maintaining the links that had been established, a scheme was set up by which a teenage member of the synagogue would stay with a Kojetin family for two weeks and then reciprocate the hospitality. This took place the following year when Graeme Trayner went there and then acted as host in return. Even though there were no subsequent exchanges, the history of the Czech scroll - which is still used as the second scroll at festivals - remains a powerful memory.

A plaque is unveiled on the wall of Kojetin church and former synagogue displaying the names of Jews from the village who were deported to the extermination camps

The Kojetin trip also served to stimulate interest in visiting other places of Jewish interest abroad. As was the Maidenhead principle when projects were mooted by members - simply going ahead and seeing if they worked or not - the choice of location and subsequent organisation was determined by whoever came forward with a good idea. Thus the next one was led by Laurie Tytel who helped take forty-one members to Warsaw in March 1997. It was chance to see Jewish life past and present both there and in Cracow. It also involved a day at Auschwitz. Its impact on everyone was typified by a report written by Josette Clift, that captured the emotional rollercoaster engendered by that experience (1):

> As long as I live, I will never forget these few days in Poland. *Unique and unforgettable*. Readers, please do not take what I am about to say as conceit, but I do not believe that anyone who was not with the forty-one of us can understand what we experienced.
>
> Never shall I forget the Orthodox *Shabbat* in Warsaw, the Jewish cemetery in Krakow, the museum in Auschwitz, the mountains of hair, of shoes, of suitcases, the sense of emptiness and desolation where so many had walked.
>
> Nor shall I forget that 'Reflections of the Day' led by Jonathan at the hotel on our return from Auschwitz. We lit six candles, we read poems, we prayed and we bared our souls, each and every one of us in their own way, we shared our grief and our tears.
>
> And after that we went to a little Jewish restaurant where we ate and we drank and we danced and we toasted LIFE. For a moment I felt guilty, but then this is what Judaism is about. LIFE. In the same way that some Jews survived the camps, we must live and not let Judaism die. And so I drank and I danced and I thanked God for being alive. Never shall I forget. Never.

When this and other articles appeared, there was an immediate demand for a second trip for those unable to go on the original one. This duly took place the following year when Laurie led a further twenty-seven members through what one described as 'a dreaded pilgrimage'. Another trip, also led by him, was to Budapest. It, too, combined retracing Jewish history with encountering contemporary Jewish life and proved equally successful, though much less traumatic.

Back in Maidenhead itself, the synagogue's engagement with the wider community locally began to expand even further. When a General Election was called in March 1992, the candidates from all three main parties were invited to address a special meeting of members at the synagogue. It had been expected that questions would primarily be about issues affecting Jewish voters - such as Israel, antisemitism or the rise of right wing parties in Europe - but in fact they largely reflected the concern of general voters and surrounded the economy, health service and education. The same applied when a similar panel occurred during the 1997 and 2005 elections. On a wider front, when the break-up of Yugoslavia led to civil war and the massacre of Bosnian Muslims in 1993, Lorna Jacobs organised a support group to raise funds to feed and clothe the many refugees. Writing in the newsletter, she appealed to members for help (2):

> I have just returned from a holiday in Israel including a visit to Yad Vashem, the Holocaust Memorial. I have been listening to radio accounts of the Warsaw Ghetto Uprising fifty years ago. Why do we remind ourselves of those horrors, except to ensure that it must never never happen again to us or to any other ethnic, religious or racial group. But history seems to be repeating itself.

One of the events to help raise money was a local charity premiere of Stephen Spielberg's film 'Schindler's List' held at the Reading MGM Cinema. It was not only very appropriate thematically, but raised £1,800. Among the two hundred members who attended was Nicholas Winton – often dubbed 'the Maidenhead Schindler' - who was invited as guest of honour. Lorna was also instrumental in starting lunches for the homeless in 1997. They were based on the theme of *Sukkot*, the time when the Israelites were wandering in the wilderness and experiencing frailty and insecurity. During the seven days of the festival, the synagogue was open at lunch-time to serve hot food to anyone in the area without regular accommodation or proper meals. An appeal to members to provide food and help with the cooking brought an enthusiastic response from many. It was not without controversy, though, with some members worrying about the effect of inviting into the synagogue individuals some of whom were grubby, alcoholic or drug-users. There was also concern over endangering the security of the synagogue. However, the obvious social good that it achieved outweighed these issues and it became an annual event. An equally important aspect was having members present who simply sat with and chatted to those attending, so that it was not just food that was being served but the warmth of human contact for those often lacking it.

By the middle of the decade, Maidenhead's reputation for both its welcoming approach and high energy were not only well-known in the Jewish world but were evident in wider circles. *The Times* had a column entitled 'At Your Service' in which its Religion Correspondent, Ruth Gledhill, reported each week on a different church around Britain and awarded stars according to its merits. In a rare exception to this pattern, she came to Maidenhead to cover a synagogue, attending a Friday night service, attending during the week of *Sukkot* with the *kiddush* being in the *sukkah* outside. She drew attention in particular to its outreach programme to Jews who felt marginalised and who had drifted away from communal life, commenting that it had 'inspired other synagogues throughout the country to emulate what had become known as "the Maidenhead experience"'. In her one-to-five star guide to the service, her verdict was (3):

ARCHITECTURE: Edwardian, in the style of a community centre in a comfortable suburb **

SERMON: Reassuring dismissal of superstitious myths, and a warning that 'tomorrow does come'. Dr Romain is without question one of this country's best contemporary preachers *****

LITURGY: Sabbath evening service from *Forms of Prayer for Jewish Worship*, the prayer book edited by the rabbis of the Reform Synagogues of Great Britain ***

MUSIC: Beautiful Sabbath songs sung with evocative bass and top line harmonies by the congregation ***

AFTER-SERVICE CARE: Lavish feast of bread and cakes under the stars ****

SPIRITUAL HIGH: Enlightening, gracious and peaceful *****

In an extraordinary publicity coup, the synagogue featured twice more that decade in the same column in *The Times* - which rarely revisited the same religious establishment: at its Communal *Seder* and at its *tashlich* (4). It was a pleasing external validation of all the efforts that had turned a part-time community into a full-time one within a short space of time. The community was forging ahead with a wide range of projects which tended to be developed as and when new ideas arose, but Robert

Goodman, who had become the President, was concerned that there should be a more co-ordinated plan for the future. In 1994 he launched moves for a 'Five Year Plan', with a series of discussion groups focusing on religious activities, education, social life, welfare, social action, premises, wider community issues and an analysis of the current situation. Members were invited to participate in their field of interest, and it was accompanied by a detailed questionnaire to the whole community about the community's strengths, weaknesses and goals.

A remarkable response rate of 55% was achieved, which was analysed by Peter Lovett and Jenny Pizer. Amongst the findings was that, for most people, membership of the synagogue was about Jewish identity rather than religion. It was also striking that members tended to become involved in communal life if they were encouraged shortly after joining, but tended not to if they were not approached immediately. It emerged that a fifth of respondents had not attended *any* service in the previous year. When asked what might encourage them to attend more frequently, the presence of a choir was cited as a major factor. Parents rated the Religion School highly for inculcating a sense of Jewish identity and knowledge, but felt it was less successful in providing a circle of Jewish friends and knowledge of Hebrew. Whilst many expressed the need for new classroom facilities, there was no clear answer as to whether the community should seek new premises or improve the present one (5).

The results of both the questionnaire and discussion groups were turned into a comprehensive Action Plan in November 1996 by Gary Webber, who had become chairman at the April AGM. It was an ambitious document, laying out both objectives and actions by which to achieve them. It aimed to attract more members to services, improve the educational opportunities for both children and adults, encourage those needing welfare help to ask for it, retain the interest of young adults, involve new members in communal life at an early stage after joining, improve the administration of synagogue affairs and enhance communication between the Council and the membership. It also firmly committed the synagogue to look for an alternative building in the area (6). This decision was taken because, although extending the building would be much cheaper and gain some extra classrooms, it would not solve the problem of existing classrooms being too small, nor prevent the problem of an inadequate hall for big events such as a *barmitzvah* or social activity, not solve the parking difficulties, nor allow sufficient space for the anticipated future growth. With hindsight, it proved to be exactly the right decision. An immediate result of the Action Plan was the establishment of a new site committee and a fund-raising team. An education and youth committee was also formed, and a number of specific initiatives that had been suggested were implemented: a communal *Shabbat* meal, all new members receiving a welcome phone call, concessionary rates of membership for those under twenty-seven, Council posts being given a detailed job description, while *Hadashot* featured both a commentary on the weekly *Torah* portion led by Barbara Rosenberg and a 'How To…' series on practical Judaism by Danny Allen.

One of the other recommendations was to consider the appointment of a professional Education and Youth Director who would develop both formal and informal education at all levels within the community. The three day-a-week post was advertised both inside and outside the community, resulting in the appointment of Jan Roseman in September 1997. An Australian by birth, she had spent a year in Israel training as a Jewish educator and had been Director of Education at the North West Reform Synagogue. As the Religion School had a well-organised structure already, her brief was to look at aspects not covered by it, as well as the educational needs of the adults. Among the projects she initiated was making a Jewish tapestry, starting a Kid's Choir, as well as arranging a visit to Beth Shalom, the Holocaust memorial in Nottingham. A key theme of hers was Family Education, with parents and children learning together, part of which was achieved by a series of *Shabbaton* experiences. She set up *Kesher* (connections) that trained members to talk about Judaism in local schools or guide groups visiting the synagogue.

Her most dramatic achievement was galvanising ninety-one members of the community to put on a production of Fiddler on the Roof as part of the synagogue's 60th anniversary year celebrations. It brought in members who were not normally active but who could use their skills in different spheres, be it as actors, dancers, singers, stage designers, carpenters, painters, costume-makers, scenery-shifters or programme sellers. There was an educational element, too, with an accompanying course on Jewish life in Eastern Europe. Performances took place in May 2000 at the Ivor Novello Theatre in Sunninghill, Ascot, with preparations starting over a year beforehand. It proved to be a stunning success theatrically. In the words of one reviewer: 'Let's be honest, you never know what to expect when going to amateur productions, but what a production it was! The acting, dancing and singing were all of such a high standard' (7). Even more significantly was its success as a cross-communal activity, involving members across a wide range of ages and interests. Amongst the many indispensable participants was the producer/director Gillian Nahum and musical director Judith Sheridan, while Evan Sugar's Tevye was universally praised.

Fiddler on the Roof cast and production team

The enthusiasm generated by the play led to the formation of a Drama Group, which organised workshops and play readings, as well as putting on a memorable Cabaret Evening. Other events to mark the 60th anniversary year were a reunion for all those who had had their *bar/batmitzvah* through the synagogue from 1940-2000, with the oldest participant being Stanley Olman, whose ceremony was in 1945. There was a similar gathering for those who had been married under the synagogue's auspices, with many being accompanied by subsequent children. That summer also saw the departure of Jan Roseman, who was offered a job nearer to her London home after three years at Maidenhead. Her successor was appointed the following year, Hila Bram, who was already a member of the community and whose energy and innovations had already benefited the community. Her job title, though, was changed to Director of Community Projects, which was a better reflection of her remit. Another change towards the end of the decade was that after ten very effective years as the Administrator, Barbara Rosenberg retired, although still remaining involved in the community in a voluntary capacity. Her place was taken by Jannette Marlow in March 1998.

Relations with neighbouring synagogues had lessened since the demise of the Association of Synagogues in Berkshire. However, the individual contacts and the positive collective memory meant that when Reading's minister changed again and there was a greater openness to inter-communal relations, the issue was revisited. In November 1995 a meeting was held between leaders of the three congregations to examine the feasibility of re-establishing links. As before, it was agreed to avoid religious or educational activities and select non-contentious areas in which they could co-operate. However, this time there were two key differences: first, that none of the rabbis should sit on the Steering Group; second, that all events should be at a neutral venue. There was no coyness, though, about publicising the new body, which became known as the Berkshire Jewish Representative Council (BJRC).

The inaugural event took place at the Masonic Hall, Sindlesham with over 120 people present from the three communities. The guest of honour was the Jewish entertainer, Frankie Vaughan, who was then living locally in High Wycombe and who was also the Deputy Lieutenant for Berkshire. The BJRC has continued ever since then, sometimes supporting activities run by one particular synagogue that is made open to the other two, and sometimes organising specific events of its own. These have included a Klezmer Evening, a Riverboat Trip, and visits to the Holocaust Museum in Nottingham and to the Cairo Genizah collection in Cambridge.

As the mutual trust deepened, some events also began to take place in the various synagogues themselves despite the initial decision not to do so. A key factor in BJRC surviving when its predecessor had failed was the willingness of successive Orthodox rabbis at best to participate in, and at worst not to object to, its activities. It was also due to the determination of the lay leadership to support it, and to make it clear to any incoming rabbi that they valued it and wished it to continue.

The decade was also marked by some other one-off events of note: in May 1996, the 3,000th anniversary of Jerusalem was celebrated with a day of activities organised by Cheryl Weale, ranging from story-telling for young children to an archaeological lecture for adults and Israeli dancing for all. A few months afterwards, Aviva Wiseman persuaded David Kossoff to present an evening of readings about Jerusalem, interspersed with songs from the synagogue choir and attended by around 150 people. Two years later, the 50th anniversary of the State of Israel occurred. Maidenhead both supported nationally organised celebrations, but also held a number of its own events. Particularly memorable was the one in which members who were in Israel in 1948 - be it as departing British soldiers, or those fighting in the nascent Israeli forces or simply living there at the time - told their stories. These included Harold Caplan who had been a pilot in the RAF during the Second World War and in 1948 was a student at Cambridge. He was approached in June by a representative of the Jewish Agency and asked to lend his technical skills to the new state. He agreed and spent six months in Israel as a *machalnik* (volunteer) at the S'de Dor airfield, north of Tel Aviv, where he was part of an internal communications and transport squadron. Another example was Maurice Mann DFC who had also served in the RAF, was demobbed in 1946 and shortly afterwards was asked to fly a much needed plane to Israel. Once there, he helped form the Israeli Air Force and served as Chief of Air Operations. He returned to Britain in 1949 and later became the manager of the Maidenhead Marks and Spencer store. Someone who made the reverse journey was Moshe Heskey who was born in Czechoslovakia and later settled in Palestine. He was appointed Deputy Director of the Philatelic Service during the period of the Mandate. When the United Nations voted in November 1947 to create an independent Israel, he was covertly put in charge of preparing Israel's first stamps, one of the tangible signs of the end of the British rule and the beginning of a new era. When he showed the new Prime Minister, David Gurion, a set of the very first stamps, the latter told him: 'This is proof that the State of Israel exists'. He moved to England in 1968 and settled in Hedgerley, Farnham Common, where he became known as George Heskey. Another settler from abroad was Rudi Sheldon who came to Maidenhead from the Continent, served as a Councillor for many years, and was Deputy Mayor in 1995. He was Mayor's Consort when his wife, also Jewish, was Mayor the following year, although neither had any active involvement with Jewish life locally.

A very moving commemoration took place in July 1998: an outdoor service of remembrance in Carpenters Wood, Pinkneys Green at the site where a Halifax bomber plane had crashed in 1944, and which had been unmarked until then. The crew – described in greater detail in Chapter 5 - had included two Jewish airmen. The service was led by the former Chaplain-in-Chief to the RAF, the Venerable John Hewitt-Wilson, along with Rabbi Romain. Family of the airmen and veterans of 578 Squadron also attended, along with Air Marshall Sir John Curtiss. The Last Post and Reveille concluded the service. By coincidence, mention of the service brought back strong memories for one member of the synagogue, Ruth Ibbetson (8):

> At the Religion School Assembly I sat listening to Jonathan telling the children of his visit to the crater and the Memorial Service when, at the name of Jan Fink, the image of a slim young man in RAF uniform appeared before me.
>
> It was on the last day of his leave before returning to his unit in the North to take up operational duties. He had come down to my war-time home in Hitchen to see his sister, Mira Lesser who

was staying with us along with her little daughter, in order to avoid the bombs in London. They spent a happy day together. Jan had just returned from Canada where he had received his training.

I almost experienced again that feeling of shock we all felt when Mira's husband came down suddenly, early the next morning, to tell us that Jan's plane had blown up in the air and he had been killed. There was no further information.

I had not thought of it for many years and had lost touch with Mira. But now the loose ends have been tied, Mira has visited the site, said a proper goodbye to her brother and learned the details of his brave death.

Memorial service for the Halifax bomber crew

The community itself sustained many losses during the decade, but four had an impact far beyond their own circle of family and friends. Harry Philipps and Harry Madenberg both passed away at the beginning of 1990. The former had been active in numerous ways over many years, from education to services to fixing whatever went wrong in the building; the latter had been a member since the 1940s, and then served as a

Council member, Marriage Secretary and Funeral Sexton for over three decades. Whereas both were retired when they passed away, Gil Poulos was only three years old when he died following a car accident in 1994. His parents, Darrel and Suri, responded by establishing the Gil Poulos Memorial Trust to fund projects both within the synagogue and the wider community that improved the quality of life for children and adults. The synagogue itself benefited in several ways via items purchased for the Ganon and Religion School, as well as the creation of a children's playground for the under-5s in the back garden. Scholarships were provided for teenagers attending leadership courses in Israel. Amongst many external ventures, the Trust supported new facilities at the Stoke Mandeville Hospital, at Camp Mohawk in Wargrave, and at homes for disabled children in Henley and Sonning Common. It also created a sensory garden for the blind in Henley.

For many, the end of an era occurred when Alec Belkin passed away in October 1996, almost exactly forty years after he had started serving the community, both teaching at the Religion School and helping take services at the High Holy Days, *Simchat Torah*, *Purim* and the Communal *Seder*. The many tributes paid to him at his funeral, *shivah* and in letters to *Hadashot* reflected the high degree of affection in which he was held and the way in which he had been involved in the lives of countless families, singing at their weddings or teaching their children their *bar/batmitzvah* portions. This was enhanced by his cheerful manner and modest personality, not to mention his constant flow of amusing stories that inevitably began 'Have you heard the one about….?' He was also an essential part of the 'altneu' character of Maidenhead, which managed to maintain a traditional flavour to its modern services. Moreover, at a time when most Reform synagogues had switched to having a choir at their High Holy Day services, he occupied a unique position as the sole surviving Reform *chazan* (cantor). One effect of his death was to change the role of the choir from having a backing role to central one, and it became a much more prominent part of synagogue services. Alec's wife, Peggy, who had been his constant companion at all Maidenhead events throughout those four decades, died five years later.

A revolution of a different sort affected the synagogues's means of communication. *Hadashot* had continued to thrive under a series of hard-working editors, but the arrival of the Internet opened up new opportunities. The synagogue's website was set up by Adam Osborne in 1999 and subsequently managed by Jill Ziegler. It proved a useful means of offering wider information than could be squeezed into the newsletter, as well as advertising the synagogue to those thinking of moving into the area and trying to find out about its Jewish life from afar. At the same time, the use of emails both cut postage costs and enabled urgent communications to members to be made more quickly. By this stage, the community consisted of 700 households, with 195 children attending the Religion School.

At the same time as all these developments and events, a constant pre-occupation of the Council was the search for new premises. This had been one of the priorities of the Five Year Plan, but was becoming increasingly urgent because the Religion School contained so many children that three classes had to be held off-site at other venues on Sunday mornings. A variety of possible locations were examined, including Alwyn School, the Maidenhead and Reading College of Art and Design in Raymond Road, and Stafferton Lodge in Braywick Road. However, a constant problem was that any venue suitable for a spacious community centre would also be large enough on which to build houses or flats, and therefore of interest to developers who could easily outbid whatever the synagogue offered. This happened a number of times. Meanwhile, funds were slowly being accumulated through a Buy a Brick campaign, which enabled both wealthy members and those with limited means to contribute. Although a professional firm had been engaged to hunt for possible land, it was a synagogue member, who found the plot at the beginning of 2000 that was to be its new home: Grenfell Hostel in Ray Park Road.

The site was originally part of Ray Lodge, and it was on land once owned by William Henry Grenfell (Lord Desborough) who, coincidentally, had been the first owner of Studlands. The building itself was thirty years old and was used as a residential centre for children with various difficulties, but was being sold by the Borough Council. At 1.48 acres, it was three times the space of the existing building and offered rooms that could easily be adapted, with the hall becoming the prayer hall, the bedrooms being converted into classrooms and plenty of other rooms for social and cultural usage. In addition, the front garden could be turned into a large car park, but with the extensive back garden still leaving plenty of green space for recreation. It also had the advantage of being near the Thames and technically within the flood plane, and therefore not a viable option for property developers. A bid was both made and accepted in March, which then unleashed a frenzy of activity to raise sufficient funds for the purchase price (£1.8 million) as well as the refurbishments necessary. It meant that a total of £2.2 million pounds had to be found by the completion date of early August. Letters, phone calls, tours of the site, personal visits to major donors, and appeals to non-members who had connections with the area eventually produced an amount just short of the desired sum, with a bank loan bridging the difference (along with the cash-flow time-gap caused by the fact that many of the pledges were to be paid over a several year period and so not all the promised money was available immediately).

It was a phenomenal achievement for a community whose members may have been reasonably comfortable but were generally not wealthy. It could only have happened with a high degree of commitment to the synagogue, with members believing strongly that it served a vital purpose irrespective of whether they themselves participated regularly or not. Moreover, the fact that approximately 80% of members did contribute – whether financially or through practical help or both – ensured that the sense of 'ownership' that had been hoped for did indeed materialise. Planning consent was approved for the change of use from residential to religious and educational, and on September 5th the synagogue formally acquired its new building, whose name was altered to Grenfell Lodge. Meanwhile the Boyn Hill Avenue site was marketed and it was sold early the following year for £595,000 to become a nursery run by Childbase.

At the same time as the fund-raising efforts, Project Bezalel – named after the artist who helped create the Tabernacle for the Israelites in the wilderness according to Exodus 35.30 – was launched. It oversaw all aspects of the refurbishment, from major construction work to the detailed design of each room, using the talents of members. This was partly to save money on professional contractors, but just as much so as to engender a sense of personal relationship with the new building through members being responsible for its creation. As the then chair, Suri Poulos, put it (9):

> Our synagogue will feel more like a home if we make it with our own hands. Our membership will feel a stronger connection and commitment to our new home if we have participated in creating it. We will also feel a greater sense of pride when we see the results of our labours.

Some of the initial hopes for the new site – that it would include space for some sheltered homes or that it would house a permanent Holocaust Exhibition for local schools and other groups to visit – had to be dropped because of structural or cost implications. However, the Bezalel Project proved highly successful in involving members with a wide range of skills – be it with spades, drills or tapestry looms. Contact was also made with the synagogue's new neighbours to let them know of its plans and ensure that good relations were established. It was envisaged that a permanent caretaker would be needed to clean and maintain a building of its size. One of the synagogue's own members, Nick Helm, was appointed. He moved into the house on the site, and was thus a presence there even when the rest of it was unoccupied for several months during building works.

The final service at Boyn Hill Avenue took place on 28th April 2001. It included a pause in the middle for members to reflect on their memories of the years there and, if they so wished, to share their experiences. It ended with the scrolls being taken out of the Ark and passed one by one between every member of the congregation until they reached the far door, ready for the journey to their next home. The Ark doors were – for the first time ever – left open, symbolising that the heart of the synagogue, its religious teachings, were no longer present. A long poignant *shofar* blast by Simon Jacobs signalled the final departure from 'Studlands' forty-eight years after it had become the focal point for Jewish life in the area. For the next five months, communal life was spread over a variety of venues: services and the Religion School were held at Claires Court School, Ganon happened in the hall of St Joseph's Church, Welcome Mat was at the home of Barbara Rosenberg, Mothers & Toddlers at that of Dawn Kohn, and other events took place in members' houses. At the same time, the Grenfell site was a hive of activity with an enormous variety of members helping to build, mend, extend, clean and decorate it. Inevitably, unforeseen problems arose, causing both time delays and increasing costs. It meant that some of the changes intended – such as an entrance conservatory – had to be postponed, but by September the building was inhabitable and the community made ready to enter its new home.

1. *Hadashot* (April 1997) 8
2. *Hadashot* (May 1993) insert
3. *The Times* (28 October 1995)
4. *The Times* (18 April 1998, 18 September 1999)
5. For full details of the survey results, see *Hadashot* (September 1996) 8-9
6. For the full text, see *Hadashot* (January 1997) insert
7. *Hadashot* (July 2000) 5
8. *Hadashot* (October 1998) 10
9. *Hadashot* (June 2000) 2

Chapter 16

2001: Grenfell Lodge

A new era in the life of the synagogue began on 21st September when the first service was held at Grenfell Lodge. According to the subsequent report in *Hadashot,* the fresh paint and newly laid wooden strip flooring gave the building an added gleam, although it was so packed that it was hard to see much of the walls or floor. Amid all the novelty of the surroundings, there were also familiar features from the old synagogue at Boyn Hill Avenue, such as the Ark and reading desk, deliberately retained as a sign of continuity. The service began with Harry Pitch blowing the *shofar*, the congregation saying the *shehecheyanu* blessing (giving thanks on doing something for the first time), and the scrolls being brought in by Darrel Poulos and David Norman, and then placed in the Ark. The sense of occasion was captured by Jill Ziegler who wrote afterwards: 'As Jonathan observed, to be present at the inauguration of a synagogue happens maybe once in a lifetime, and for most people, never. We felt truly privileged and uplifted to participate in such a historic and significant moment in the history of our synagogue' (1).

There were two subsequent events to celebrate the new building. In October there was a Grand Opening, aimed at the entire community, young and old, using the entire premises and gardens, with a range of 'taster sessions' for all the different social and cultural activities that were planned, from book club to genealogy group to bridge circle to youth activities to play-reading sessions. The following month saw the official Dedication Service, to which the wider community was invited. The dignitaries included two Lords, three bishops, Sikhs, Muslims, the local MP, Theresa May, and even ITV cameras recording the event for their news programme the next day. A plaque commemorating the event was unveiled by Lord Janner of Braunstone, former President of the Board of Deputies. The rabbi's sermon emphasised the high hopes that all felt were expressed by the move:

> The synagogue should serve three functions: first, as a home for members where everyone felt welcome and with a part to play; second, that it would continue its pioneering role in British Jewry as one of the few synagogues to grow at a time of general decline, integrating Jewish values with modernity, Jewish law with common-sense; third, that it would be an asset to the area and the wider community.

Lord Janner unveiling the plaque at the Dedication Service, alongside Suri Poulos and the rabbi

Among the guests was the Religion Correspondent of *The Times*, Ruth Gledhill, who included the visit in her weekly column 'At Your Service'. Noting that the ceremony occurred not long after the September 11 terrorist attacks in the United States and at a time when religion was associated in many people's minds with conflict and atrocities, she quoted part of the rabbi's sermon: 'Yes, every faith has its fanatics who abuse the religion to which they say they subscribe, and who hijack its name and tarnish the reputation of the vast majority who do abide by tenets of love and justice and truth and mercy...but this synagogue will help reinforce the good in religion'. In her one-to-five star guide to the service, the verdict of Ruth Gledhill – who had returned yet again on behalf of *The Times* - was (2):

ARCHITECTURE: Homely modern style, white walls and blue plastic seats ***

SERMON: Humorous, historical overview with a serious message as well ****

MUSIC: Congregational prayers and psalms ***

LITURGY: Collection of evocative readings, meditations and prayers book ****

SPIRITUAL HIGH: Symbolic of growth, hope, faith and unity *****

AFTER-SERVICE CARE: Sandwiches, cakes, tea and coffee ****

It was the only occasion that the long-running column reported on the opening of a new synagogue and typified the fact that Maidenhead not only served the local Jewish community, but sought to spread its message far afield.

One of the notable features of the transformation of Grenfell Lodge from a residential youth centre to synagogue was how much of the work was done by the members with particular skills rather than by external professionals. This ranged from designing the lighting to laying the flooring, from landscaping the garden to painting the walls. In addition, the decorations for the prayer hall were all created by members, such as the textile wall-hangings in a rainbow of rich jewel colours, and the hand-painted blinds for the windows, patterned with a gold lattice design in the shape of Stars of David. There was also a pelmet along the wall opposite the Ark with gold, cream and silver embroidered letters, spelling out in Hebrew a verse from the Psalms: 'One thing I ask of God, that only do I seek: to live in Your house all the days of my life' (27.4). In time, other features were added, such as a partition between the main section of the prayer hall and the annexe, which featured a lavish depiction of the Tree of Life. Elsewhere, the walls of the long corridors in the education block were hung with paintings by members. The combined effect of these was both to beautify the building and to give it a sense of personal belonging: the new synagogue was not the product of hired builders but the creation of members themselves.

The extensive grounds were also put to use: the beds around the car park were populated with trees and plants that are mentioned in the Bible, along with a plaque quoting the relevant verse. It was intended both for internal purposes, to give the gardens 'a Jewish feel', but also to be of interest to the many outside groups visiting the synagogue. The different parts of the garden at the back were gradually transformed to serve several functions: a football area for the Religion School children, a general play area, a basketball area, a playground for the under-fives, a hut for the teenagers. To the side of the building, a patio area was created with tables and chairs for general socialising or for outdoor discussion groups. It also had a structure around which the *sukkah* could be decorated annually.

Jon Berman at work in the Prayer Hall: typical of the countless members who helped build and decorate the new Synagogue

Amid all the excitement and elation, two sombre moments affected the community. The 11th September attacks on New York's Twin Towers, along with other targets in the United States, not only shocked the world but affected the thirty American families who were members of Maidenhead, some of whom knew those caught up in the atrocity. The rabbi phoned all of them to check on their situation and invite them to attend a special remembrance ceremony held as part of the following *Shabbat* service. Two weeks later, a more local loss was the unexpected death of the synagogue's President, Robert Goodman. The widespread sadness reflected his long-standing involvement in communal life over several decades, whether serving on Council or teaching Adult Education classes or working on projects. His election as President in 1990 had been not just in recognition of his past contributions to communal life, but to keep his wisdom and experience at the heart of the leadership. A memorial fund was established in his honour, which resulted in a water fountain being created at the front of the synagogue entrance. Another addition was the Memorial Wall at the back of the synagogue annexe, a striking visual feature made up of fabric squares hanging from the ceiling which had inscribed on them the names of loved ones who had died. The synagogue also benefited from the Elvira Room, an extension to the classrooms in 2005 in memory of Elvira Kirchhoff-Gordon. Amongst other losses was that of Jo Osborne at the very end of the decade, who had taught continuously at the Religion School for over twenty-five years. As a tribute to her efforts in the world of education generally, 'Jo's Box' was created, which contained all the artefacts needed for those giving talks to local schools about Jewish life.

The opportunities presented by the new building were seized upon with the launch of a variety of new activities: Roger and Barbara Rosenberg began a Film Club that held a monthly showing of films connected with Jewish life or Israel. It proved very successful, particularly in appealing to those who did not come regularly to other activities but found film evenings a 'safe space' where they could enjoy themselves without feeling challenged as to their level of Jewish knowledge or involvement. A number of special interest groups also emerged: a chess club was set up by Frank Rich, while one for amateur photographers was formed by Irving Lomon, which culminated in a exhibition of their works. Poetry Evenings were started by June Fingret, which attracted a loyal following that still continues. A singing group arose, using the talents of Judith Sheridan to lead those interested, while later on a knitting group was initiated by Lorna Jacobs. Certain activities also took place in members' homes, such as the Friday night meals organised by Jeannette Kupfermann. At the same time, pre-existing groups that had waned were re-started, such as the Music Circle, Bridge Club (which later became Duplicate Bridge), the *Rosh Hodesh* women's circle, Roaring Forties (40+) group and Mothers and Toddlers (variously known as Noah's Ark, and then Bumps and Babes).

On the pastoral side, the Shalom Counselling Service was formed shortly after the move to Grenfell. It consisted of members of the community who worked professionally as trained counsellors and who formed a group to offer their services to other members in need. The service was free and provided up to six sessions on a range of personal problems, including relationship issues, depression, trauma, work stress and major life changes. Spear-headed by Laurie Tytel, its object was to be both of direct help to members and also to be seen as a 'safe place' for those who might not otherwise approach anyone for counselling. The counsellors applied their usual professional skills, but the fact that they were Jewish often help reassure those who called up the Service, as they felt the counsellors would understand them better or not need complicated explanations about Jewish family life and expectations. Since its inception at the end of 2001, it has been in use regularly by those who either find it supplements the assistance they are receiving from other agencies, or who turn to it alone. Another valuable addition to communal help was a Telephone Chatline established five years later and operated by Pauline Glendinning. It did not offer professional advice but simply the ability to have a chat, and was aimed at those who either lived by themselves or had worries that they felt they could not share with those close to them. The idea had arisen from when Pauline had been organising the *kiddush* rota and had found that a quick call about a particular date often turned into a lengthy conversation about that person's private life. Both the Shalom Counselling Service and the Telephone Chatline also acted in a referral capacity if it became obvious that those contacting them needed more specialised help or should speak to Social Services.

Many of the activities that already already existed before the move thrived even more so at Grenfell. Among these were the Ulpan summer camp for children, which was later renamed *Kaytana* (summer camp), and took full advantange of the larger premises and gardens. One permanent reminder of the many years' worth of activies is a unique model of the Temple in Jerusalem, which was specially constructed by Windsor-based Legoland for one of the camps. The annual Jubilee Lecture maintained its ability to attract leading personalities, and also huge audiences, including Howard Jacobson, Maureen Lipman and former Lord Chief Justice Harry Woolf, as well as one of the synagogue's own members, Gerald Ratner. Another local speaker connected with the synagogue was Heston Blumenthal. Other 'big names' spoke at the meetings of Council of Christians and Jews, such as John Sentamu, then Bishop of Birmingham and about to be Archbishop of York. Other ventures saw a significant expansion: thus the fortnightly group for the retired, Welcome Mat, became weekly, while the Lunches for the Homeless changed from just being held at *Sukkot* to being once a week. It had long been recognised that those without proper accommodation needed meals throughout the year and now the synagogue was able to provide it. Despite the vast increase in both physical help and food donations required to sustain the weekly lunches, members responded enthusiastically. A further development occurred a few years later as a result of the increasingly close inter-faith contact locally. Much of the latter had been pain-stakingly built up by Nigel Cohen, who realised that the best way to further relationships was not so much talking together but doing together. This could apply particularly to cooking together and it led to a monthly inter-faith cook-in of representatives of all local faiths that took place at the synagogue and provided food to a shelter for abused women in Slough.

The combination of the new facilities with the energy and ideas of the recently appointed Director of Community Projects, Hila Bram, proved a particularly successful coincidence. She launched a Sunday afternoon programme called *Keshet* (rainbow), which offered a range of educational, cultural and sports activities for adults and children alike. For parents with nothing to do on a Sunday morning while their children were at the Religion School, she revived ASK (Adult Seeking Knowledge), a weekly learning group. The *Kiddush* hall was transformed into *Café Chaverim*, providing coffee and Danish pastries for those who just wanted to socialise. Meanwhile its walls were used for a display of works of arts by members of the community, both professional and amateur, which changed every three months. At the same time, she organised a group of involved members to wear badges to indicate that they could be approached by newer members for queries about any aspect of synagogue life. Whilst many of these programmes proved both successful and enduring, some were surprisingly poorly supported. An example of the latter was the bi-monthly 'Great Debates' which explored major topical issues such as whether drugs should be legalized and if Israel should be a state for Jews or a Jewish state, yet hardly attracted any interest.

Within the Religion School, she initiated two fortnightly classes for parents that became a regular feature: one for parents of children new to Religion School, which looked at Jewish home life and ways of bringing up children as Jewish, as well as the many questions the parents had about their own Jewish identity; the other for those whose children were in the *bar/batmitzvah* class, tackling the issues facing Jewish teenagers, as well as the challenge of being a parent of a Jewish teenager. This in turn led to the parents of the *bar/batmitzvah* class taking a *Shabbat* morning service in 2003 - both to show an example to their children and to improve their own familiarity with the liturgy - which then became an annual tradition. Another result, as a practical expression of *gemilut hasidim* (good deeds), was a series of visits by *bar/batmitzvah* families to Ravenswood Village, the Jewish residential centre in nearby Crowthorne for those with learning disabilities. Some members also worked there, either professionally or as volunteers, while others occasionally took services there when the staff were not able to do so. In 2009, both Suzanne Cohen and Noya Noble met the Queen on her visit there.

Hila Bram was also instrumental in creating a cross-communal venture, Thames Valley Limmud. This built on the template already in operation in other areas of a study day with a wide range of different sessions led by teachers from all Jewish groupings both locally and elsewhere. It was organised in co-operation with members from Reading Hebrew Congregation and Thames Valley Progressive Jewish Community. There were over forty presenters at the first one, held at Leighton Park School, Reading, with almost three hundred people attending. It became a triannual event, with subsequent ones being equally successful.

Her Majesty the Queen at Ravenswood pottery class, with Noya Noble (far left) and Suzanne Cohen (standing).

Alongside all these strides - often dependent on individual initiatives - there was concern that there be a strategic plan for making the best use of Grenfell. On becoming Chair in 2002, Jenny Pizer launched a consultation process on all aspects of communal life, leading to a Development Plan. After a lengthy process, a number of recommendations were made and implemented. The constitutional changes included reducing the size of Council slightly and drawing up clear terms of reference for all Council posts. The new focus on youth meant that the previous position of Education and Youth was split into two separate posts, while the future direction was also given expression by the creation of two new Council positions, Communications and Welfare (3). It was also decided that Council members could remain in a particular post for three years rather than two, in order to give them more time to develop and complete projects. Under her successor, Daniel Cameron, it was decided in 2004 to incorporate the synagogue, thereby changing it into a company limited by guarantee. This had been recommended by the Charity Commission in order to protect members from liability should the synagogue experience any financial problems.

Further afield, synagogue trips abroad continued on a periodic basis, with thirty-eight members going for a four-day visit to Berlin in 2004, led by David Simon, and another thirty travelling for a long weekend in Morocco four years later. A smaller contingent went to Ethiopia in 2010, spear-headed by Hila Bram and Sybil Romain, with a second trip the following year, to visit the country and also meet the Jewish community in Gonder. It led to a series of exhibitions and fund-raising initiatives to help both those seeking to emigrate to Israel and those wishing to remain and enhance Jewish life in Ethiopia. Several attempts to arrange another trip to Israel had failed over the years through lack of support owing to the dangerous security situation there. However, a ten-day tour did eventually take place in 2011, organised by Roger Rosenberg, with twenty-five members covering a wide area of the country. Even more members, thirty-eight, went on a visit to Ukraine the following year, led by Daniel Cameron. One reason for the latter's popularity was that for many members it was a 'heritage tour', with their families having roots that stretched back to that part of Eastern Europe around the early 1900s.

There had been efforts at increasing the synagogue's contact with Israel long before the trip. The frequent vilification of Israel in the British media, along with the discomfort that even some Jews felt because of its association with occupation of Palestinian lands, led to support of Israel, once taken for granted, now being much more ambivalent. It was decided that, rather than being involved in general Israel activities, it would be more fruitful to identify with a particular project of special interest. A regular visitor to the country, Adrienne Kessly, established a twinning group with the Reform congregation, Kehilat Birkat Shalom, which was located on Kibbutz Gezer, not far from Ben Gurion airport. However, despite visits there by a handful of members, no inter-communal relationship developed and the connection petered out. At a time when other British Reform synagogues maintained very active Israel committees, Maidenhead as a whole seemed to lack a strong identification with Israel despite the enthusiasm of individuals within it. Despite attempts to promote Israel from time to time, the community never sustained a continuous Israel group for more than a few years. Among the occasional bursts of Zionist activity was that from 2006 Maidenhead began to participate in the annual Magic Moments project. This was organised by UJIA (United Jewish Israel Appeal). It was a scheme through which over a hundred Israel teenagers came to Britain for a week, dividing up into small groups of six or seven, each of whom stayed with a different Jewish community for that time, hosted by families with similar aged children. The object was for the British and Israeli youths to meet and establish a relationship. It also resulted in the Israelis learning about what Diaspora life entailed, while the British teenagers gained a sense of what it meant to be an Israeli Jew. The visits were designed to coincide with *Yom Ha'atzmaut* (Israel Independence Day) and also involved a major activity for each community as a whole led by the visitors. Moreover, in 2008, Israel's sixtieth anniversary, there were a variety of other celebratory events, culminating with a visit by the Israel ambassador, Ron Prossor.

The community also maintained its interest wider affairs, beyond Jewish life or Israel: *Hadashot* published articles on the atrocities in Darfur, efforts on behalf of victims of a major earthquake in Pakistan, and the suffering caused by the catastrophic tsunami in the Indian Ocean. The latter led to a campaign driven particularly by Nigel Cohen, along with Sarah Kelen and in co-operation with other local faith groups, to help rebuild the devastated communities. The funds they raised led to the complete rebuilding of an entire village in southern Thailand, Ban Laem Pom, which had been swept away by the Tsunami. It had consisted of around two hundred people, half of whom were killed at the time. The village cost around £100,000 to rebuild and the group had initially raised £20,000 through their efforts locally. One of the members was invited to talk about the project at the St Paul's Cathedral memorial service in front of the Queen and Prime Minister, Tony Blair. The BBC heard what was said and asked to be taken to the former village to film what life was like for the survivors. During the process, the remaining £80,000 needed was raised. Further funds contributed towards building an orphanage in Ban Nam Khem for twenty-two children who lost their parents in the disaster, and which also provided activities, companionship and meals for over two hundred deprived children locally. It was estimated that the group had involved the contributions of around a thousand people in and around Maidenhead through donating, organising or lending their expertise in other ways. The synagogue also participated in a wide range of other local charitable activities, from the Lions Club Swimarathon at the Magnet Leisure Centre to the Macmillan Cancer Support coffee mornings.

Relations with local churches, which had long been cordial, continued through both personal contact and meetings of the Council of Christians and Jews. There was, however, a notable increase in contact with the large Muslim community. Immediately after the September 11 attacks, Rabbi Romain arranged a joint prayer session with Dr Hafiz Saleem, the Imam of Maidenhead, whereby he went to the mosque and said a prayer for peace in Hebrew, while the Imam came to the synagogue and said a prayer for peace in Arabic. It was a message to both communities that whatever the political problems elsewhere, there was no religious discord between the faiths and no reason why Jews and Muslims could not co-exist harmoniously in Maidenhead. A series of joint ventures took place in subsequent years, including the Imam giving a public lecture in the synagogue. Links with other religions continued through the inter-faith group, previously known as Maidenhead Community Consultative Committee, which then became the Windsor and Maidenhead Community Forum (WAMCF). Its activities ranged from shared exhibitions to talks to sports events, with strong bonds growing between the participants and filtering down to their respective communities.

Amid all these adult activities, the youth group for the 8-12 year olds had been running with reasonable success, although always facing the struggle of persuading parents who lived far away to bring their children to the club. However, it received a big boost when the Post-*bar/batmitzvah* group won the national Reform Synagogue Youth (RSY) *Purim* Spiel competition held in Manchester in 2006 with a film they had made of a contemporary version of the Esther story. As the convention was that each year's competition was hosted by the previous year's winners, this meant that some two hundred teenagers descended on Maidenhead the following year for a weekend of activities, sleeping over in the synagogue and showing local families the benefits of being part of a national youth movement. Maidenhead was to win it again in 2010.

Even more noteworthy was the appointment of a professional youth worker. This had been mooted for some time, but in 2006 the idea became a reality when the part-time post was advertised nationally and Nathan Servi was selected. The twenty-three year old was born in Florence and partially educated in America, and proved a great asset, both appealing to the youth and giving youth activities a greater structure. Among the many projects he introduced was a *hadrachah* (leadership) course for sixteen year olds that gave them a sense of responsibility to be involved in the community, helped developed their own personal skills, provided role models for younger children and ensured a succession of assistant youth leaders. As well as club for the younger children on Sundays after Religion School, midweek club for the teenagers became a regular feature of synagogue life. He also encouraged much greater participation in RSY weekends, summer camps and Israel tours, and the number of Maidenhead children attending them rose greatly. They in turn brought back an added enthusiasm to club activities and eventually became youth leaders themselves. The individuals concerned gained enormously from the responsibilities they took on, while the members of the youth group had the bonus of teenage leaders whose appeal was always much greater than that of adults.

Nathan's efforts were given external recognition in the national Massuot Community Youth Awards in 2010 when he was announced as winner of the Outstanding Youth Worker Award. It was no coincidence that three members of Maidenhead's youth club received 'Honourable Mentions' at the same ceremony for their contributions: Benni Grossman, Zoe Jacobs and Sapir Tal. Shortly afterwards, Nathan led Maidenhead to winning the *Purim* Spiel for a second time. When he resigned later that year to take up a full-time position elsewhere, it was a tribute to his success in galvanising the youth that there was no question of discontinuing the post. As one of the very competent youth leaders whom he had helped nurture was on a gap year, Zoe Jacobs, she was asked to take over. This she did very successfully, and upon her departure to university, Gal Farchi was appointed. The twenty-five year old Israeli had been an Intelligence Officer in the Israeli Army, reaching the rank of captain, and was about to study music in the UK. He proved an ideal choice, building on the work of his two predecessors and having an inspirational relationship with club members themselves. The involvement with RSY took another leap forward when one of the club graduates, Aaron Cameron, went on the year-long leadership course in Israel, *Shnat*, following the footsteps of Matthew Dunston who had gone previously.

Another change in the professional team came when Hila Bram stepped down as the Director of Community Projects in 2007 after six highly successful years. She was replaced by another member, Barbara Grossman, who was already involved in communal life as a Religion School teacher and had served on Council. She brought skills from the other worlds she had inhabited as a medical writer and editor of a classic car magazine. Among the various new ventures she introduced were weekly badminton sessions, a series of midweek painting or jewellery sessions, car boot sales, and outings to places of Jewish interest**.** A concerted effort was also made to combine social and religious life, as well as catering for those without families, by holding either Friday evening meals before the *Erev Shabbat* service or lunches after the Sabbath morning services. Although these were enjoyed by those that attended, they did not attract as many as might have been expected. As so often happened with other events, the hardest part was not organising them but persuading people to come. As one Council member put it 'I work very hard to force people to enjoy themselves'. The issue was not so much the distance people had to travel, but motivating both them and nearby members to think that the community had something worthwhile to offer them and could be a significant part of their lives – not just religiously but socially and culturally - alongside the other regular activities in which they engaged. Another such attempt was the monthly T-Group she started, which provided a monthly speaker on a wide variety of topics, not necessarily Jewish, ranging from art in the Bible to consumer rights, followed by discussion and refreshments.

The growth in both membership and activities of the synagogue led to further developments in the way the community was organised. Sue Kayne joined Jannette Marlow in sharing the work of Administrator. Juliette Lockwood was appointed part-time financial administrator, and was succeeded by Nigel Murphy after some years. It was noticeable that all - along with caretaker Nick Helm - were members of the community and this reflected the policy of seeking to give employment to members as a first option, along with Maidenhead's strong sense of self-sufficiency.

Jonathan Romain celebrates 25 years at Maidenhead with former chairman during that period (l to r:) Peter Holt, Stephen Sommer, Gary Webber, Suri Poulos, Michael Lansman, Daniel Cameron, Jenny Pizer, Ivor Shafran, Richard Charon, Hanna Peyman and Howard Lamb

It was during this period that the rabbi celebrated his 25th year with the community. When he had arrived in 1980, he had been told that the community's small size meant that it had sufficient funds only to support a three year post and that there could be no guarantees after that.

However, its spectacular growth rendered that warning irrelevant. As he explained at the ceremony to mark the occasion: 'Whereas most rabbis start with a small congregation, leave for a larger one, then move to a middle-size one and continue to graduate upwards, I was able to stay put while the community changed around me'. The event also saw the unveiling of new mantle for the scrolls, which were embroidered in a rich mix of strong colours and hexagonal designs by Karen Broude. Apart from his congregational work, the rabbi's contribution to other areas of Jewish life also received recognition during the decade: he was presented with the Inter-Faith Gold Medallion by Sir Sigmund Sternberg, founder of the Three Faiths Forum, for fostering inter-faith dialogue both locally and nationally. In 2004 he received the MBE at Buckingham Palace for his pioneering work in the field of mixed-faith marriages, while in 2007 he was voted number nine in the *Jewish Chronicle's* first ever 'Power 100' listing the top one hundred Jews in Britain in terms of influencing the life and direction of British Jewry (4).

The community at large also attracted national attention: in 2004 it was selected by BBC World Service to provide two programmes for its Sunday morning series *In Praise of God* which broadcasted religious services across the world to an audience of forty-three million people. As the then choirmaster Stephen Chaytow commented, 'As the choir normally sings to an audience of a hundred people, the thought of being heard by millions across the globe galvanised us into a frenzied bout of rehearsals, both to polish existing hymns and master new material' (5). Four years later, the BBC returned, this time its online department, to film a Sabbath morning service to accompany its website section Judaism. Later that year it was the turn of BBC television, who recorded the synagogue choir for an edition of *Songs of Praise*, focusing on the Psalms in both Jewish and Christian tradition.

Music of a different sort – bagpipes – was heard at a Burns Night in 2007 for all Scottish members of the community (plus English admirers), but that proved a one-off event whereas the Golf Day became an annual feature. Amongst other innovations was a lunch for volunteers in the community to show how much they were appreciated, with an astonishing total of 149 being invited, indicating the wide number of members who contributed in different ways to communal life. Meanwhile Jill Ziegler introduced the idea of designated 'hosts' being present at every service to welcome newcomers, guests, latecomers and generally provide a friendly face.

In 2005 a Family *Seder* was started for those whose children were too young to stay up for the Communal Seder and were better served by one in the afternoon and that was also shorter and more age-commensurate. It proved an instant success and became a regular event. Equally popular was *Shabbat* Together - whereby young families met for a Sabbath meal and experience at the synagogue. The festival services also saw certain additions: an *etrog* tree had been grown from seed by Ruth Milton and then nurtured by Jeff Silver. It bore a unique Berkshire-grown *etrog* for use every *Sukkot*. In 2010 those attending the High Holy Day services gasped in admiration at the tapestry created by Karen Broude and Suri Poulos. Depicting the prayer *El Rachum* along the side of a giant *shofar*, it was twenty-two metres wide and six metres high, and added considerably to the atmosphere. In all, thirteen kilometres of gold machine thread were used to produce it. Alongside these positive developments, attendance at *Erev* Seventh Day *Pesach* services again began to prove problematic despite the innovations that had been introduced, When only one person turned up for the 2004 service, the decision was taken to abandon them, although the morning services were maintained.

*Members of the choir perform for the BBC
including (l to r) Alice Chaytow, Michael Jonason, Irene Cameron,
Muriel Simons, Lorna Rhodes, Sandy Lambert, Pearl Berman*

The needs of the Religion School meant that yet another teachers training course was arranged via the Leo Baeck College, with no less than 15 members graduating with a diploma in 2007: Lorraine Alfert, Jean Cross, Regine de Frettes, Shirley Fox, Aaron Kader, Keren Kader, Clare Lewis, Ruth North, Jeff Rosenbaum, Sheila Sather, Sam Seabrook, Anina Selve, Rachael Shaer, Susie Stein, Leah Tal. The following year, the School took part in the recently established national *Mitzvah* Day project, which entailed a variety of practical acts that helped members of the community, wider society and the environment. Over the following years it was widened to involve adults too and included packing food parcels for the poor, cleaning up the cemetery, making an illustrated dictionary for immigrant children, planting trees in local parks, collecting food outside Sainsbury's, and gathering books to donate to children's wards in nearby hospitals. In later years, other faith groups were invited to join in the activities, with Muslim adults and children being particularly keen to participate.

The decision of Maidenhead's umbrella organisation, the Reform Synagogues of Great Britain, to change its name to the Movement for Reform Judaism (MRJ) had little effect locally. The synagogue continued not to include the word 'Reform' in its title, preferring to have a name that was neutral and implied it served the area generally, whereas an adjectival one would have had an appearance of limitations. Much more significant was the new edition of the Daily and Sabbath prayer Book issued by the MRJ in 2008. Among key innovations was a greater choice of readings, inclusive language used for the English translation and explanations about the prayers. Although some members who were comfortable with the old format resisted the changes, it was largely welcomed and particularly because of the fact that all Hebrew prayers were transliterated. Whereas some synagogues had public meetings to vote on whether to adopt the new edition, at Maidenhead it simply happened and there was a smooth transition. The links between the synagogue and the Movement took another step forward when Jenny Pizer was elected as the latter's chair in 2011 after serving for some years on its Board.

A venture that attracted some raised eyebrows initially but quickly proved a welcome success was the attitude towards the environment and energy sources. The synagogue had long recycled paper and glass (the latter largely being empty bottles of *kiddush* wine), but now it also began to use fair-trade products, especially coffee and tea, and seek to use glass cups rather than throw-away plastic ones. The drive for more efficient energy-use was spear-headed by Danny Allen and Ellen Salazar, and became part of the 10:10 campaign, to reduce one's carbon dioxide emissions by 10% during the year 2010. It led to establishing a Green

Committee which grew vegetables in the synagogue garden - including carrots, cucumbers, lettuce, marrow, onions and tomatoes - which were then used for the Welcome Mat as well as the lunches for the Homeless. It also resulted in the synagogue putting solar panels on its roof. This not only made use of natural energy but greatly reduced the electricity bills. At the same time, the synagogue itself occurred no costs as the panels were funded through donations and a sponsor-a-solar-cell campaign that was fully subscribed.

The need to look after members who were elderly or infirm, especially those living by themselves, was a constant concern. A telephone rota was established by Sari Stacey to phone all those in the community over eighty years old at least twice a year, which was then extended to those over seventy-five. This proved an excellent way of keeping in touch with members, and for them knowing they had someone to turn to if needed. However, it was felt that a more pro-active approach was necessary, as well as having greater resources for providing practical help. There were some voices opposed, who felt that caring should be the responsibility of the whole community and not made that of one person, but the general view was that it still required someone to co-ordinate the efforts of others. As a result, the part-time post of Community Care Co-ordinator was established, with Caroline Morris being appointed in September 2010. However, despite her best efforts, it became apparent that the main demand for help was for lifts to synagogue events or to medical appointments and did not justify a professional position. Given the wide dispersion of the community, personal visits for keeping someone company were best organised locally through the Networks, while more serious issues were best dealt with by Social Services. Caroline resigned after a few months and it was decided that the post should be discontinued, seen as an experiment worth trying but not appropriate long-term

There were two features of communal life that could have been very pronounced but were largely absent. The first was controversies. The rows and walk-outs that sometimes characterised other synagogues' Council meetings were almost unknown. It was not that strong personalities did not exist, nor that no issues were ever disputed, but that discussions were kept even-tempered and did not become acrimonious. The few isolated instances were the exceptions that proved the rule. This was partly due to the fact that all Council members had particular tasks, so that meetings were predicated on achieving results rather than being, as a former Council member of another synagogue put it, 'a talking shop when you just sat around criticising others'. It was also due to the culture of the community, set by the rabbinic leadership, which strongly encouraged it to be cohesive and which set a high value on camaraderie. This applied to wider communal life, and *Hadashot* was noticeable for its lack of irate letters or hostile articles over the years. The only subject that did cause some dissension in print was that of Israel, once a unifying cause within British Jewry in general but one that had become increasingly divisive. Thus some members objected to its policies towards the Palestinians and others defended its actions (6).

The High Holy Day tapestry

The second absentee was anti-semitism. Despite periodic attacks on Jewish targets elsewhere – synagogues being daubed, cemeteries vandalised, pupils at Jewish day schools harassed – there were no incidents locally. This was also despite the fact that the synagogue had a high profile nationally because of the rabbi's activities in the media. This absence could be ascribed to a mixture of factors, including the economic stability of the area generally, making it fairly harmonious and not riven with discontent. It was also due to the strenuous efforts at good inter-faith relations between all the different communities which had been maintained over the years, building up into a high degree of mutual respect. When the extreme right-wing party, the National Front, put up at candidate for the first time in the Windsor and Maidenhead constituency at the 1979 General Election, it only managed to gain 1.4% of the overall vote. This sank to 0.9% at the 1983 General Election, after which the party disintegrated nationally. It was succeeded by the British National Party, by which time the constituency had split in two. It achieved 1.5% in Maidenhead in the 2005 General Election, while in the 2010 one it gained exactly the same in Maidenhead and 1.9% in Windsor. The mere presence of such candidates did cause concern, but the electoral results showed that they were soundly rejected by the population at large.

      The end of the decade coincided with a worsening economic situation nationally and the country going into recession. In response to the job losses that accompanied the downturn, the synagogue once again established a 'Looking-for-Work' group, with Simon Jacobs acting as a co-ordinator. The synagogue also offered members use of classrooms that were occupied only on Sunday mornings but empty midweek as office space for start-up businesses. There had been plans to revamp the building, extending the synagogue and *Kiddush* hall, but the financial climate made it impossible to think of approaching members for funds and the project was postponed indefinitely. At the same time, income from synagogue subscriptions dipped, as many members had to ask for reductions because of their own difficulties in paying bills. The policy was always to agree to such requests, taking the view that, although it relied on such income, the synagogue was a community not a bank, and wished to support members facing problems. It also made sense to keep members at a low, if not negligible subscription, so as to be able to receive fuller amounts once their circumstances improved. The synagogue was fortunate to have received some major legacies that softened the shortfall, while its outreach activity continued unabated, thus bringing in new members and extra income. In November 2010, despite the country at large struggling economically, the synagogue reached the total of 800 households on its membership list.

1. *Hadashot* (November 2001) 4
2. *The Times* (13 April 2002)
3. *Hadashot* (March 2004) 5
4. JC (27 April 2007) 1
5. *Hadashot* (March 2004) 8
6. *Hadashot* (September 2006) 17; (November 2009) 11; (December 2009) 9

Chapter 17

Trends and Changes

Analysis of the three decades from 1980 (for which period accurate records are available) reveals some dramatic changes in both communal trends and cycle of life rituals. Some of these may be unique to Maidenhead as non-metropolitan community, but others may be replicated elsewhere in British Jewry.

The overall birth rate in the community grew in line with the increase in membership

Decade	Male births	Female Births	Total
1980s	56	42	98
1990s	69	65	134
2000s	93	88	181

Baby blessings in synagogue shortly after birth became a regular feature, and whereas they were initially for girls - as an equivalent welcoming ceremony to that of circumcision for boys – they increasingly became common for both sexes. This was partly because some parents found circumcision traumatic and wanted to also enjoy the more relaxed atmosphere of a baby blessing; and partly because circumcision was usually carried out at home, with only family and close friends present, whereas a baby blessing was shared in synagogue with the wider community.

Normally only families who had Jewish children – ie where the mother was Jewish – requested a baby blessing. However, there were increasing instances in which the mother was not-Jewish, and so the child lacked Jewish status, but the Jewish father wanted the child to have a blessing, with the mother being happy to concur. These began to happen from 2000 onwards, with the rabbi seeing it partly as a way of welcoming a new arrival with a Jewish heritage, and partly as a first step that might lead to the family becoming involved in synagogue life and perhaps the child acquiring full Jewish status, either through the mother converting or in its own right.

Another change from previous years was the number of parents who opted not to circumcise their sons, feeling that it was no longer an appropriate ritual. In the decade beginning 2000, this happened on average in two births per year, although hardly at all beforehand. The number of male children known not to be circumcised during the decade was nineteen out of the ninety-three males born in the community, a rate of just over 20%. However, it is noticeable that in virtually all these cases, the father was not Jewish and may have been reluctant to permit a ceremony that was not only alien to him personally but often labelled in wider society as 'barbaric' or 'mutilation'. The increase in non-circumcision may therefore be directly related to the increase in mixed-faith marriages.

Mixed-faith marriage also brought instances of those lacking Jewish status wishing to opt into Jewish life. One example was children of non-Jewish mothers attending the Religion School. This was permitted, so long as parents appreciated that this gave the children a Jewish education but did not confer Jewish status per se. The only limitation, therefore, was that the children could not have a *bar/batmitzvah*, as that was conditional on being Jewish. In some cases, the children did adopt Jewish status during their time at the school; those who did not do so were treated equally in all other respects and, for instance, participated in services taken by their class, and stayed on for both the Post-*bar/batmitzvah* and GCSE Judaism classes.

The number of *bar/mitzvahs* increased over the three decades in line with the membership growth - from 110 in the 1980s to 120 in the 1990s to 176 in the 2000s, although the figures also relate to the national birth rates thirteen years earlier in each decade. The proportion of *batmitzvahs* stayed almost exactly the same at 43% or 44% of the total number of ceremonies in each decade. This was in great contrast to what happened prior to 1980, when they were not automatic and only happened occasionally. Another development was the number of adults having a *bar/batmitzvah*. In many cases, this was by proselytes who wished to have the ceremony that they had missed when they were thirteen years old, as they were not Jewish then. Adult ceremonies were also undertaken by those who were born-Jewish: in the case of men, it was often a re-run of their original ceremony on a special anniversary; for women it was usually because they had belonged to Orthodox synagogues in their childhood, and so were not permitted to have a full *batmitzvah* and they now wished to reclaim the Jewish opportunity they felt had been denied to them. In many instances this was prompted by their own daughter approaching – or having recently had – their *batmitzvah* and awakening the realisation that they had 'missed out' on theirs.

Another issue arising from mixed-faith families - and also those in which one partner had converted - was the involvement of non-Jewish relatives attending a *bar/batmitzvah* in the participatory roles in the service, such as opening and closing the Ark. Normally these were performed by close family and only by Jews, but with a growing number of cases where one set of grandparents of the child concerned were not Jewish, it was decided that it would be churlish not to let them participate if they so wished, particularly if they had been supportive of the family's Jewish involvement. In such instances, the two grandfathers might do the first ark opening and closing, and the two grandmothers do the second one. This both ensured that one Jewish person was involved, while it also helped guide the non-Jewish partner who was unfamiliar with synagogue rituals. However, this was not usually permitted in most other Reform synagogues.

As for the pupils themselves, the old joke often told about *bar/batmitzvah* - that rather than thirteen being the age of intensifying one's Jewish involvement, it was the time of leaving synagogue - was gradually proved out-dated, with many children staying on at the Religion School until sixteen or eighteen. In addition, the *bar/batmitzvah* year was made much more of a family occasion rather than an individual task, with a preparation course for the family being launched a year in advance and parents being asked to attend fortnightly classes during the year itself.

The Ganon class practise the Sabbath blessings

There was an average of four marriages a year over the three decades. This was very small compared to the number of *bar/batmitzvahs* a year, and reflected the high rate of Jews who entered mixed-faith relationships and who therefore could not have a synagogue marriage, as synagogues were legally empowered only to marry couples in which both partners were Jewish. Moreover, the figures indicate (see Appendix 5) that 75 of the 115 ceremonies involved one partner who had converted to Judaism, a proportion of 65%. This further echoed the intermarriage rate, albeit with a percentage of the non-Jewish partners then choosing to become Jewish so as to unify the family faith. It also reflected local factors: both the greater likelihood of Jews not marrying a fellow Jew when they were living in an area of low Jewish density, as well as the openness of the synagogue to those wishing to convert for marriage reasons. In most cases, the conversion took place before marriage, with the ceremony being both a civil and religious one. However, the 27 ceremonies that were religious only were usually those where the conversion took place some time after the couple were already married civilly – either because they had wanted to marry quickly for legal or fiscal reasons and then convert and have a religious ceremony too, or because the idea of converting only developed at a later stage.

The number of weddings that were conducted inside the synagogue itself decreased over the period, with 50% in the 1980s to 30% in the 2000s. This was partly because of the many scenic spots available locally, be it along the river or country gardens. The government decision in 1997 to licence hotels and other venues for marriage did not affect Jewish weddings, as they could always take place wherever there was a registrar present, but it did alert members to options they may not have previously considered. Whereas some synagogues were not willing to perform ceremonies elsewhere, Maidenhead did not discourage them and, in fact, specialised in outdoor ceremonies, with 44 out of the 115 being in the open and with the remarkable record of none of them suffering from rain. Sadly, almost a fifth of the marriages had resulted in divorce by 2012, while almost a quarter of the total number of marriages contained one partner who had already been divorced. In almost a tenth of the ceremonies, both partners had been divorced. The weddings were largely conducted according to the prayer book, but variations were encouraged to make each one as distinctive as possible – from additional songs and blessings to the bride stamping on a glass in the same way that the groom did. In addition, family and friends often participated in reading the seven blessings.

In many cases, the bride and groom were not only living togther beforehand but had done so for many years. The wedding was increasingly seen as a confirmation of a well-established relationship rather than the start of it. Moreover, there was a noticeable rise in each succeeding decade: in the 1980s, 7 out of the 21 couples having a civil wedding under the synagogue's auspices were registered as having the same address; in the 1990s, it rose dramatically to 28 out of 33 couples; and in the 2000s it was 26 out of the 29 couples. Almost all young coupes who lived together eventually had a wedding, and it was rare for a couple to be permanently living together unmarried. The handful that did so were older couples who had been widowed or divorced, and who were reluctant to make formal ties again or complicate inheritance arrangements for their children.

Another marital issue was that of same-sex couples in the community and the growing acceptance of homosexuality as being determined by one's genes from birth. Thus it was natural for those concerned, and no longer seen as an abnormality, perversion or sin. There were at least two homosexual and one lesbian households in the community - although this was far below the national average of homosexuals and begs the question of whether other couples avoided synagogue affiliation for fear of rejection. Whilst it was becoming increasingly common for Jewish gays to openly identify themselves, others still felt obliged to hide their sexual identity. There were also two cases of divorce when husbands who had repressed their homosexuality 'came out' and left their wives for another man. When the lesbian couple already mentioned asked the rabbi to do a private ceremony of thanksgiving after having lived together for twenty-five years, he saw no reason not to do so.

The funeral statistics (see Appendix 6) show that during the three decades, there were a total of 421 ceremonies. The number of members compared to non-members was 236 to 185, indicating a moderately larger number of member-ceremonies, which is not surprising as one reason for joining a synagogue is for funeral rites. However, if each decade is separated, the figures are much more stark:

Year	Total	Members	Non-members
1980s	134	56	78
1990s	129	71	58
2000s	158	108	50

It indicates a sharp decline in the number of non-member funerals over the three decades, compared to a growth in member funerals. The most likely explanation is that this coincided with the pursuit of an active membership drive: thus many who lived in the area and might otherwise have died as non-members were persuaded to join the synagogue whilst alive, and by the time of their death were members.

The funerals were almost evenly split between burials and cremations (214-207), which is a far higher proportion of cremations than took place under the auspices of other Reform synagogues. Figures for the Jewish Joint Burial Society, which arranges funerals for Reform synagogues in the South of England, showed in 2010 an overall balance of 62% opting for burial and 38% for cremation. There was virtually no distinction between men and women in terms of their preference for either type of ceremony. However, there was a marked preference by members for burials (57%) and a similar inclination amongst non-members for cremations (56%). This is in keeping with a greater sense of tradition amongst those who join synagogues compared to those who do not.

Whilst the type of funeral was very much a matter of personal choice, there were two groups of members who tended to opt for a cremation. One was continental Jews who had come to England in the 1930s to escape the growing Nazi menace. It might have been thought that as so many of their generation had been killed subsequently in extermination camps and then cremated, they might have have shied away from cremation. However, it was common amongst Reform Jews in Germany and Austria long before Hitler and so they merely carried on an already existing custom. The other group was mixed-faith couples, who were faced with the dilemma of deciding in which cemetery to be buried - Jewish, Christian or non-denominational? This was compounded by the added complication that most Jewish cemeteries only permitted Jews to be buried in them, and so that meant dividing the couple. Being cremated solved the territorial problem, as crematoria are operated by the local authorities and open to those of all faiths. As for disposal of the ashes, only a few of those cremated chose to have their ashes buried in the Jewish cemetery – 15 out of the 207 - with the vast majority having them scattered in a garden of remembrance at the crematorium or a spot that held personal significance.

A noticeable development in funeral services was the increased participation of mourners, with it being common from the mid 1950s not just for the rabbi to speak but for family and friends to add their tributes. In many cases, the formal prayers were supplemented with additional readings, often from English literature or poems specially written for the occasion. In addition, there were twelve funerals carried out for non-Jews, all of whom were the partners of Jews. In all cases, the deceased had no faith of their own; in some instances, they themselves identified with the Jewish community through their partner's involvement, if not their own;

in other instances, it was the wish of the Jewish partner that the funeral rites were done in a Jewish context because they themselves felt more comfortable with it. Although the numbers are small, two patterns emerge: first, the growth in numbers (three each in the 1980s and 1990s, but six in the 2000s). This reflected the rise in the number of mixed-faith couples, especially in the 1950s and who were now beginning to pass away, along with the greater willingness to welcome such couples and be open to their needs. Second, that whereas initially they were cremations, from 1998 they were largely burials in the Jewish cemetery at Braywick, as they and their Jewish partner wished to be buried together and this was permitted. The rabbi took the attitude that those who had been together in life should not be separated in death, nor should the family be forced to visit them in different places. The only proviso was that they were placed in in-depth graves, with both coffins thereby being in the same plot. This meant that 'the Jewish character' of the cemetery was maintained – because each plot contained a Jewish person – which was important for some within the community, especially those whose relatives had been buried there in earlier decades. This was not possible in the main Reform cemetery at Cheshunt until 2012.

The summer Ulpan recreates the Temple

The three decades also involved the synagogue officiating at ceremonies for five stillbirths, while two members donated their bodies to science and so did not have a funeral, although a memorial service took place for them. In addition, there were six suicides, four of whom were men of thirty years old or under, along with a man and a woman both over fifty.

Analysis of the membership as it stood in 2010 reveals some dramatic results: of the 800 households, 261 were made up of Jewish couples, whereas 305 were mixed-faith ones, with the remaining 234 being single persons. Of the latter group, 76 were divorcees, 51 never married, 84 widows and 23 widowers. The overall profile is a major departure from the traditional image of synagogues comprising of happily married Jewish families; at Maidenhead, the majority were either intermarried or unattached. This reflects a combination of two factors: the low Jewish density of the area, making Jewish-Jewish marriages less likely; and the active outreach programme that brought such couples into the community who might otherwise not have joined. The latter applies also to divorcees who can also feel marginalised and unwanted, but who were made to feel welcome. The number of the Jewish members who had been divorced is higher than the 76 living by themselves, for another 81 had remarried: 25 to Jewish partners and 56 to non-Jewish ones. This produces an overall divorce rate of 19%, far below the national average. It is noticeable, though, that the number of divorcees who remarried non-Jews is over double those who married within the faith a second time. The likelihood of this statistic is to be expected due to a number of factors: the Jewish partner is now older and less subject to family influences; they may have moved to non-Jewish areas because of work or house prices, and thus be away from Jewish social life; they may feel less obliged to marry another Jew, having done so already and it proving a failure (1).

The 2010 figures reveal a significant number of proselytes in the community. Of the 800 households, 113 included someone who had converted; in 20 cases, they were males, in 93 cases they were females. This imbalance is not surprising given that Jewish status is handed down through the maternal line and therefore there is a far greater incentive for a woman to convert if Jewish children are desired. In addition, prospective male converts have to face the hurdle of undergoing circumcision, which discourages applicants who might otherwise apply (2). Given that Jews married to a proselyte had initially found a partner outside of the faith (who then converted), if the households with a proselyte is combined with those in which there is an existing mixed-faith marriage, 305, it comes to 418 – just over half of the entire community and indicative of the high rate of Jews finding partners from the population at large.

The conversion programme run by Maidenhead itself saw 175 adults take the tuition course and pass their interview at the Reform Beth Din in the years 1980-2009, almost six per annum. For the reasons cited above, the great majority were female – 127, compared to 48 males. In the overwhelming number of cases, the person was either converting in order to marry their Jewish partner (79) or was already married to a Jew (43) and wished to join their faith. In a further 28 cases, the person converting had Jewish family roots through a Jewish father or grandfather, along with a Jewish identity, but lacked Jewish status and wished to regularise it. In only 17 instances did the person converting have no Jewish connections at all, and was approaching the faith purely for religious reasons. This number of *l'ishma* ('for it's own sake') cases would have been much higher but for the rabbi's deliberate policy of turning down many such applicants and giving preference to those applying with Jewish partners. This was because the latter group were already involved with Jewish circles and family, whereas it was much harder for those without that support to become part of a faith that centred so much around domestic life. In a handful of instances, the proselytes had non-Jewish partners, and thus were creating a mixed-faith household, although the other partner had no objections and was fully supportive. There were also four couples where neither partner had any Jewish family links, but both had decided to convert to Judaism. There were three cases of adoption of non-Jewish children by Jewish couples, who took them to the Reform Beth Din to give them Jewish status. From 1992, a number of parents took advantage of the relatively new procedure developed by the Reform Movement by which children of non-Jewish mothers and Jewish fathers could acquire Jewish status in their own right. These were cases where the mother was unwilling to convert for personal reasons, but happy for the children to be brought up Jewish. Thirty-seven children appeared before the Reform Beth Din in this way during the three decades. There were no known cases of reversion to a previous faith, although there were individuals who ceased being members of the synagogue after a period, even though they were still living in the area. In some cases, this was because their Jewish-born partner dropped out of synagogue life and so they simply followed the same course. In the other cases, it followed a divorce from their born-Jewish partner, and rejecting the latter's faith and culture was part of the acrimony that resulted. In two instances, a proselyte decided to re-convert under Orthodox auspices after a few years, because they had become more traditional in their observance and thinking.

Maidenhead may be a Reform synagogue but its membership in 2010 shows a fascinating diversity of Jewish backgrounds. The membership form asked applicants to state their previous synagogue. Of the 800 members, just under half (366) filled in this section. In some cases, this section may simply have been overlooked, but in most cases the rest of the questions on the form were filled in. Thus the assumption can be made that in the vast majority of cases, they were not transferring from another synagogue but left it blank because they were not currently synagogue members. This is compatible with the fact that in most instances, the members were found and approached by the rabbi, rather than them contacting the synagogue. Of the 366 who did respond, just under half (144) had previously been members of an Orthodox synagogue (137 from the United Synagogue or corresponding Provincial ones; 3 from Sephardi ones; 4 Federation ones). 110 families came from Reform synagogues, 73 from Liberal ones, 1 from the Masorti and another 38 from communities abroad whose name gave no indication of their denomination. The figures indicate that only 1 in 8 families had transferred directly from a Reform synagogue, while the majority of affiliated members came from Orthodox backgrounds. It also implies that many joined Maidenhead because it was the local synagogue or because of the facilities it offered, and not out of ideological reasons.

Members of the Youth Club
l to r: Clara Lehmann, Anna Compton, Olivia Rome, Vicky Moran, Sulia Celebi, Gabie Reiff, Andrew Knight, Sam Harris, Roie Tal, Georgina Lockwood, Natan Bram, Sapir Tal, Gal Farchi

The place of marriage of members in 2010 is equally revealing. Details were given in 465 out of the 800 membership forms (given that another 234 households consisted of only one person, this was a fairly full response). 115 were married in an Orthodox synagogue (111 in the United Synagogue or corresponding Provincial ones; 4 in Sephardi ones), 69 in Reform ones, 27 with the Liberals. This makes a total of 311 and shows that, as with the statistics concerning the previous synagogue at which they were members, just under half came from the Orthodox. There were also 190 civil marriages that took place in Registry Offices. This reflects once again the high number of mixed-faith marriages in the community. Even more astonishing is the 9 forms that recorded the marriage being in Church. It indicates both the extent to which some Jews had veered away from Jewish life, and the fact that Maidenhead was able to reach out to some of those individuals and bring them back into the Jewish fold. It may be that there were some more instances of Church weddings by members who left this question unanswered. There were also 55 weddings that took place abroad at synagogues whose affiliation was unspecified.

The geographical spread of the 800 households in 2010 (see Appendix 4) shows that although the town with the largest number was Maidenhead (100), it also meant that the vast majority of members lived outside the town. Moreover, they were scattered throughout Berkshire and Buckinghamshire, as well as in Oxfordshire and Surrey, and spilling into parts of Hampshire. To the west, Reading was the second largest centre, with 83 homes. To the south, Bracknell, Wokingham, Ascot, Camberley and other towns provided 100 households, while to the east there were over 40 in the Slough and Windsor area. Going North, there were around 100 addresses encompassing Marlow, Cookham, Bourne End, and High Wycombe; in the north-east, towns such as Beaconsfield, Gerrards Cross, Amersham and the Chalfonts added over 60 more, while north-west there were 30 in Henley. There were also smaller clusters in more outlying areas, covering a wide arc around the entire area, such as Aylesbury, Oxford, Basingstoke and Guildford. The remaining members were dispersed in small numbers across a wide range of towns and villages, some being the only known Jewish family in the locality. Most members lived within a thirty minute drive of the synagogue, but very few lived in walking distance. There were also some eighty households located out of the area – from Dover to London – as well as a handful abroad. These were members who had moved away, but wished to retain their membership because of family in the area or a strong personal connection to the community.

The age profile in 2010 revealed a fairly balanced spread: of the 1,533 individuals in total, with a significant number found in most of the ten year age-brackets:

0-9 years: 184	(approx. 11% of the total)
10-19 years: 267	(approx. 17% of the total)
20-29 years: 86	(approx. 6% of the total)
30-39 years: 115	(approx. 8% of the total)
40-49 years: 209	(approx. 14% of the total)
50-59 years: 221	(approx. 14% of the total)
60-69 years: 224	(approx. 15% of the total)
70-79 years: 139	(approx. 9% of the total)
80-89 years: 73	(approx. 5% of the total)
90-99 years: 14	(approx. 1% of the total)
100+ years: 1	(less than 1% of the total)

Apart from those over 80 years old, the smallest tranche were in their 20s, an age when many who had grown up locally moved away to cities, while not yet the age at which others moved to the area to settle down with families. The total number of those under 50 years was 861 compared to 672 being over 50, thus giving the community a relatively young profile, and which accounted for the large Religion School.

The membership campaign that had produced such startling growth also revealed high levels of disinterest in affiliation. During the period 1980-2009 the rabbi either phoned or visited a total of 3,113 households of those who had either moved to the area recently, or had been living locally for several years, but were not members. 1,758 of them joined the community, a success rate of over 50%. However, that meant there were 1,355 households that did not join. In some cases, they already belonged to a synagogue, be it another one in the area (168) or in London (141). The latter reflected those who had moved out of London but retained their existing membership, either out of habit or because they wished to maintain their burial rights. More significant were the 1046 Jews in the area who did not belong to any synagogue and said they had no interest in doing so. By not expressing their Jewishness through synagogue-affiliation and, in the absence of any other Jewish institutions in the area, they were effectively cutting themselves off from Jewish life. Their lack of any meaningful Jewish contacts, combined with the fact that they were living in a non-Jewish area, was likely to mean that they (and any children) would quickly assimilate and be lost to the Jewish community at large. The figure tells a story applicable to the 'drop-out' rate for British Jewry as a whole, where it has been estimated that approximately 1 in 3 Jews do not belong to a synagogue (3). The ability to 'buck the tend' with an active outreach campaign is highlighted not only by the synagogue's success rate in the wider area but even more so locally. In the 2011 Census, 475 Jews are recorded as residing in the Windsor and Maidenhead Unitary Authority, while synagogue records show that 383 adults and children within it belonged to the synagogue, an affiliation rate of 81%. In time, Maidenhead became a byword for reaching out to the unaffiliated, with many other synagogues wishing to emulate its success in this area. The Reform Synagogues of Great Britain held a seminar at which Rabbi Romain explained the methods used and the approach behind them. This was then turned into a booklet published by the movement entitled *How To Grow* and was later replicated as training video. Eventually the growth rate slowed, largely because all the Jews 'hiding' in the area had been found. By 2005, although there were still a few long-term residents who were detected after escaping notice for many years, the majority of new members were those who moved into the area and were either reported to the Synagogue by existing members (who had become well trained in this respect) or contacted it of their own volition.

The fact that the vast majority of new members had joined not because they approached the Synagogue but because the Synagogue located them had certain consequences. It meant that, as a generalisation, they were religiously lapsed, otherwise they would have been sufficiently motivated to join of their own accord. Thus although they were then happy to become involved in the social and cultural life of the community, which boomed, the attendance at a services did not increase in any way commensurate with the membership growth. In the 1980s the average attendance was 33 individuals on a Friday evening and 26 on a Saturday morning (discounting *bar/batmitzvahs* when numbers rose due to visiting family and friends). In the 1990s Friday evening attendance remained the same average and Saturday mornings went up slightly to 31, while in the 2000s both rates fell to 25. This decline is surprising given the steady increase in membership. One explanation might relate to the general decline in worship among Jews even if they still identify culturally. Another might be the more pressing economic climate which left less time for leisure pursuits at weekends. It may also be connected with the general trend in Britain of people still having spiritual needs but being less inclined to express them through institutional religion (4).

The occupations of members in 2010 varied enormously, and included a cartographer, a cartoonist and a cattle breeder. Members were also in the police and armed forces. Not surprisingly, given Maidenhead's proximity to Heathrow, several were connected with the airline business, whether as pilots, cabin crew or groundstaff. In an area often dubbed as 'Silicon Valley' because of the high number of computer firms present, the greatest number of members were connected with that industry. Amongst the other occupations attracting the highest numbers were the professions: while there were only 2 dentists, there were 26 doctors and surgeons, 33 accountants and 35 practising law (8 barristers and 27 solicitor). There were also many in different parts of the 'caring industries': 7 social workers, 8 counsellors, 35 school teachers and a further 11 university lecturers.

*The Wednesday Social Club hold a play-reading session
l to r: Flora Gale, Jenni & Roy Woolf, Rita Jacobs, Rose Danzinger, Regina Presser, Gay Koss, Myra Garnet Pell, Sally Heilbut, Steven Pordes, Jenny Cooper*

The overwhelming majority of members in 2010 were British born, but there were also certain clusters of others nationalities: 31 households having one or both partners who were South African, 36 having one or both partners who were American, and with 46 having one or both partners who were Israeli. No other nationalities had more than 9 households, with those from France, Germany and Russia being the larger groupings.

The steady gains in membership over the three decades are all the more pronounced given the high losses that happened at the same time, with a total of 913 households leaving the community. In the majority of cases (595), this was because they moved out of the area. Some of these were older couples retiring to smaller accommodation elsewhere or to be nearer their children, but most were working families and reflected the mobile job market. Just over half of that figure (358) were Jews from abroad who returned to their respective countries or British Jews going to work overseas. Moreover, the high number of American families who came to the area for three to five year contracts accounted for 136 of that number. Another 262 households resigned because they decided they did not want to maintain contact with the Jewish life locally. This is not surprising in view of the fact that most new members did not contact the synagogue but were approached by the rabbi. Thus they were persuaded to join, rather than initiating it themselves, and so a certain number dropping away was to be expected. There were also 52 households who resigned because they wished to join another synagogue in the area, usually Reading Orthodox or South Bucks Liberal. For them, the Maidenhead style of services was not what they wanted and they chose another community where they felt more comfortable. A further two households resigned in order to convert to Christianity, while two more were asked to leave because of inappropriate behaviour (one being a Jew for Jesus who engaged in missionary activity, the other after molesting another member).

****

The year 2011 marked the tenth anniversary of the community's stay at Grenfell Lodge. The move had been an important step in consolidating Maidenhead as the largest non-metropolitan community in Britain. The new building had emphasised in a concrete way the philosophy of Maidenhead and the change of culture it sought to engender, with the synagogue being not just a place of worship but a community centre and open to all Jews, whatever their level of identification. It was accepted that there were many ways of being Jewish. A frequent saying of the rabbi that echoed this approach was that 'you don't have to be religious to be Jewish', while he often cited the view that 'to be a good Jew, you don't have to believe in God, you just have to do what God says'. It emphasised that one could play an active role in synagogue life even if one had doubts in theological matters. The acquisition of Grenfell allowed expansion of the social and cultural activities that defined Maidenhead as much as its religious services.

The enthusiasm generated by the new facilities, and the energy of countless individuals over the years, had led the community from a hut rented by evacuees in 1940 to a thriving hub of Jewish life, that was now thoroughly etched into the Jewish map of England.

The fountain in memory of Robert Goodman at the entrance to the Synagogue

1. Romain (1996) 76ff
2. Romain (2000) 21ff
3. Miller, School & Lerman (1996) 10
4. Linda Woodhead, 'Redrawing the Lines', in *New Humanist* (November 2012)

Appendix 1

Communal Leadership

Initially the leader of the community was designated as the President, but from 1959 the President was changed to a figurehead role, while executive authority was invested in the new position of Chairman.

AGM year	President
1945	Leslie Paisner
1950	(not known)
1953	Sidney Rich
1954	Victor Afia
1955	William Goldstein
1956	Israel Madenberg
1957	Israel Madenberg
1958	Israel Madenberg

AGM year	Chairman	President
1959	Victor Afia	Israel Madenberg
1960	Victor Afia	Israel Madenberg
1961	Laurence Misener	Israel Madenberg
1962	Laurence Misener	Israel Madenberg
1963	Laurence Misener	Israel Madenberg
1964	Laurence Misener	Israel Madenberg
1965	Laurence Misener	Israel Madenberg
1966	Laurence Misener	Israel Madenberg
1967	Laurence Misener	Israel Madenberg
1968	Bernard Feldstein	Israel Madenberg
1969	Bernard Feldstein	Laurence Misener
1970	Ronald Bernie	position vacant
1971	Ronald Bernie	Murray Bernie
1972	Ronald Bernie	Murray Bernie
1973	Gerald Cohen	Murray Bernie
1974	Gerald Cohen	Murray Bernie
1975	Harry Madenberg	Murray Bernie
1976	Harry Madenberg	Murray Bernie
1977	Robert Goodman*	Murray Bernie
1978	Robert Goodman	Murray Bernie
1979	Ivor Shafran	Murray Bernie

1980	Ivor Shafran	Murray Bernie
1981	Michael Lansman	Murray Bernie
1982	Michael Lansman	Murray Bernie
1983	Ian Scott	Murray Bernie
1984	Ian Scott	Murray Bernie
1985	Peter Holt	Murray Bernie
1986	Peter Holt	position vacant
1987	Peter Holt**	position vacant
1988	Stephen Sommer	position vacant
1989	Stephen Sommer	position vacant
1990	Hanna Peyman	Robert Goodman
1991	Hanna Peyman	Robert Goodman
1992	Richard Charon	Robert Goodman
1993	Richard Charon	Robert Goodman
1994	Howard Lamb	Robert Goodman
1995	Howard Lamb	Robert Goodman
1996	Gary Webber	Robert Goodman
1997	Gary Webber	Robert Goodman
1998	DannyAllen	Robert Goodman
1999	DannyAllen	Robert Goodman
2000	Suri Poulos	Robert Goodman
2001	Suri Poulos	Robert Goodman
2002	Jenny Pizer	position vacant
2003	Jenny Pizer	position vacant
2004	Daniel Cameron	position vacant
2005	Daniel Cameron	position vacant
2006	Daniel Cameron	position vacant
2007	Martin Silverman	position vacant
2008	Martin Silverman	position vacant
2009	Danny Allen	position vacant
2010	Danny Allen	position vacant
2011	David Simon	position vacant
2012	David Simon	position vacant

* Maurice Davis was nominated as chairman but suffered a heart attack, Harry Madenberg stayed on as acting-chair for a while and then Robert Goodman took over

** the AGM was changed from November to April, so as to coincide with the financial year, with the result that Peter Holt remained chair for six months more than the usual two year period.

Trustees

Trustees were appointed when the property at 9 Boyn Hill Avenue was acquired. The appointment was for an indefinite term, having no executive responsibilities but holding the deeds of the synagogue building on behalf of the membership. Changes were made only when a trustee died in office or resigned. However, those appointed were considered stalwarts of the community who could act in its best interests if a major decision regarding the future of the community and its assets arose.

1953	Victor Afia, Arthur Duran, Israel Madenberg and Sidney Rich
1968	Israel Madenberg, Victor Afia, Laurence Misener, Hugo Schwab, Benjamin Jewell
1969	Victor Afia, Laurence Misener, Hugo Schwab, Benjamin Jewell, Hary Olman
1974	Benjamin Jewell, Harry Olman, Robert Goodman, Harry Madenberg
1977	Benjamin Jewell, Robert Goodman, Harry Madenberg, Willy Frank
1985	Benjamin Jewell, Robert Goodman, Willy Frank, Mark Diskin
1994	Robert Goodman, Mark Diskin, Peter Holt, Stephen Sommer
2000	Robert Goodman, Mark Diskin, Clive Lewis, Nigel Cohen
2002	Mark Diskin, Clive Lewis, Nigel Cohen, Sam Geneen

In 2004 the synagogue was incorporated and the members of the Council all became Trustees in addition to the previously appointed ones.

Appendix 2

Association of Synagogues in Berkshire
Contact List - May 1987

The original list also had home phone numbers besides everyone's name, but they have been omitted below

Position	Maidenhead Synagogue Community	Reading Hebrew Congregation	Thames Valley Progressive Jewish
Chairman	Peter Holt	Jack Album (president)	Bill Meyer
ASB Liason Officer	Jonathan Romain	Geoffrey Fairfield	Cyril Selinger
AJEX	Otto Pordes	Barney Collings	Cyril Selinger
Board of Deputies	Herta Orchudesh	Jack Album	-
CCJ	Julian Marks	Jessel Hazleton	Stephen Phillips
Cultural Society	Hilda Bronstein	Marcia Perkin	Bill Meyer
Friendship Club	Barbara Rosenberg	Sophie Avner	Mila Harris
Gan/Toddlers	Sybil Romain	Sarah Firsht	Mila Harris
Israel	Herta Orchudesh	Geoffrey Fairfield	Maddy Gozman
League of Jewish Women	-	Sheila Levy	Myrtle Osorio
Soviet Jewry	Debra Brunner	Marcia Perkin	Diz Adelman
Unattached 35+	Freda Lambourne	-	-
WIZO	-	Karen Ross	Lisa Klein
Young Marrieds	Sharon Epps	Sue Fuhr	-
Kosher Shop	Richard Gow	Hilary Meyer	-
Judaica Shop	John Cummings	Karen Ross	-
Security	Clive Creager	David Firsht	-

Appendix 3

Bar/batmitzvah Statistics

Year	13 year olds			Adults		
	Total	Bar	Bat	Total	Bar (Pros)	Bat (Pros)
1980	4	4	0	0	0	0
1981	7	5	2	0	0	0
1982	12	5	7	0	0	0
1983	15	7	8	0	0	0
1984	20	10	0	0	0	0
1985	8	4	4	2	1	1
1986	16	11	5	1	0	1
1987	11	6	5	1	1 (1)	0
1988	8	6	2	1	0	1
1989	9	3	6	2	0	2 (1)
1990	9	5	4	1	0	1 (1)
1991	7	4	3	1	0	1 (1)
1992	13	7	6	1	1 (1)	0
1993	9	7	2	0	0	0
1994	14	7	7	0	0	0
1995	10	6	4	1	0	1 (1)
1996	12	8	4	1	0	1
1997	17	9	8	0	0	0

1998	19	9	10	0	0	0
1999	10	7	3	3	1 (1)	2
2000	19	11	8	1	1	0
2001	17	12	5	0	0	0
2002	15	9	6	0	0	0
2003	18	12	6	2	0	2 (1)
2004	16	7	9	1	0	1
2005	18	8	10	2	1	1
2006	14	7	7	2	0	1
2007	22	13	9	1	1 (1)	0
2008	20	11	9	0	0	0
2009	17	10	7	2	1	1
	406	230	176	26	8 (4)	17 (5)

Abbreviations:
Bar = *Barmitzvah*
Bat = *Batmitzvah*
Pros = Proselytes

The bar/batmitzvah class of 2000/2001 prepare to take a service

l to r: Joanne Williams, Stephen Wiltshire, David Segal, Alice Chaytow, Rianna Poulos, Jonathan Helm, Roy Green, Daniel Norman, Jonathan Romain, Tim Alfred, Jordan Green, Simon Altman

The Jewish section at Braywick cemetery

Appendix 4

Map of Maidenhead Synagogue Membership

Below is a map of the towns and villages with three or more Jewish households covered by the 2010 membership of Maidenhead Synagogue. They account for 740 of the 800 households, with the remainder being scattered amongst other locations, as well as some being out of the area completely. Towns in which medieval Jews also had association are in capitals.

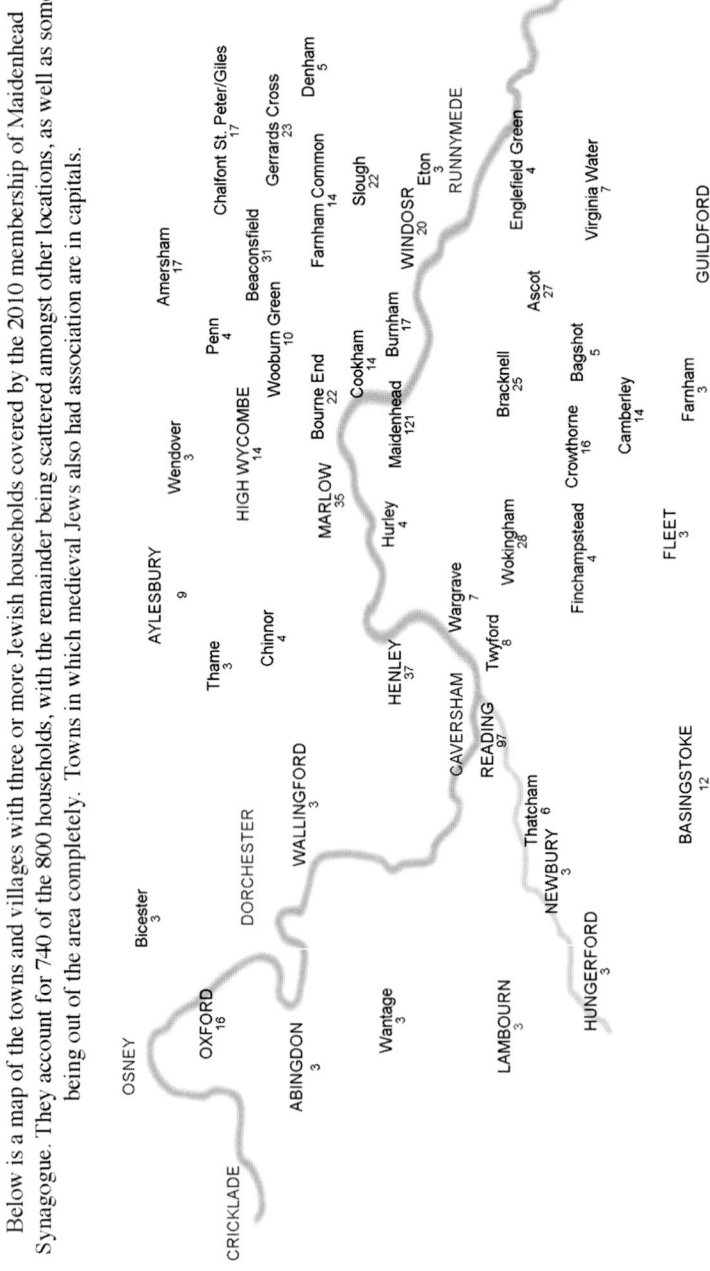

Appendix 5

Marriage Statistics

Year	Total	Civil & relig.	Relig. only	One pros.	One div.	Both div.	Venue: syn.	Venue: other	Sub. div.
1980	0	0	0	0	0	0	0	0	0
1981	1	1	0	0	0	0	0	1	0
1982	3	2	1	3	1	0	1	1	0
1983	2	2	0	1	0	0	1	1	2
1984	5	3	2	5	0	1	4	1	0
1985	3	3	0	2	2	0	2	0	2
1986	4	1	3	2	1	0	1	3	2
1987	6	6	0	2	1	1	2	3	0
1988	7	5	2	5	2	1	4	1	3
1989	1	1	0	1	0	0	0	1	1
1990	5	5	0	4	2	0	2	2	1
1991	9	7	2	6	0	2	6	3	0
1992	5	5	0	5	2	0	3	2	2
1993	3	2	1	2	1	0	3	0	1
1994	6	5	1	3	1	0	4	2	1
1995	5	1	4	3	1	0	5	5	2
1996	2	2	0	2	1	0	2	0	1
1997	2	1	1	1	1	0	1	1	0

Year									
1998	1	1	0	1	0	0	1	0	0
1999	6	4	2	4	2	0	1	5	2
2000	4	4	0	3	1	0	2	1	0
2001	1	0	1	1	0	0	0	1	0
2002	3	3	0	2	0	0	2	1	1
2003	2	2	0	1	0	2	1	0	0
2004	6	3	3	4	2	0	1	4	1
2005	3	2	1	2	0	2	1	0	0
2006	2	2	0	1	1	0	0	1	0
2007	8	7	1	4	1	1	1	2	0
2008	5	5	0	2	1	0	1	0	0
2009	5	3	2	3	1	1	3	2	0
	115	88	27	75	25	11	55	44	22

Abbreviations:

Civil & relig. = marriages that had both civil and religious effect
Relig. = marriages that had religious effect only
One pros. = one partner was a proselyte
One div. = one partner was already divorced
Both div. = both partners were already divorced
In syn. = ceremony held inside the synagogue
Venue other = ceremony held at a different venue to the synagogue
Sub. Div. = the couple were subsequently divorced

Appendix 6

Funeral Statistics

Year	Funerals Total	M	F	B	C	Mm	Non	Burials M	F	Mm	Non	Cremations M	F	Mm	Non
1980	13	8	5	3	10	5	8	1	2	2	1	7	3	3	7
1981	7	4	3	3	4	0	7	3	0	0	3	1	3	0	4
1982	11	6	5	5	6	3	8	3	2	1	4	4	2	2	4
1983	12	5	7	5	7	5	7	3	2	3	2	3	4	2	5
1984	7	5	2	5	2	4	3	4	1	4	1	1	1	0	2
1985	16	8	8	10	6	4	12	5	5	3	7	3	3	1	5
1986	19	7	12	9	10	12	7	5	4	3	6	7	3	3	7
1987	14	7	7	8	6	6	8	4	4	3	5	3	3	3	3
1988	11	7	4	5	6	7	4	3	2	3	2	4	2	4	2
1989	24	16	8	9	15	10	14	5	4	6	3	10	5	5	10
1990	8	7	1	2	6	6	2	2	0	2	0	5	1	4	2
1991	7	2	5	3	4	2	5	1	2	2	1	1	3	0	4
1992	18	5	13	7	11	9	9	2	5	4	3	3	8	4	7
1993	13	9	4	7	6	8	5	5	2	4	3	4	2	2	4
1994	13	5	8	8	5	10	3	3	5	6	2	2	3	4	1
1995	15	9	6	8	7	8	7	5	3	5	3	5	2	3	4
1996	19	6	13	8	11	6	13	2	6	3	5	5	6	3	8

Year														
1997	12	8	4	7	5	5	7	5	2	4	3	3	2	1	4
1998	10	4	6	7	3	7	3	3	4	5	2	1	2	1	2
1999	14	7	7	8	6	10	4	4	4	6	2	4	2	4	2
2000	11	6	5	7	4	7	4	4	3	5	2	2	2	2	2
2001	19	10	9	7	12	16	3	3	4	6	1	7	5	10	2
2002	16	7	9	10	6	12	4	4	6	7	3	3	3	5	1
2003	16	10	6	10	6	12	4	5	5	7	3	5	1	5	1
2004	15	7	8	10	5	8	6	5	5	6	4	2	3	3	2
2005	17	7	10	10	7	8	8	5	5	6	4	2	5	3	4
2006	16	10	6	9	7	11	5	6	3	5	4	4	3	4	3
2007	18	8	10	9	9	12	6	5	4	5	4	3	6	7	2
2008	20	9	11	11	9	16	4	4	7	10	1	5	4	7	2
2009	10	5	5	4	6	5	5	2	2	2	2	3	3	3	3
	421	214	207	214	207	236	185	111	103	128	86	112	95	98	109

Abbreviations:
M = male
F = female
B = burial
C = cremation
Mm = member of the synagogue
Non = non-member

Appendix 7

Timeline since 1940

Maidenhead Synagogue	Wider events
1940 Community founded	
	1948 State of Israel established
1953 Premises at Boyn Hill Avenue bought	
1954 Maidenhead becomes a member of the Reform movement	
First *barmitzvah* takes place	
1955 First wedding takes place	
1957 Schwab Hall built	
	1963 Profumo Affair at Cliveden
	1967 Six Day War
1971 Jewish section in Braywick Cemetery opened	
	1972 Maidenhead linked to the M4
	1974 Royal Borough of Windsor and Maidenhead created
1980 Full-time rabbi appointed	
	1986 Berkshire Council of Christians and Jews formed (CCJ)
1987 Association of Synagogues in Berkshire formed (re-established as Berkshire Jewish Representative Council in 1995)	

Synagogue is redeveloped at Boyn Hill Avenue

1987 Maidenhead Community Consultative Council formed (MCCC) – known from 2006 as Windsor and Maidenhead Community Forum (WAMCF)

1988 Administrator appointed

1990 50th anniversary of the synagogue attended by Princess Margaret

1997 Education and Youth Director appointed (later known as Director of Community Projects)

1998 Berkshire County Council abolished and Royal Borough becomes a unitary authority

2001 Move to Grenfell Lodge

2006 Youth Worker appointed

2010 Community Care Co-ordinator appointed

Bibliography

1. Books and academic publications

Alderman, Geoffrey (1987) *The Federation of Synagogues 1887-1987* (London: The Federation of Synagogues)
Alderman, Geoffrey (1992) *Modern British Jewry* (Oxford: Clarendon Press)
Ansell, Gerald (2000) *The Way It Is* (New York: Keshet Press)
Asquith, Herbert (1928) *Memories and Reflections* Vol. II (London: Cassell)
Barnett, Arthur (1961) *The Western Synagogue Through Two Centuries* (London: Vallentine Mitchell)
Bermant, Chaim (1971) *The Cousinhood* (London: Eyre & Spottiswoode)
Black, Gerry (1992) *Lender to the Lords, Giver to the Poor* (London: Vallentine Mitchell)
Blake, Robert (1966) *Disraeli* (London: Eyre & Spottiswoode)
Brand, Paul (2005) *Plea Rolls of the Exchequer of the Jews - Vol. VI* (London: Jewish Historical Society of England)
Cassell, Curtis (unpublished mss.) *D.W. Marks - The Father of Anglo-Jewish Reform*
Causton, Anne (2007) *Medieval Jewish documents in Westminster Abbey* (London: Jewish Historical Society of England)
Cheesman, E.C. (1946) *Brief Glory* (Chippenham: Antony Rowe Ltd)
Cluse, Christoph (2004) *The Jews of Europe in the Middle Ages* (Turnhout, Belgium: Brepols)
Cohen, Melvin (1999) *Habonim in Great Britain 1929-1955* (Israel: Irgun Vatikei Habonim)
Cohen, Sarah (2005) *Plea Rolls of the Exchequer of the Jews Vol. V* (London: Jewish Historical Society of England)
Danby, Frank (1887) *Dr Phillips: A Maida Vale Idyll* (London: Vizetelly)
Davis, M.D. (1888) *Hebrew Deeds of English Jews* (London: Jewish Chronicle Publications)
Emanuel, Muriel & Gissing, Vera (2002) *Nicholas Winton and the Rescued Generation* (London: Vallentine Mitchell)
Encyclopaedia Judaica (1972) (Jerusalem: Keter Publishing House)
Endelman, Todd (1990) *Radical Assimilation in English Jewish History 1656-1945* (Indianapolis: Indiana University Press)

Endelman, Todd & Kushner, Tony (eds) (2002) *Disraeli's Jewishness* (London: Vallentine Mitchell)
Fry, Helen (2007) *The King's Most Loyal Enemy Aliens (*Stroud: Sutton Publishing)
Godden, Jeremy (unpublished mss.) *The Steinhardts and the Cedar Boys*
Gollancz, Herman (1916) *Sermons and Addresses* (London: Chapman & Hill)
Goodman, Susan (1986) *Spirit of Stoke Mandeville: The Story of Sir Ludwig Guttmann* (London: Collins)
Gray, Rosemary & Griffiths, Sue (1980) *The Book of Wargrave,* (Wargrave: Wargrave Local History Society)
Grenville, Anthony (2010) *Jewish Refugees from Germany and Austria in Britain 1933-1970* (London: Vallentine Mitchell)
Hadas, Moses (2001) *Fables of a Jewish Aesop* (Boston: Nonpareil Books)
Henriques, Robert (1966) *Sir Robert Waley Cohen* (London: Secker & Warburg)
Hole, Bridget (1998) *Are You Married, Or Do You Live In Maidenhead?* (Maidenhead: Acorn Forum)
Hunter, Judith (1995) *A History of Berkshire* (Chichester: Phillimore)
Hyde, H. Montgomery (1967) *Lord Reading* (London: Heinemann)
Inglis, Ruth (1989) *The Children's War* (London: Collins)
Jackson, Carlton (1960) *Who Will Take Our Children?* (London: Methuen)
Jackson, Stanley (1936) *Rufus Isaacs* (London: Cassell)
Jacobs, Joseph (1893) *The Jews of Angevin England* (London: David Nutt)
Jenkinson, Hilary (1929) *Calendar of the Plea Rolls of the Exchequer of the Jews* Vol. III (London: Jewish Historical Society of England)
Jewish Quarterly Review (Pennsylvania: University of Pennsylvania Press)
Jewish Year Book (1896 ff) (London: Vallentine Mitchell)
Joseph, Simon (1994) *Didactic Love* (London: Multifarious Publications)
Joseph, Zoe (1988) *Survivors: Jewish Refugees in Birmingham* (West Midlands: Meridian)
Kershen, Anne & Romain, Jonathan (1995) *Tradition and Change: A History of Reform Judaism in Britain 1840-1995*, (London: Vallentine Mitchell)

Knibbs, Ray (1989) *Furze Platt Remembered* (Maidenhead: Cliveden Press Ltd)

Krisman, Sue (2001) *Portrait of a Community, Reading Synagogue 1900-2000* (Reading: Reading Synagogue)

Kushner, Tony (1989) *The Persistence of Prejudice* (Manchester: Manchester Univesity Press)

Lipman, V.D. (ed) (1961) *Three Centuries of Anglo-Jewish History* (London: Jewish Historical Society of England)

Loewe, Herbert (1932) *Starrs and Jewish Charters* Vols. II & III (London: Jewish Historical Society of England)

Manix, Pam (2012) *Beneath Our Feet: Oxford's Medieval Jewish Cemetery* (Oxford: Roke Elm Books)

Manix, Pam (2013) *Oxford Town Hall and The Medieval Jewry* (Oxford: Roke Elm Books)

Masters, Peter (1997) *Striking Back: A Jewish Commando's War Against the Nazis* (New York: Presidio Press)

Middleton, Tom (1975) *The Book of Maidenhead* (Buckingham: Barracuda Books)

Middleton, Tom, (1979) *Royal Berkshire* (Buckingham: Barracuda Books)

Miller, Stephen, Schmool, Marlena & Lerman, Antony (1996) *Social and Political Attitudes of British Jews* (London: Institute of Jewish Policy)

Miscellanies of the Jewish Historical Society of England, Vols. I - VI (1925-1962) (London: Jewish Historical Society of England)

Mundill, Robin R., (1998) *England's Jewish Solution,* (Cambridge: Cambridge University Press)

Newman, Aubrey (1976) *The United Synagogue 1870-1970* (London: Routledge & Kegan Paul)

Newton, Clare (2001) *My Grandmother Rachel* (Bakewell: Country Books)

Over, Luke (1984) *The Story of Maidenhead* (Newbury: Local Heritage Books)

Over, Luke, & Oppenheimer, Nicky (2001) *Waltham Place* (Maidenhead: Nicky Oppenheimer)

Phillips, Daphne (1983) *The Story of Reading* (Newbury: Countryside Books)

Powell, Arnold (2010) *A Touch of Chutzpah* (Milton Keynes: AuthorHouse)

Prais, S.J. & Schmool, M. (1967) 'Statistics of Jewish Marriages in Great Britain' *Jewish Journal of Sociology* Vol. 9, No. 2 (London: World Jewish Congress)

Revue des Etudes Juives (Leuven, Belgium: Peeters Publishers)
Richardson, H.G. (1960) *The English Jewry Under Angevin Kings* (London: Methuen)
Richardson, H.G. (1972) *Calendar of the Plea Rolls of the Exchequer of the Jews* Vol. IV (London: Jewish Historical Society of England)
Rigg, J.M. (ed) (1902) *Select Pleas, Starrs and other records from the Rolls of the Exchequer of the Jews 1220-1284* (London: Jewish Historical Society of England)
Rigg, J.M. (ed) *Calendar of the Plea Rolls of the Exchequer of the Jews* Vols. I (1905) & II (1910) (London: Jewish Historical Society of England)
Rokeah, Zefirah Entin (2000) *Medieval English Jews and Royal Officials* (Jerusalem: Magnes Press, Hebrew University)
Romain, Jonathan (1984) *How to Grow* (London: Movement for Reform Judaism)
Romain, Jonathan (1985) *The Jews of England* (London: Jewish Chronicle Publications)
Romain, Jonathan (1991) *Faith and Practice: A Guide to Reform Judaism Today* (London: Movement for Reform Judaism)
Romain, Jonathan (1996) *Till Faith Us Do Part* (London: HarperCollins)
Romain, Jonathan (2000) *Your God Shall be My God* (London: SCM)
Rosenthal, Chrissy & Danks, Ann (2004) *Maidenhead Voices* (Stroud: Tempus)
Roth, Cecil (1938) *The Jewish Contribution to Civilisation* (London: Macmillan)
Roth, Cecil (1949) *The Jewish Chronicle 1841-1941* (London: The Jewish Chronicle)
Roth, Cecil (1950) *The Rise of Provincial Jewry* (London: The Jewish Monthly)
Roth, Cecil (1951) *The Jews of Medieval Oxford* (Oxford: Clarendon Press)
Roth, Cecil (1962) *Essays and Portraits in Anglo-Jewish History* (Philadelphia: Jewish Publication Society of America)
Roth, Cecil (1964) *A History of the Jews of England* (Oxford: Clarendon Press)
Stebbing, David (Ed) (2003) *Jewish Memories of the Twentieth Century* (London: Evelyn Kent Associates)
Stokes, H.P. (1913) *Studies in Anglo-Jewish History* (London: Jewish Historical Society of England)
Stroud, Oswald (1974) *The Story of the Stroud Family* (private

publication, Anglo-Jewish Archives, Southampton)
Titmuss, Richard (1950) History of the Second World War (London: Longman, Green & Co.)
Transactions of the Jewish Historical Society of England, Vol.1 (1893) - Vol. 44 (2013) (London: Jewish Historical Society of England
Weizmann, Vera (1967) *The Impossible Takes A Little Longer* (London: Hamish Hamilton)
Wicks, Ben (1989) *The Day They Took the Children* (London: Bloomsbury Publishing Ltd)
Woolf, Stanley (1988) *The Lumie Tree* (Buckingham: Barracuda Books)

2. Journals, local papers and archives
(abbreviations in brackets as appropriate)

AJR Journal (London: Association of Jewish Refugees)
Bucks Examiner (High Wycombe)
Hadashot (Maidenhead Synagogue)
Hashomer (Maidenhead Synagogue)
Jewish Chronicle (JC) (London)
Jewish Guardian (London)
Kindertransport (London)
London Jewish News (London)
Maidenhead Advertiser (MA) (Maidenhead)
Manna (London: Movement for Reform Judaism)
Minutes, Assembly of Ministers (later: of Rabbis)
Minutes, Association of Synagogues in Great Britain (ASGB)
Minutes, Maidenhead Synagogue Council (MSC)
Minutes, Reform Synagogues of Great Britain (RSGB)
Minutes, United Synagogue Council
New Humanist (London: Rationalist Association)
Second Generation Voices (London: Association of Jewish Refugees)
Slough & Windsor Observer (Slough)
Synagogue Review (SR) (West London Synagogue)
Update (London: Central British Fund)
ULPS News (London: Union of Liberal and Progressive Synagogues)

Index

Names are listed in the way they appear in the book.
Medieval Jews are usually listed by their forenames.
Families members who appear together are listed together.
Titles are not given unless no other means of identification is possible.

Aaron Crespin of London 26
Aaron of Canterbury 37
Aaron of Colchester 51
Aaron of Dorchester 35
Aarons, Nathan 63
Abraham fil Muriel 25-6
Abraham of Berkhamsted 31-2
Abraham of Guildford 42
Abraham of Kent 37
Adelman, Diz 310, 366
Adelman, Joshua 182
Adelman, Lou 175, 182
Adler, Hermann 62
Afia, Peter 198
Afia, Philip 198
Afia, Robert 198, 211
Afia, Rose 197, 199, 214-5, 221
Afia, Victor 188, 197, 199-203, 208-9, 212, 216, 363
Agnes of Wallingford 32
Ahrend, Bertha (nee Goodman) 161
Album, Jack 283, 366
Alexander II (Scotland) 36
Alexander II (Russia) 62
Alfert, Lorraine 343
Alfred, Tim 369
Allen, Danny 319, 343, 364
Alon, Yigal 194
Altman, Simon 369
Altman, Sue 312
Amar, Mr & Mrs 153
Anne, Queen 6
Ansel, Gerald 180
Ansell of Wycombe 36

Anson, Alice (nee Gross) 140
Anterra, daughter of Leo 39
Argy, Edith (nee Tintner) 141
Arancy, Peter 141
Aris, Hans & Ernst 132
Ascher, Claus 131
Ascher, Leo & Sophie 143
Asher, son of David of Oxford 37
Asquith, Herbert 70
Astor, Waldorf 81, 110
Astor, Nancy 81, 110
Austin, Freddie 187
Avner, Sophie 366
Baker, Gerald 187
Balfour, Arthur 70
Ballantine, Reg 188
Banks, David 280
Bannard, Mr 101
Barclay, Susan 252
Barnard, H.D. 213
Barnett, Helen (nee Levenson) 124
Barnett, Jacob 51
Barnett, Mr & Mrs 160
Barnett, Ronald 104-5
Barrington-Baker, Mr 173
Bassa (of Hungerford) 40
Baum, Rabbi 169
Bechman, Ted 249
Beckhardt, Kurt 130
Beer, Ronald 223
Behrman, Tom 195
Belaset of Wallingford 34-5
Belia of Hungerford 40
Belkin, Alec 7, 217, 219, 220-1,

233, 235-6, 246, 261, 265, 267, 304, 324
Belkin, Evelyn 221
Belkin, Peggy 221, 324
Benedict of Lambourn 41
Benedict, (fil Abraham of Kent) 36
Benedictus, David 225
Benedictus Le Puncteur 45
Benjamin of Canterbury 45
Benjamin, Philip 249
Bennet, Sydney & Alice 104
Berechiah ben Natroni Ha'Nakdan 45
Berg, Charles 222
Berger, Cyril 187
Berk, Mrs 228
Berkshire, Earl of 58-9
Berman, Bernard 187
Berman, Jon 274, 331
Berman, Pearl 267, 342
Bermant, Chaim 306
Bernard, Leo 207
Bernie, Frances 93, 177, 197, 221
Bernie, Judith 233-4, 249-50
Bernie, Len 183
Bernie, Murray 190, 197, 229, 235, 241, 304, 363-4
Bernie, Phil 249
Bernie, Ronald 187, 208-9, 245, 363
Bernie, Yetta 214
Bernstein, Leslie & Manon 269
Bernstein, Ruth 307
Bessa, wife of Elias of Warwick 39
Best, George & Angie 299
Bidmead, G. 126
Bilsky, Max & Jabe 104
Birnstingl, K.S. 86
Bischoffsheim, Henry 84
Bissley, James 92
Blairman, Leila 285
Blank, Mikhail & Elena 309

Bloch, Sonny 154
Blooman, Jessica 7, 188, 246, 254-5
Blue, Lionel 235
Blumenau, Ralph 117
Blumenthal, Heston 333
Blumenthal, Tony 188
Bodenheimer, Hans (Hanan) 136
Bogod, Mr & Mrs 161
Bona of Wallingford 32
Bonamy of Henley 28
Bonafey/Bonevie of Newbury 38-9
Bonevie of Oxford 32
Bonevye son of Jacob 28
Borovinsky, Semion & Natalia 288-90, 309
Bowes-Lyon, Lady 22
Brace, William 99
Bram, Hila 310, 320, 334, 336, 339
Bram, Natan 356
Brazil, Rev. 175, 184, 195, 197
Bressler, Leon 219
Brodie, Israel 168-9
Brodie, Morris 188
Brodin, Ashley 309
Bronstein, Hilda 366
Brookman, Adam 272-3
Brookman, Daniel 272
Brookman, David 299
Broude, Karen 341-2
Brown, Beverley 275
Brown, Helga 150
Brown, Len 268, 313
Brown, Mendel 102
Brown, Polly 102
Brown, Shirley 302
Brown, W.W. 142
Brunel, Isambard Kingdom 6
Brunner, Debra 309, 366
Burns, Frank 213, 233
Burnside, Michael 117
Burton, Montague 174

Cahn, Warren 252
Caine, Jack & Mabel 160
Cameron, Aaron 339
Cameron, Daniel 336, 340, 364
Cameron, Irene 342
Caplan, Steven 275
Caplan, Harold (son of Rube & Ada) 125, 182-4, 215
Caplan, Harold 321
Caplan, Leon 125
Caplan, Rube & Ada 125, 197
Cashdan, Louis 134
Cassell, Curtis 213
Castelfranc 59
Catherine of Aragon 51
Catsell, Bob 187
Celebi, Sulia 356
Chapman, Florrie 79
Chapman, John 80
Charles I 6, 58
Charles II 6, 58
Charon, Richard 340, 364
Chaytow, Alice 342, 369
Chaytow, Stephen 341
Chodosh, Morris 187
Christian, Princess 77
Chumaceiro, Henrietta 102
Churchill, Winston 230
Clift, Josette 272, 315
Clore, Charles 242
Cockerel (fil Abraham of Kent) 37
Cohen, Abraham 59
Cohen, Arthur 76
Cohen, Barbara, Pamela & Marion 125
Cohen, Celia, Renee & Hazel 125
Cohen, Gerald 245, 255-6, 367
Cohen, Harvey 125, 182
Cohen, Israel 76
Cohen, Israel & Annie 76
Cohen, Jack & Annie 125
Cohen, Joost 245

Cohen, Joseph & Marie 76
Cohen, Leon Gaston 104
Cohen, Mick & Cissie 125
Cohen, Nigel 333, 337, 365
Cohen, Paul 125
Cohen, Philip 228
Cohen, Solomon & Eva 102
Cohen, Sidney & Millie 102
Cohen, Suzanne 334-5
Cohen, Tom & Esther 125
Cohn, Ernst 209
Cohn, Susan 140
Collings, Barney 366
Collins, Joseph 60
Compton, Anna 356
Conn, Werner 150
Cooper, David 268, 300
Cooper, Jenny 360
Cooper, Maurice & Renee 188, 271
Cooper, William, Doris & Mary 143
Copin of Worcester 22
Coppel, Mitchel 249
Copyn fil Bonavita 29
Corman, Jack 168
Corne, Ashley 265
Cotton, Jack 242
Cowan, Albert 188
Cowan, Sam & Jean 198, 203, 214-6
Cowan, Lewis 198, 211
Cowan, Susan 198
Cox, Charles 99
Crabbe, Anne 129
Creager, Cherrie 266
Creager, Clive 303, 366
Creamer, Mr & Mrs, & Victoria 160-1
Cresse (son of Lumbard of Winchester) 24-5
Cromwell, Oliver 51, 58
Cross, Jean 343

Cummings, John 366
Curtis, Michael 239
Curtis, Raymond 309
Curtiss, John 322
Curshen, Andy 251
Daltroff, Charles, Frank, George 93
Daniel, I. 158
Danziger, Hans-Wolfgang 133
Danzinger, Rose 360
David of Oxford 37
Davidson, M. 162
Davis, Alfred 187
Davis, Alfred E. 75
Davis, Arthur 65
Davis, Ben, Fay & Lee 133
Davis, Bernard 240
Davis, Ian & Sandy 273
Davis, Jacob 65
Davis, John 65
Davis, Maurice 364
Davis, Vivienne 271
De Frece, Walter 104
De Frettes, Regine 343
De Gaulle, Charles 111
De Lissa, Samuel 86
Delman, Ivor (Deitchman) 155, 272-3
De Payba, Isaac Carriao 65
Dessler, Eliyahu 156
Devereux, Mr 148
Diei of Wallingford 32
Diener, Sophie 146
Dieulecresse of Oxford 21-2
Diskin, Mark 276, 365
Disraeli, Benjamin 7, 70-2, 154
Disraeli, Mary-Ann 71
D'Israeli, Isaac 71
Doff, Kenneth 27
Doniger, Ruth 198, 252
Dresner, Maurice 225
Dubrov, Boris & Hannah 309
Dubs, Alfred 138

Dunkel, Ernest 104
Dunkel, Mina 104
Dunkel, Walter 104
Dunston, Matthew 339
Duran, Arthur & Nita 198, 200, 203, 215-6, 365
Duran, Diana 215
Ebner, Cecilia (Celia) 144
Eckman, Sid 118
Edelman, Maurice & Tilly 31, 154
Edward the Confessor 6
Edward I 6, 31, 35, 43, 58
Edward IV 6
Edward VI 6, 58
Edward VII 77, 81
Edward VIII 146
Eglington, W. 98
Ehrentreu, Yisroel 156
Ehrentreu, Meir Zvi & Chanoch 156, 158
Elderton, Pat 268-9
Elias of Bedford 28
Elias of Warwick 39
Elijah of London 32
Elizabeth I 58
Ellis (Elias) of Fleet 36
Ellis, John 183-4
Engelberg, Philip 242
Englander, Hilke 230-1
Englander, Regina 197
Epps, Sharon 366
Ethelred the Unready 13
Evans, Eva & Gertrude 144-5
Fairfield, Geoffrey 366
Falk, Bernard 254
Farchi, Gal 339, 356
Feldman, Rachel 194
Feldman, Valerie 252
Feldstein, Bernard 194, 243, 363
Fenn, Bertram 104
Fenton, Rosie 103
Ferber, Hirsh 161

Ferber, Jacob 161-2
Finestein, Israel 306
Fingret, June 332
Fink, Jan 113, 322
Firsht, David & Sarah 366
Fisher, Doris 30
Flanagan, Bud 111, 242
Flather, Shreela 252
Floria (wife of Abraham of Berkhamsted) 32
Floria of Guildford 42
Fluria of Newbury 39
Fogelman, Mr & Mrs 93
Fogelman, Reuben & Mary 127, 190
Fogelman, Myrna (Julius) 127, 184
Fogelnest, S. 103
Formosa (of Guildford) 42
Fox, Rebecca 211-2
Fox, Jacob Samuel 102
Fox, Shirley 343
Frank, Amelia 233-4, 249
Frank, David 249
Frank, Willy 233, 236, 239, 246, 256, 365
Frankau, Julia 75
Frankl, Robert & Charlotte 253-4
Fraser, Joe 161
Fredman, Braham 272-3
Freed, H. 160
Freedman, Paul 211
Freeman, Isaac & Betty 104
Freedman, Jack & Miriam 197, 200
Fry, Mr & Mrs D. 185
Fuhr, Sue 366
Furman, H. 160
Galas, Yechiel 166, 172-6, 180, 184, 187
Gale, Flora 360
Gale, Reuben 91
Galinski, David 91
Gamliel of Oxford 41

Gardner, Ernest 78
Garnett Pell, Myra 360
Gartner, Helen 312
Gavento, H. 162
Geneen, Sam 365
George IV 6
George VI 168
Geppert, Morton 196
Gert, Geoffrey 135
Gertler, Alfred 187
Girling, Rev. 134
Gledhill, Ruth 317, 329
Glendinning, Pauline 333
Gluecksmann, Mr & Mrs 149
Gold, Hannah 311
Goldberg, David 157
Goldberg, Marta 189
Goldbluhm, Mr & Mrs J. 161
Goldman, Isaac 59
Goldman, Raymond 8, 209, 241
Goldsmid, Francis Henry 60-1, 165
Goldsmid, Isaac Lyon 60
Goldsmith, Ron 274
Goldstein, Freda 198, 214-5
Goldstein, Henry 228, 239
Goldstein, Jack & Jenifer 246, 258
Goldstein, Morry 214
Goldstein, William 198, 200, 216, 363
Goldstone (nee Ellis) 112
Goldwater, Marion (nee Danziger) 133
Gollancz, Hermann 63
Goodhardt, Ian 285
Goodman, Celia 120
Goodman, Elie, Simon & Jo 173
Goodman, Harry Aron 169, 172, 174, 176, 189-90
Goodman, Howard 301
Goodman, Jan 266-7
Goodman, Joseph 173
Goodman, Robert 227, 235-6, 239,

243, 257-9, 268, 304, 308, 331, 362-5
Gordon, Hortense 141
Gordon, Jeremy 216
Gould, Isobel 168
Gould, Mr & Mrs Lewis 166-7
Goulston, Michael 239
Gow, Jenny 274
Gow, Richard 366
Gozman, Maddy 366
Grayeff, Marianne (nee Zanders) 139
Green, A.A. 79
Green, Jack 188
Green, Phil & Busie 161
Green, Roy & Jordan 369
Greenberg, B. 169
Greenberg, Florence 161
Greenberg, Sue 252
Greenspan, Philip 184
Greenwood, Samuel & Rita 104
Greenwood, Sonia 74
Grenfell, William Henry 201, 325
Grenville, Anthony 8
Grossman, Barbara 339
Grossman, Benni 339
Gryn, Hugo 369
Gunzberg, Mr & Mrs 102
Guttmann, Ludwig 148-9
Gwyn, Nell 6
Haakon, King of Norway 111
Haggai of Oxford 30
Hagin of Wallingford 32
Hagin (son of Moses of London) 26
Hake of Windsor 23
Hakelot (of Reading) 29
Halford, Jeanette 224
Hall, Marjorie 222
Halter, Roman 194
Hambury, Alec & Golda 198, 202, 212, 215-6, 250
Hammerson, Alfred & Leah 126

Harris, Hilary 312
Harris, Jack 102
Harris, Mila 366
Harris, Raphael 301
Harris, Sam 316
Hart, Julius 207
Hayes, Maurice 232
Hawkins, Sarah 66-7
Hazleton, Jessel 366
Heilbut, Sally 360
Heilbut, Samuel 86
Hellman, Hans (Jack) 135-6
Helm, Jonathan 369
Helm, Nick 327, 340
Henna, wife of Leo 39
Henry I 6
Henry II 29
Henry III 18, 22, 25, 30, 32, 36
Henry IV 51
Henry VI 51
Henry VIII 6, 51
Henry of Eton 51
Henry of Windsor 51
Herman, Sonny 239
Hertz, Joseph 152
Herzl, Theodor 81
Heskey, Moshe (George) 322
Hewitt-Wilson, John 322
Hillaby, Jo 8
Hirschfeld family 154
Hoffner, Charles 117
Hoffnung, Abraham & Esther 86
Hole, Bridget 8
Holt, Max 236
Holt, Peter 301, 308, 340, 364-6
Hubbers, Alice, (nee Engel) 133
Hurley, Griselda 8
Hyamson, Naomi 280
Ibbetson, Ruth 322
Illoway, Paul & Ilse (nee Fuehrenberg) 144
Indech, Jonah 154

Isaac Le Eveske 28
Isaac of Dorchester 35
Isaac of Norwich 38
Isaac of Oxford 26
Isaac of Southwark 42
Isaac of Wycombe 36
Isaacs, Gerald Rufus 89
Isaacs, Henry 65
Isaacs, Joseph 165
Isaacs, Lionel 165
Isaacs, Michael Rufus 89
Isaacs, Nathaniel 165
Isaacs, Rufus 7, 87-8, 165
Isaacs, Simon Rufus 89
Jacob of Oxford 31
Jacob of Wycombe 17, 36
Jacob (fil Moses of London) 17, 23
Jacobs, David & Julius 147
Jacobs, Fritz & Toni 224
Jacobs, Gaskell 168
Jacobs, John 155
Jacobs, Joseph 168
Jacobs, Lorna 316, 332
Jacobs, Louis 169, 306
Jacobs, Rita 360
Jacobs, Simon 289, 327
Jacobs, Zoe 339
Jacobson, H. 93-4
Jacobson, Howard 333
Jaffe, Albert 104
Jakobovits, Immanuel 168
Jakobovits, Julius & Paula 166-9
Jakobovits, Shulamit 167
James, Mike 272-4
James, Miri 304
Janner, Greville 328-9
Janner-Klausner, Laura 313
Jewell, Ben 188, 365
Jewell, Ruth 161, 188, 254
Jobson, Cirques 51
John (King) 25-6
Joiette (of Odiham) 37

Jolles, Michael 8
Jonason, Michael 342
Jones, Harold 201
Jordan, Gretel 193
Josce of Aylesbury 36
Josce of Guildford 42-3
Josce of Newbury 36, 40
Josceus of Wallingford 32
Joseph, David 181, 183-4
Joseph, Gerald 124
Joseph, Miriam 181, 184
Joseph, Simon & Beatrice 127, 166, 175, 181-4, 186, 196
Joseph, son of Isaac 26
Jospin of Basingstoke 37
Jospin, son of Solomon of Marlborough 32
Joyce, William 190
Judith, daughter of Belaset 35
Jung, Julius 157
Kader, Aaron & Keren 343
Kahan, George 254
Kahan, Mr 154
Katz, Arthur 161
Kaufman, Mr & Mrs H. 102
Kaufmann, Anna Lisa 143-4
Kaufmann, Jean 193
Kaye, Martin & Marion 252
Kayne, Sue 340
Kelen, Sarah 337
Kellman, Edward & Sadie 186
Kent, Duke of 279
Kessly, Adrienne 336
Kessly, Edward 127
Khan, Mr & Mrs 161
King, Max 103
Kingsley, Sidney 207
Kirchner, Max 154
Kirschoff-Gordon, Elvira 332
Klausner, A.L. 180
Klein, Kurt (Robert) 132
Klein, Lisa 366

Knight, Andrew 356
Kohn, Dawn 327
Konig, Micha 260
Koppel, Marion 146
Koppelman 102
Koss, Gay 360
Kossoff, David 321
Kremer, Michael 183
Krestin, Jack 198, 216
Krestin, Sharon 198
Kupfer, Mr & Mrs 149
Kupfermann, Elias & Mina 8, 196, 312
Kupfermann, Jeannette 332
Kutner, Bob 132
Kuttner, Henry 134
Lamb, Howard 340, 364
Lambert, Sandy 342
Lambourne, Freda 272, 366
Landau, F.M. 158
Landau, Hermann 72
Lang, Cosmo 149
Lang, David 163
Langton, Stephen 30
Langtry, Lillie 6
Lansman, Michael 340, 364
Lansman, Robin 276
Lansman, Veronica 252
Lask, Jack 188
Laurie, Jerry (Jerome) 182-3
Lawrence, Alex 188
Lawton, Clive 306
Lazarus, Lawrence 66, 165
Leapman, Dennis & Ann 188, 271
Leapman, Peter 114
Leese, Arnold 107
Leftkewich, Leo 185
Lehmann, Clara 356
Leigh, Michael 213, 228
Leo, son of Deuleben 38
Lesser, Mira 322
Levene, David 273

Levene, Millie 103
Levene, Mr & Mrs 103
Levenson, Barney & Bob 124
Levenson, Ellis 144, 188, 197, 202, 205, 212-3, 216-7, 221, 227
Levenstein, Herbert 225
Lever, Cllr 99
Lever, Stuart 159
Levine, Barnett 102
Levy, Alexander M. 92, 225
Levy, Jacob 66
Levy, Mr & Mrs M. 153
Levy, Sheila 360
Levy-Lawson, Edward 72
Levy-Lawson, Harry 72
Lewis, Clare 343
Lewis, Clive 365
Lewis, David 274
Lewis, Frances 271
Lewis, Hyman & Annie 104
Lewis, Lester 285
Lewis, Sam & Ada 7, 76-8
Licoricia of Winchester 36
Lilienthal, David 245, 249-50
Lipman, Maureen 333
Lissak, Mrs 155
Littaur, Mr & Mrs 104
Littlestone, Gerald 183
Lockwood, Georgina 356
Lockwood, Juliette 340
Loewe, Herbert 80
Lovett, Peter 318
Lucas, Victor 213, 239
Ludner, Charles 187
Lumbard of Basingstoke 36-7
Lumbard of Marlborough 37
Lumbard of Windsor 23-4
Lumley, Julian Arthur 76
Lunt, Raymond 189
Luper, Rosalind 310
Luxembourg, Grand Duchess 111
Lustig, Fritz 139-40

Lyon, Alan 188
Lyond, Edna 188
Madenberg, Harry 186, 188, 209, 211, 216, 219, 252, 323, 363, 365
Madenberg, Israel (Isidore) 112, 144, 197-8, 200, 203, 216-7, 224, 228, 233, 240-1, 245, 363, 365
Madenberg, Sarah 197
Manasses (of Blicestone) 20
Magnus, Philip 106
Maly, Dobromil 313
Manix, Pam 8
Mann, Arthur & Florrie 187, 197
Mann, Maurice 322
Manuel ben Hayyim Levy 65
Maple, John Blundell 79
Marcovitch, Shalom & Edie 120-1
Margai, Yoram 290-1
Margaret, Princess 306-8
Margo, Monte 230-1
Markham, Mr & Mrs S. 186
Markovitch, Mr 194
Marks, David Woolf 82-3
Marks, Frances 82
Marks Geoffrey 188
Marks, George 155
Marks, Harry 162
Marks, Julian 272-3, 289, 366
Marlow, Jannette 275, 310, 320
Marmur, Dow 239
Martin, Arthur 106
Matilda, Queen 20-1
May, Theresa 328
Mayer, J. 160
Mayer, J.P., Lola & Peter 147
Mees, Eric 189
Meir of Hungerford 40
Meir of Oxford 50
Melichan, Harry 216, 221
Menachem of London 45

Mendel, Leonard 223
Menon, Krishna 195
Merran, Leonard 126
Merran, Stanley 129
Merton, Walter de 23
Meyer, Bill 366
Meyer, Hilary 366
Michaels, Maurice 313
Michaels, Yetta 126
Michaelson, Bernard 166
Michaelson, Clare (Newton) 194
Middleton, Tom 252
Mikardo, Ian 164-5
Milman, Henry Hart 59
Miller, Edward & Nita 144, 187, 198
Miller, Tony 196, 215
Miloslower, M. 160
Milton, Ruth 267, 342
Mirner, D 102
Misener, Iris 198
Misener, Laurie 114, 198, 203, 209, 220-1, 227, 229, 232-4, 236, 238-240, 363, 365
Moher, Michael 196, 274
Montagu, Samuel 62-3
Montefiore, Claude 62
Montfort, Simon de 32
Moore, Vanner 106
Moran, Sandra 312
Moran, Vicky 356
Morris, Belle 102
Morris, Caroline 344
Morris, Laurence 249
Morris, Yeshayahu 194
Morrison, Maxwell 127, 182
Morris, Newrnan 160
Mortara, Edgar 60
Moses, Ellen 147
Moses of Aylesbury 17, 36
Moses of London 37
Moses of Wycombe 36

Moses of Wallingford 21, 31
Mosley, Oswald 107
Moss, Lewis 188, 254
Mosse-Mokke (Norwich) 19
Muehlstein, Lea 313
Muer, M. 102
Mundhill, Robin 8
Munk, Rabbi 127, 175, 184
Muriel, sister of Leo 39
Muriel, wife of David of Oxford 37
Murphy, Nigel 340
Musgrave, Beatrice 132
Mushlin, Max & Fanny 102
Myer, Ernest A 100
Myer of Cricklade 50
Myers, Elizabeth & Sara 84
Nahum, Gillian 319
Nathan, Kurt 155
Nathan, Lyon 59
Neufield, Mr & Mrs 149
Newman, Aubrey 152
Newman, Ron 272
Newman, Simon 200
Newton, Edward & Sylvia 214
Noble, Noya 334-5
Norman, Daniel 369
Norman, David 328
North, Alan 291
North, Jule 276
North, Ruth 267, 343
Novello, Ivor 6
O'Connor, Ellen Odette 84
Oldershaw, Alderman 189
Olman, Annie 197, 252
Olman, Harry 188, 197, 216, 245, 305
Olman, Stanley 183-4, 193, 320
Olman, Suzanne 184
Oppenheimer, Ernest 84
Oppenheimer, Gustav & Cecily 84
Oppenheimer, Kurt (Keith Orpen) 145

Oppenheimer, Louis & Charlotte 84
Oppenheimer, Nicky & Orcillia 84
Oppenheimer, Raymond 84
Orchudesh, Herta 256, 271, 304, 366
Ord, Hazel 225
Osborne, Adam 324
Osborne, Jo 310, 332
Osborne, Sidney & Lily 126
Osorio, Myrtle 366
Otter, Harry & Renee 197, 203, 216
Otter, Charles & Gillian 198
Over, Luke 8, 13-4
Paisner, Leslie 175, 179, 182, 189, 195, 197, 363
Patterson, David 194
Pearl, Chaim 120
Pearce, J.D.M. 79
Pell, David & Freda 124
Perkin, Marcia 366
Perkins, Eric 205, 212-3
Perlzweig, Maurice 105-6
Peskin, Edward 188
Peter, King of Yugoslavia 111
Pettle, Sidney 210
Peyman, Hanna 308, 340, 364
Philip the Convert 30
Philipps, Harry 264, 267, 323
Philipps, Marianne 235, 270
Phillips, Estelle 269
Phillips, Laurie 289
Phillips, Stephen 366
Picciotto, Alfred & Edith 86
Pinkerton, Lesley 310
Pinkerton, Stuart 280
Pitch, Harry & Ruby 265, 277-8, 280, 328
Pizer, Jenny 318, 335, 340, 343, 364
Podguszer, Sophia 127
Polack, James 79
Polack, Joseph 79

Polack, Lazarus 79
Poliakov, Arthur 124
Pollock, Brian 273
Pordes, Otto 366
Pordes, Steven 360
Porter, Lesley 187
Poulos, Darrel 272, 324, 328
Poulos, Gil 324
Poulos, Rianna 369
Poulos, Suri 269, 309, 324, 326, 329, 340, 342, 364
Prashner, Jacob 76
Presser, Regina 360
Profumo, John 6, 375
Prossor, Ron 337
Pucelle (of Newbury) 39
Rabinowitz, Isy 114
Radges, Gus 207
Raine, Chris & Simon 249
Ratner, Gerald 333
Rantzen, Esther 138
Rapaport, Isaac 154, 158-9
Reich, Abraham 180
Reich, Phyllis 180
Reigate, Mr & Mrs 132
Reinhart, Harold 134, 204-5, 207, 209
Reiff, Gabie 356
Reisz, Karel 138
Restall, Gerald 281
Reuben, Danny 249
Reynolds, John 301
Rhodes, Lorna 342
Rich, Barbara & Margaret 198
Rich, Frank 332
Rich, Jean 198, 215
Rich, Sidney 7, 198-203, 205, 216, 222, 298, 363, 365
Richard I 29
Richard of Cornwall 31-2
Richards, Helga (nee Nettel) 131
Richardson, M. 162

Rimel, Maurice 173
Ritson-Smith, Leslie 113
Robert of Reading 29-30
Robertson, Juliana 224
Robinson, Bryan 307
Romain, Daniel 188
Romain, Jonathan 245, 257-8, chapters 13-17
Romain, Sybil (Sheridan) 280, 287, 310-1, 336, 366
Rome, Olivia 356
Roos, Harry 186
Rose, A. 213
Rose, Aubrey 125
Rose, D. 162
Rose, Kate 166
Roseman, Jan 319-20
Rosen, Kopul 196
Rosenbaum, Jack & Judy 228, 245
Rosenbaum, Jeff 343
Rosenbaum, Walter & Hans (John Rosen) 133
Rosenberg, Barbara 270, 273, 280, 302, 310, 319-20, 327, 332, 366
Rosenberg, Frank 114
Rosenberg, Roger 272-3, 336
Rosenberg, Rosita (nee Gould) 119, 166-8, 193
Rosenblum, Erwin 203-5, 209, 212, 215-6, 218-9, 221-3, 228, 240
Rosenheim, Adella 182
Rosenheim, Jacob 174, 182
Ross, Karen 366
Roth, Mr & Mrs 149
Rothschild, Alice 67, 69
Rothschild, Alfred 69-70
Rothschild, Anthony 67-9
Rothschild, Ferdinand & Evelina de 67-9
Rothschild, James & Dorothy de 135-6
Rothschild, Leopold 67

Rothschild, Lionel 67, 69
Rothschild, Lionel Nathan 68-9
Rothschild, Lionel Walter 68-9
Rothschild, Louise 72
Rothschild, Mayer Amshel 66, 68-9
Rothschild, Nathaniel 63
Rothschild, Nathaniel Meyer 67-9
Rothschild, Nathan Mayer 66, 69
Ryz, Kurt 146
Sagan, M. 182
Sainsbury, Lord 133
Sakal, Jenny 276
Sakal, Joan 250, 252
Sakal, Vivian 188, 245, 252
Salazar, Ellen 343
Saleem, Hafiz 338
Saleshaln, Mr & Mrs Sam 104
Salmon, Bobby 245
Salmon, Mark 250
Salzberger, Georg 136
Sampson, Jennifer 160-1, 193
Samuel, Edgar 8
Samuel, Judah 65
Samuel of Wallingford 31
Sanders, Tom & Margit 264
Saperstein, Marc 8
Sarah (of Windsor) 7, 23, 25
Sarner, Marie 268-9
Sather, Sheila 343
Saville, Annie (nee Baskier) 117-8
Savitt, Martin 239
Sawady, Ernest Konrad 209
Schimunek, Mr & Mrs 149
Schindler, Alma 117
Schneider, Fay 161
Schonfeld, Solomon 166, 182
Schonfield, Daniel 213
Schreiber, Hermann 136
Schwab, Hugo 222-3, 237, 240 242, 245, 365
Schwab, Sigmund 229
Scott, Mrs Hyam 104

Scott, Ian 188, 262-3, 268, 299, 303, 364
Scott, Tanya 263
Seabrook, Sam 343
Segal, David 366
Segal, Marcus 80
Seldon, Anthony 281
Selinger, Cyril 283, 366
Sella, Uri 136
Selve, Anina 343
Sentamu, John 281, 333
Servi, Nathan 338-9
Shackman, Rube 125-6, 190, 198
Shackman, Rose 93, 125, 198
Shaer, Rachael 343
Shaffer, Barbara 280
Shafran, Ivor 340, 363
Shakespeare, William 58
Shear, Alf 175, 197, 214, 217, 219-21, 228, 231-2, 235
Shear, Sam 197, 231
Sheldon, Rudi 322
Sheridan, Judith 319, 332
Sherman, Henry 250
Sherman, Jack 188
Shieldhouse, Brian 245-6
Shinerock, Abraham 102
Shire, Michael 310
Shire, Ruth 134
Shorrick, Alan 312
Sichel, Leo 283
Sigge, daughter of Leo 39
Silver, Jeff 342
Silver, Manny 122
Silverman, Carrie 235
Silverman, David & Hetty 175, 178, 195, 197
Silverman, Henry 231-5
Silverman, Martin 364
Silverman, Maurice 178, 184
Silverman, Robert 245
Simmonds, Meyer 102

Simon, David 336, 364
Simon, Natasha 311
Simon de la Haye 47
Simons, Muriel 342
Simons, Victor 130
Simpson, W.W. 189-90
Skitten, Isaac 59
Skinner, Annie 127
Slema, daughter of Isaac of Southwark 42
Smith, Boyd & Helen 124
Sokolow, Nahum 70
Solomon Episcopus (of Dorchester) 35
Solomon, H.L. 161
Solomon (of Odiham) 37
Solomon, Myer 65
Solomon, Sidney 175
Somerville, A. A. 107
Sommer, Carolin 8
Sommer, Stephen 272-3, 285, 304, 306, 308, 340, 364-5
Spencer, Charles 239
Spencer, Stanley 6
Spielman, Meyer 86
Spiers, Sydney 187
Spivack, Barney 168
Stacey, Sari 310, 344
Stanton, Jerry & Toby 187
Starkoff, Victor 113
Stein, Ernst 245
Stein, Susie 343
Steiner, Daisy 184
Steinhardt, Hugo & Lilly 135-6
Steinhardt, Lore & Helga 135
Stephen (King) 20
Sternberg, Sigmund 104, 341
Sternberg, Hazel (nee Jones) 104
Stobieka, Ulrich (Uri Sella) 136
Stollerman, Bernard (Philip) 177
Stollerman, Isaac 93, 177, 190
Stollerman, Jack 7, 177, 190

Stollerman, Sydney 177-8
Strauss, Joseph 76
Street, Isabel 268
Stuart, Samuel 99
Stuchberry, T.W. 201, 205
Stungo, Mr 124
Suffolk, Earl of 58
Sugar, Evan 319
Supper, George 188
Suswin, Len, Nini & Muriel 124
Swift, Harris 154, 158-60
Swift, I. L. 175
Swift, Morris 159-60
Szablewski, Varda 312
Tal, Leah 343
Tal, Roie 356
Tal, Sapir 339, 356
Tobias, Mr & Mrs 102
Trayner, Graeme 314
Trobe, Lewis 187
Tull, Jethro 6
Turner, J.M.W. 6
Tytel, Laurie 264, 276, 315, 332
Upson, Cllr 99
Ursel of Marlow 28
Vanderlinde, Simon 100
Van der Zyl, Nikki 134
Van der Zyl, Werner 207, 209, 217-8, 223, 232-3
Vanner-More, Mrs E.A. 189
Van Zwanenberg, Ies & Dorothy 130
Vaughan, Frankie 321
Vellerman, Mr & Mrs 160
Veniar, Sheila 262, 310
Vicar of Bray 6
Vickers, Enid 188
Victoria, Queen 6, 71
Vivant of Hungerford 40
Wagen, Michael 168
Waldorf, Beryl (nee Bloch) 119
Waley Cohen, Robert 85

Wallach, Michael 215
Wallerstein, Henry Louis (Heinrich Ludwig) 83
Walsh, Barry 273, 289
Walters, John 187
Walton, Rhiannon & Ruth 211
Ware, Michael 232
Warren, Michael 273
Weale, Cheryl 310-11, 321
Webster, Harriette 73
Webber, Gary 318, 340, 364
Weinman, Mrs 162
Wender, Chaim 245
Westerman, Mr & Mrs 212
Westrich, Mr & Mrs George 102
Wheeler, Michael 236
White, Neville 258
Wieser, Amy 118
Wilde, Oscar 6
Wilhelmina, Queen (Netherlands) 111
William I 6, 13, 16, 58
Williams, Denise 310, 312
Williams, Joanne 369
Williams, Michael 245
Willis, Rita 213
Wiltshire, Jill 310
Wiltshire, Stephen 369
Windsor, Duke of 146
Wingate. Monica 161
Wingate, Orde 161
Winston, Clive 310
Winton, Nicholas 7, 136-9, 316
Wiseman, Adolphe 197, 200, 202, 205, 216, 218
Wiseman, Aviva 321
Wiseman, Minnie 197, 215, 221
Wiseman, Michael 188
Wiseman, Patricia 198
Wolf, J. 163
Wolff, Caroline 87
Wolff, David 188
Wolff, Harry 114
Wolff, Willy 245
Wolfgang, Jacob 56
Womersley, Walter 148
Woolf, Daphne, Ursula & Diana 123
Woolf, Roy & Jenni 360
Woolf, Harry 333
Woolf, Stanley 91
Woolfe, Alec 177
Ximenes, David 65
Ximenes, Moses (Maurice) 65
Zanardo, Andrea 313
Zeffert, Michael & Pauline 104
Ziegler, Jill 324, 328, 341
Zimmels, Erla 8
Zimmerman, Paul 114
Zipporah, wife of Isaac of Southwark 42
Zog, King of Albania 111

The ark and reading desk.

*The Hebrew inscription reads:
'The breath of life in every creature shall praise You, God'*